The
Law-Growth
NEXUS

The
Law-Growth
NEXUS

The Rule of Law and
Economic Development

Kenneth W. Dam

BROOKINGS INSTITUTION PRESS
Washington, D.C.

Copyright © 2006
THE BROOKINGS INSTITUTION
1775 Massachusetts Avenue, N.W., Washington, D.C. 20036
www.brookings.edu

Library of Congress Cataloging-in-Publication data

Dam, Kenneth W.
    The law-growth nexus : the rule of law and economic development
/ Kenneth W. Dam.
        p.   cm.
    Summary: "Examines the underlying mechanisms through which the
law, judiciary, and legal profession influence the economy. Analyzes
enforcement, contracts, and property rights—the concepts collectively
defining rule of law—and examines their roles in the real estate and
financial sectors. Extended China analysis assesses the importance
of the rule of law"—Provided by publisher.
  Includes bibliographical references and index.
  ISBN-13: 978-0-8157-1720-1 (cloth : alk. paper)
  ISBN-10: 0-8157-1720-2 (cloth : alk. paper)
  1. Economic development. 2. Rule of law. I. Title.
HD75.D357 2006
338.9—dc22   2006027764

9 8 7 6 5 4 3 2 1

Typeset in Minion

Composition by Cynthia Stock
Silver Spring, Maryland

Printed by R. R. Donnelley
Harrisonburg, Virginia

Contents

Foreword

W e often deal with hard data at Brookings. No statistic about today's world is more important and less acceptable than this one: more than 1 billion people—a sixth of humanity—live on less than $1 per day. The persistence of global poverty is all the more daunting given how much effort has gone into promoting inclusive economic growth. In the years after World War II, policymakers tried to stimulate development through foreign aid. In the 1980s, they put their faith in liberalization and economic reform. But since the end of the 1990s, the persistence of global poverty has led many experts to conclude that we must look beyond neoclassical economics in order to understand the causes of growth. The "Washington consensus" is looking increasingly wobbly, while a new belief in the power of institutions is on the rise.

The idea that institutions matter—and in particular, legal institutions—has attracted a large following among academics and policymakers alike. Among economists, it has also provoked a highly technical and at times acerbic debate over such questions as the relative value of common and civil law. But to date, the new consensus has not generated much in the way of practical advice. It tells policymakers that law is important, but it is virtually silent on what they should do.

With this book, Ken Dam steps confidently and constructively into the breach. It is difficult to imagine anyone better qualified to do so. A lifelong student of comparative law and a pioneer in the field of law and economics, he has served three presidents. He occupied key posts at the Office of Management and Budget and at the White House and served as deputy secretary in both the State and the Treasury Departments, which makes his résumé just about the perfect one for a master of geo-economics.

At the University of Chicago, he initiated generations of students into the subtleties of U.S. and foreign law. And he is no stranger to the world of business and the global economy, having served for seven years as corporate vice president for law and external relations with IBM.

Ken is also a long-time member of the Brookings family. In 1964 we had the honor of publishing his first book, *Federal Tax Treatment of Foreign Income*, written with Lawrence Krause. He became a Brookings trustee in 1988 and a senior fellow in 2004, after retiring from full-time teaching at Chicago. At Brookings, he has been a key participant in the Economic Studies and Global Economy and Development programs, among other activities.

In *The Law-Growth Nexus*, Ken offers a penetrating analysis of the law and finance literature, based on his expertise as both a scholar and a policymaker. In clear and elegant prose, he explains why legal institutions are important to economic development and which institutions matter most. But that is far from being his main goal. Instead, the great contribution of this book lies in Ken's determination to help policymakers use this knowledge to foster growth. By spelling out the concepts that underpin the rule of law—property rights, contracts, and enforcement—he brings legal institutions out of the ivory tower and down to earth. By tracing their role in the land and financial sectors, he identifies the challenges and opportunities facing policymakers interested in reform. And as a parting salvo, he takes on the greatest contemporary challenge to the "law matters" perspective: China's rapid growth, despite its manifest failings when it comes to the rule of law. Ken's work complements the research conducted by Brookings scholars in the John L. Thornton China Center and the Global Economy and Development program, particularly the work of Cheng Li on the development of China's legal system and civil society and of Wing Thye Woo on poverty and inequality in China.

For all these reasons, we feel fortunate to have Ken as a colleague and to have the imprimatur of the Brookings Institution Press on this, his latest contribution on a subject of vital importance.

Strobe Talbott
President

October 2006
Washington, D.C.

Acknowledgments

This book required the encouragement, assistance, and careful reading of colleagues and experts from several different fields, both in academia and in the public policy world.

For encouragement and helpful discussions, I would like to thank a number of colleagues at the University of Chicago and the Brookings Institution, especially Cass Sunstein at Chicago and Robert Litan and Peyton Young at Brookings.

For assistance, I was blessed with a number of able research assistants, whom I wish to thank, especially Wonbin Kang at Chicago and Eric Haven, Heather Milkiewicz, and Rebecca Vichniac at Brookings. Also in that category are the students in several seminars at the University of Chicago who were forced to help me think through my initial thoughts on the subject. Finally, I want to thank the incomparable assistance of the able staff of the University of Chicago Law School Library, especially Margaret Schilt. Research support was provided by the John M. Olin Foundation at Chicago and by the Brookings Institution.

Various experts on particular subjects read relevant parts of the book. From academia I would like to mention my Chicago colleagues Douglas Baird, Ruoying Chen, Dick Helmholz, and Robert Rasmussen (then visiting at Chicago and regularly at Vanderbilt), as well as Richard Cooper, Robert Madsen, Susan Shirk, and Marina Whitman. From the policy community I benefited greatly from conversations (based on their reading of parts of the book) with Jin Chen, Lyric Hughes Hale, Albert Keidel, and Steven Radelet. A number of lawyers, including Jia Zhao, Larry Kwok, and Preston Torbert, also aided me considerably by reviewing parts of the book. I appreciated particularly the willingness of international civil servants with great day-to-day expertise to read and comment, including John Bruce, Natalie Lichtenstein, and Matthew Parish from the World Bank; X. Peng from the Asian Development Bank; and Maria Dakolias from the U.K. Department of Constitutional Affairs. Finally, I would like to thank several anonymous referees for constructive suggestions.

I particularly want to recognize and thank Sidney Hyman for the enormous contribution he made to the conception and execution of this book. From his deep background as a scholar and professional writer, he deserves credit for helping to make this effort into a book rather than a set of essays.

Finally, I should like to acknowledge my intellectual debt to Ronald Coase, a colleague at the University of Chicago Law School, who—through countless conversations and by stimulating me to undertake several new lines of law and economics research—first introduced me to what would later become known as neoinstitutional economics.

Why This Book?

Emerson once laid it down as a rule that when friends meet after a time apart, they should greet each other by asking one question: Has anything become clear to you since we were last together? The sense of his rule applies to the subject of the book now in the hands of the reader.

In the last decade the issue of how best to improve the rate of economic growth of the poorer nations of Africa, Asia, and Latin America has come to be approached along lines quite different from those in the decades after the Second World War. Economists in the academy and practitioners in national and international aid agencies—as well as influential participants in public debate—now increasingly hold that neither traditional development theory nor neoclassical economics fully answers the complex problems of economic development. The ascendant view is that *institutions*—as the term is used in what has become known as neoinstitutional economics—matter for economic development, and that they do so in a major way.

Neo and Other Economics

An interest in institutions is not new. A movement focused on business enterprises, labor unions, and other organizations that flourished in the United States in the 1920s and 1930s is associated with the names of Thorstein Veblen and John R. Commons. The movement, which relied heavily on description rather than mathematics, failed to gain respect among those neoclassical economists who focused on economic concepts rather than on organizations. The neoclassical school of economics can be thought of as an updated version of the teachings of Adam Smith and later "classical econo-mists" such as David Ricardo, John Stuart Mill, and Alfred Marshall. Neoclas-sical economists gradually extended their reach beyond microeconomics (the initial focus of classical economics) into macroeconomics (involving issues such as inflation and employment) and even into adjacent social science fields. When a new focus on institutions—concerned with the way rules, con-tracts, and property function in the economy—developed in the second half of the twentieth century, it was called neoinstitutional economics. The objec-tive of the name was both to distinguish it from the institutional economics of the prewar period and to contrast it with neoclassical economics.[1]

Neoinstitutional economics is associated with the names of two Nobel Prize winners of the 1990s, Ronald Coase and Douglass North. Ronald Coase's Nobel citation states that he won the prize "for his discovery and clar-ification of the significance of transaction costs and property rights for the institutional structure and functioning of the economy."[2] North's contribu-tion, according to his Nobel citation, was to renew "research in economic his-tory by applying economic theory and quantitative methods in order to explain economic and institutional change."[3]

North's influential 1990 work—*Institutions, Institutional Change, and Eco-nomic Performance*—used history to illuminate the economic and institu-tional factors that have driven economic growth since the Middle Ages and that contribute to economic development in the third world today.[4] In his analysis *institutions* means *rules*—not just legal rules but social norms and other determinants of behavior—rather than organizations.

North's work, like all major intellectual achievements, had antecedents. Two equally remarkable figures who deserve consideration in the history of what is now called neoinstitutionalism are Max Weber and Friedrich Hayek. While Weber, usually thought of as a sociologist, is renown for his work in

---

1. On the influence of neoclassical and neoinstitutional economics on development pol-icy, see Meier (2001, pp. 26–28, 37–39).

2. The Bank of Sweden Prize in Economic Sciences in Memory of Alfred Nobel 1991 (nobelprize.org/economics/laureates/1991/index.html). Douglass North described the rele-vance of Coase's work to his own in North (1987, p. 419).

3. North shared his Nobel Prize and citation with Robert Fogel, also an economic histo-rian, who focused on U.S. history. Although the reference in the joint citation to the applica-tion of "quantitative methods" presumably refers primarily to Fogel's work, North had pub-lished several influential quantitative articles. See The Bank of Sweden Prize in Economic Sciences in Memory of Alfred Nobel 1993 (nobelprize.org/economics/laureates/1993/ index.html). See also North and Wallis (1982) and North (1987).

4. North (1990).

many fields, two works stand out. The most famous is *The Protestant Ethic and the Spirit of Capitalism,* which was a forerunner in considering the relevance of culture to economic growth.[5] But perhaps more directly relevant to this book is *Law in Economy and Society.*[6]

Perhaps a more immediately important predecessor is Hayek, also a Nobel Prize winner. He is particularly interesting in the context of any inquiry into legal institutions because of his focus on legal ideas, well conveyed in the titles of two of his most ambitious works, *The Constitution of Liberty* and *Law, Legislation and Liberty* (published in three volumes).[7]

Just as North's work had predecessors, so too many scholars have tried to expand on his concept of institutions. Dani Rodrik, whose work is relied on at various points in this book, has written on the various forms that institutional solutions take in different countries. One message of Rodrik's work is that there is no single institutional route to economic development.[8] Masahiko Aoki, building in part on the experiences of such diverse venues as Japan, China, and Silicon Valley, has sought to broaden the perspectives of neoinstitutionalism to include private sector arrangements.[9] More generally, Aoki emphasizes relations among institutions as the rules of the game, organizations—the players in the game, including not just governments and private parties—and the equilibrium these various players achieve over time across various domains.[10]

Since the purpose of this book is not to expand on the intellectual, historical, and economic aspects of neoinstitutionalism but rather to unpack its implications for legal institutions, the focus in later chapters is on the various legal issues that arise in any effort to spur economic growth through legal reform.

Stages in Economic Development Thinking

After World War II, and especially during the decades when many former colonies of Great Britain and France (as well as Belgium, the Netherlands, and Portugal) won their independence, practitioners in the field of economic development concerned themselves with the factors that might bring about

5. Weber (1958).
6. Weber (1954).
7. Hayek (1960, 1973, 1976, 1979). See also Mahoney (2001).
8. Rodrik (2000, 2003).
9. Aoki (2000).
10. Aoki (2001).

economic growth in those former colonies, most of which were quite poor. Three major stages in economic development thinking can be defined, albeit with considerable oversimplification and loss of interesting detail.

Initially, during the first few decades, the focus was on the simple economic proposition that production was a function of capital and labor. The poor countries of this time usually had a large supply of labor, with many unemployed or at least underemployed workers, and capital was scarce.[11] What could be simpler than transferring capital to these countries, thereby presumably increasing production? Economic aid programs in the developed world and the expansion of World Bank and regional development bank lending were directed toward this goal.[12]

Regrettably, many of the developing countries viewed industrialization as the primary goal and to that end cut themselves off from international trade by pursuing import substitution policies while using massive public expenditures to build infrastructure and to subsidize new industries. One unfortunate result was serious inflation in many countries, which in turn (especially with the fixed exchange rates that were the rule in those days) led to exchange controls to prevent the currency from depreciating. The exchange controls further reduced international trade.

The response to these problems, in the second stage of economic development thinking, was to apply the insights of neoclassical economic policy, not just to opening domestic economies to imports and to freeing prices from controls but also especially to macroeconomic stabilization.[13] At the policy level these goals became embedded in what was called structural adjustment lending, where loans were made not for projects but for general government support in exchange for commitments to economic reform, prominently macroeconomic reform.[14] The side effect of the focus on economic stability, however, was perceived to be (and often proved to be) slower economic growth than had been enjoyed in earlier decades. Emphasis broadened in the 1990s to include so-called microeconomic reforms, including privatization of state-owned industries and reforms of financial and labor markets.[15]

11. Meier (2001, pp. 14–16).
12. Easterly (2001, pp. 27–28).
13. Yusuf and Stiglitz (2001, pp. 229–32).
14. Easterly (2005); Dollar and Svensson (1998).
15. Krueger (2000). Krueger explained that the microeconomic reforms were divided into two stages: "big picture" reforms such as privatization of state-owned industries and "second generation reforms" concerned with labor and other markets. See generally Kuczynski and Williamson (2003) and Lora and others (2004, pp. 24–39).

The search for new solutions led to an increasing focus on how poorly many developing country governments functioned and especially on widespread inadequacies, even corruption, of public regulatory bodies and of the legal system. As this emphasis on the weaknesses of developing country governments grew, the intellectual rise of neoinstitutional economics seemed to provide an answer. Institutions came to matter in this third stage of economic development thinking. It is with the policy implications of this third stage, especially insofar as legal institutions are involved, that this book is primarily concerned.

Legal Institutions: The Law and Finance Literature

Toward the end of the 1990s, a group of economists, specializing in finance and building upon the emerging emphasis on institutions, conducted cross-country econometric research to determine what legal rules best contributed to strength in the financial sector and thereby to economic growth. Their studies in Law and Finance represented an unprecedented focus on microeconomic analysis of the influence of legal rules on economic growth.[16] Their seminal work led to an explosion of research by other economists and by lawyers into the role of legal institutions in economic development.

A major conclusion reached in their studies was that countries whose legal systems originated in the English common law have enjoyed superior per capita income growth compared with so-called civil law countries, whose law is based on European codes, especially those countries whose law is based on the Napoleonic codes and hence on French law. As this book shows, their conclusions have drawn criticisms on various grounds, especially because many civil law countries—not only those in Western Europe but also some developing countries—have enjoyed superior economic growth and because many common law countries in the third world have done quite poorly in the economic growth tables.

Despite such criticisms of these economists' specific results, the idea that institutions and especially legal institutions are crucial to the process of economic development is now broadly accepted in the academies and in the research departments of international financial institutions such as the World Bank. The term "crucial" is not meant to imply, however, that legal institutions are necessarily more important than other aspects of government policy. Educational and health care institutions have their own crucial roles to

16. See, for example, La Porta and others (1998). For a fuller discussion, see chapter 2.

play in advancing economic growth. One can say that they complement good legal institutions in the way that separate fingers of the hand combine to make for a solid grip; it is pointless to argue over which finger has the highest priority.

The Dual Aims of This Book

What has just been said lies behind the dual aims I have set for this book. The first is to analyze the reasons why legal institutions are important to economic development, and what aspects of the law are of particular importance. The second and related aim is to try to grapple with a task too seldom addressed—perhaps because it is shot through with slippery imponderables. The task I have undertaken is to lay out the policy implications and especially the policy means for following through on the new accent on legal institutions as a major factor in economic development. In short, the key question I address is what it means to act on the premise that the *rule of law* is essential to economic development.

I bring to the matter at hand the perspective of a law professor in the law and economics tradition, an early interest in comparative law, and extended experience as a policymaker at the "nuts and bolts" subcabinet level in three U.S. administrations between 1971 and 2002. I know through personal involvement in traditional debates over economic development that it is easy and convenient for policymakers to call for more economic assistance to distressed countries and to insist on their adherence to better fiscal and monetary policies. Today it is even easier to deliver sermons about the need for "good government"—or, to use the current phrase, "better governance."

I also know that the first instinct of lawyers, which is simply to transplant world-class legal institutions to developing countries, will most likely produce little more than a harvest of dead leaves. The institutions important to development are more likely to bear fruit if they evolve out of roots already growing in the soil of particular countries. How to do that systematically is, of course, still well beyond the current state of the art. Nevertheless, despite the problems and the complexities of the analysis to unfold in this book, there is an urgent need for policymakers, in both the developed and developing worlds as well as in the international institutions that are the financial and technical intermediaries, to grasp the relationship between institutions—legal institutions in particular—and economic growth. The reason can be compressed into a single declarative sentence. Parts of the developing world have ceased to develop. Put differently, per capita incomes are failing to increase significantly in all too many countries. And to use a more popular term, the poor in those unfortunate countries remain trapped in poverty.

Economic Regulation and Corruption

If everything must be treated in a book, nothing can be. To limit the inquiry to manageable proportions, I have necessarily and regretfully excluded from the discussion certain topics that fall within the framework of law and institutions.

In rough order of importance, the first topic that is *not* discussed is economic regulation of business, labor markets, land use, and new business formation.[17] The World Bank has focused particular attention on this last topic—the question of how many, and what kind of, legal steps must be taken to start a new business. The reasons for this focus can be deduced from two extracts from a recent World Bank study:

> It takes 2 days to start a business in Australia, but 203 days in Haiti and 215 days in the Democratic Republic of Congo. There are no monetary costs to start a new business in Denmark, but it costs more than 5 times income per capita in Cambodia and over 13 times in Sierra Leone. Hong Kong (China), Singapore, Thailand, and more than three dozen other economies require no minimum capital from start-ups. In contrast, in Syria the capital requirement is equivalent to 56 times income per capita, in Ethiopia and Yemen, 17 times, in Mali, 6 times.

> Teuku, an entrepreneur in Jakarta, wants to open a textile factory. He has customers lined up, imported machinery, and a promising business plan. Teuku's first encounter with the government is when registering his business. He gets the standard forms from the Ministry of Justice, and completes and notarizes them. Teuku proves that he is a local resident and does not have a criminal record. He obtains a tax number, applies for a business license, and deposits the minimum capital (three times national income per capita) in the bank. He then publishes the articles of association in the official gazette, pays a stamp fee, registers at the Ministry of Justice, and waits 90 days before filing for social security. One hundred sixty-eight days after he commences the process, Teuku can legally start operations. In the meantime, his customers have contracted with another business.[18]

17. World Bank (2005, p. 108).
18. World Bank (2004a, p. xi).

In truth, economic regulation has not received the attention it deserves, in part perhaps because it is often a highly technical subject, with the nature of regulation differing from sector to sector and from regulatory agency to regulatory agency, even within a single government. A recent book by William Lewis, based on the work of the McKinsey Global Institute, argues rather powerfully that a prime cause of development failure is overregulation.[19] He refers not to typical public utility regulation so well known to economists, political scientists, and lawyers, but rather to regulation of the minutiae of everyday business life. To take two examples, Lewis points out that India has reserved hundreds of products for small-scale producers (which in practice are so small that they are high-cost producers) and that Indian zoning laws rule out large retail stores of the kind so well known in the developed world. Since average per capita incomes are ultimately correlated with productivity levels, economic regulation is a neglected aspect of legal institutions. (After all, regulation is usually written into law and often administered by a special regulatory body with enforcement responsibilities.)

Another problem that I have omitted from this discussion is corruption. It is a huge subject, and arguably the most important factor inhibiting economic development in several countries. World Bank research estimates the total of annual bribe payments in the world at $1 trillion annually.[20] Corruption is, of course, related to issues of social norms that I do discuss. More important, corruption can influence the way in which legal rules operate in practice: "Not only do formal rules matter, but also the institutional environment in which those rules are applied and enforced," write three World Bank economists.[21] I have assumed, without attempting to prove, what seems to me obvious—that honesty and trustworthiness in commercial dealings and an absence of corruption in dealings with government agencies, including the judiciary, would be conducive to more rapid economic growth. But honesty and trustworthiness do not appear to be fully achievable goals for public policy, although, of course, a legal system may cause dishonest and untrustworthy businessmen to act in a way that they would not act if they were inherently honest and trustworthy. What the elements of such a legal system are, especially to the extent that culture and social mores work against the legal system rather than complementing it, is one of the major themes of this book.

The problem of corruption, however, is a bit different. Although here too culture and social norms play a role, the legal changes and government

19. Lewis (2004).
20. World Bank (2004b).
21. Kaufmann, Kray, and Mastruzzi (2005, p. 39).

programs best able to combat corruption are not obvious. Government policies may themselves invite corruption. For example, the complex requirements for starting a business not only invite corruption but in some cases
may indeed have been imposed as a lure for bribes for those who dispense the
needed licenses and permissions. In any event, I have decided to leave the
question of corruption for another day.

To put the case directly, I focus in particular on rule-of-law issues: the protection of property rights, the enforcement of contracts, and the role of the
judiciary in achieving those goals. And I illustrate the applications of these
institutional questions in a few especially important economic sectors: land
(since most developing countries are primarily agricultural, and legal
improvements such as titling and land registries are common proposals for
reform) and, in keeping with the Law and Finance literature, equity and
credit markets. My hope is that concentrating on this subset of legal issues
will provide a framework for further work on the role of legal institutions in
economic development.

Economic Growth: The Big Picture

Since this book is about economic development, it is best to say straight off
that the overall record of economic growth in the half century from 1950 to
2000 is not to be dismissed as, to use the American vernacular, "peanuts." In
that period the developed world grew roughly fourfold in real per capita
income and the developing world threefold.[22] The "onefold" is a big difference, certainly not peanuts; it is, of course, necessarily equivalent to average
per capita real incomes in 1950. Yet the growth in the developing world as a
whole was much greater than had been predicted at the outset of the period.[23]
Moreover, in the 2001–04 period, emerging economies grew two and one-
half times faster than advanced economies, which were plagued by recessions,
and, in Europe and Japan, by uncommonly slow growth.[24]

Not least of all, the developing country growth was much better when
viewed from two more points of comparison and contrast. First of all, the
2.3 percent annual per capita growth in the developing world as a whole from
1960 to 2000 was much more rapid than the 0.6 percent growth from 1820 to
1950. Second, and more striking, the developing world's 2.3 percent growth
in the four decades from 1960 to 2000 exceeded the U.S. growth rate of

22. Maddison (2003).
23. Cooper (2005).
24. "Coming into Flower; Emerging Economies," *Economist,* October 16, 2004.

1.8 percent during the heyday of its pathbreaking development during the half century before World War I; it was also better than British growth of only 1.3 percent during the half century from 1820 to 1870.[25]

Still, the variability in growth rates between countries in the developing world has been remarkably large, with whole regions suffering subpar economic growth for long periods. And many countries have in recent decades experienced a serious slowdown in growth.[26]

TO RESTATE THE aim of this book, I address the implications of the view, now in the ascendancy in the academy and many international organizations, that institutions—and the rule of law in particular—provide the keys to unlocking the full growth potential of the developing world. Second, I examine the preconceptions about the role that different legal systems may play in economic development. The thrust of the analysis is to unpack the still rather general notions of the kinds of problems that the ascendant view would call upon developing countries to confront and the legal rules and arrangements that could be expected to address those problems successfully.

25. Rodrik (2005); Maddison (2001, p. 265, table B-22).
26. Maddison (2002, pp. 36–37).

Perspectives on Law
and Economic Development

Four perspectives that I explore in this first part lay the basis for the detailed substantive chapters in the remaining parts.

The first chapter concerns the concept of the rule of law itself. Whatever the value of that concept for lawyers and political scientists, policymakers and policy analysts will want to know its relevance for economic development policy. A further question is how the rule of law fits into the current focus on institutions.

The second chapter explores the Law and Finance literature that has been so crucial in popularizing the notion that the origin of a country's law is important to the pace of economic development. Since that literature depends on the distinction between the common law and civil law traditions, the chapter begins with a discussion of the difference in those two traditions, emphasizing how they came to dominate the developed world's law and how, despite the variety in civil law systems (the French, the German, and the Scandinavian being considered the three "origins" of civil law), the countries in today's developing world have nearly without exception either common law or French law origins. The reader should be aware that the objective of analyzing the Law and Finance literature is to consider the choices developing countries have in improving their legal institutions in furtherance of economic development.

The third chapter examines explanations other than legal origin for the difference in rates of growth, especially between the developed and the developing world. The emphasis is on geography and on culture. Explanations based on geography usually include temperature, soils, and vegetation, as well as tropical disease and landlocked location. Under culture the inquiry in this chapter looks at dimensions such as trust, social capital, social norms, and religion.

The fourth and final chapter in this part steps back to ask some basic questions about how today's developed world achieved the rule of law, imperfect though it may still be. After all, if the leaders of today's developing world should conclude that economic development depends on the quality of their legal institutions, they would surely be wise to ask themselves how today's developed world achieved the rule of law. As the reader will see, it was not easy. Any thoughtful policymaker will realize, of course, that while the accumulated legal learning of past centuries is certainly helpful, it contains few recipes that can be directly applied to a particular developing country with its own special history and institutions.

1

Where Does the Rule of Law Fit in Economic Development?

W hat is this thing we call the *rule of law*? Advocating the rule of law as a key to development is much too vague a prescription to be meaningful to policymakers in developing countries or to foreign assistance agencies in international organizations and individual developed countries. Before turning in later chapters to the meaning of the rule of law in particular economic sectors, it is important to have some sense of the concept's history and general meaning.

The concept has a long history. The rule of law was a preoccupation of writers in civilizations from Greece to early England and on to the birth of the American republic. Plato wrote that "the state in which the law is above the rulers, and the rulers are the inferior of the law, has salvation, and every blessing which the Gods can confer."[1] In early England Bracton wrote that the King was subject to "God *and the law*."[2] John Adams, later president of the United States, arranged in 1780 to include in the Massachusetts constitution a phrase that echoes down to today: "Ours is a government of laws, not of men."[3] The phrase was placed front and center in American constitutional law by Chief Justice John Marshall in 1803 in the fundamental Supreme Court opinion establishing the power of judicial review, *Marbury* v. *Madison*.[4]

---

1. Plato (1952, p. 682).

2. The quotation is from Plucknett (1940, p. 5). Issues have arisen about how much of the work known as Bracton the man known as Henry of Bratton (or Henri de Bracton) really wrote and what his views on the relation of the king and the law really were (Barton 1993; Tierney 1963).

3. Bartlett (2002, p. 351). Adams used the phrase in the *Boston Gazette* in 1774; see *Columbia World of Quotations* 2824 (www.bartleby.com/66).

4. 5 U.S. 137, 163 (1803).

Today, unfortunately, most rule-of-law discussions are so general and abstract as to have little direct relevance to the formulation of economic development policies. Perhaps the rule of law is something that we know when we see it, as Justice Potter Stewart said of pornography in a U.S. Supreme Court case involving a motion picture.[5] My own focus, in developing the root concept of the rule of law, is on how the protection of property and enforcement of contracts can contribute to economic development.

One of the reasons for taking this apparently narrow approach is precisely to avoid the ambiguities of a broader approach involving political liberties, human rights, democracy, and constitutionalism, even though these ideas may indeed play a role in economic development, especially if one adopts Amartya Sen's approach stressing that development is much more than higher incomes.[6] Even if development is measured simply as an increase in GDP per capita, however, a fuller treatment than permitted by the scope of this book would have to consider, for example, the evidence that one of the reasons democracies on the whole grow faster than autocracies is that democracies tend to have stronger institutions.[7] Any attempt to deal with the indisputably important issue of human rights would have to confront the absence of empirical information on the relation of human rights to economic development. Most discussions of human rights are either aspirational or devoted to the recounting of horror stories about abuses.[8]

I recognize that even when restricting the discussion to protection of property and enforcement of contracts, the rule of law cannot be cabined into a discussion of property law and contract law. And for one simple reason: A major threat to protection of property and enforcement of contracts is the government itself. In earlier times the threat came from the ruler (a king, for example) who would often act predatorily to take a subject's property or to renege on a contract with a subject—say, by failing to repay loans (which were often advanced in the first place only because of coercion from the ruler).

5. *Jacobellis* v. *Ohio*, 378 U.S. 184, 197 (1964), J. Stewart concurring.
6. Sen (1999).
7. Halperin, Siegle, and Weinstein (2005, pp. 58–63). Even the proposition of a correlation between democracy and growth has been contested, however. A review in 1993 of eighteen studies, which generated twenty-one findings, revealed that eight found that democracies developed faster, eight found that authoritarian regimes grew faster, and five found no difference (Przeworski and Limongi 1993, p. 60). In any event, the form and history of democratic institutions can be expected to make a difference (Persson 2005). On the impact of a transition from authoritarianism to democracy, see Rodrik and Wacziarg (2002).
8. For a promising start to producing quantitative information on the relation of human rights to economic development, see Kaufmann (2004b).

So even narrowing the subject to the protection of property and the enforcement of contracts, I still must deal not just with relations between economic actors in the economy but also with the broader question of relations between the government and the people. In modern times, the broader question involves the structure of government, especially the overlapping and separation of the executive, legislative, and judicial powers.

Similarly, at the other end of a continuum starting from the structure of government, the core ideas of property and contracts themselves have to be unpacked. Take property: It is not just a question of real estate—houses and land. If that were all that were involved, legal restrictions could be focused on expropriation and on the policing of criminal invasions of private houses and land. But property is a much broader subject. A share of stock is also property. Yet who is it who owns a corporation? And who is it who owns the corporation's property? Although the subject is protection of property, contemporary problems of corporate governance and self-dealing by corporate officers and directors cannot be avoided. In considering economic development in, say, Africa, policymakers must confront the very large questions of how communal property fits into a modernizing economy and whether tribal members should be accorded individual property rights.

Just as the protection of property expands into a myriad of issues, so too the enforcement of contracts explodes into a host of problems ranging from contracts for sale or use of property to the entire spectrum of financial relations and instruments. Finance is largely about contracts. To take a simple example, bank deposits and bank loans are contracts.

In short, the rule of law concerns two spheres of institutions and legal rules. The first has to do with the state, specifically with the relations among its structural parts—namely, the executive, the legislature, the judiciary, and regulatory agencies. Under this first heading an important issue is how those structural parts relate to the country at large; where economic development is at issue, the concern is with economic actors in the economy, including not just human beings but also corporations and other economic entities.

The second sphere has to do with the interactions among those economic actors. There the focus is on the content of the legal rules, not only subject by subject but also the ways the rules fit together in a legal system. As discussed in the next chapter, one highly influential line of research concludes that, at least in the financial sector, Anglo-American legal rules, originating in English common law, are superior to civil law originating in continental Europe, and especially civil law originating in France.

The Content of the Rule-of-Law Concept

Whether the focus of the discussion on the rule of law falls within the first sphere involving the structure of government and its relation to economic actors or into the second sphere involving relations among economic actors, an important question has to do with whether there is something about a state's legal system and rules that is a base requirement for regarding it as a rule-of-law state. In other words, are the state's actions and its courts governed by the rule of law?

Many scholars have written at length about the content of the rule of law. Much of the writing has to do with limitations on the state's power to persecute individuals. This is, of course, the focus of references to the rule of law in discussions of human rights. But aside from human rights abuses, the rule of law is likely to be compromised even in purely private law matters if the leadership of a country or if privileged individuals can act arbitrarily against others. Rules applicable between private parties may mean entirely different things when one of the parties has the power of the state behind it—say, through political influence (crony capitalism) or corruption. Scholars have therefore tried to find bedrock principles that must be followed if a rule of law is to prevail. While the approach in the vast literature of the rule of law varies, the most basic ideas are:

1. Legal rules should be written down and available to all residents of the realm: No secret law.

2. Rules should apply, and be enforced, equally and dispassionately for all, regardless of position or station. Further, the state and the ruler should also be subject to the law: Nobody is above the law.

3. Individuals have a right to have rules that favor them enforced for their benefit. In other words, they are entitled to access to justice on a nondiscriminatory basis no matter who they are and who the defendant may be.[9]

It would be a diversion in this discussion of economic development to go further, although a great deal of elaboration and extension of rule-of-law principles is possible. Nonetheless, it should be recognized that a certain tension exists between these principles and some that are popular in some

9. The reader may wish to consult, to cite just a few of the many fine discussions of the rule-of-law concept, Fuller (1964), Raz (1983, pp. 210–29), Summer (1999), and Sunstein (1995, pp. 968–69). See also Cass (2001) and Hayek (1960). See also the 1885 lectures of Albert Venn Dicey, available in Dicey (1893). For a discussion of the fundamental differences between the Anglo-American rule of law, the German *Rechtsstaat,* and the French *État de droit* concepts, see Rosenfield (2000–2001).

non-Western nations. For example, Confucian notions that compromise and conciliation should be promoted over litigation with its up-or-down, winner-take-all characteristics do not necessarily accord with Western rule-of-law principles. Similarly, any system, whether it be a military dictatorship or a communist state, that makes the welfare of the state or the government the dominant standard is bound to infringe to a greater or lesser extent on rule-of-law principles. In particular, the rule of law is to be distinguished sharply from rule *by* law—that is, the use of legal instruments by those holding power to impose their arbitrary will.[10] Finally, many rule-of-law issues are raised in any state constructed on religious principles where those principles are determined by a religious hierarchy rather than by democratic processes.

What Is the Problem that a Rule-of-Law Approach Addresses?

One way to start to look at the rule-of-law question is by showing why this apparently narrow approach has gradually moved to the fore in contemporary discussions of economic development. To do that one must start with the economic development problem for which legal institutions are increasingly proposed as a partial solution.

As noted already, the stark fact is that many parts of what is optimistically called the developing world have stopped developing. Between 1973 and 1998 real GDP per person grew only 0.99 percent a year in Latin America and only 0.1 percent a year in Africa (compared with 2.52 percent and 2.07 percent, respectively, between 1950 and 1973).[11] In fact, in many parts of Africa per capita GDP has actually declined in the last several decades—to the point where some African nations have made no progress in per capita GDP in the forty-plus years of independence.

The problem for much of the rest of the developing world is more one of a slowdown in otherwise promising growth. The remarkable part of the experience of recent decades is the great diversity among regions and among countries within regions. During the half century from 1950 to 2000, Asian developing countries grew fivefold, Latin American nations twofold, the transition economies (former Soviet Union and Eastern Europe) less than twofold, and African countries only about two-thirds.[12] China has, of course, experienced spectacular growth, though from a very low per capita level,

10. See, for example, Cooter (1997).
11. Maddison (2001, p. 126, table 3-1a).
12. Maddison (2002, pp. 31–32).

while a number of sub-Saharan African countries have declined over the half century, as have a few others, such as Haiti, Cuba, and some oil exporters.[13]

On the bright side, some developing countries have done exceedingly well. Radelet found twenty-one countries whose per capita income growth was at least as fast in the 1960–2001 period as any currently developed country (other than Japan) had ever grown over any forty-year period in its entire history. Moreover, these twenty-one countries include not just the East Asian Tigers and China but countries in Africa (Botswana, Cape Verde, Egypt, Lesotho, Mauritius, and Tunisia), the Caribbean (Dominican Republic), and Asia (India, Indonesia, Sri Lanka, Thailand, and even Pakistan). In contrast, no Latin American country is on that list.[14]

Some regional contrasts are quite remarkable. While most of sub-Saharan Africa has done very poorly, Botswana—the world's poorest country in 1950—has grown by more than 5 percent per capita a year in recent decades.[15] And of course South Korea presents a startling contrast with North Korea, despite the common language and the fact that before the Korean War, the North was the industrialized part of the peninsula. A similar contrast could be found between West and East Germany before reunification, and this contrast continues to some extent even after a decade and a half of unification.

The Korean and German contrasts are, of course, the most dramatic proof that institutions matter. But before asking how institutional differences might explain the other intra- and interregional differences, it is worth observing that economic history fails to repeat itself, at least over long periods. What is remarkable about the situation of the developing world over the last several centuries is that it could hardly have been predicted from its much earlier history. The developing regions, including some that are suffering from the recent slowdown, encompassed polities that were once the richest in the world. Many of the former colonies of European nations have done poorly, even though before colonization they were comparatively rich. Acemoglu, Johnson, and Robinson have called this the "Reversal of Fortune."[16] Examples can be readily seen in India, Mexico, and Peru:

---

13. Cooper (2005).

14. Radelet (2005, table 1).

15. Cooper (2005).

16. Acemoglu, Johnson, and Robinson (2002). For a related discussion of a reversal of fortune, see Diamond (2005), which emphasizes environmental factors and, especially, some of the collective decisionmaking factors (at pp. 427–36) discussed later in this book.

Societies like the Mughals in India, and the Aztecs and the Incas in the Americas were among the richest civilizations in 1500, yet the nation states that now coincide with the boundaries of these empires are among the poorer societies of today. In contrast, countries occupying the territories of the less-developed civilizations of North America, New Zealand and Australia are now much richer than those in the lands of the Mughals, Aztecs and Incas.[17]

Though war and disease can explain what happened to groups such as the Aztecs, the reversal of fortune is noteworthy because while Europe was relatively well off in 1500, the challenge is to explain why some of the then-rich areas did so poorly while others were able to do well. To pick up the theme of this book, is the explanation institutional or is there a better explanation? And if it is institutional, are legal institutions at the heart of the explanation? Whatever the explanation across the sweep of five centuries, it is, of course, more directly relevant to explain what has happened during the postcolonial period, particularly for those countries that became independent only after World War II.

The Role of Foreign Assistance

To the differential but generally disappointing record of the last few decades must be added a growing perception that aid—foreign development assistance—has not contributed significantly to improving growth rates. To some extent, economic studies have strengthened this perception. Perhaps the most influential article was by Burnside and Dollar, published in 2000. Their econometric analysis led to somewhat pessimistic conclusions about how much difference foreign assistance had made in the developing world: "Consistent with other authors, we found that on average aid has had little impact on growth. . . ."[18] But the paper also had an optimistic aspect, and consequently their article was widely cited for their additional conclusion that aid can make a difference in countries that follow good policies.

A variety of articles, especially in the press and in foreign assistance agency publications, cited Burnside and Dollar for the proposition that aid can be made to work and therefore that foreign assistance budgets should be

17. Acemoglu, Johnson, and Robinson (2004, p. 21).
18. Burnside and Dollar (2004, p. 864).

increased. Less than two years later, in 2002, President George W. Bush proposed a U.S. Millennium Challenge Account that would increase U.S. aid by 50 percent, with the increase going to those countries able to demonstrate that they followed good policies.[19]

Subsequent econometric analysis has thrown some doubt on even the modestly optimistic Burnside and Dollar results. A study by Easterly, Levine, and Roodman used additional data based on alternative definitions of aid, good policy, and growth, as well as alternative time periods, to test the Burnside and Dollar results. According to an advance summary by Easterly, their study found "no support for the conclusion that 'aid works in a good policy environment.'" Easterly did concede that in some cases foreign assistance had been "strikingly successful" but added that there were also "numerous examples of aid failing."[20] The full article by Easterly, Levine, and Roodman was more circumspect in its conclusions. It avoided arguing that policies made no difference but rather concluded that adding additional data to the earlier Burnside and Dollar study "raises new doubts about the effectiveness of aid and suggests that economists and policy makers should be less sanguine about concluding that foreign aid will boost growth in countries with good policies."[21] A response by Burnside and Dollar merely said that a conclusion that "aid has no effect on growth in all environments" would be "too negative a conclusion to draw," citing theoretical considerations and case studies to support their original conclusion.[22]

Even assuming that Easterly and his colleagues are correct that good policies alone cannot make foreign assistance work to improve economic growth, it is still possible that the quality of government itself and specifically the quality of legal institutions can make a difference, indeed a systematic difference. The "good policies" referred to in the debate were "good fiscal, monetary, and trade policies."[23] But that leaves open the possibility that good institutions, as opposed to macroeconomic policies, can make a big difference in enhancing the effectiveness of aid.

From a public policy point of view, it was particularly discouraging for foreign assistance proponents when in 2005, the head of the International

---

19. Remarks of President Bush to the Inter-American Development Bank, March 14, 2002. See Brainard and others (2003).

20. Easterly (2003, pp. 27, 36).

21. Easterly, Levine, and Roodman (2004, pp. 779–800).

22. Burnside and Dollar (2004, p. 783). For a paper arguing that certain kinds of aid have a relatively strong favorable impact on economic growth, see Clemens, Radelet, and Bhavnani (2004).

23. Burnside and Dollar (2000, p. 847).

Monetary Fund's research department, Raghuram Rajan, co-authored two working papers. The first paper found "little evidence of a robust positive (or negative) relationship between aid inflows into a country and its economic growth" and, perhaps more debatable, "no evidence that aid works in better policy or institutional or geographic environments, or that certain kinds of aid works better than others."[24] The second paper contributed to the pessimistic view by finding that "aid flows have systematic adverse effects on a country's competitiveness, as reflected in the share of labor intensive and tradable industries in the manufacturing sector," resulting from "the real exchange rate overvaluation caused by aid inflows."[25] In other words, aid inflows push up the exchange rate and thereby discourage manufacturing exports, a problem popularly known as the "Dutch disease."[26]

At the same time, several points need to be kept in mind to avoid undue pessimism about the **effecti**veness of foreign aid. First, a majority of studies do in fact show that aid is effective in some circumstances.[27] Second, some aid—such as humanitarian food aid in disaster situations (tsunamis, earthquakes, and civil strife)—is not intended to promote economic growth, and hence the failure to show greater growth than in the years before the disaster is hardly surprising. This circumstance points to a particular weakness in cross-country regression studies that lump all types of aid together and then test for growth impacts over a short period of time.[28] Finally, aid (like many other policy interventions) has diminishing returns, and it is indeed likely that massive aid to some countries has gone well beyond those countries' absorptive capacities.[29] The upshot is that even critics of aid, such as Rajan, concede that aid can work in some circumstances.[30]

Looked at from a skeptical policymaker's point of view, foreign assistance has not worked, consistently at least, because there is no assurance that the money will be used for investment rather than consumption and because too often foreign assistance has led to an increase in corruption and economic

24. Rajan and Subramanian (2005a).
25. Rajan and Subramanian (2005b). Rajan (2005) later stated that he was "not fully persuaded" by the Clemens, Radelet, and Bhavnani (2004) study arguing that certain kinds of aid have a relatively strong favorable impact on economic growth.
26. The Dutch disease refers to the experience of the Netherlands when North Sea gas was discovered and the resulting increase in foreign currency earnings caused the exchange rate to rise, reducing exports of traditional Dutch products.
27. Hansen and Tarp (2000). This article reviews, of course, only studies that predated it.
28. Clemens, Radelet, and Bhavnani (2004).
29. Clemens, Radelet, and Bhavnani (2004).
30. Rajan (2005).

waste. Assistance for industrial development stands indicted in many eyes by monuments of rusting steel mills or underutilized raw materials processing plants that simply add to world surpluses in basic industries. Infrastructure development can help if properly conceived, though toll roads and bridges that no one uses come to the skeptical mind, and the emphasis on dams and hydroelectricity raises profound sustainability questions about environmental effects and large movements of population. The emphasis on macroeconomic stability that developed in the 1980s was presumably correct, but a consensus has emerged that macroeconomic stability is simply a necessary condition for consistent economic growth and does not itself guarantee that growth. Even within the foreign assistance community, writes Nicolas Van de Walle, doubts grew in the 1990s about the effectiveness of the aid that "for 50 years . . . has been the central policy instrument with which the international community has promoted economic development." Such doubts were particularly focused on the poorest countries where "despite a large volume of aid . . . a core set of the poorest countries has known little improvement in poverty rates [and] little or no economic growth."[31]

These conclusions leave the chastened optimist with institutional solutions. Surely the third world must improve institutions and then perhaps it can develop as the currently developed world has done in the past.

Some Preliminary Questions about Institutions

The foregoing considerations lead to a conceptual question about the institutional approach, especially as applied to rule-of-law issues: What do we mean by institutions? Douglass North was clear that in emphasizing institutions, he was not talking about organizations. Institutions are the "rules of the game," he said, and therefore include "any form of constraint that human beings devise to shape human interactions." They include not just law but social norms, customs, and unwritten codes of conduct as well as formal and informal enforcement measures.[32]

Organizations, in contrast, include—according to North—every way in which "individuals bound by some common purpose to achieve objectives" organize themselves, from governments through political parties, labor

---

31. Van de Walle (2005, pp. 1–2). Heckelman and Knack (2005) found that higher levels of aid had the effect of slowing economic reform in the 1980–2000 period. Nevertheless, aid levels, in twenty-two countries already above 50 percent of government expenditures, continue to rise. See Moss and Subramanian (2005).

32. North (1990, pp. 4, 6).

unions, churches, and so forth.[33] Most readers will find this institutions-organizations distinction counterintuitive. First, it does not correspond to common parlance. Second, each organization has rules, which are humanly devised constraints and therefore are "institutions" according to North. And third, the essence of the organization sometimes lies in the rules: a central bank that is not independent of the finance ministry is a different animal from a central bank that has true independence.

At the same time, North's concept of institutions has a great virtue when talking of law: it keeps one's mind on the fact that what counts is not only the written rule but all of the factors that shape the rule's influence, from enforcement to social norms to corruption. Unlike neoclassical economics, which has traditionally dealt primarily with the substance of economic policies and legal rules, neoinstitutional economics puts rather more focus on what actually happens on the way from a policy or rule to its application and practical result. Neoinstitutional economics also looks more often to history and experience than to mathematics for its analysis.

Despite the terminological clarity of limiting the term institutions to rules of the game and using the word organizations to describe what in popular usage is termed institutions, this distinction is actually too confining in a discussion of law. The reason is simple. Substantive rules on the books do not capture the essence of a legal system. This is true whether law is made by the legislature or by the judiciary. The nature of a country's judiciary and the role it plays not only in enforcing the law on the books but also in modulating and even in the outright changing of the substantive law is perhaps even more important, as we shall see. Therefore, broadly conceived, the nature of a country's judiciary becomes institutional in the sense that it interacts with substantive law to give the true rules of the game for the economy. Thus the judiciary is not a mere organization and is therefore referred to in this book as a legal institution.[34]

An Advance Look at Some Conclusions

To give the reader some idea of where this book is leading, I set forth here, in an uncaveated and unvarnished manner, some of the conclusions that I reach in succeeding chapters. The qualifications of those conclusions lie in the

33. North (1990, p. 5).
34. For an analytical discussion of the concept of institutions in the context of economic growth, see Nelson and Sampat (2001).

chapters themselves, but I hope that this approach will give the reader a sense of what lies ahead and why it may be worthwhile persevering.

In the first part I reach three main conclusions. First, although much has been written in support of the proposition that developing countries that inherited a common law system have a development advantage over those that inherited a civil law system, I conclude in chapter 2 that for several reasons there is little merit to that idea. This conclusion about the so-called legal origins thesis is illustrated in several later chapters. Second, in chapter 3, I conclude that competing explanations for differences in growth rates in the developing world have some merit. Both geographical differences and especially cultural differences appear to have some effect on growth rates, although the explanations for these differences offer little insight to the policymaker. Third, in chapter 4, I step back to ask how Europe acquired the rule of law, and my answer is that it did so with great difficulty and that centuries were required to accomplish that great transformation. Implicitly the message is that developing countries have the advantage of being able to see how the rule of law works in many developed countries, but it would be unwise to be too impatient with their difficulties in acquiring the rule of law for themselves.

In the second part, I take up three main rule-of-law topics: the judiciary, contracts and property, and land. I conclude that the judiciary is of key significance because enforcement is usually more important than the details of substantive law in creating the conditions for economic development. Contracts and property turn out to be the two key concepts for analyzing the substantive law problems that developing countries face. Land is a key issue in the developing world because many, perhaps most, residents of the developing world do not have state-recognized property rights in their farms and dwellings. At the same time developing countries should not be pushed into universal titling schemes so quickly that communal land arrangements, most of which are relatively economically efficient, are undermined.

In the third part, the subject shifts to the financial sector, which much economic research shows is the most important sector for sustained economic development. After revisiting the legal origins theory, showing how it fails to illuminate the issues, I conclude in a chapter on equity capital that the essence of the problem of achieving the great advantages of the corporate form lies in corporate governance issues, particularly in protecting minority shareholders from majority shareholders. That is an especial problem in the developing world where most corporations' shares are held by a few controlling "blockholders" rather than, as in the United States and some of Europe, being held by a widely diverse shareholding public. Turning then to credit markets, which are much more important—especially in the developing world—than equity markets, I make three main points. Banks are of central importance, but they are also prone in much of the developing world to multiple kinds of abuses by their concentrated owners; secured lending law is far more important than bankruptcy even though economic research has been devoted overwhelmingly to bankruptcy, and the same research rather badly misconceives how bankruptcy works in practice and why it may work poorly in many developing countries.

In the final part of the book, after tracing the implications of a rule-of-law approach to economic development, I take up the case of China. How can it be asserted, as it so universally is, that the rule of law is essential to economic development when China, the fastest-growing country in the world, is by any measure far short of having achieved a rule of law? The answer is too complicated and also provides too useful an insight into how the rule of law can actually be achieved for me to attempt a single-sentence summary. But the question is also too important not just to China but also to the world as a whole to be ignored.

2 | Legal Institutions, Legal Origins, and Governance

Two legal families central to the discussion of the relationship between the rule of law and economic development are English common law and continental civil law—in particular, French civil law. An overview of these two families is warranted at the outset, if only to indicate what the concept of legal origins as a determinant of economic development entails.

Common Law

When William conquered England in 1066, he set in train a flow of events that eventually divided today's Western world between common law and civil law countries. At that time the Roman law system that had distinguished the Roman empire no longer held sway in western Europe, where law was local or at best regional. In the Eastern empire, Roman law had been written down. But in the West the empire centered in Rome had already collapsed, and so the law was a series of customs, often unwritten, that varied from place to place.

William was crowned King of England in Westminster on Christmas Day 1066, and in the space of a few decades he and his successors and their officials had imposed Norman law, effectively displacing the existing Saxon law. The new English kings gradually established a bureaucracy complete with its own law and courts as well as a feudal system, based on Norman custom, for the holding of land.[1] Carrying out a promise to his key supporters, William seized the land of his Saxon opponents and divided it among his most important

1. Van Caenegem (1988, pp. 96–97). See further discussion of feudalism in chapter 4.

followers. Under the system he established in England, based on the continental feudal system, all land was ultimately held by those who actually worked the land in a chain of ownership leading back to the king.[2] In the early days English common law was largely a law of real property.[3] Vestiges of the adaptation of the common law to its feudal heritage are found in common law countries to this day.

The new court system, centered in London, began using traveling royal judges to cover the country, thereby ensuring a unified common law for all of England that left only a minor role for local custom.[4] The quick consolidation of law—a *common law* for all of England—was remarkable.[5] A leading German comparative law text notes that France did not achieve any comparable common legal rules until the sixteenth century and Germany did not do so before the nineteenth century. Consequently, the text authors point out that "there never existed in England one of the essential motor powers behind the idea of codification, which even on the Continent rested on the practical need to unify the law as well as on the philosophy of the Enlightenment and the thinking of natural lawyers."[6]

Substantive English law, being nevertheless customary (albeit at root Norman custom), was not written down in a comprehensive way. Rather it was based on a series of writs (that is, writings) that were "forms of action," one for each of the multitude of law proceedings that a plaintiff might wish to bring. But each writ presumed a particular wrong and a particular remedy, and it was up to the plaintiff to choose the right one on pain of having his remedy denied.[7] These forms of action also lingered in English law until legal reform finally eliminated most of the last vestiges in the twentieth century.

The writs, though in writing, were not themselves statements of substantive law, and indeed the substantive law of England cannot be said to have

2. Holdsworth (1956, pp. 17–32). See further discussion in chapter 7.

3. Holdsworth (1909, p. 204).

4. Von Mehren, Taylor, and Gordley (1977, pp. 12–13); Danziger and Gillingham (2003, p. 179). The Magna Carta required the royal courts to be held "in a certain place," which could be Westminster (Hudson 1996, p. 224). Itinerant judges were nonetheless still sent out about the country, with important cases referred back to Westminster, thereby preserving the uniformity of the law (Dawson 1968, p. 6, n. 11).

5. Common law, in its core meaning, "applies throughout the realm" and is "territorial, applying to people because they are within the realm, in contrast with a system of 'personal' law, where a person's nationality determines the type of law to which he or she is subject" (Hudson 1996, pp. 16–18).

6. Zweigert and Kötz (1992, p. 191).

7. Milsom (1969, pp. 22–32).

been written down until the publication of the treatise known as Bracton.[8] But even though its author, or authors, knew some Roman law and were influenced by it, the book was explicitly based on court records, thereby recognizing a central principle of the common law that the law is at base what the judges say it is.[9] New writs were regularly being invented to meet new felt needs, statutes were occasionally passed, and the king's imposition of the feudal land system was in effect creating law, but common law techniques of finding and extending law had not yet developed.[10]

Later, common law judges began to elaborate on their rulings with written opinions. These opinions, which sought their justification in earlier cases, began to create the distinctive approach of the common law that characterizes it even today. This approach treats formerly decided cases as controlling precedent and requires judges to reason from case to case, distinguishing cases that could be said to be conflicting precedents, in order to find the controlling principles for new fact situations. It is this process of reasoning from case to case that is what most people today think of as the essence of the common law. Indeed, today the words common law are usually taken to mean judge-made law, rather than just unified law.

To be sure, the English parliament began to pass important statutes, but they were regarded for some centuries, at least by some judges, as embellishments to the body of common law. Indeed, it was understood that statutes that contravened the common law rule were to be narrowly construed to avoid changing more than parliament had clearly intended. But in time it became customary that statutes had their own independent status, independent of the common law, and that statutes could even change common law rules. Nonetheless, judges used methods of interpreting ambiguities in statutes that echoed their methods in nonstatutory fields. In particular, judges relied on earlier decisions on the interpretation of a particular statute and generally considered these earlier rulings as binding on later courts. These characteristics, which are recognized even today by every beginning law student in common law countries as the common law method, can be contrasted with the civil law system that came to reign on the European continent.

---

8. Some scholarship raises doubts about how much of the book Henri de Bracton actually wrote; see Tierney (1963).

9. Dawson (1968, p. 2).

10. Hamowy (2003, p. 249) states that more than 470 writs had been created by the end of the reign of Henry II in the thirteenth century, but that the creation of new writs "had stopped altogether" by the end of the fourteenth century because by that time "common law judges opposed the issuance of writs that had no precedent."

Civil Law

The civil law system developed only slowly. In the early centuries of the common law, continental western Europe was still divided among the remnants of the Roman empire, with customary local law still governing issues involving land, contracts, torts, and the like. This remained true even with the rising importance of the Holy Roman Empire, which exercised little of the sovereign power that is normally associated with law, that power remaining in the various kingdoms and principalities within the Holy Roman Empire.

Nonetheless, over the centuries interest grew in continental western Europe in Roman law, leading to what was known as the "reception" of Roman law. This reception occurred predominantly in the German-speaking areas of Europe (which was the territory where the Holy Roman Empire of the German Peoples, as it was called, had its primary influence). But Roman law remains to this date an important influence on the law of, for example, Scotland.

The interest in Roman law led to a situation in which its concepts and procedures were overlaid on local traditions, being especially influential in areas such as contracts and torts. Law still varied from place to place, but students were increasingly taught Roman law; hence a sense of continuity and unity grew in what became known as the *jus commune*—a kind of common law at least for German-speaking parts of the continent (though quite different from the common law of England).[11] Curiously the Roman law texts were those collected in the *Corpus Juris Civilis* of the Eastern emperor Justinian I in the sixth century, after the collapse of the Western empire. The split between the Reformation and the Counter-Reformation states and the rise of nationalism led to national codifications, the first in Denmark in 1683. By the time Napoleon came to power in France in 1799, the codification movement was well advanced. Napoleon set out to promulgate the codification of all codifications, the French Civil Code, which went into effect in 1804.

Napoleon took a great interest in his code. He personally chaired many of the meetings of the consul committee reviewing the work of the drafters. No doubt Napoleon, the man of action, insisted on the practicality of the code and perhaps its clarity and simplicity.[12] He certainly was proud of his work; after the defeat at Waterloo, he proclaimed: "My true glory is not that I have won 40 battles; Waterloo will blow away the memory of those victories. What

11. Rheinstein and Glendon (2003).
12. Zweigert and Kötz (1998, p. 83); Rabel (1949–50a, pp. 107–08).

nothing can blow away, what will live eternally is my civil code."[13] That was perhaps why Napoleon wanted the code understandable by the common man. But it was drafted by professors and reflected their approach, rather than that of men of practical affairs, and certainly not that of merchants.[14]

Being the product of professors, the French Civil Code was abstract, reflecting the "abstract reasoning [that] had characterized the French approach to law and to life in general" during the Age of Reason. But its generality and its emphasis on understandability meant that one had often to take into account a variety of provisions to determine the legal rules covering a given set of facts. Its very generality gave it staying power, with no important changes made until 1880 (except for the repeal of divorce in 1816 when the Catholic monarchy was restored).[15] And indeed even today the core provisions of Napoleon's code remain in place despite increasingly numerous statutory changes. No doubt it was its generality and clarity of language[16]—Napoleon's army and French imperialism aside—that made the French Civil Code so influential in much of the nineteenth century world that is spoken of today as the developing world. Alan Watson has made the point that when countries choose the law of another country, the prestige of the legal system under consideration counts.[17] No doubt about it, the French Civil Code was prestigious.

The French Civil Code contrasts nicely with the German Civil Code, which came almost a century later in 1900. Why was the German Civil Code so different? Some would say that the explanation lies in the difference in the style of thinking in the two countries, but history played a big role. It was in the German-speaking territories that the greatest "reception" of Roman law occurred. This is not to say that Roman law did not have a major influence on the French Civil Code, but the influence in France was for a different reason than its influence in Germany. One of the reasons Napoleon wanted a code was to unify the law of southern and northern France. Whereas the law in the north was customary law, the law in the south, derived from Roman law, was already written down (*droit écrit*).[18]

In contrast, a major form of German legal scholarship in the decades between the adoption of the two codes was devoted to the study of Roman law. Out of that strain of scholarship came a group of law scholars, the Pandectists,

---

13. Quoted in Aucoin (2002).
14. See Aucoin (2002) and Merryman (1985, p. 56).
15. Rheinstein and Glendon (2003).
16. Rabel (1949–50a, p. 109).
17. Watson (1977, pp. 98–99).
18. Zweigert and Kötz (1998, pp. 77–82); Jolowicz (1982, p. 89).

who devoted themselves over some decades to the elaboration of a German civil code.[19] The style of that code is quite different from the French code. In contrast to the French Civil Code, which was written to be understandable by a moderately literate Frenchman, no one would expect the ordinary German to read the German code, much less understand it. Concepts are carefully defined in the German code, and any given legal term is used in the same way throughout the entire code.[20]

For the purposes of considering contemporary economic development issues in this book, the bulk of our attention on the influence of civil law can be focused largely on the French Civil Code. We can do so for quite pragmatic reasons. Putting aside the transition countries of Eastern Europe and the former Soviet Union, few developing countries are influenced by German law, and those few—such as South Korea and Taiwan—are already high-income countries. (Of course, South Korea and Taiwan had much lower incomes just a few decades ago and thus their legal development would merit investigation.) Scandinavian countries had a few colonies, but today no developing country is regarded as being part of the Scandinavian legal family. The dominant influence in private law (as opposed to, say, constitutional law) in the great bulk of today's less developed world came from either English common law or French civil law.[21]

Legal Origins as a Theory of Development

The essence of the legal origins approach, as applied to economic development, is to use regressions to show that the origin—say, English common law or French civil law—of a particular country's law is associated with that country's rate of economic growth. An alternative approach to the relevance of legal institutions to a country's economic growth looks at the role of "governance." It includes an important role for the rule of law in overall

19. Dawson (1968, pp. 450–61).

20. Ernst Rabel, the foremost comparative law scholar of his generation, held a set of lectures in his new home in the United States after leaving Germany, in which he was unsparing in his comparison of the French and German civil codes. On the question of style, he described the French Civil Code: "The language, crystalline and beautiful, has not had its equal before or afterward; there have been celebrated French poets who like to read some chapters for encouragement in prose" (Rabel 1949–50a, p. 109). For the German code, he reserved pejorative descriptions: "ponderous," "overaccurate pedantry," "innumerable wheels and gadgets," and "ugly" (Rabel 1949–50b, pp. 270, 275).

21. The statement in the text ignores China, which was never a colony and never felt the need to adopt Western law, as did Japan in the late nineteenth century, at least in part.

governance. The two approaches complement each other, and I take up the governance approach below as a useful contrast to the legal origins approach.

Most of the legal origins work began in finance. An early, and perhaps still the most influential, legal origins article is "Law and Finance," published in 1998 by four economists—Rafael La Porta, Florencio López-de-Silanes, Andrei Shleifer, and Robert Vishny—whose work has become so well known that they are universally cited as LLSV.[22] Even though the four authors did not set out to apply their work to economic development policies, it has often been interpreted as throwing important light on economic development outcomes.

Building on earlier work showing that stronger financial sectors led to more rapid economic growth in the economy as a whole, LLSV used a sample of forty-nine countries to show a statistical relationship between the character of legal rules concerning the financial sector and the origin of a country's laws. [23] The most interesting part of this body of research was its finding that countries whose law derived from the common law had stronger legal systems for financial development and hence faster economic growth than civil law countries. An obvious conclusion was that the common law provided a superior legal base for a country (and this was true whether new countries received their law through conquest or colonization).

Equally striking was the finding that French law was the worst among civil law systems for the development of the financial sector and that German and Scandinavian legal systems were situated between common law and French legal systems. And in a related 1997 article, "Legal Determinants of External Finance" (which was based on the same research involving the same countries), LLSV showed that common law origin countries had grown faster than French origin countries—4.30 percent per capita versus 3.18 percent.[24]

In their "Law and Finance" article, La Porta and his colleagues looked at "enforcement variables" such as the "efficiency of legal system," "rule of law," and so forth. But mostly they looked at substantive legal provisions, particularly rules concerning the protection of shareholders and creditors, finding that the common law countries offered the most protections, followed by the German and Scandinavian law countries, with French law countries trailing.

22. La Porta and others (1998).
23. Levine (2004) reviews the considerable research, dating back to the early 1990s, showing a causal link running from financial development to economic growth. See also Beck, Demirgüç-Kunt, and Levine (2004a), who find that "financial development reduces income inequality by disproportionately boosting the incomes of the poor."
24. La Porta and others (1997a, p. 1138, table II).

The main body of their work was in the financial sector, raising perhaps a systemic issue about the policy implications of the legal origins work (important as the financial sector undeniably is to growth, particularly in the middle-income countries). Indeed, an oddity of their work on the financial sector was that it concerned primarily the protection of minority shareholders under corporate law and the protection of creditors in bankruptcy law. Yet both corporate law and bankruptcy law are legal areas where most countries—common law and civil law countries alike—rely on statutory law, much of it quite recent, rather than judge-made common law or nineteenth century civil law codes.[25] This circumstance raises serious questions about the leading interpretation of their results to the effect that the common law method of judge-made laws is superior to legislative enactments in building stronger financial sectors and hence in enhancing economic growth.[26]

In 2000 LLSV followed up with another article, which referred to their earlier work and to new work by other economists. Summarizing those works, they said that "an exogenous component of financial market development, obtained by using legal origin as an instrument, predicts economic growth."[27] They therefore reached the policy conclusion that "the evidence on the importance of the historically determined legal origin in shaping investor rights . . . suggests at least tentatively that many rules need to be changed simultaneously to bring a country with poor investor protection up to best practice."[28]

A different approach is to be found in an article by Mahoney, who rejected the notion that the prime influence of legal origin on economic growth was through financial development. He favored an explanation concerning the greater role for the state relative to the individual citizen in French law. Mahoney explicitly tested the relation of legal origin to economic growth, finding that common law countries grow at least 0.7 percent faster than civil law countries.[29]

A short narrative version of the legal origins theory, which generates the dominant view of the superiority of the common law, is that France under Napoleon adopted elegant civil and commercial codes at the beginning of the nineteenth century, which became the base for the legal systems of much

---

25. In fact, large bodies of American common law have been replaced by statutes (Cross 2005 at n. 116–19).

26. Pagano and Volpin (2005, p. 1006).

27. La Porta and others (2000, p. 16).

28. La Porta and others (2000, p. 20); see also, La Porta and others (2002, pp. 1148–49).

29. Mahoney (2001, p. 516, table 2).

of southern Europe (Napoleon made sure of that through his armies) and later for French Africa and, derivatively through Spain and Portugal, for Latin America. Thus, if those African and Latin American countries grow less rapidly—as they have been doing recently, the regressions suggest rather strongly that it must have something to do with the origin of their legal systems. Mahoney attacked the issue of African and Latin American countries' poor showing by including dummy variables for both sub-Saharan Africa and Latin America and found that common law countries still grew faster but to a lesser extent and with lower statistical significance, suggesting that the LLSV results on legal origin are a less important predictor of economic growth than might otherwise have been thought.[30]

Nearly a century later, in 1900, Germany adopted its own distinctive civil and commercial codes. Those codes became the base not just for German-speaking Austria and multilingual Switzerland but also the point of origin for the codes in Japan, South Korea, and Taiwan; these countries have been growing more rapidly than most of the rest of the developing world, thereby, according to a common intuition, supporting the view that German law is superior to French law for developing countries. (We can ignore the Scandinavian countries, since their few colonies are not developing countries today, and so the Scandinavians influenced only each other.) Meanwhile, the common law countries, such as the United States, Canada, and Australia, have flourished, even if the overall results in terms of growth are weighed down by the Kenyas and Zimbabwes of the world—common law countries in terms of "legal origin." One can thus see a certain intuitive plausibility that noneconomists quickly came to attach to the LLSV regression results.

All of this work on legal origins was based on cross-country regressions with only the most general comparative law analysis. Nonetheless, the legal origins literature set forth legal and institutional hypotheses that, coupled with economic studies on the contribution of financial development to economic growth, have been taken by many scholars and policymakers as the reason why common law countries grow faster than civil law countries. These hypotheses, including the supposedly uncontroversial classification of countries by legal origin, are examined at length in this book. The choice of indicators of what substantive law provisions constitute superior protection of shareholders and creditors is examined in Part III on the financial sector. As shown in later discussions, the LLSV choice of indicators and their interpretation of those indicators are weak elements of their legal origins work.

30. Mahoney (2001, p. 517, table 3).

In the many economic articles, by LLSV and others, there is a broad recognition that the enforcement of contracts and the protection of property are vital to financial development. Although finance is an ideal sector to demonstrate this point, especially because the profusion of data lends itself to econometric methods of proof, it can hardly be doubted that the same principle should apply outside the financial area. After all, economies are more than finance, even if the concept of finance is interpreted broadly to include corporate governance; in the real economy, as opposed to the financial, the same principles should apply. One of the many legal areas outside financial markets where legal origin should therefore be important, but is much less studied in cross-country regressions, is the real estate sector. It is examined in a chapter on land in Part II. This is a particularly important sector in many developing countries where more than half the population works in the agricultural sector and where the growth of megacities has made security of urban real estate, and underlying concepts of title and registry, particularly important.

Although the legal origins literature is focused on financial markets, and especially on substantive legal rules concerning shareholder and creditor protection, LLSV do recognize, as noted above, that enforcement of the rules, and hence the role of the judiciary, is important. Their approach to using legal origin to study these issues is also discussed in Part II in a chapter on the judiciary. Obviously the judiciary has a role transcending the financial sector.

Before reaching these nonfinancial applications of the legal origins analysis, quite a number of issues about the entire legal origins approach need to be fleshed out. The rest of this chapter is devoted to those questions, and the following chapters ask what history can teach about the role of legal institutions in the development of economies.

Preliminary Questions

Although my focus on the legal origins literature is not on the authors' regressions as such, I nevertheless raise some preliminary questions about the data on which the regressions are based. These questions are offered as a basis for raising more fundamental questions about the legal and policy implications for economic development and to suggest several lines of inquiry for a more qualitative analysis.

What is it about law that makes its origin important? Why should law play an important role in economic development, and therefore what differences in legal systems make a difference in rates of economic development? Many alternative qualitative questions spring quickly to mind, and in fact the economists who have conducted these studies have not been shy about suggesting answers to these and similar questions even though their answers do not flow, strictly speaking, from their econometric work. Rather their answers are derived from their understanding of legal institutions, for which they usually cite a few legal surveys, particularly in the field of comparative law.

More specifically, I focus on a pressing, if also problematic, question: What are the policy implications of the legal origins research for economic development? If legal origin does in fact make a decisive difference in economic growth, what policies should policymakers in the developed country foreign aid agencies, in the international financial institutions, and, above all, in third world governments adopt?

No one would suggest, to take an extreme example, that Latin American countries should simply adopt U.S. or English law and legal institutions from one day to the next. (On the supposed superiority of common law over civil law, see box 2-1.) Indeed, even if such adoption were possible, it would take perhaps two generations before one could reasonably expect Latin American law and legal institutions to function like those in the United States or England. Even assuming that culture, social norms, and history have little role in the functioning of a legal system, a time lag would occur for the simple fact that a legal system works through a legal profession and a judiciary. Even if law faculties could be changed overnight to meet their new function, it would still take two generations before the leaders of the profession and the senior judges trained in the old system would be replaced by those trained in a common law system.

This realistic view of how law evolves does not mean that no changes are possible in a shorter run. Quite the contrary, much of the burden of my argument is that the many changes of the past several decades, both in market economy developing countries and in communist countries transitioning to a market economy, offer quite a good deal of experience in what works and what does not work. Moreover, these experiences do not need to be discussed in the abstract but can be examined in specific fields of law. For example, following the popular "sloganized" definition of the rule of law, one can look at the enforcement of contracts and the protection of property rights. One can look at specific areas where law affects the economy in a powerful way—land law, corporate law, bankruptcy law, and the like. And especially one can look at the role of law and legal institutions in financial markets, where the legal origins research focuses.

Any inquiry into policy implications has to go beyond regression results to the underlying mechanisms through which the law, the judiciary, and the

Box 2-1. *Why Should the Common Law Be Superior?*

Whatever the methodology and the results of cross-country statistical studies, a lawyer is left with the question why a common law system should be superior to a civil law system. American legal scholars have not been shy about offering suggestions as to the best answer, and the American legal literature is impressively large on the subject. The proffered explanations mostly have to do with the supposed advantages of reasoning from case to case, but there is little agreement among the authors of the essays. The reasoning, much of which suggests analogies of the case law system to Darwinian natural selection with good precedents replacing bad precedents, largely ignores two crucial points: First, most law today, especially that involving the economy, is statutory in both common law and civil law countries. And second, civil law countries have extensive bodies of case law.[a]

Cross, in a thorough review of the arguments, came to the conclusion that whatever differences may once have existed between common law and civil law systems, "it would be surprising to see a remarkable effect from the nation's choice of common or civil law [and], surely, the convergence between the approaches would have at least muted the effect of the distinct systems."[b] Cross does find a possible difference based on a greater independence of the judiciary in common law systems. In this respect, Cross follows in the footsteps of Mahoney, whose work was briefly reviewed earlier in this chapter. Cross, however, is relying on a perception of greater judicial independence gleaned from a World Economic Forum survey. His conclusion underscores again the greater importance of public law than private law in investigating legal origins.

The policy "takeaway" for developing countries from the Cross review is thus the need to focus on how a judiciary can be made more independent constitutionally and how judges can be enabled and encouraged to behave more independently, subjects taken up in chapter 5.

a. Cross (2005).

b. Cross (2005, nn. 125, 126).

legal profession influence the economy. Therefore, it is worth deepening the understanding of the possible role of legal origins in economic development. One way of doing so is to look at some of the factual anomalies in the studies and then to look for alternative explanations of differential rates of economic growth. But the reader should be aware that the purpose of such an examination is not to reach some final conclusion as to the validity of legal origins theory but rather to use the examination as an entry point to a deeper consideration of the relationship between legal institutions and economic development.

Some Anomalies

The legal origins literature does not purport to be a study of economic development. It treats developed countries and developing countries alike and simply asks whether certain origins are better for certain purposes. In the key legal origins article, all forty-nine countries, developed or developing, are treated as equal, including the origin countries themselves, and no consideration is given to the size of the population or to the geographical region.[31] The central inquiry is to determine which legal families have the best substantive law for financial development, using substantive legal criteria determined by the authors.

On the few occasions when the authors attempt to determine whether the countries differ based on their per capita income levels, they come to some surprising results. As is spelled out in a later chapter, where the legal origins authors choose to categorize countries by their stage of development, the startling result is that the poorest one-third of countries have better substantive law than the richest one-third by the authors' own definition of the crucial substantive law rules![32]

Even among developed countries there are some oddities if one were to interpret the legal origins literature as directly relevant to economic growth. One might suppose on a casual reading that Britain, the source of the common law, has a better growth story to tell than France, which provided what the legal origins literature says is the worst legal origin. Nothing could be further from the truth. Taking the period from 1820 to 1998 as a whole, France outpaced Britain in the rate of per capita growth. A study by Maddison showed, moreover, that this was true from 1820 to 1913 (France had an

---

31. La Porta and others (1998).
32. See chapter 9.

annual average compound growth rate of 1.13 percent versus 0.96 for Britain), 1913 to 1950 (1.12 percent to 0.80 percent), and 1950 to 1998 (2.77 percent to 2.10 percent).[33] An appendix to Maddison's study, however, tells a more nuanced tale: breaking the time periods differently, the data show that from 1820 to 1870 Britain outpaced France, as it did again from 1973 to 1998.[34] Still, for the entire period, France came out ahead.

In fact, from 1870 to 1976 Britain grew only fourfold whereas an arithmetical average of sixteen "advanced countries" grew sixfold, stimulating a leading British financial journalist, Samuel Brittan, to note that the "lag in British growth rates goes back at least a century."[35] Of course, Brittan wrote in 1978, before the privatization and deregulation that began in the Thatcher period and were in place thereafter. One therefore might say that the reason Britain outperformed France in more recent years has more to do with those microeconomic policy initiatives than with any superiority of common law over French law. In 1979, the year Margaret Thatcher became prime minister, French per capita income was $14,970, compared with $13,164 in the United Kingdom (a difference of $1,806, or about 12 percent). In 2001 France was still ahead at $21,092, compared with the United Kingdom at $20,127 (a difference reduced to $965 and less than 5 percent).[36]

Consider, moreover, that throughout the nineteenth century French per capita income had been much lower than British per capita income, but despite two world wars fought on French territory, by the late 1960s French per capita income was able to pull ahead.[37] Hence, if one looks at developments from the beginning of modern financial development in the mid-nineteenth century to the beginnings of Thatcherite reform, one would conclude that the French legal system is superior to the British legal system for economic growth.

Perhaps with this economic record in mind, Merryman wrote an astute article in 1996, before the legal origins literature appeared, advancing the thesis that French law may be fine for France but is unsatisfactory for former French colonies.[38] His reasoning reflects the importance of separating substantive

33. Maddison (2001, p. 90, table 2-22a).
34. Maddison (2001, p. 186, appendix table A1-d).
35. Brittan (1978, p. 246).
36. Maddison (2001, pp. 276–77, table C1-c).
37. Maddison (2002, pp. 62–65, table 1c). For a detailed argument that any superiority of financial development in common law countries over civil law countries is to be explained by twentieth century economic destruction and national occupations rather than legal origins, see Roe (2006).
38. Merryman (1996).

rules of law from questions of enforcement, as well as of taking a realistic view of how judicial enforcement actually operates. Noting that the most important aspect of the Napoleonic legal revolution was to limit the power of judges and particularly their ability to "make law," he pointed out that limiting the role of judges to make law by interpreting ambiguities in statutes was quickly perceived to be impracticable and that a number of fields of French law are in fact principally judge made. As Jolowicz explains, in France:

> Development of law through judicial decisions, though not altogether new, came to be openly recognised as a fact by all except, of course, the Judges themselves when they came to give the formal reasons for their decisions. No one denies today, either for France or for Germany, that great areas of the law are in truth the products of the courts; if any common lawyer still supposes that for the civil law systems case law does not exist, a glance at any Continental textbook with its wealth of case citations will quickly convince him of his error.[39]

Merryman, in his critique, went on to contrast French law in France with French law in former colonies, arguing that when other countries adopted French law, they were not so practical:

> The attempt to depict the judicial function as something narrow, mechanical and uncreative and to portray judges as clerks . . . has had a self-fulfilling effect. Judges are at the bottom of the scale of prestige among the legal professions in France and in the many nations that adopted the French Revolutionary reforms, and the best people in those nations accordingly seek other legal careers. One result has been to cripple the judicial systems in a number of developing countries. In France, where everyone knows how to do what needs to be done behind the separation of powers façade, misrepresentation of the judicial function does not have severe consequences. But when the French exported their system they did not include the information that it really does not work that way, and they failed to include a blueprint of how it actually does work. That has created, and continues to create, problems in nations with limited legal infrastructures and fragile legal systems . . . .[40]

The point that enforcement is more important than the substantive rules of law is one that recurs throughout this book, but for now the important

39. Jolowicz (1982, p. 93).
40. Merryman (1996, p. 116).

point is that the legal origins literature indirectly maligns the French legal system even as it actually operates in France, and it tends to lead the casual reader of that literature to erroneous conclusions about the rule-of-law challenges facing the developing world.

FACTUAL ANOMALIES

Once one goes into the details of the legal origins literature, some important factual anomalies also emerge. Two stand out. The first is that, at least in the early studies, the focus was heavily on private law—especially corporate and commercial law—rather than what might seem far more important to economic growth, namely, public law—that is, constitutional law bearing on the powers of the government, administrative law bearing on the powers of the bureaucracy, regulatory law bearing on the way in which the government regulates business, and the like.[41] As Schlesinger and his comparative law colleagues stated: "The economic and social changes which have taken place during the [twentieth] century . . . mostly are reflected in the growth of such *public law* fields as administrative law, labor law, social security, taxation, nationalization, and public corporations. Many of these changes, therefore, are only faintly reflected on the face of the modern private law codes."[42]

It is important to understand that the French and German civil codes dealt with private law, as opposed to public law. Indeed, those two civil codes are primarily concerned with what are referred to in common law circles as contracts, torts, property, family law, and inheritance. Because its focus is on the financial sector, much of the legal origins literature has to do with corporate and commercial law, which is found largely in the French and German commercial codes. Neither the civil nor the commercial codes have much at all to do, especially today, with the relationship between the state and the individual citizen or enterprise. This is not to say that the details of corporate and commercial law are not important to economic growth; on the contrary, their importance is stressed in later chapters. But they are arguably less important to the concept of the rule of law, which in the economic sphere has much to do with the protection of property rights and the enforcement of contracts. Lack of enforcement of property rights in the developing world has more to do with public law than with private law. The biggest threats to property

41. See, however, chapter 5 for an analysis of an important article on judicial checks and balances; three of four authors were LLSV authors (La Porta and others 2004). More recently, the same three LLSV authors have turned their attention to securities regulation (La Porta, López-de-Silanes, and Shleifer 2006).
42. Schlesinger and others (1998).

rights are the state itself and favoritism toward friends of the government. Difficulties in enforcing contracts do not normally arise from weaknesses in substantive law.

THE CODING QUESTION: THE LATIN AMERICAN EXAMPLE

A second anomaly is that in the process of applying regression analysis— the coding of particular third world countries as, say, French law countries— is quite an oversimplification.[43] To see this point most easily, one has only to consider Latin America, which represents more than 40 percent of the French civil law countries in the LLSV legal origins database.[44]

First of all, Spain did not adopt its civil code until 1889, and until that time its private law was based on Roman law (although it did adopt a commercial code applicable to merchants' transactions in 1829). Hence the law of property and contracts in Spanish- and Portuguese-speaking Latin America (not only during the colonial period but also during the years when the newly independent countries were establishing their legal systems) was based on Roman law—which is exactly what the French civil code system was intended to replace.[45] Even after 1889 the Spanish Civil Code followed the French Civil Code only in the law of obligations (roughly, contracts and torts). In other words, well after the legal die had been cast in most of Latin America, the Spanish Civil Code codified indigenous Spanish rules, especially in family law and inheritance. While those legal areas are arguably not crucial for commercial growth, those countries maintained the family law and inheritance rules that kept together the traditional great families with their vast estates and hence may not have been the best model for economic development in Latin America.[46]

Thus the Latin American codes in force today, while indisputably based on a civil law rather than a common law approach, certainly did not follow the French Civil Code down the line. As the president of the Spanish Supreme Court, seeing as many Spanish and Portuguese elements as French elements in Latin American law, observed:

---

43. The authors recognized that their reliance on a standard legal source led to difficulties in some countries, but apparently the requirements of regression studies—necessitating that each country be assigned one and only one legal origin—required the oversimplification. See La Porta and others (1997a, p. 1138, table II).

44. For similar points about other regions of the world, see Siems (2006).

45. Berkowitz, Pistor, and Richard (2003b, p. 180).

46. Mirow (2004, pp. 150–54).

The influences that have acted on the law of the countries of Iberic origin have been many and varied, but they have not been able to erase its own and original characteristics nor blot out the Spanish origin. It is a mistake to include in the French group, as many times has been done, such Iberic-American legislations as Chile, Peru, Argentine, Colombia, Brazil, Venezuela and Mexico, just because in these civil codes of these, and the other American countries, there can be seen directives and norms that come from the French Civil Code, because they are also influenced by the Spanish, the Portuguese, and the Italian laws, and even by the German and Swiss Codes.[47]

Take Mexico as an example: According to its code commission, the 1871 Mexican Civil Code was based on "principles of Roman law, our own [Mexican] complicated legislation, the codes of France, Sardinia, Austria, [and] Portugal . . . in addition to past drafts completed in Mexico and Spain."[48] In the area of commercial codes, one finds that until 1884 Mexican bankruptcy law was based on the 1737 *Ordenanzas of Bilbao*. From 1890 to 1943 the source of Mexican bankruptcy law was the 1829 Spanish commercial code. And even the 1943 Mexican bankruptcy law was drafted by a Spanish lawyer; it was based on Spanish law and on a 1665 Spanish book, although for the first time "Italian and French influences" could be found in Mexican bankruptcy law.[49] Yet Mexico is unambiguously coded as being of French legal origin with respect to bankruptcy law.

As for Brazil, Zweigert and Kötz explain: "In addition to the Code civil [of France] it [Brazil] was able to draw on the Portuguese and Italian codes, as well as those of Germany and Switzerland. The structure of the Code, especially its 'General Part,' is largely traceable to German influence."[50]

The case of the Chilean civil code of 1857 is perhaps the most instructive, because it was subsequently adopted in Colombia, Ecuador, El Salvador, Honduras, Nicaragua, and Venezuela and was the main source for the civil codes of Guatemala, Mexico, Paraguay, and Uruguay. The draftsman of the Chilean civil code, Andrés Bello, was born in Caracas in 1781 and lived in England from 1810 to 1829, when among other things he worked on the papers of Jeremy Bentham. After moving to Chile in 1829, he taught Roman

---

47. Castan Tobeñas (1988, pp. 105, 140).
48. Quoted in Merryman, Clark, and Haley (1994, p. 467).
49. American Law Institute (2003, pp. 21–23).
50. Zweigert and Kötz (1998, p. 118).

law and became a citizen and a senator in Chile. His code "successfully wove together modern European codes, particularly the French Civil Code of 1804 (the *Code Napoleon*), the medieval Spanish law of the *Siete Partidas*, and Roman law . . . . Numerous factors played into Bello's construction of the code, including the works of von Savigny [German], the French commentators on the civil law and the French civil code, the writings of Jeremy Bentham, and various European codes of civil law."[51]

The story of the civil code of Argentina is essentially similar, except that the draftsman's name was Ocampo rather than Bello. Ocampo was an Argentine, who had studied law in Spain and later taught law in Chile. In addition to colonial Spanish law and the *Ordenanzas de Bilbao*, he based the Argentine commercial code on "the commercial codes of France, Spain, Portugal, Holland, Brazil, and Wurtenberg, as well as many treatises on commercial law."[52]

However one characterizes the origins of Latin American private law, it is certainly true that in recent decades North American influence on private law has grown. The Anglo-Saxon device of the trust has taken deep root in Latin America.[53] Usually used for family financial matters, the trust also has found abundant use in secured lending and corporate finance in the United States and potentially, therefore, is of considerable relevance, particularly in the financial sector, for those many Latin American countries that have imported this legal device.[54] As Mattei has commented:

> It is no wonder therefore that, despite the very peculiar institutional background in which the [English and American] law of trust has developed, as soon as its potential became clear to the economic and legal community, this institution became very fashionable . . . . Many South American civilian systems have adopted the institution of trust by legislation . . . . [The] trust has obtained an easy and well-deserved victory in the competition in the market of legal ideas.[55]

In the area of public regulation of corporate transactions, U.S. notions of securities regulation have been important influences on the financial sector, starting with Mexico's legislation in 1953 based on the U.S. securities legislation.[56] But even much earlier than this, Latin America had been heavily

---

51. Mirow (2004, pp. 137–38). See also Valencia (1958).
52. Mirow (2004, pp. 158–59).
53. Schlesinger and others (1998, p. 291); Eder (1950); Kozolchyuk (1979); Clagett (1952).
54. Mirow (2004, p. 212).
55. Mattei (1997, p. 124).
56. Mattei (1997, p. 169).

influenced by U.S. and British law and practice, whatever the underlying commercial codes might provide.[57]

Sometimes these two anomalies—the emphasis on private law (civil and commercial) and the multiple origins of particular third world countries' law—interact. As we have seen, the coding of the Law and Finance studies somewhat misrepresents the private law legal heritage in some important countries, and it certainly is based on a misconception when it comes to public law.

Legal Origins and Public Law

In Latin America there are two major public law influences, one from the United States and one from the Iberian peninsula. Indeed, certain characteristics of Latin American public law are special to the area, perhaps best explained as products of the history of the region.

The first and perhaps predominant influence on Latin American constitutions is the U.S. Constitution, which was certainly more important than the successive French constitutions. As Schlesinger and his colleagues noted: "Yet, common law ideas (especially the elements of common law entrenched in the U.S. Constitution) have had a considerable impact on Latin American legal systems, primarily in the area of public law. The notions of due process and habeas corpus, for example, have been incorporated into the constitutions and statutes of a number of Latin American nations."[58] Merryman, Clark, and Haley put it this way:

> In the structure of the various branches of government, in the idea of the nature and function of a constitution, in the approach to review of the legality of legislative, administrative, and judicial action, Latin America was strongly affected by the United States model. This feature of Latin American legal systems can be simply, with only partial accuracy, summarized by saying that Latin American public law is more North American than European in character.[59]

A second influence comes from the Iberian peninsula rather than France. Spain and Portugal were authoritarian countries, both during the period before the nineteenth century Latin American revolutions that created the

57. Eder (1950, pp. 438–39).
58. Schlesinger and others (1998, p. 291).
59. Merryman, Clark, and Haley (1994, p. 463).

present-day nation states and throughout the period of initial constitution writing, and even well into the second half of the twentieth century. In Wiarda and Kline's view:

> Political theory in Iberia and Latin America, in contrast, views government as good, natural, and necessary for the welfare of society. If government is good, there was little reason to limit or put checks and balances on it. Hence, before we fall into the trap of condemning Latin America for its powerful autocratic executives, subservient parliaments, and weak local government, we must remember the different assumptions on which the Latin American systems are based.[60]

Douglass North emphasized the influence of European ideas, probably more Iberian than French, that shaped nineteenth century Latin America and were carried over into the twentieth century—"a long heritage of centralized bureaucratic controls and accompanying ideological perceptions of the issues."[61] The results were unfortunate. In Mexico, "centralized, bureaucratic traditions carried over from its Spanish/Portuguese heritage" were "perpetuated." North wrote:

> The interventionist and pervasively arbitrary nature of the institutional environment forced every enterprise, urban or rural, to operate in a highly politicized manner, using kinship networks, political influence, and family prestige to gain privileged access to subsidized credit, to aid various stratagems for recruiting labor, to collect debts or enforce contracts, to evade taxes or circumvent the courts, and to defend or assert titles to lands. Success or failure in the economic arena always depended on the relationship of the producer with political authorities—local officials for arranging matters close at hand and the central government of the colony for sympathetic interpretations of the law and intervention at the local level when conditions required it. Small enterprise, excluded from the system of corporate privilege and political favors, was forced to operate in a permanent state of semiclandestiny, always at the margin of the law, at the mercy of petty officials, never secure from arbitrary acts and never protected against the rights of those more powerful.[62]

From the standpoint of enforcement of contracts and protection of property, these nineteenth century conditions of governance in Latin America

---

60. Wiarda and Kline (2000, p. 59).
61. North (1990, p. 103).
62. North (1990, pp. 116–17), quoting from Coatsworth (1978, p. 94).

have little to do with the French tradition of a strong bureaucratic state or with the principles of the Code Napoleon. The constitutional structure of France coming out of the French Revolution was far from devoted to perpetuating the power of local economic and social interests. The new French constitutional arrangements were based on the sovereignty of the legislative branch. Indeed, that was the central theory of French constitutional theory until de Gaulle came to power in 1958, when the French constitution was amended. This amendment was a condition of his willingness to assume the helm of the French state. The new 1958 French constitution granted the executive the power to make law in certain areas by decree.

Yet the theory of Latin American constitutions has traditionally been the opposite of the pre-1958 French constitution; these Latin American constitutions granted great power to the executive. And, as North points out, Spain was the source of these Latin American institutions: "There was a centralized monarchy and bureaucracy in Castile, and it was Castile that defined the institutional evolution of both Spain and Latin America."[63] As Wiarda and Kline further explain:

> Virtually all Latin American constitutions have provided for the historical, three-part division of power among executive, legislature, and judiciary. However, in practice the three branches are not co-equal and were not intended to be. The executive is constitutionally given extensive powers to bypass the legislature, and judicial review until recently has been largely outside Latin American legal tradition.[64]

With regard to judicial review—that is, the power of the courts to declare acts of the legislature unconstitutional—it is quite wrong to code Latin American countries' law as based on French law. Indeed, the institution of judicial review has recently become more common in Latin America. Yet in France, judicial review is not available at all, except in a special, essentially nonjudicial council in advance of enactment (and even that review became available only in 1958, many decades after judicial review became common in Latin America).[65]

In the case of administrative law, while French law provides for acts of government administration to be reviewable, that review takes place only in specialized administrative courts and not in the regular judicial system (that is, administrative law is not reviewable by the ordinary courts that also handle

63. North (1990, p. 114).
64. Wiarda and Kline (2000, p. 60).
65. Bell (1992, pp. 29–56).

cases among private parties).[66] Just the opposite is true in most of Latin America. Many Latin American countries have developed a remedy, usually called *amparo* (similar to but broader than the English and American writ of habeas corpus), that can be used to attack a broad range of administrative acts. In fact, unlike most European countries that allow administrative acts to be reviewable only by a specialized administrative court, *amparo* can normally be brought in the ordinary court system.[67] One therefore could ask why Latin America is not coded for regression purposes in the same category as the United States, at least to the extent that the underlying theory of the rule of law in economic development depends on the relationship between the state and the economy.

If one looks to legal culture, it may be the case that even in public law, the legal culture of many Latin American countries leads to different results in public law controversies than one would anticipate by looking only at the rules on the books. And it may be that the Latin American legal culture in some way can be said to reflect a French approach to the legal profession and the judiciary. But a defense of the legal origins approach on this subtle ground merely leads to a second set of questions that may be the most important ones when one begins to look for policy implications for developing countries.[68]

Still a different kind of anomaly arises from treating Anglo-Saxon countries as in the same box simply because they adopted the common law. Insofar as public law is concerned, one can ask—for example—why Britain and the United States should be placed together. As a continental European legal scholar puts it: "[I]t is clear enough that British and American constitutional law are not part of the same 'family.'.... For the study of public law ... the idea of legal families does not work."[69]

While the reasoning of courts in both countries places more emphasis on judicial precedent than is normal in many civil law countries, Britain has never recognized judicial review of statutory enactments.[70] Parliament is sovereign (just as the French Assembly is sovereign) and has been since the

66. Schlesinger and others (1998, p. 552).

67. For a discussion of *amparo* in Latin America, see Merryman, Clark, and Haley (1994, pp. 740–45) and R. Baker (1971). See also Clark (1975, pp. 432–34).

68. The question of culture as an alternative to legal origins in explaining economic growth is discussed in the next chapter.

69. Koopmans (2003, pp. 39–40).

70. A species of judicial review is now required to a limited extent by U.K. membership in the European Union, but this exception is based on an interpretation of Parliament's will as expressed in the EEC Act of 1972; see Carroll (2003, pp. 97–98).

Glorious Revolution of 1688–89. (Before 1689 neither Parliament nor the king—the latter being generally recognized as sovereign—would recognize judicial review.[71]) As a matter of fact, Britain—unlike France, Germany, and nearly all other countries in the world—does not even have a written constitution. To the extent that Britain has a constitution—based on legislation and conventions and practice going back to the Magna Carta—it is not just subject to many interpretations but is considered more a question for Parliament than for the courts. Indeed, Parliament can change the constitution by its enactments, just as it can change a statute, without any special constitutional amendment procedure.[72]

Governance as an Alternative Theory

The governance approach to explaining the rate of economic growth, though useful as a contrast to the legal origins literature, has in common with it the use of econometric techniques by economists. The governance work has been done largely by economists at the World Bank Institute, a research component of the World Bank. The original legal origins work, in contrast, was almost entirely the product of economists in academia, although some offshoots from it have been funded and extended by the World Bank. An important reason for the difference in where the work is done is probably that the governance work had to be preceded by the collection of a great deal of special survey data. The administration of the survey questionnaires involves more than 200 countries, and their continuation year after year is obviously easier for an international organization than for academic researchers.

The governance work has several advantages over the legal origins literature in explaining comparative economic growth. The larger number of countries included allows many more interesting comparisons. Moreover, many more developing countries are included in the governance studies than were considered in the original Law and Finance literature. Especially noteworthy are the number of common and civil law countries in Africa, compared with the Law and Finance literature, which had no African civil law countries (other than Egypt, which is quite different in most respects from sub-Saharan Africa). The governance indicators suggest some obvious and

---

71. Lord Coke suggested in *Bonham's Case* in 1610 that legislation could be set aside if it was contrary to the common law, but that concept of judicial review proved to have no future in England; see Van Gerven (2005, p. 105) and Koopmans (2003, p. 39).

72. The canonical citation for this proposition remains Dicey (1893); see Carroll (2003, pp. 79–80).

practical modifications to development strategy beyond the law on the books and especially beyond legal origin, which by definition cannot be changed. The amount of data collected over an eight-year period allows judgments about how changes in governance may have affected countries' growth. Kaufmann noted, for example, that "a simple review of recent data suggests a much higher correlation between FDI [foreign direct investment] and governance than between FDI and macroeconomic variables," leading him to the conclusions that "maintaining macroeconomic stability ought to continue to be regarded as a necessary precondition for growth and for FDI, yet it is far from sufficient," and that "particular emphasis on governance factors is warranted, since at the present juncture it appears to constitute a binding constraint."[73]

Another important difference is that the governance inquiry has been much broader than the legal origins approach. In the minds of the governance analysts, there are three dimensions of governance of a country, each of which is in turn broken down into six dimensions: "voice and external accountability"; "political stability and lack of violence, crime, and terrorism"; "government effectiveness"; "lack of regulatory burden [sometimes abbreviated as regulatory quality]"; "rule of law"; and "control of corruption."[74]

The core of the analysis in the succeeding chapters of this book is thus the fifth component, the rule of law, although elements of the other five components also play a role in some legal origins work. In turn, the governance research implicitly looks to factors other than legal origin, although it does provide some insight into the legal origins work product.

One aspect of the governance research is that it permits one to rank countries by "rule of law" and, to the extent that the research results are based on surveys, to chart progress between compilations of the surveys, not just for countries but for regions of the world. So, for example, the surveys provide quantitative evidence of what one normally finds in qualitative writing, such as the extent to which judicial independence varies by region. The surveys show that judicial independence is greater among the members of the Organization for Economic Cooperation and Development (OECD) than in the East Asia industrialized countries, which in turn rank higher than the transition countries (Eastern Europe and the former Soviet Union), with emerging market countries slightly lower than the transition countries. The surveys

73. Kaufmann (2004a, p. 139).
74. Kaufmann (2004a, p. 142).

also show that the Eastern European countries have done much better in judicial independence than the countries of the former Soviet Union.[75]

Looking at changes from one compilation to the next, one finds the less obvious and more worrisome fact that, from 1998 to 2003, judicial independence deteriorated slightly in all regions (other than the East Asian industrialized countries).[76] And still more interesting, judicial independence is no higher in Latin America and the Caribbean's emerging countries than it is in Eastern Europe's transition countries, despite the pernicious influence of Communist parties on judicial independence until the early 1990s.[77]

Similarly worrisome is the major deterioration experienced by low-income countries in all six governance dimensions from 1996 to 2003. A number of low-income African countries, such as the Central African Republic, Côte d'Ivoire, and Zimbabwe, suffered "significant" deterioration in all six categories, including the rule of law. In contrast, some low-income countries made significant improvements in five or six categories, showing that improvement even in the lowest-income countries is definitely possible.

Another insight comes from survey questions such as "In your industry, how commonly would you estimate that firms make undocumented extra payments or bribes connected with influencing laws and policies, regulations, or decrees to favor selected business interests?" (with seven possible answers ranging from "common" to "never occurs").[78] Of course, surveys depend on questions, and it is common knowledge that different individuals interpret questions differently, and that this is especially true with regard to individuals in different countries. For example, some individuals, and probably even more so some cultures, tend to be more pessimistic than others about the state of values of other people and hence are inclined to assume that corruption is more common among other firms than perhaps is warranted. A comparable reservation about comparisons with regard to judicial independence is prudent. Trends over time within regions, and especially within countries, may thus be more important than cross-country and especially cross-regional comparisons. Still, the general cross-regional results from the surveys support, rather than contradict, judgments commonly expressed in qualitative commentary.

75. Kaufmann (2004a, p. 143, table 1).
76. Although one may have statistical doubts about whether a deterioration has been conclusively shown, Kaufmann (2004a, p. 139 n. 8) points out that the "statistical confidence in the statement that there is no evidence of a positive trend in any governance dimension is very high."
77. Kaufmann (2004a, p. 140, figure 1b).
78. Kaufmann (2004a, p. 160, table A2).

The findings showing sharp differences between developed and developing countries on rule-of-law issues raise the same problem that plagues the legal origins studies, namely, the direction of causality. Do more independent legal institutions cause higher incomes? Or is it a case of reverse causality? In other words, do higher incomes provide the resources that lead to a higher rule-of-law level? One can see, for example, that with more money, judges can be paid more and be provided with more computers and better libraries, thereby insulating them better against political pressures and the temptation of bribes.

In dealing with the issue of reverse causality, legal origins studies can rely on the analytical point that because the legal origin of a country was determined more than a century earlier, the country's current income level cannot determine its legal origin.[79] Governance studies have no such recourse. However, governance researchers have used a different approach that allows them, in their judgment, to find not just that there was no reverse causality but "a *large direct causal effect* from better governance to improved development outcomes."[80]

The governance literature provides a platform for evaluating the legal origins literature. Specifically, the governance surveys, together with expert assessments from a wide variety of governmental and nongovernmental groups, provide country-by-country data on the state of the current rule of law. These country results can then be run back to see how different origins rank on the rule-of-law criterion. This cross-methodology exercise does find, "controlling for other factors, on average a small advantage for countries with common law over civil law origins."[81] But it also raises a number of reservations about the utility for public policy of the common law–civil law distinction. If one divides countries into two categories, high-quality and low-quality rule of law, one can further sort by legal origin and current income levels and then can see how many of the civil law developing countries actually enjoy high-quality rule of law and how many of the common law developing countries suffer from low-quality rule of law. French law countries include, for example, Chile and Costa Rica, countries that are usually considered to rank relatively high on rule of law. And the common law countries include many lower-quality rule-of-law countries, not just in Africa (such as Kenya, Liberia, Nigeria, and Somalia) but also in Asia (Bangladesh and Pakistan). German

79. See La Porta and others (1998, pp. 1150–52) on the use of instrumental variables.

80. The World Bank Institute approach to reverse causality is explained in Kaufmann (2004a, p. 145).

81. Kaufmann (2004a, p. 147).

law is not found to any great extent in the developing world because of the lateness and weakness of German colonial expansion, but it includes high-quality rule-of-law countries such as Korea and Taiwan in Asia and Estonia, Hungary, and Slovenia in Eastern Europe.[82]

A further virtue of the governance literature is that it includes some 200 countries, whereas the key Law and Finance article included data on only 49 countries. Although 49 countries may be enough for an academic paper aimed at a general conclusion (and at the time a new perspective), serious problems arise when one is attempting to arrive at policy recommendations for a subset of those countries—namely, developing countries.[83] Then questions about the selection criteria become important. The governance literature uses data from essentially all developing countries.

Furthermore, the difference by legal origin among the governance literature's seventy-five low-income countries (which are especially important for economic development policy) provides a common law–civil law comparison on governance indicators as a whole (that is, all six dimensions and not just the rule-of-law dimension). The results show, for example, that in those countries, common law countries come out slightly ahead of civil law countries on three components (voice and accountability, government effectiveness, and rule of law); even with civil law countries on regulatory quality; and slightly behind civil law countries on political stability and control of corruption.[84] From this perspective, the public policy problem to be addressed in low-income countries is governance across the board and not just the legal origin aspects of governance.

Even with respect to legal origin as such, Kaufmann found that while there was "evidence of a small but significant correlation between legal origins

---

82. Kaufmann (2004a, p. 147).

83. The LLSV (La Porta and others 1998, p. 1117) criteria for inclusion required that the country have at least five domestic, nonfinancial, publicly traded firms with no government ownership in 1993. These criteria made sense for a study of the development of financial sectors without special focus on special issues involving developing countries but left out information that would be important if one were primarily interested in developing countries. The legal origins authors have somewhat increased the number of countries in their database over time; see, for example, Djankov and others (2005), in which seventy-two countries are used. But the LLSV Law and Finance database remains much smaller than Kaufmann's governance database. Some of the legal origins authors, particularly Djankov, who did not participate in the original Law and Finance studies, have participated in the World Bank *Doing Business* series, but that series is focused on regulatory issues that are beyond the scope of this book. Some of LLSV's later work, discussed in chapter 5, uses larger data sets to analyze other issues.

84. Kaufmann (2004a, p. 148, figure 3b).

and governance" in the complete set of some 200 countries, when he focused on the 75 lower-income countries, "the differences between common law and civil law essentially disappear." Yet, as Kaufmann points out, it "is precisely within this group of countries, many of which exhibit dysfunctional governance, that the most daunting governance challenges lie."[85] In short, the concept of legal origins is interesting from a scholarly point of view, but from the point of view of public policy formation for the poorer developing countries, legal origin appears to be of dubious relevance.

In trying to understand these governance results, one must consider subjectivity and related survey issues. Kaufmann's answer to the subjectivity concern is that subjective measures of governance contain important information often not captured by objective indicators, particularly in emerging economies.[86] This answer is no doubt correct in view of the serious shortcomings of the LLSV "objective" indicators reviewed in this and later financial sector chapters, but there is still reason to consider the shortcomings of subjective measures.

For example, a judicial corruption question was: "In your industry, how commonly would you estimate that firms make undocumented extra payments or bribes connected with getting favorable judicial decisions?" A score of 1 means "common" and a score of 7 means "never."[87] Here, as in the legal origins work, policy implication issues arise: Bribes have both a supply and a demand side, and the research gives little insight into how to work to lower the incidence of judicial corruption. Especially when one is talking about judicial corruption, it is unclear how enforcement of anticorruption legislation can be achieved in those countries where it is most needed.

In the case of judicial independence, the respondents were asked to what extent they agreed with the following statement: "The judiciary in your country is independent from political influence of members of government, citizens, or firms."[88] These types of questions were asked of 6,000 enterprises in more than 100 countries, and therefore the answers are primarily a business view of the judiciary, which is certainly not the only view that counts and perhaps not even the most important one.

85. Kaufmann (2004a, p. 147). See also Kaufmann (2003).
86. Kaufmann, Kraay, and Mastruzzi (2005).
87. Kaufmann (2004a, p. 141, figure 1c).
88. Kaufmann (2004a, p. 140, figure 1b).

One therefore might be inclined to object that perceptions do not necessarily reflect reality, and to some extent that is no doubt true.[89] But perceptions can have independent force. If business firms believe that the courts are not independent, they are likely to make less use of the judiciary to resolve disputes. And if the dispute is with a governmental institution, they may be more likely to choose bribery as less expensive and more certain than litigation.

Although one might quarrel with the choice of business respondents, an important by-product of focusing on business perceptions is that Kaufmann and colleagues were able to construct an index of "crony bias"—defined as the business respondents' assessment of the special influence of firms close to the government as compared with the influence of their own trade association. Among the nonobvious results was that crony bias was substantially higher in Latin America than in the sub-Saharan Africa and the Middle East–North Africa regions.[90]

What should one conclude to be the relative merits of the legal origins and governance approaches? The governance work suggests that the public policy implications in the rule-of-law area are complicated and that rule-of-law performance may well depend on institutions and organizations unrelated to the law; voice and accountability seem particularly important and can be influenced by legal rules, such as a constitutional guarantee of freedom of speech and press. But at least one can say that while legal origin cannot be changed, the governance work adds greatly to our understanding of what rule-of-law problems need to be worked on in the developing world whatever the legal origin of the countries involved.

89. K. Davis (2004, p. 150), who provides a critical review of efforts to assess the rule of law in developing countries, has pointed out that some business respondents in surveys may not have been residents of the country in question and therefore their perceptions may not have been based on personal and direct knowledge.

90. See Hellman and Kaufmann (2002).

3 | Competing Explanations

Economist Dani Rodrik has trenchantly observed that econometric tests of the causes of growth are inherently suspect:

> Econometric results can be found to support any and all . . . categories of arguments. However, very little of this econometric work survives close scrutiny . . . or is able to sway the priors of anyone with strong convictions in other directions. Moreover, there is little reason to believe that the primary causal channels are invariant to time period, initial conditions, or other aspects of a country's circumstances. There may not be universal rules about what makes countries grow.[1]

Rodrik's observations suggest that factors other than legal rules, or even legal institutions more broadly defined, may provide competing explanations to the ultimate puzzle of what actually accounts for high per capita GDP levels and economic growth. Why have some countries grown rapidly over the last few centuries and others have not?

One answer sympathetic to poor countries in hot climates is to say that the issue is mostly about geography. Under this approach it is no accident that the successful countries in the GDP per capita game are those that lie in temperate climates.

A different approach is to say that culture explains relative rates of economic growth. Historically one of the most influential works was *The Protestant Ethic and the Rise of Capitalism*, written by German scholar Max Weber

---

1. Rodrik (2003, pp. 9–10).

in the early twentieth century.[2] Religion aside, Harvard historian David Landes claims that "culture makes almost all the difference." By culture he means nothing more complicated than "work, thrift, honesty, patience, tenacity."[3] On examination, the cultural explanation has a number of subthemes: not only religion, but also trust, social capital, and social norms.

Let us take these competing explanations—geography and culture— in turn, with a view not to passing judgment on the value of the legal origins and governance literature but rather to placing that literature in proper context for an analysis of how legal institutions influence economic development.

Geography

Geography is not a new explanation. In the mid-eighteenth century Montesquieu devoted Book XIV of *The Spirit of the Laws* to "Laws in Relation to the Nature of the Climate," in which he considered the impact of various climates on a broad range of human activity. Montesquieu's work today seems idiosyncratic, even racially prejudiced, but climate still plays a large role in geographic explanations.

On the surface of things, geography matters. As Acemoglu wrote in 2003, "Locate the poorest places in the world where per capita incomes are less than one-twentieth those in the United States. You will find almost all of them close to the equator, in very hot regions that experience periodic torrential rains and where, by definition, tropical diseases are widespread."[4] Even though some economists have published studies showing that geography does not add anything once one controls for institutions, it can hardly be doubted that economic growth presents a greater challenge in the tropics for a number of reasons. [5]

A vocal proponent of the geography thesis is Jeffrey Sachs. He emphasizes two points: the health problems arising from tropical diseases, and the lower productivity in the tropics of staple crops, especially rice, wheat, and corn (maize).[6] According to one Sachs study, malaria transmission directly affects per capita income levels even after controlling for institutional differences.[7]

---

2. For an English translation, see Weber (1958).
3. Landes (2000, p. 12).
4. Acemoglu (2003, p. 27).
5. On institutions and geography, see Rodrik, Subramanian, and Trebbi (2004).
6. Sachs (2001).
7. Sachs (2003a).

Although Sachs agrees that institutions matter, he simply argues that geography also matters and therefore that special efforts are needed, especially in places like sub-Saharan Africa.[8]

A different view of the Sachs thesis has been advanced by Easterly and Levine. Using cross-country regression methods, they found that the Sachs explanation involving disease and agricultural products affects economic development only through institutions.[9] But that conclusion merely raises the question why, among tropical countries, some have better institutions than others.

A second line of support for the geography thesis addresses the institutional question more directly. This line of argument finds that two kinds of institutional structure were developed during the colonial period, the difference in institutions depending on the geographical characteristics of the colony. In realms suitable only for mineral exploitation or plantation farming and where Europeans could not easily survive because of tropical disease, the Europeans enslaved the indigenous population and did not themselves form permanent settlements.[10] But in the poorer lands, like New England, where the natives were not easy to enslave and where there was no way to organize mass exploitative activities, the Europeans were forced to form their own tiny settlements.

Glaeser and colleagues (who include three of the four LLSV authors) have examined this second version of the geography thesis and argued that it was not so much the institutions that settlers brought with them to North America but rather their human capital—in other words, not just democratic institutions and the rule of law, but more particularly their education and the educational values and systems—that laid the foundation for future economic development.[11] The relationship among education, human capital, and institutions is, of course, an important question. If human capital is essential to well-functioning institutions, it would, of course, possibly shed some light on why, according to Merryman, French law works well in France and less well in countries where French law was adopted (as well as shedding light on the fact that English law has not produced outstanding economic growth in many countries of sub-Saharan Africa).[12]

8. Sachs (2003b).
9. Easterly and Levine (2002).
10. Acemoglu, Johnson, and Robinson (2001). See also Beck, Demirgüç-Kunt, and Levine (2003).
11. Glaeser and others (2004).
12. Merryman (1996).

These latter versions of the geography explanation, unlike the Sachs version, are compatible with neoinstitutional and legal origins thinking. After all, the French seemed on the whole to favor the tropics and the Spanish were especially interested in gold and silver mining, while the British had to make do with less romantic places like New England, Canada, Australia, and South Africa. Napoleon, according to a perhaps apocryphal story, is said to have considered trading Guadeloupe for Canada, but abandoned the idea of trading the lush island for "a patch of snow."[13] This version of the geography thesis leaves in place the insight that institutions not only count but are a crucial influence. But that insight by itself does not prove that only institutions count.

Geography is not totally immutable in the sense that, for example, health measures can mitigate the negative effects of a tropical location. Yet the diverse growth patterns of countries outside the tropics and lying contiguous to each other suggest that institutions can make a huge difference. As Daniel Kaufmann asked in expressing reservations about the somewhat different question of using cross-country regressions to test any theory of the causes of economic growth: "What accounts for the rather different institutional paths taken by Argentina and Chile in spite of their very similar cultural, geographical, colonial, and (civil) legal code systems? Or by Poland and the Ukraine? Or by both Koreas?"[14] Using a similar argument-by-example approach, a publication of the International Monetary Fund (IMF) argues that if "geographical factors were the only determining factor . . . , it would be difficult to reconcile the strong economic performance of Botswana with the severe difficulties in neighboring countries such as Angola and Zimbabwe, or the high standard of living in Singapore with the much lower incomes in many other equatorial countries."[15] The foregoing questions are particularly forceful in evaluating the geography thesis if one's focus is on legal institutional reform. And if the geography explanation is at least partly correct, the broader development challenge for the international community is that "adverse geography does not fundamentally alter the fact that the effectiveness of assistance depends heavily on the institutions of the recipient country."[16]

13. Britain occupied Guadeloupe, but France retook the island during the revolutionary period. Sokoloff and Engerman (2000, p. 217) report a related story about Voltaire characterizing the war between the French and the British in North America in the 1756–63 period as "fighting over a few acres of snow."

14. Kaufmann (2003a, p. 311).

15. IMF (2003, p. 101).

16. Birdsall, Rodrik, and Subramanian (2005).

Another aspect of geography lies in the recognized importance to development of openness to international trade.[17] Trade involves both exports and imports. A small, poor, and landlocked country may find it difficult to develop export markets. Being landlocked is not as favorable geographically as being situated where oceangoing vessels can reach world markets.

Culture

Several social scientists and historians have found strong evidence that culture explains at least some differences in the rate at which countries develop.[18] An economic history view is that, in the words of David Landes, "if we learn anything from the history of economic development, it is that culture makes almost all the difference."[19]

The variability in growth rates among developing countries and the link of that variability to cultural differences have been highlighted by Huntington:

> In the early 1990s, I happened to come across economic data on Ghana and South Korea in the early 1960s, and I was astonished to see how similar their economies were then. These two countries had roughly comparable levels of per capita GNP; similar divisions of their economy among primary products, manufacturing, and services; and overwhelmingly primary product exports, with South Korea producing a few manufactured goods. Also, they were receiving comparable levels of economic aid. Thirty years later, South Korea had become an industrial giant with the fourteenth largest economy in the world, multinational corporations, major exports of automobiles, electronic equipment, and other sophisticated manufactures, and a per capita income approximating that of Greece. Moreover, it was on its way to the consolidation of democratic institutions. No such changes had occurred in Ghana, whose per capita GNP was now about one-fifteenth that of South Korea's. How could this extraordinary difference in development be explained?[20]

Huntington went on to argue that "culture had to be a large part of the explanation," noting that "Koreans valued thrift, investment, hard work, education, organization, and discipline," and that "Ghanaians had different values." Huntington's conclusion is encapsulated in the title of the book, *Culture Matters*.

17. Sachs and Warner (1995).
18. See generally Guiso, Sapienza, and Zingales (2006).
19. Landes (2000, p. 2).
20. Huntington (2000, p. xiii).

As powerful as Huntington's argument may appear, it leads to an obvious question. How is one to explain that Ghana and South Korea were at the same level of development (well above subsistence levels) in 1960 if, as Huntington says, Ghanaian culture is so inferior to South Korean culture? If the answer is that in 1960 Ghana was part of the British Empire, that explanation points to the strength of British institutions. Should one conclude that institutions therefore trump culture, rather than the other way around?

Whether or not culture determines differences in economic development, it cannot be denied that Huntington rightly points out that the variability in growth rates of developing countries has been enormous and not easily explained. Certainly a legal origins approach helps little. Ghana inherited the common law and at the least the outer trappings of democracy from Britain (even though "2001 witnessed the first peaceful transfer of power between democratically elected governments in Ghana's 44-year history").[21] And South Korea inherited, through Japan, a civil law tradition and experienced authoritarian government during its early growth years. Thus the Ghana–South Korean contrast casts doubt on both a legal origins and a pro-democracy rule-of-law thesis.

Harrison offered another reason for concluding that culture must make some difference. In "multicultural countries," he wrote, ". . . some ethnic groups do better than others, although all operate with the same economic signals, [for example,] the Chinese minorities in Thailand, Malaysia, Indonesia, the Philippines, and the United States; the Japanese minorities in Brazil and the United States; the Basques in Spain and Latin America; and the Jews wherever they have migrated."[22]

Although much of the work on the influence of culture on economic growth has been done by historians and noneconomist social scientists, the economics profession has begun to turn its attention to the subject. The answer is that, yes, culture can affect economic outcomes both directly and through the political process.[23] For example, Tabellini, using data from European regions, found that historical indicators of culture (literacy as of 1880 and differences in historical political institutions within regions that are currently within a single country) were an important determinant of current economic performance.[24]

---

21. *Encyclopedia Britannica Almanac 2003*, p. 483.
22. Harrison (2000, p. xxiv).
23. A thorough review is to be found in Guiso, Sapienza, and Zingales (2006).
24. Tabellini (2005).

Cultural explanations for differential growth rates are challenging to refute (or to confirm) because culture is hard to define and to measure. Some economists, therefore, have preferred to avoid cultural explanations. Solow famously wrote that if culture was to be more than a "buzzword," it "should somehow be measurable, even inexactly," but "measurement seems very far away."[25] Nevertheless, some of the most prolific of the researchers using regressions to analyze the legal origins approach to economic development research have been willing to try to examine the contributions of various aspects of culture to development. LLSV, for example, started by looking at comparative levels of "trust" across countries; they used a forty-country survey, the World Values Survey, that asked such questions as the following: "Generally, speaking, would you say that most people can be trusted or that you can't be too careful in dealing with people?"[26]

One important reason for thinking that culture is not just a support for law but can even be a partial substitute for it lies in the area of enforcement of contracts. If one posits, as seems reasonable, that the development of contracting is essential to economic development, then it seems clear that the performance of contracts cannot depend solely on judicial enforcement. Although the availability of court enforcement may remain important, routine performance of contracts among unrelated parties cannot depend solely on the threat of bringing a defaulting party to court. One reason is that economic contracts of any complexity or duration are nearly always incomplete. For such contracts, it will normally be impossible or at least unduly expensive and time-consuming to write all future contingencies into the contract.[27] Hence cultural factors, such as generalized and cross-group trust of the kind referred to in the World Values Survey, are likely to be a factor in voluntary performance of contracts where contingencies arise that are not specifically covered in the contract. And since financial development is crucial to economic development (a point that is discussed later in this volume), the regularized performance of financial contracts depends not just on law but on such generalized trust. As Guiso, Sapienza, and Zingales put it:

> Since financial contracts are the ultimate trust-intensive contracts, social capital should have major effects on the development of financial markets. Financing is nothing but an exchange of a sum of money today for a promise to return more money in the future. Whether such

25. Solow (1995, p. 38).
26. La Porta and others (1997b, p. 335).
27. Guiso, Sapienza, and Zingales (2004a).

an exchange can take place depends not only on the legal enforceability of contracts, but also on the extent to which the financier trusts the financee.[28]

One reason, despite measurement difficulties, for looking at culture is that if institutions (including legal institutions) shape culture, then culture may not be a variable independent of institutions. To take one example from political institutions, Sunstein has argued that democratic governance can shape cultural values involving issues such as the environment.[29] The same should be true of cultural values involving the economy as such.

More generally, a reason for being attuned to cultural differences is that law and legal institutions introduced, in the name of good governance, into developing countries that are at odds with local culture are unlikely to succeed. This is the "legal transplant" issue that recurs throughout this book. A good deal of evidence suggests that legal transplants do not work in such circumstances. An especially dramatic set of examples of failed transplants involved the introduction of developed country law, especially in the commercial and financial sectors, in Eastern Europe and the former Soviet Union in the 1990s.[30] One important insight, compatible with an economic approach, is that just because a legal rule or institution is supplied does not mean that it will be demanded.[31] The success of a legal transplant from an alien culture therefore depends on a local demand for the new transplanted rule or institution.[32]

Pistor and her colleagues found that in some countries transplanted law has remained without influence for decades in the face of rapid economic change. In other countries, they found, the institutional base for adapting the law to changing realities was not present. And in some countries transplanted laws were changed erratically, sometimes in a retrogressive fashion, because the legal profession and lawmakers had so little knowledge of or experience with the legal field involved. In short, transplanted laws often do not operate in the host country the way they do in the home country.[33]

28. Guiso, Sapienza, and Zingales (2004b, p. 527).
29. Sunstein (1996, 1997).
30. Berkowitz, Pistor, and Richard (2003b).
31. Hendley (1999).
32. Berkowitz, Pistor, and Richard (2003a). The same principle of successful law corresponding to social norms has long been recognized even where no alien influences are involved. Holmes (1963, p. 36) observed in 1881, "The final requirement of a sound body of law is that it should correspond with the actual feelings and demands of the community, whether right or wrong."
33. Pistor and others (2003, pp. 97–108).

To begin to unpack the idea of culture, it is therefore useful to look at several different concepts that social scientists have used to analyze culture: trust, social capital, religion, and social norms.

TRUST

LLSV found that the willingness of individuals to trust others within the same country had "statistically significant and quantitatively large" effects on judicial efficiency, bureaucratic quality, tax compliance, and limitation of corruption. They even found a high association between the level of trust and per capita GDP growth.[34] As is discussed in a later chapter, trust may be especially important in the development of credit markets because trust in repayment is important to creditors, whatever the availability of legal remedies for nonpayment.

In contrast, Ronald Inglehart, a political scientist, warned against placing undue emphasis on trust as a free-standing variable, showing that "virtually all historically Protestant societies rank higher on interpersonal trust than virtually all historically Catholic societies . . . even when we control for levels of economic development." He found that interpersonal trust does not determine per capita income levels even in the developed world.[35]

SOCIAL CAPITAL

Some economists find culture easier to analyze if they can analogize it to some accepted economic concept. One such concept is "social capital," which is analogous to the well-accepted economic concept of "human capital."[36] Knack and Keefer, in an article whose title asked "Does Social Capital Have an Economic Payoff?" found that social capital did indeed have a payoff in building trust and civic cooperation. They were unable, however, to show a direct payoff in economic growth, despite their conclusion that "trust and civic norms are stronger in nations with higher and more equal incomes."[37]

Fukuyama bridged the social capital and more purely economic approaches in arguing that while it "is perfectly possible to form successful groups in the absence of social capital, using a variety of formal coordination mechanisms like contracts, hierarchies, constitutions, legal systems, and the like, . . . informal norms greatly reduce what economists label 'transactions

34. La Porta and others (1997b).
35. Inglehart (2000, p. 90 and figure 7.3).
36. See Coleman (1990). For a survey of the social capital literature, see Durlauf and Fafchamps (2005).
37. Knack and Keefer (1997).

costs'—the cost of monitoring, contracting, adjudicating, and enforcing formal agreements."[38]

RELIGION

Another cultural factor is religion. Guiso, Sapienza, and Zingales used regression techniques to find that on average "religion is good for the development of attitudes that are conducive to economic growth." This was, however, more the case for Christian religions than for Islam.[39] As between Catholics and Protestants, they found differences: "Protestants trust others and the legal system more than Catholics and they are less willing to cheat on taxes and accept a bribe [than] Catholics."[40]

Guiso and his colleagues also found an important link between religion and respect for the law. When respondents were asked whether particular actions could "always be justified, never be justified, or something in between," results from sixty-six countries showed that while "all religions result in increased trust in the legal system and reduced willingness to break legal rules," this "effect differs significantly across religious denominations." For example, they found that "Judaism [has] the strongest negative impact on willingness to cheat on taxes, Protestantism second, Catholicism and Hinduism third, and Islam fourth," but that the "negative impact" with respect to accepting a bribe is "strongest" for Buddhists "with Protestants and Muslims next, and Catholics last."[41] This summary does not do justice to the richness of the results, given the very large sample size of over 80,000, and the findings varied substantially depending on whether individuals were merely "raised religiously" or were "currently religious" (attending religious services at least once a year) or were "actively religious" (attending at least once a week).[42] The results also differed depending on whether the respondents were part of a dominant religion in a country. (The intuition behind this last inquiry is that a dominant religion has a broader cultural impact on a country as a whole; for example, Catholicism might have an independent impact on, say, Italian culture beyond the impact of any individual's religious affiliation and activity.)

In their study finding trust to be a positive factor for economic growth, LLSV also found that countries with dominant hierarchical religions

38. Fukuyama (2000, p. 99).
39. Guiso, Sapienza, and Zingales (2003, p. 280).
40. Guiso, Sapienza, and Zingales (2003, pp. 241, 264).
41. Guiso, Sapienza, and Zingales (2003, p. 264).
42. Guiso, Sapienza, and Zingales (2003, p. 256).

(Catholic, Eastern Orthodox, and Muslim) "have less efficient judiciaries, greater corruption [and] higher rates of tax evasion" than other countries, and this was true holding per capita income constant.[43]

SOCIAL NORMS

Although trust, social capital, and religion may all be factors in determining attitudes toward honesty in commercial dealings and therefore in determining a country's economic performance, broader social attitudes may also play a role in using law to enhance economic development. With this notion of broader social attitudes in mind, legal scholars, especially in the United States, have increasingly spoken of social norms.[44] The source of social norms, though clearly reflecting cultural values, is for some purposes less important than whether they exist and what they are. Indeed, from a legal point of view, social norms are in some respects like legal rules. Legal rules are norms promulgated and enforced by the state. Social norms come from the individuals of the society, and the society enforces them by social pressures and social sanctions.

When social norms—say, a norm supporting the sanctity of contracts and property—coincide with legal rules and a judiciary to back them up, social norms and law are complementary and mutually reinforcing. This is why neoinstitutional economists such as Douglass North regard social norms as part of the "rules of the game" in the same sense as law. Of course, as noted in the discussion of legal transplants, social norms can undermine law, particularly new law imported from a foreign culture.

Even where social norms do not actively undermine legal rules, they may throw light on anomalies in the legal origins approach. To take just one example, Garretsen, Lensink, and Sterken found that although common law countries in Asia had adopted the British legal system, different social norms led to "different legal institutions with respect to shareholder rights" compared with the major common law countries: the United States, the United Kingdom, Canada, Australia, and New Zealand.[45]

Values and Cultural Regions

The cultural explanation suggests that culture should be taken seriously by lawyers; law reform is not a technocratic exercise. The cultural explanation,

---

43. La Porta and others (1997b, pp. 336–37). For a different approach, see Barro and McCleary (2003).
44. See, for example, Posner (2000). For a review of the earlier literature, see Elster (1989).
45. Garretsen, Lensink, and Sterken (2004, p. 172).

however, gives little guidance to a policymaker seeking to quicken the pace of economic development. What is missing thus far is a concrete sense of what aspects of culture are crucial. Further, it would be useful to know whether any aspects of culture can be changed through public policy and in what particular respects culture inhibits law reform.

Using the notions of values and cultural regions, Licht, Goldschmidt, and Schwartz have taken important steps to measure cultural differences.[46] They pursue an analogy to the legal origins literature's use of legal families by delineating cultural regions within which particular cultural similarities predominate. To do so, they have sought to stress cultural values that are deeper (or more fundamental) than social norms and religion. They have relied on a short list of polar opposites, such as autonomy versus embeddedness, where autonomy "describes cultures in which the person is viewed as an autonomous, bounded entity who finds meaning in his or her own uniqueness," and embeddedness "represents a cultural emphasis on the maintenance of the status quo, propriety, and restraint of actions or inclinations that might disrupt group solidarity or the traditional order." Other such cultural dichotomies are hierarchy ("obeying role obligations within a legitimately unequal distribution of power, roles, and resources") versus egalitarianism ("transcendence of selfish interests in favor of voluntary commitment to promoting the welfare of others") and mastery ("getting ahead through active self-assertion") versus harmony ("fitting harmoniously into the social and natural environment").[47] It is not surprising that English-speaking countries (one of the cultural regions) rank high on autonomy, egalitarianism, and mastery (though not the highest in each instance).

Regions constructed from these values corresponded in much of the world with regions of the same legal origin (for example, English-speaking and common law). However, the data led to a distinct Far Eastern–Asian cultural region composed of roughly equal numbers of common law and civil law countries, suggesting that culture is sometimes independent of legal origin. Yet, in this cultural region, Licht, Goldschmidt, and Schwartz found that, consonant with the LLSV legal origins results, the subset of common law countries had higher corporate governance scores than the subset of civil law countries. But they also noted that the "perceived legality in the East Asian cultural region is significantly lower than in English-speaking and West European countries," leading to the conclusion that "the law on the books may

---

46. See Licht, Goldschmidt, and Schwartz (2004, 2005). See also Licht (2001).

47. Licht, Goldschmidt, and Schwartz (2005, table 1.A.). The authors also rely on a series of indexes on individualism-collectivism, power-distance, uncertainty-avoidance, and masculinity-femininity. These latter four values were taken from the work of Hofstede (2001).

play only a minor role in determining shareholder protection in practice in East Asian countries" and therefore that "caution" should be used in judging "East Asian shareholder protection solely according to legal origin."[48]

Although the data relied on in these studies have not been subjected to the same kind of peer review as were the LLSV legal origins data, a virtue of this particular analysis is that it throws light on the difficulties of basing legal reform in a particular country on foreign concepts. For example, they note that from 1992 to 1998 the average level of shareholder rights in central and eastern Europe under the LLSV measure based on law on the books advanced from substantially below the world average to well above it. And yet the reforms, based on advice from American academics, yielded poor results. Their explanation is that surveys showed that the residents of the former communist countries "strongly endorsed cultural embeddedness and hierarchy," which "correlate robustly with low perceived legality" and hence these "countries lacked the cultural foundation that is consistent with widespread, voluntary law-abidingness."[49]

Furthermore, the reforms involved emphasizing litigation based on standards over bright-line rules, but the surveys showing a "relatively high average score on Harmony" suggest "that the populace may be inclined to avoid the court system." The authors' somber conclusion was that "engendering beneficial social change through legal reform thus faces massive hurdles in such societies."[50] Whether that conclusion ultimately proves right or wrong, it certainly raises important questions for an economic development program based on transplanting law from countries with quite different cultural values.[51]

Legal Culture

Culture and legal origins may not be entirely contrasting explanations. It would be surprising if they were because, for example, the law of England and of France emerged from the societies of those countries. It is a common observation that the common law reflects a sense of pragmatism and practicality associated with English thinking and behavior. Be that as it may, one

---

48. Licht, Goldschmidt, and Schwartz (2005, p. 27).
49. Licht, Goldschmidt, and Schwartz (2005, pp. 31–32).
50. Licht, Goldschmidt, and Schwartz (2005, p. 32).
51. On the reforms in the former communist states, see Black and Kraakman (1996). See Glaeser, Johnson, and Shleifer (2001), suggesting that enforcement by state regulators worked better than enforcement by litigation in Eastern Europe.

aspect of culture that cannot be avoided in looking at the influence of law on economic development is the legal culture. Since whether laws on the books are enforced (and whether they are enforced promptly at a reasonable cost to the complainant) is at least as important as whether a particular substantive rule is on the books, legal culture is an important, if frequently overlooked, subject.

Although the legal origins literature began with a focus on substantive rules of law, economists working in that tradition have increasingly introduced the quality of enforcement. Obviously a rule of law that is not easily enforced is likely to have limited influence. Hence the quality, integrity, and attitudes of judges are a central consideration. As is argued in a subsequent chapter, those characteristics of judges are as much a cultural phenomenon as a technical question of court organization, funding, computerization, and the like. In other words, legal education, judicial career patterns, the experience and prestige of the judiciary as a profession, along with similar factors involving the lawyers who appear before the judges, have a great deal to do with the rules of the game in actual practice.

Left open are such questions as whether the legal culture of a country reflects the general political culture of a country, including ideology and nationalism, as well as broader political attitudes toward the economy, the role of government, and the like. For example, Roe has emphasized social democratic politics as a determinant of legal rules.[52] Rajan and Zingales have emphasized interest group politics in which incumbent financial firms resist financial development because it breeds competition for them.[53]

These political issues, and more generally the question of the ultimate source of cultural attitudes, are not addressed in this book because the focus is on how the legal rules actually adopted affect economic development and what policy measures might prove feasible as options realistically within the reach of the developing world. From the standpoint of this objective, therefore, the main conclusion from reviewing the legal origins story and the cultural literature is a recognition of the importance of law while being sensitive to the difficulties of relying primarily on legal reform as the key to economic development. In the next chapter the importance of the process of legal change is explored. One insight is that large-scale legal change does not necessarily occur either rapidly or as a result of sudden change but rather through an evolutionary process.

52. Roe (2003).
53. Rajan and Zingales (2003a).

4 | *Institutions and History*

If one wants insight into how the developing world can attain the rule of law, one good place to start would be to ask how countries in today's developed world did it. Although the developed world now stretches well beyond the countries of western Europe where the rule of law first arose, developed countries such as the United States, Canada, and Australia—and, in a less direct fashion, Japan—achieved a successful transplant of western European legal institutions. Perhaps the western European experience can provide insights into how this process of legal institutional development can succeed in developing countries where the transplant remedy is obstructed by historical, societal, or other differences from western European nations. Western Europe, after all, was not blessed with a rule of law in the Middle Ages but successfully achieved it over a number of centuries.

The first step in this analysis is to recognize that rule-of-law institutions are not essential for economic activity (although they are relevant to economic growth). In every country goods and services are exchanged, usually against money. In fact, in some of the poorest countries, the level of economic activity in local marketplaces is intense, truly something to marvel. And yet this exchange takes place without law playing a significant role.

Consider the public market, or bazaar—the primary economic institution of the medieval world and even today a common sight in the developing world. After seller and buyer reach a verbal agreement, the seller hands over the goods and the buyer hands over the money. The quid and the quo are exchanged simultaneously. But, as Greif put it, suppose the quid and the quo are separated.[1] They can be separated in time, as when the buyer promises to pay later but wants to take the goods with him. What will then give the seller confidence that he will be paid as promised? In the absence of law (or some ongoing relationship between seller and buyer), the seller is likely simply to refuse to sell except against money pressed into his hand. The same problem arises where goods are to be made to order with the seller requiring advance payment.

These problems were compounded in the medieval world when the buyer and the seller were geographically separated. True, seller and buyer could negotiate in writing or through a traveling agent. But the separation in place meant that the goods would have to be produced and delivered before payment could be expected, the seller thereby taking what he might well consider an unreasonable risk that the buyer would change his mind. Or payment could be made before the goods were produced, in which case the buyer would be taking the risk.

In these cases, the quid and the quo were separated in both space and time. Of course, most goods were simply taken physically to distant bazaars where they were offered for sale. The problem for the producer in that situation was twofold. If he was cheated in the bazaar, he had to trust the local authorities to protect him and not to discriminate against him as a foreigner. And second he would normally have to choose some kind of agent to act as a salesman for him. If the agent absconded with his goods or with the payment received in exchange, the producer's remedies might be limited.

These kinds of problems were acute in the Middle Ages, not so much within the city-states that were the dominant economies of the time in Europe but whenever long-distance trade had to be conducted.[2] The city-states had domestic legal systems, but they could not easily enforce contracts in which their citizens were cheated when selling or buying goods in distant city-states.[3] And so intercity trade was limited. These kinds of problems extended beyond trade and its financing to purely financial contracts and insurance contracts, both of which necessarily had the same separation between the quid and the quo as the trade examples.

Even where the parties were bargaining in good faith, the separation of the quid and the quo created the possibility that one party, however well-intentioned ex ante, would find it to his advantage ex post to reopen the

1. Greif (2004a).
2. Greif (2004b).
3. M. Smith (1928, pp. 213–16).

bargaining or simply renege on the deal. This incentive to renegotiate agreements after one party had performed, a common occurrence even today, can be referred to as ex post opportunism; it creates severe economic inefficiencies whenever an adequate legal system is not in place. In other words, the enforcement of contracts is important to ensure that contracts will be performed voluntarily.

These kinds of problems exist across the entire spectrum of economic activities whenever a system of law is not in place or does not work effectively to give parties confidence that contracts will be carried out. This is the essence of the rule-of-law problem in many developing countries where the legal system does not, for whatever reason, work effectively.

Nevertheless, some trade can take place even though the parties are separated if the party at risk has confidence in the performance of the other party. That confidence may come from the reputation of the other party, though that statement begs the question of how the requisite reputation can be created. Of course, if the parties have repeated transactions, confidence may be created because each party knows that a failure to perform will end the business opportunities between the two. (Readers familiar with the theory of games will recognize the repeated game phenomenon, which offsets the incentive for someone in a two-player game to defect.[4]) Similarly, if the parties have some other relationship, such as being members of the same family, that relationship may be sufficient to give the requisite confidence. Consider the success of the extended Chinese families spread across Southeast Asia in carrying on trade even across countries that did not yet enjoy the rule of law.[5]

Early European Substitutes for the Rule of Law: Boycotts and Reputation

In considering the evolution of long-distance trade in Europe during the Middle Ages, one must recognize, however, that even in that period some solutions were found to these kinds of trade problems, at least in certain instances. The solutions, however, illustrate why a rule of law is essential to the efficient functioning of a modern economy.

One early solution was the community responsibility system.[6] Under this system, city-states (communities) would hold all members of a foreign

4. Baird, Gertner, and Picker (1994, p. 203).
5. Bardhan (2000, pp. 219–20); Redding (1990).
6. The description of this system draws heavily on Greif (2004a) and earlier Greif articles cited therein. See also Greif (2004b).

community responsible when any member of that foreign community cheated, or failed to pay a debt to, a local citizen. If the foreigner refused to make compensation, goods of that foreigner's compatriots within the local community would simply be impounded for the benefit of the local citizen. In effect, the presence of a debtor's compatriots provided de facto collateral. The system worked because the debtor's community would be motivated, in view of its dependence on long-distance trade, to force its own citizen-debtor to pay because trade opportunities would otherwise be limited by what amounted to a boycott by the creditor's community. The system worked both for trade in goods and for financial transactions.

The system was, however, imperfect. In a sense the sanction was too powerful. In the first place, impoundment of goods of all foreigners from a given city disrupted trade between the two cities, at least until the dispute was settled. Nearby city-states, therefore, sometimes entered into treaties to regulate the implementation of the system, as in the Pisa-Florence Treaty of 1214.[7] And the sanction was too strong in a further sense; it gave the local creditor less reason to investigate the creditworthiness of his counterpart foreign debtor before entering into the transaction.

Clearly third-party enforcement would have been preferable to the community responsibility system. But no appropriate third party was available where the two communities were not subject to a common sovereign. Neither Italy nor Germany had a single ruler because they were not unified states. In England the Normans created a centralized legal system in Westminster covering the part of England subject to royal control through traveling judges, but it was a costly and uncertain form of third-party enforcement, and so the community responsibility system played a role in England as well.[8]

---

7. Greif (2004a, p. 130, n. 58).

8. In 1166 "a system of sending royal judges from the center to go on circuit through the counties" was established; see Danziger and Gillingham (2003, pp. 186–87). In view of the common belief that in the Middle Ages only churchmen could read and write, it is worth noting that the overwhelming majority of this new class of judges were laymen, men learned in a law that depended for its regular functioning upon documents. "Everywhere they went these judges applied the same laws, a common law all over England, which is why the king who sent them out is commonly regarded as the founder of the Common Law," Danziger and Gillingham wrote (p. 189). This practice was similar to circuit riding in the United States. In early U.S. Supreme Court history, "riding circuit for justices meant bouncing thousands of miles over rutted, dirt roads in stagecoach, on horseback, and in stick gigs to bring the federal judiciary to the American communities strewn along the Eastern seaboard. More so than the representatives of the federal postal system, the justices appeared despite rain, snow, sleet, and the hazards of traveling" Baker (1976, p. 63).

An effort was made in England to create an alternative adjudication system. The Statute of Westminster I of 1275 outlawed the community responsibility system among communities within England by declaring that "no stranger who is of this kingdom is to be distrained . . . for what he is neither debtor nor pledge for."[9] As a substitute, a voluntary registration system was established eight years later in which debtor and creditor could jointly register a debt, thereby allowing designated local officials to foreclose on the movable property of the debtor in the case of nonpayment.[10] This registration system was in effect a primitive mortgage or pledge system for the enforcement of contracts involving the separation of the quid and the quo.

Another medieval solution to the problem of the separation of two parties to a transaction involved merchant guilds. In northern Europe, guilds, which already existed for other local purposes, developed a way of dealing with the mistreatment of their members operating outside the town of their origin. Some guilds created what amounted to a multilateral system of boycotting foreign communities whose citizens cheated, stole from, or imprisoned guild members. This multilateral arrangement was one of the major features of the association of German towns and merchant communities (known as the Hansa or the Hanseatic League) surrounding the Baltic and North Seas and their tributary rivers.[11] Such a coordinated boycott was, for example, successful in forcing the Belgian city of Bruges to deal fairly with the German expatriate business community in that city.[12]

That example involved boycotts, but other systems based on reputation rather than boycott were adopted in the period before the nation-state. Just as local traders within a town could rely on local knowledge and experience based on past trading (in other words, on reputation), additional means were established to build on the reputation concept.

For example, Jewish traders, known as the Maghribi traders, operated in the area surrounding the Mediterranean in the eleventh century. The system they developed involved the use of foreign merchants acting as agents for merchants seeking to sell their goods in distant towns. The problem to be solved was how the foreign agent could acquire the reputation needed to be entrusted with the goods when ongoing communication between principal and agent was ruled out by distance and the primitive communications

9. Douglas (1975, p. 404); see also Moore (1985, p. 104).
10. Plucknett (1949, pp. 138–43). The new system evolved from the Statute of Acton Burnell, 1283 (Douglas, 1975, pp. 420–22).
11. Tanner, Previté-Orton, and Brooke (1932, pp. 216–47).
12. Greif, Milgrom, and Weingast (1994, pp. 759–62).

technology available to them. The level of knowledge of conditions—prices, customs duties, and the like—in the agent's town was not just asymmetric between principal and agent but often the principal would have no current knowledge at all.

The solution adopted by the Maghribi traders involved a means by which the agent could convince the principal ex ante that the agent would be honest ex post. The Maghribi traders formed what amounted to a coalition that promoted the level of knowledge and communication so that any cheating by an agent could be catastrophic to the agent's business; he could expect that his cheating would become known among all Maghribi traders. Maintaining a reputation for honesty could thus be expected to result in favorable terms and conditions for the agent. The system worked because the Maghribi traders were a distinct social group not just within the trading community but within the Jewish communities of the Mediterranean world, a condition that promoted trust as well as the communication on which trust could be based. The system was thus built on a multilateral reputation mechanism.[13]

The Maghribi traders system was geographically localized in the Mediterranean world and disappeared by the end of the eleventh century. But a different system, also based on reputation, was being created in northern Europe. This was the law merchant. It was not a system of law enacted by a legislature or handed down by a ruler, and therefore some scholars are reluctant to call it "law."[14] But it worked. Trading communities, normally guilds, established their own private tribunals. The law they adopted to govern commercial transactions was initially rooted in the rules followed in the most developed European cities of the time, the Italian city-states, and was more or less uniform across Europe. But it was private law established and applied by private tribunals. One can call it customary law, but it was custom of a different kind than the customary law applied in small communities across Europe for local matters such as inheritance.

The law merchant can be seen as based on reputation because it was created and applied by merchants and was more or less uniform across northern Europe. Any word that a particular merchant had flouted a law merchant decision would result in the destruction of that merchant's reputation for honesty, and he would no longer be trusted in long-distance trade or credit transactions. Moreover, that merchants knew and applied this standard law

13. Greif (1989).

14. See, for example, Donahue (2004) and Kadens (2004). See also comments in Epstein (2004, p. 3), which state that "the debate is as much about the definition of law as it is about the historical origins and development of the Law Merchant itself."

meant that word of a decision could be communicated simply and expected to travel quickly. Eventually the law merchant grew beyond simple sales to include credit, bills of exchange, insurance, and other trade-promoting legal devices.

A system related to the law merchant was used to promote honesty and fair dealing at fairs (in Champagne and elsewhere in Western Europe), which were one of the principal means of long-distance trade during this period. At these fairs buyers and sellers met, normally once a year. A number of localities held fairs.[15] The fairs had means of resolving disputes that arose at fair time, and some detail exists about the Flanders fairs, which had their own legal system. Beginning in 1252, foreign merchants were exempted from trial by combat and from reprisals; only their personal goods could be confiscated, although imprisonment for debt was permitted. But the important point was that any case involving a merchant had to be judged within a week. Cases, once brought, could not be delayed or adjourned. In short, disputes were resolved before the parties left the fair. It seems likely that a defendant would find it difficult to leave earlier or, if he succeeded in leaving, ever to return in view of the power of the authorities to exclude merchants from fairs. Moreover, many towns sent consuls to fairs to represent their own merchants in disputes before fair courts.[16] And some towns established their own courts at distant fairs: a Flemish guild court traveled with Flemish merchants to handle internal disputes among the Flemish merchants at fairs in England.[17]

The Nation-State

The development of the nation-state in Europe provided a more centralized means to solve long-distance trade problems. These nation-states were monarchies, and the monarch had not only the means to create courts that could coerce compliance with contracts but also some motivation to promote trade, which meant some incentive to treat foreign traders fairly.

Initially the problems of long-distance trade could be resolved only to the extent that the parties were subject to the same government. Even in England, which had an early start with the Norman conquest and the centralization of the English court system in Westminster, it took a long time for the legal system to evolve to support even the rudiments of what we take for granted as necessary for a modern economy, with secured credit, business enterprises in

15. Pirenne (1937).
16. The foregoing paragraph is based on Postan, Rich, and Miller (1965, pp. 132–37).
17. Moore (1985, pp. 96–99).

corporate form, and markets in shares.[18] Moreover, the existence of a monarch with nominal sovereignty over large areas did not mean that the writ of his judges necessarily ran so broadly. One has only to read Shakespeare's historical plays to realize that the rebellion of regional nobility was a repeated occurrence and a constant preoccupation in England.

In short, even with the rise of the nation-state, the ability of a King's courts to protect long-distance trade must have been largely theoretical for some centuries as justice remained mostly local.[19] For example, even in a country as relatively centralized as France, the law was not fully unified until the Napoleonic codifications at the beginning of the nineteenth century. Germany and Italy did not become united nations until later in the nineteenth century. And as long as justice was local, the temptation to favor local merchants over traders from distant parts, even merchants of the same kingdom, presented problems for the growth of long-distance trade and the development of modern financial and insurance techniques. Flourishing foreign trade requires protection against discrimination in the enforcement of contracts and the protection of property.

Much as we may admire the legal systems of present-day developed countries, those legal systems have evolved a great deal. England, for example, had a number of competing court systems over many centuries. These different courts might produce different outcomes in factually similar disputes. A prime example would be the difference between outcomes in Common Pleas, a common law court, and Chancery, a tribunal designed to "do equity"—in short, to provide a remedy not available at common law.[20] There were, moreover, various prerogative courts that enforced rules proclaimed by the King independent of Parliament or the common law in the exercise of the King's prerogative powers.[21]

Predation and the Rule-of-Law Dilemma

With the growing power of monarchs came not just court systems but also a new threat to the emergence of the rule of law. The monarch himself might

---

18. Milsom (1969, pp. 15–22).

19. In the twelfth and early thirteenth centuries, according to Ibbetson (1999, p. 17), "pleas concerning the debt of laymen . . . belong[ed] to the crown and dignity of the lord king" and therefore were nominally within the jurisdiction of the courts, but "private agreements" were "not customarily dealt with by the king's courts."

20. Hanbury and Maudsley (1989).

21. Berman (2003, pp. 202–13).

disavow his own contracts or seize property of a subject for his own purposes. Today in authoritarian regimes in the developing world there sometimes are what might be called predatory rulers. And predatory is exactly what a number of European monarchs were in earlier centuries.

Social scientists sometimes describe the resulting rule-of-law dilemma in the following terms: a ruler strong enough to enforce contracts and protect private property is also strong enough to take predatory action against subjects.[22] If citizens cannot trust their government to keep its hands off their property, they are unlikely to invest as much, at least in certain kinds of property. Investment in diamonds, jewelry, and gold is still common in the contemporary world in countries where precisely this kind of fear holds back investment in wealth-creating property. Failure to resolve the dilemma can therefore not only impede economic development but stimulate counterproductive behavior by citizens of the country.

Thus history teaches that resolution of this fundamental dilemma takes time and is likely to be an evolutionary process. Attempts to jump-start the process can prove dead ends. For example, one way in which rulers have sometimes tried to enrich themselves while still favoring economic development has been to create an alliance with chosen business interests. For example, Mexican development took that form in the nineteenth and early twentieth centuries.[23] It is fair to say that Mexico, despite its proximity to a rapidly growing U.S. market, was held back by this coalition between autocratic rulers and what today might be called "oligarchs."

That today's developed countries have largely solved not just the quid and the quo problem but also the predatory ruler problem is not the result of the work of great legal scholars or brilliant legal architects. On the contrary, the transition to a rule-of-law state has in most countries been the result of an evolution over several centuries.

Legal Evolution in England

The evolution in England has been the best documented of these transitions. Although many people of Anglo-Saxon heritage romanticize English history, often jumping to the conclusion that the Magna Carta of 1215 created a rule-of-law state, the facts are rather different. In truth, the Magna Carta, or Great Charter, was more a partial settlement of a dispute between King John and

---

22. Weingast (1993, p. 287).
23. Haber, Razo, and Maurer (2003).

the English barons.[24] Schama well captures the limited scope, yet immense promise for a future rule of law, of the Magna Carta:

> No one should read the Magna Carta as if it were some sort of primitive constitution. . . . Inevitably, many of [its] prohibitions amounted to tax relief for the landed and armoured classes. . . . So, if the Magna Carta was not the birth certificate of freedom it was the death certificate of despotism. It spelled out for the first time, and unequivocally . . . that the law was not simply the will or the whim of the king but was an independent power in its own right, and that kings could be brought to book for violating it. . . . All this, in turn, presupposed something hitherto unimaginable: that there was some sort of English "state" of which the king was part (albeit the supreme part) but not the whole.[25]

If the rule of law is in part about the protection of property, it is well to recall that Henry VIII, in seizing the monasteries, carried out one of the largest expropriations in history, surpassed perhaps only in the twentieth century with the advent of Communism in Russia. The monasteries, the accumulated physical manifestation of centuries of donations by the faithful, constituted "approximately one-fourth of the landed wealth of England."[26]

The dissolution of the monasteries thus provided the Crown with vast lands, which were gradually sold to finance the needs of the Crown, especially wars.[27] Although the seizure of the monasteries was part of the struggle with Rome, the truth is that Henry VIII, as English kings before and after, had to run his governments largely out of his own resources, in part because no one had enough confidence in the king or in their legal rights against the king to lend to him. Nevertheless, the Crown did have limited sources of public revenue. Kings successfully claimed the right to impose customs duties as part of the royal prerogative. Taxation was limited, often to what the king was able to coerce out of Parliament on special occasions. For example, the first Parliament of the first Stuart king, James I (1603–25), granted him the power to impose additional duties on imports and exports in view of the debts run up on behalf of the Crown by Queen Elizabeth.[28]

As for direct taxes, when Charles I became king in 1625, "Parliament refused to grant the usual lifetime taxes allowed to a new monarch, and

24. Plucknett (1960, pp. 66–88); Danziger and Gillingham (2003, pp. 160–84).
25. Schama (2000, p. 162).
26. Berman (2003, p. 209).
27. Tawney (1941, pp. 23–25). See also Rajan and Zingales (2003b, pp. 136, 141) and Maddison (2001, p. 91).
28. Berman (2003, pp. 213–14).

Charles resorted to forced loans, imprisoning those who refused to give them."[29] Perhaps as a consequence, the Stuarts expanded the practice of borrowing to finance wars, largely from goldsmiths and non-English lenders, but they destroyed the confidence of their creditors by failing to pay on time and sometimes by repudiating debts.

The showdown came after the restoration of the Stuart monarchy in the latter half of the seventeenth century. At one point Charles II defaulted on the debt in the famous "Stop of the Exchequer" incident in order to free revenues for military purposes.[30] Stuart King James II desperately sought funding for the war against France but could not raise adequate funds. The resulting concatenation of decisive events led to an alliance of convenience between Tories and Whigs to replace James II with the Dutch Prince of Orange (who became King William III) and his English wife Mary. These events had a series of legal by-products that created the foundation for a rule of law in England.[31] These fundamental changes are today called the Glorious Revolution, not just because they were essentially bloodless but also because they created a constitutional foundation for ensuring that the English monarchy was no longer in a position to be predatory.[32] Today social scientists refer to these changes as creating a "credible commitment" that English rulers would no longer take their subjects' property without compensation nor repudiate debts.[33]

Among these changes was that the king could spend from public funds only what Parliament appropriated for that purpose. Some of the key steps in creating this new order were enacted by the Convention Parliament in the 1689 Bill of Rights. This famous document declared that "levying money for or to the use of the crown . . . without grant of parliament . . . is illegal," thereby giving the legislature exclusive fiscal powers.[34] The king was now truly "King in Parliament," not king separate from and in effect over Parliament.[35]

29. Berman (2003, p. 215).

30. Carruthers (1996, pp. 122–27); Stasavage (2003, p. 63); Dickson (1967, pp. 43–45). As noted in Clapham (1945, p. 12), the Stop of the Exchequer was not a repudiation of debt but rather a suspension of interest payments.

31. Weingast (1997a).

32. The Glorious Revolution is conventionally dated 1688 when James II took flight to France and the future king of England arrived in England, but the decisive constitutional events awaited the meeting of the Convention Parliament in 1689; indeed they continued to the Act of Settlement in 1701, which established the proposition that Parliament would thenceforth determine the succession to the throne. See Plucknett (1960, pp. 444–65).

33. North and Weingast (1989, p. 803).

34. Williams (1960, p. 28); Maitland (1931, p. 309).

35. Maitland (1931, p. 300). Dicey (1893, p. 38), relying on Blackstone, expressed the concept as follows: The king, the House of Lords, and the House of Commons "may be aptly described as the 'King in Parliament,' and constitute Parliament" and "Parliament thus defined

The Parliament responded by voting an annual appropriation for the Crown.[36] By the end of William's reign in 1702, the annual "civil list" appropriation specified in some detail what the money would be spent for.[37] When the Bank of England was created in 1694 (before it was given monetary regulatory duties as a central bank), it was intended to be an intermediary from whom the Crown might borrow, but it was specifically forbidden to lend to the Crown without consent of Parliament, thereby giving Parliament further leverage over the king.[38]

Parliament also established the supremacy of its lawmaking, again in the Bill of Rights, by declaring illegal the "pretended power of suspending laws, or the execution of laws, by regal authority, without the consent of Parliament." A second, almost parallel clause similarly made illegal "dispensing with laws, or the execution of laws, by regal authority." "Dispensing" referred to the king's previous practice of declaring certain statutes inapplicable to specified individuals, whereas "suspending" referred to the declaration of statutes as inapplicable to all persons. [39] That this was not a unilateral statement by Parliament, but rather part of the bargain between the two political parties of the day, the Whigs and the Tories, and a bargain by them with the Crown is shown by an amendment to the traditional Coronation Oath, in which William, unlike earlier monarchs, swore to govern "according to the statutes in parliament agreed on, and the laws and customs of the same."[40] It is significant that, thereafter, "William and his successors duly refrained from any attempt to exercise a suspending or dispensing power."[41]

Parliament's power vis-à-vis the Crown was made clearer in the 1701 Act of Settlement, which regulated the succession to the monarchy.[42] Thereafter the monarchy became a statutory office not only because its powers were circumscribed by legislation but also because even the person to succeed to that position would be determined, albeit perhaps indirectly, by the legislature.[43]

More important still for the rule of law was a provision of the 1701 Act of

---

has, under the English constitution, the right to make or unmake any law whatever; and, further, that no person or body is recognized by the law of England as having a right to override or set aside the legislation of Parliament."

36. "English History," *Encyclopedia Britannica 1970.*
37. Maitland (1931, p. 310).
38. Giuseppi (1966, p. 10).
39. Williams (1960, p. 28).
40. Williams (1960, p. 3); Maitland (1963, pp. 287–88).
41. Thompson (1938, p. 198).
42. Plucknett (1960, p. 504).
43. Dicey (1893, p. 41).

Settlement that further defined the separation of powers by establishing the basis for an independent judiciary. Judges were granted life tenure on good behavior, thereby ending a pattern in which the Crown had threatened judges in key cases and dismissed them when threats failed.[44] Soon thereafter salaries of judges became fixed during their tenure, and they could be dismissed only if convicted of a criminal offense or by "the address of both houses" (similar to the U.S. impeachment process).[45] These major steps toward an independent judiciary supplemented earlier measures to limit or eliminate the prerogative tribunals controlled by the Crown. The Star Chamber had been used, until abolished in 1641, not just to escape the safeguards and procedures of the common law courts, including the use of juries, but also to punish violations of royal proclamations and other crimes designated by the Crown—in short, crimes that were not created or defined by Parliament or by the common law courts.[46]

The abolition of the Star Chamber and several other prerogative courts did not put an end to prerogative bodies. With the restoration of the Stuart monarch after the Civil War, James II, in 1686, created a new prerogative commission to govern the church and the clergy (with a view to reestablishing the dominance of the Church of Rome).[47] In response the 1689 Bill of Rights stated flatly that this latest effort to create a prerogative court, as well as a "court of commissioners for ecclesiastical causes, and all other commissions and courts of like nature are illegal and pernicious."[48] This last provision was implicitly acceded to by King William in the new Coronation Oath by his acknowledgment that he must govern "according to the statutes in parliament agreed upon, and the laws and customs of the same."[49] The suppression of the prerogative courts was, as Weingast has observed, a major step by which "royal control over the judiciary was abolished, creating the . . . 'independent judiciary.'"[50]

44. Plucknett (1960, pp. 463, 464–66).
45. Maitland (1931, p. 313).
46. Maitland (1931, p. 302); Finer (1997, p. 1347). For a general discussion on the court, see "Court of the Star Chamber," *Encyclopedia Britannica 2004*, Encyclopedia Britannica Online.
47. Maitland (1931, p. 312).
48. Williams (1960, p. 28).
49. Williams (1960, p. 3). A remaining prerogative body, the Court of Requests, was abolished by the end of the century. For a general discussion, see "Prerogative Court," *Encyclopedia Britannica 2004*, Encyclopedia Britannica Online.
50. Weingast (1997b, p. 220).

Other steps creating a modern separation of powers were designed to give Parliament independence from royal arbitrariness. Parliament, by the Triennial Act of 1694, now met in regular sessions, assuring that it could not be sent home for long periods when its majority was opposed to the Crown or kept in session for long periods when parliamentary majorities favored the Crown.[51] Although the Triennial Act set a limit to the length of any particular Parliament and ensured that the Parliament would meet at least every three years, the previously mentioned provisions on the king's income and expenditures were perhaps more important because they changed the incentives so that it was now in the king's interest to see that a Parliament was in session at least every year.[52] Parliament now controlled both the king's income (or at least his use thereof) and his borrowings. Although the king still had his traditional sources of income (such as customs duties and the profits of lands he held personally), these sources were inadequate. He had to turn to Parliament every year to supplement them; as Berman noted, "Parliament, which from November 1685 until November 1689 did not meet at all, and met in only 75 of the entire 130 years of Tudor-Stuart reign, has met every year since 1689."[53]

In addressing the elements of the British evolution toward a rule of law, two aspects must be considered: the constitutional structure, and the underlying legislation that supported the growth of economic activity. The Glorious Revolution established the constitutional basis. The evolution from the abolition of the Star Chamber in 1641 through the Bill of Rights of 1689 and the Triennial Act of 1694 to the Act of Settlement of 1701 created a solid legal and constitutional base for the rule of law. In addition to cementing the independence of the judiciary, these developments fashioned a new relationship between the king, as ruler, and Parliament. Certainly the discretionary powers of the king vis-à-vis Parliament were drastically reduced: "of the discretionary powers exercised . . . by the pre-Revolutionary English monarchy in

51. Plucknett (1960, p. 526).

52. Kemp (1957, pp. 32–36). The Triennial Act states: "That from henceforth a parliament shall be holden once in three years at the least;" and "that from henceforth no parliament . . . shall at any time hereafter be called, assembled or held, shall have any continuance longer than for three years only at the farthest" (quoted in Williams 1960, p. 50). The Septennial Act of 1716 extended the period from three to seven years but did not change the principle of a maximum term for a particular Parliament and therefore elections and turnover (Kemp 1957, pp. 39–40). Meanwhile, as the text explains, parliamentary control over the king's income and expenditures assured that there would be annual parliamentary sessions.

53. Berman (2003, p. 227).

relation to legislation, only one—the ultimate power of veto—remained by 1690 [and] after 1708 it was never resorted to again."[54]

Although the new structure was focused on the relationship between king and Parliament, one cannot say that by itself it created the kind of relationship between the ruler and the people that one associates today with the rule of law. To be sure, Parliament in some sense represented the people, and one can certainly say that protection of Parliamentary power served to protect the people. Of course, one should not confuse the resulting structure with "democracy" in view of the severe limitations on the voting franchise. But the same objection can be made to the system created by the U.S. Constitution of 1787. Both the English and U.S. systems represented a balance between legislative and executive powers, providing an answer to the predatory ruler problem and a further balance achieved through an independent judiciary.[55] In the case of England, the Glorious Revolution provided a strong base for later enjoyment of the fruits of the industrial revolution and for an economic evolution that made England arguably the wealthiest country in the world for a considerable period of time.

Assessing the Glorious Revolution

The Glorious Revolution has been celebrated by economists largely for its role in enabling the British Crown to borrow to finance wars. A broader and ultimately more important perspective, however, concerns the creation of a rule-of-law state, which has broader development implications.

The large volume of recent studies examining interest rates and other financial indicators in the period after the Glorious Revolution to determine its financial effects is important but somewhat beside the point. Interest rates fell, though there is debate about how soon, how much, and for how long.[56] Certainly the creation of a new international debt market in English government securities was somewhat of a hit-and-miss affair.[57] But the ability of the English sovereign to borrow new money at all was noteworthy in view of the earlier behavior of the Stuart kings. Especially remarkable was the ability to borrow to the extent of increasing the debt seventeenfold between 1688 and

54. Holmes (1993, p. 222).

55. The Act of Settlement of 1701 did not provide security of tenure to judges during the lifetime of the appointing king. This exception was eliminated in 1761; see Klerman and Mahoney (2005, pp. 11–12).

56. See Stasavage (2002) and Quinn (2001). On the effect of judicial independence, see also Klerman and Mahoney (2005).

57. Dickson (1967, pp. 46–75).

1697.[58] One reason was that Parliament greatly increased taxes, thereby cementing, in the famous phrase of North and Weingast, a "credible commitment that the Crown would not default."[59] A land tax was introduced that raised large amounts of revenue. But the important point was that the land tax was voted by the same landed classes that controlled Parliament, thereby signifying that Parliament was prepared to pay for the wars that were engulfing England.[60]

The larger accomplishment for future centuries of these great constitutional events surrounding the Glorious Revolution was, as already noted, the creation of a functioning rule of law, the first in the world.[61] And these accomplishments paid off. English per capita GDP, already some 30–35 percent higher than French per capita GDP in 1700, grew by 35 percent in the 1700–1820 period while French per capita GDP grew only 25 percent.[62] North gives credit to the rise of the power of Parliament, which "caused the nature of English property rights to diverge from the Continental pattern."[63]

Perhaps the best way to explain the institutional advance over continental countries is to emphasize that the Glorious Revolution took care of the predatory ruler problem. But in celebrating the Glorious Revolution's achievements, one should not overlook the fact that much of what was required to protect property against other private parties had already been accomplished in part by the evolution of common law rules, which dealt especially with land and inheritance. Also important was Parliamentary legislation as well as acts of private contractual ordering by merchants enforced by the common law. An early work by North points to such seventeenth century developments as "the creation of the first patent law to encourage innovation; the elimination of many of the remnants of feudal servitude, with the Statute of Tenures; the burgeoning of the joint stock company, . . . [and] the

---

58. Rajan and Zingales (2003b, p. 137).

59. North and Weingast (1989).

60. Stasavage (2003, p. 108). For the facts, but with a somewhat different interpretation, see Brewer (1989, pp. 95–100). Commercial interests, particularly those engaged in Atlantic trade, also favored the constitutional changes, according to Acemoglu, Johnson, and Robinson (2005, pp. 562–66).

61. The Dutch Republic has perhaps some claim to be the first rule-of-law nation state. Stasavage (2003, p. 55). Certainly it grew faster than England for a time after it became independent of Spain in 1579 (Maddison 2001, p. 75). Maddison and North attribute this growth rate to its position in international trade rather than to its domestic political arrangements (Maddison 2001, p. 75; North 1981, pp. 152–54).

62. Maddison (2003, table 1c).

63. North (1981, p. 156).

development of the goldsmith into a deposit banker issuing bank notes, discounting bills and providing interest on deposits."[64]

Well before the Glorious Revolution, English property law already constrained the English king in a way that the French and other kings were not constrained. Under French law the sovereign owned subsurface resources. But the English sovereign had no such power. Nef observed that this was one factor in explaining how the industrial revolution came earlier to England than to France:

> The tendency in England during the hundred years from 1540 to 1640 was not, as in France, for the sovereign to extend his authority over mining and metallurgy. Under the influence of decisions in the common-law courts, and under the pinch of financial necessity, the royal authority contracted at a time when the rapid expansion in the output of copper, lead, iron, and especially coal gave the mining and metallurgical industries a much greater importance in England than in France.[65]

In short, the legal measures surrounding the Glorious Revolution taken together with earlier common law decisions and Parliamentary legislation established a set of rules protecting property rights and enforcing contracts, free from arbitrary actions of the Crown. These rules enabled Britain in the eighteenth century not only to enjoy faster growth of the economy but also led the way into the industrial revolution.[66]

Constitutions

Although the Glorious Revolution is primarily to be seen as creating a constitutional structure, it did not result, as most revolutions do today, in a single written document and certainly not one that those involved chose to call a constitution. Constitutions did not become fashionable until the U.S. Constitution was ratified a century later. (And, of course, the British Constitution even to this day is not a single written document.)

Relations between the government and the people are now often thought of as a matter for constitutions. For that reason constitutional development is essential not only for the protection of human rights but also, as the English example shows, for economic development. That is one of the shortcomings of the legal origins literature, which focuses on only one side of the

---

64. North and Thomas (1973, p. 155).
65. Nef (1940, p. 101).
66. North (1981, pp. 171–86).

economic development question—the private law side—and pays less attention to the public law side. Public law concerns not just constitutions—where the influence of the U.S. Constitution with its separation of powers is an important if often overlooked element in nineteenth century economic development—but also the way in which the public bureaucracy is controlled, if at all, by an independent judiciary. These issues are discussed in a later chapter on the judiciary.

Constitutions can, of course, have a major impact on the rule of law, particularly in the realm of personal liberties and human rights. These latter subjects are beyond the scope of the current discussion, but they are certainly relevant to the protection of property; it is hard to visualize a system that does not protect people but does adequately protect property. Put differently, if a person's life and personal freedom are at risk, then that person's physical property can hardly be safe. Nevertheless, one can observe developing countries with rapid growth but without satisfactory human rights protections—China being a prototypical example.

One completely different constitutional issue that has some bearing on economic development is federalism. In some cases federalism can contribute to economic growth. Certainly allocating some governmental power to constituent units of a country, as in the case of the United States, acts as a constraint on abuse by the central government. And as Weingast has pointed out, federalism can also favor economic development by preserving markets.[67] This possibility is explored in a discussion of federalism in China in a later chapter. But perhaps just as often, federalism creates barriers to economic development, as the case of Russia in the 1990s suggests.[68] In any event, federalism is not essential to economic development, as the case of present-day, still highly centralized France demonstrates.

Nonconstitutional Elements of the Rule of Law

For now it is important to return to the nonconstitutional aspect of the rule of law—the part that is referred to when developing countries are urged to protect property rights and enforce contracts. On its face this is a simple dictate. But it is not an easy policy to implement. Worse still, it is a slogan, more than a directly implementable policy. Just as in the case of the public law side involving the relation between government and the people, achieving the

67. Weingast (1993, 1995).
68. de Figueiredo and Weingast (2001).

property-contract rule-of-law goal in private and commercial law has proved to be more of an evolutionary process than a simple exercise in decisionmaking and legal drafting.

One of the problems is that the apparently crystal clear injunction to protect property and enforce contracts is inherently ambiguous. To show why this is so, it is useful to review what the draftsmen of the French Civil Code had in mind when they began their work. We cannot get too far with our analysis if we start with the legal origins conclusion that French law falls short. After all, the French Revolution and the Code Civil were precisely about private property and freedom of contract.

Rather the French code drafters were primarily interested in changing the social structure of France. Protection of property in the Napoleonic period meant predominantly an end to feudalism and thereby the subversion of the power of the aristocracy. The 1791 French Constitution, although it did not survive, perfectly reflects the revolutionary intentions: "There is no longer nobility, nor peerage, nor hereditary distinctions, nor feudal regimes. . . ."[69] Feudalism in Europe meant originally a complex hierarchical system in which an ordinary owner's interest was dependent on the interest of a higher-level person.[70] By the time of Napoleon it meant the aristocratic practice of primogeniture, which by ensuring that only the eldest son inherited land guaranteed the survival of landed estates in the same families generation after generation and hence the perpetuation of the aristocracy's wealth and thereby its power. Napoleon's solution in the Code Civil was to require the division of property at death among all children.[71] A person with children could dispose of only one-tenth of his property by will.[72] The obvious purpose was revolution by evolution: over several generations the great landed estates would be divided and subdivided and the aristocracy would lose its prestige and power.

One perhaps not so minor detail is that the 1791 French Constitution also stated that only one hierarchical feature from the past would not be abolished: ". . . nor any other superiority [was to be allowed] than that of public functionaries in the performance of their functions."[73] This can be interpreted as a belief in the bureaucratic state, with an emphasis on the public sector; that particular revolutionary heritage may be more important historically

---

69. Merryman, Clark, and Haley (1994, p. 446).
70. Berman (1983, pp. 303–32); Lawler and Lawler (1940, pp. 3–22). See the discussion of feudalism in England (which came to England from Normandy) in chapter 7 of this volume.
71. M. Smith (1928, pp. 171–73).
72. Merryman, Clark, and Haley (1994, p. 447), quoting from Zweigert and Kötz (1987).
73. Merryman, Clark, and Haley (1994, p. 446).

than the Code Civil. Indeed, even without the exaltation of the public functionary, the draftsmen's intent to eliminate all previous law had a similar consequence. Merryman, Clark, and Haley concluded that even during the more temperate postrevolutionary days of the Civil Code, a subtext underlay the declared purpose of writing on a clean slate:

> One reason for the attempt to repeal all prior law, and thus limit the effect of law to new legislation, was statism—the glorification of the nation-state. A law that had its origin in an earlier time, before the creation of the state, violated this statist ideal. So did a law that had its origin outside the state—in a European common law, for instance.[74]

Thus, if, as I argued in chapter 2, the origin of public law is at least as important as the origin of private law, this underlying theory of French constitutional arrangements, with its background of glorifying the nation-state and the public functionary, may well be more important for economic development than the Code Civil. Certainly many developing countries with a French law background accord the state (especially the top political leadership and a large public bureaucracy) a powerful role in the economy. Yet it is also true that private sector arrangements lingered on in French law countries despite the modernizing changes Napoleon introduced into his codes. For example, a long time was required to eliminate vestiges of feudal land ownership in the present developing world. Take Latin America as an example: it was not just that French private law was not adopted in Latin America for many decades after independence. In addition, as seen in the previous chapter, even though French law may have been an influence, the French Civil Code was rarely adopted outright. Rather Spanish law and Roman law, perhaps more supportive of feudal ideas, played a role in Latin America. In doing so, this cafeteria approach helped to perpetuate the societal role of the descendants of the early Spanish and Portuguese settlers.[75] Likewise, in modern times, it would be wrong to assume that the French Civil Code was the only influence determining the protection accorded by Latin American governments to newer forms of property, such as rights in intangible property or shareholder rights.

The same counterintuitive story about protection of property can be told about the French revolutionary draftsmen's intentions with regard to the

---

74. Merryman, Clark, and Haley (1994, pp. 449–50).

75. For a general discussion on Latin American social and economic influences on rule-of-law issues, see Rosenn (1990, pp. 20–30).

constitutional provisions on "freedom of contract." In practice that phrase meant that certain limitations on contracts that came largely from the influence of the Roman Catholic Church were invalidated. A prime example was the abolition of usury restrictions on contracts. If there was to be freedom of contract, then legal restrictions on the rate of interest could not be tolerated.[76] This element of French revolutionary law was not widely followed in French law countries and in fact was later abandoned in France.

A final aspect of the Code Civil bearing on the rule of law is that it was drafted in the context of other changes designed to reduce the role of the judiciary to a mechanical interpretive role in order to avoid *gouvernment des juges* and assure the dominance of the legislature. The judges were simply to apply the enactments of the legislature to the letter, just as a bureaucrat would be expected to do. Whether a judiciary with such a limited role can assure the rule of law is an important question.

At a superficial level, the French revolutionary emphasis on property and freedom of contract might seem to be the keystones of a move toward the rule of law, especially in the simple-minded modern "protect property rights" and "enforce contracts" version. But the French Civil and Commercial Codes (and one could argue at greater length, civil law in general) do not necessarily equate to the rule of law. More is required. In the next chapter, I explore one of these additional requirements—an independent and effective judiciary.

76. Herman (1984, pp. 612–14).

part II

Enforcement, Contracts, and Property

Proponents of the rule of law in the context of economic development often express the core of their position, as noted in part I, by emphasizing the need to "enforce contracts and protect property rights." This second part of the book takes up the three separate ideas underlying this simple phrase: enforcement, contracts, and property rights.

The initial chapter in this part is about enforcement, specifically enforcement by an independent third party, which typically means enforcement through a court system, even though some tribal areas still retain the right to use communal enforcement systems. Even arbitration can work only if there is an underlying right to enforce an arbitration award through a court. Hence the initial chapter, chapter 5, concerns the judiciary.

Chapter 6 is about the underlying substantive concepts of contracts and property. A contract is best thought of as a promise that the courts will in principle enforce if the party making the promise fails to carry it out. Many promises, such as the promise a parent may make to a child to serve pizza for dinner, are not legally enforceable. This book is concerned with mutual promises between two (or more) parties. Unlike the common law, however, where the traditional doctrine of consideration requires that the promisee must either make a reciprocal promise or pay something of value in order to enforce a promise, civil law systems (and even on occasion the common law) will enforce a promise made with sufficient solemnity or formality, especially where another party relies on the promise.[1]

1. Zweigert and Kötz (1998, pp. 388–99).

Chapter 6 then turns to another core concept—property. The phrase *property rights* is often used, but the rule of law also encompasses protection of property as such. A country seeking to develop rapidly must protect against theft by a private party and, if it is a rule-of-law state, against takings by the state without compensation as well.

Though many contracts do not involve property and many property disputes do not involve contracts, a large proportion of transactions and disputes particularly relevant to economic development clearly do involve both contract and property. Even agricultural land is most useful if it can be mortgaged and sold, but both mortgage and sale involve contracts with the land as a subject matter. In the realm of financial markets, discussed in part III, we will see that financial interests are normally the subject of contracts; a bank account is simply a contract between a depositor and the bank. A loan is a contract between a lender and a borrower. But when the loan is collateralized, the collateral is a "thing"—in other words, property—perhaps land or perhaps movable property such as an automobile. In equity finance, the organizing shareholders normally enter into a contract with one another, and once the corporation is formed, the shareholders hold property interests in an artificial legal entity known as a corporation. Therefore, the most important legal issues in economic development often arise at the interface of contract and property. Certainly it would make little sense for a government interested in economic development to say that contracts would be enforced but, for ideological or other reasons, property would not be recognized, or vice versa.

In the final chapter in this part, chapter 7, attention will turn to the application of enforcement, contract, and property in one of the most important sectors in developing countries, the agricultural sector. Here the key asset is land. The protection of rights in land and the ability to buy and sell land are important issues, particularly in those countries where tribal communal land systems still operate.

5 | *Judiciary*

A recurring theme in this book is that no degree of improvement in substantive law—even world "best practice" substantive law—will bring the rule of law to a country that does not have effective enforcement.[1] A sound judiciary is key to enforcement. No doubt some technical laws can be enforced by administrative means, but a rule of law, in the primary economic sense of protecting property and enforcing contracts, requires a judiciary to resolve disputes between private parties. And protection against the state itself is made easier where the judiciary can resolve a controversy raised by a private party against the state based on constitutional provisions or parliamentary legislation. One conclusion widely agreed upon, not just in the economic literature but also among lawyers and legal scholars, is therefore that the judiciary is a vital factor in the rule of law and more broadly in economic development. A number of studies show some of the positive benefits of strong, effective judiciaries. The degree of judicial independence is correlated with economic growth.[2] Better-performing courts have been shown to lead to more developed credit markets. A stronger judiciary is associated with more rapid growth of small firms as well as with larger firms in the economy.[3] Economic studies show that within individual countries the relative competence of provincial and state courts affects comparative economic

1. Indeed, some evidence exists that law can be "bad" when it is not enforced. Bhattacharya and Daouk (2004) find that the cost of equity actually rises when a country introduces an insider trading law but does not enforce it. See also Beny (2005).
2. Feld and Voigt (2004).
3. Islam (2003, pp. 7–8).

competitiveness. According to a World Bank report, "studies from Argentina and Brazil show that firms doing business in provinces with better-performing courts enjoy greater access to credit. New work in Mexico shows that larger, more efficient firms are found in states with better court systems. Better courts reduce the risks firms face, and so increase the firms' willingness to invest more."[4]

Surveys illustrate some of the deleterious effects of weak judiciaries on economic expansion. As the same World Bank report stated, "Firms in Brazil, Peru, and the Philippines report that they would be willing to increase investment if they had more confidence in their nation's courts. Firms in Albania, Bulgaria, Croatia, Ecuador, Moldova, Peru, Poland, Romania, Russia, Slovakia, Ukraine, and Vietnam say they would be reluctant to switch suppliers, even if offered a lower price, for fear they could not turn to the courts to enforce the agreement." Still other country surveys of firms show the impact of lack of confidence in courts on extending trade credit and in the willingness to do business with anyone other than those they know well.[5]

An ineffective judiciary may have extraordinary and far-reaching effects on a country. Brazil provides an example.[6] A critique in the *Financial Times*, under the telling headline "Brazil's judicial nightmare brings gridlock for growth," relates one unusual aspect of such effects: "The vast majority of claims stuck in the judicial system are against the public sector. Their total value is unknown, but [a public prosecutor] reckons the government's 'judicial liability' is roughly equal to Brazil's public debt. . . . [The prosecutor states that] if the delays in the judiciary were removed, all levels of government (federal, state and municipal) would go bankrupt the next day."[7] In other words, Brazil's public debt is understated by 50 percent. But from an economic development perspective, the worst aspect is perhaps that the Brazilian private sector has enormous assets (equal to the value of the claims it is unable to vindicate through the court system) on which it is not able to earn interest currently or otherwise benefit.

The *Financial Times* critique also laid out the perverse incentives produced by the poorly functioning Brazilian judiciary:

---

4. World Bank (2004b, p. 86).
5. World Bank (2004b, p. 86).
6. In 1997, according to one estimate, Brazil had a backlog of 6 million cases (with each judge having a backlog of 700 cases); according to another estimate, the backlog was 50 million cases (Dakolias 1999, p. 110 and n. 88).
7. Wheatley (2005).

Brazil's dysfunctional judiciary . . . is increasingly seen as an obstacle to national development. It is a system that allows debtors of all kinds to abscond at will, knowing that none but the most determined of creditors will pursue them through the courts. It forces banks to lend at astronomical rates of interest because they cannot foreclose on debts. More worryingly, it means that vital infrastructure projects are stalled because investors cannot be sure the judiciary will uphold their rights.[8]

Even where the judiciary is competent and independent, national legal culture may place limits on improving substantive law when the improvements involve transplanting substantive law from other legal cultures. Kanda and Milhaupt give the example of the inclusion in the Japanese Commercial Code in 1950 of the "duty of loyalty," taken directly from U.S. law and generally considered today to be a key judicial tool in the United States for assuring good corporate governance: "For almost forty years after it was transplanted, the duty of loyalty was never separately applied by the Japanese courts, and played little role in Japanese corporate law and governance."[9]

Where the legal institutions such as the judiciary are not effective, an improvement in substantive law may make very little difference. Studying the transition countries of Eastern Europe and the former Soviet Union, Pistor, Raiser, and Gelfer came to the conclusion that despite the great improvement of corporate and bankruptcy law in those countries from 1992 to 1998, improvement in financial markets occurred only to the extent that legal institutions became more effective. These authors explicitly considered changes in the substantive corporate and bankruptcy law as measured by the legal indicators used in the LLSV "Law and Finance" study, as well as additional indicators of substantive law change. They found that progress in such financial measures as market capitalization and private sector credit could be attributed primarily to improvement in the effectiveness of legal institutions: "Our regression analysis shows that legal effectiveness has overall much higher explanatory power for the level of equity and credit market development than the quality of law on the books. . . . [G]ood laws cannot substitute for weak institutions."[10]

Their study was based on surveys, which are inherently subjective, and the surveys did not target judiciaries but rather more general measures of legal

---

8. Wheatley (2005).

9. Kanda and Milhaupt (2003, p. 888). See further discussion in chapter 8.

10. Pistor, Raiser, and Gelfer (2000, p. 356).

effectiveness. The study nevertheless is powerful evidence that relatively too much emphasis has been placed, especially in the financial sector, on improvement in the details of substantive law compared with the effectiveness of legal institutions, including judicial effectiveness.

An Effective Judiciary: The Question of "Formalism"

Every lawyer in a developed country can point to numerous shortcomings in his own country. Yet judiciaries in developing countries frequently fall far short of developed country standards. In recent years efforts have been made to develop cross-country measures of judicial effectiveness. By all odds, the most ambitious effort was a study, prepared for the World Bank's *World Development Report* of 2002, measuring how effectively judicial systems dealt with the simple cases that fill courtrooms around the world.[11]

For this purpose four economists, including three of the LLSV authors, organized a large-scale but relatively simple and straightforward study of the procedures used in 109 countries to resolve two hypothetical disputes in which the merits of the cases in favor of the plaintiff were overwhelming, but the defendant chose not to settle.[12] The two cases were designed to be "run-of-the-mill"—typical of the cases facing every country's judicial system. The first was an action to evict a residential tenant for nonpayment of rent; the second an action to collect on an unpaid check. Lex Mundi, an international association of law firms, worked out the exact factual specifications of the disputes to facilitate cross-country comparison. This association also developed a questionnaire designed to produce data from each of the 109 countries concerning each of several subject matter areas ("variables" in the language of economists). The most significant variables were whether the proceedings involved professionals or laymen; were written or oral; involved legal justification being set forth in the complaint and the court's judgment; were legally constrained with regard to the use of evidence; and were subject to review by superior courts, especially during the pendency of the case in the court of first instance. Particularly significant were estimates for each country of the duration of the legal proceedings as well as an assessment of the incentives of the parties that bore on speed and efficiency.

One upshot of the economists' analysis was the construction of a "formalism" index based on the foregoing five variables plus two others. Formalism

11. World Bank (2001b).
12. Djankov and others (2003).

is not a concept in the average lawyer's vocabulary since each lawyer tends to take his own national legal system as given. In fact, the word *formalism* is perhaps not as useful for legal purposes as the term *procedural complexity*.[13] Formalism is a concept invented by the four economists to measure what they considered to be differences among countries bearing on judicial efficiency. Their view was essentially that the two Lex Mundi hypothetical cases were the simple kinds of disputes that in some societies could be resolved by a neighbor of the two parties without any formalities whatever.

Against that standard of highly efficient resolution (though atypical because dependent on the cooperation and good faith of both parties), the authors implicitly judged national legal systems from the following a priori criteria: limited jurisdiction (special purpose) courts are better than general purpose courts; nonprofessional judges are better than professional judges; the less the need for professional legal representation the better; the greater the use of oral evidence and arguments (which they christened collectively as "orality"), as opposed to written presentations and argument, the better; the less the need for "legal justification" for the complaint and the court's judgment the better; the more informal the rules of evidence the better; the fewer the requirements for conciliation and for notice the better; the less the control of the proceedings by an appellate or superior court the better; and the fewer the procedural stages the better.

The authors did not assert that absence of formalism was better for complex cases, but rather they judged that formalism was not efficient for the two cases in the Lex Mundi study (which are, however, illustrative of the kinds of cases that are most numerous in many court systems).[14]

No doubt many lawyers will be shocked by these implicit judgments. The reason is that many procedural rules the four economists disliked are implicitly or explicitly based on a set of criteria designed to produce an accurate and just result. Rules of procedure and evidence are designed to reduce "errors" in the judging of the facts and to ensure that the facts are judged by the right substantive law standards. (This, of course, requires more rules where a lay jury is involved than where a judge tries the case, and so lawyers in the United States—which is one of the few countries, perhaps the only

---

13. Islam (2003).

14. K. Davis (2004, p. 159) has argued that the two simple cases used to construct the formalism index and to measure efficiency do not provide an overall measure of the enforceability of contracts: "For example, in many jurisdictions residential tenants are granted significant levels of protection from eviction for ideological reasons that have no application in cases involving commercial contracts."

remaining country, where a jury trial in noncriminal cases is still common—are especially sensitive to miscarriages of justice arising from too informal a set of procedures.) So, too, review by superior courts is designed to reduce legal errors and thereby further the objective of justice by treating similarly situated parties in a like manner.

Nevertheless, even lawyers who value formalities for reasons of accuracy and justice understand that for routine cases or for cases with very little at stake, a legal system cannot provide a readily available forum for the population at large if the formalism useful in complex cases is not attenuated. The traffic court and the small claims court are common examples where nearly all lawyers understand that there is a trade-off between accuracy and efficiency. Or to put the point differently, such disputes are sufficiently minor that the prompt settlement of the dispute one way or the other is arguably the most important value.

One other legal reservation about the published analysis of the Lex Mundi study is that the mode of inquiry, especially the focus of the analysts on formalism, tends to bias the results against some of the basic assumptions of a civil law system, especially as known in continental Europe and in many developing countries. Except for rules constraining the use of certain kinds of evidence (which one finds in common law systems when there is a jury), the rules that the economists disliked tend to be more frequent in civil law systems, especially the use of written evidence and argument and the existence of "stages" of the proceeding. Indeed, the authors include as variables rules that exist only in one or two common law countries but in the majority of civil law countries.[15] The reasons for adoption of these rules in civil law countries normally have to do with the relatively greater role for the judge as opposed to counsel for the parties in a civil law system.

At a high level of generality, it can be said that civil law systems are based on the notion that a judge, normally a professional career judge, will run the proceedings and will know when oral evidence from a party or witness is useful; otherwise, documentary evidence and written submissions by the parties will suffice. And at the same high level of generality, it can be said that common law judges assume that the parties in noncriminal cases will more or less run the proceedings, coming to the judge only to resolve disagreements and for interim rulings and, finally, assuming that the parties have not worked out a settlement, for trial. Because of these differences, many civil law countries do

15. These variables include "legal representation mandatory," "oral interrogation only by judge," and "mandatory prequalification of questions."

not even have a trial in the sense of an oral proceeding involving presentation of evidence conducted on consecutive days—sometimes called a concentrated hearing—because the judge will call for oral testimony when needed.[16]

The *International Encyclopedia of Comparative Law* sums up these differences and the consequences as follows:

> In civil law . . . nations the ratio of judges to attorneys tends to be greater than in common law countries. Civilian judges are more actively involved in both civil and criminal proceedings with the goal of reaching the correct result than common law judges with their more privatized judicial procedure that delegates most evidence gathering to the parties' attorneys. . . . The role of judging in civil law nations involves much more responsibility for gathering evidence and moving the process forward. . . . Civil law judges also take on more of the effort of analyzing law . . . while common law judges rely on the attorneys to brief them on the legal issues.[17]

The encyclopedia author points out the obvious consequences for the ratio of judges to lawyers: "In Germany . . . 13 percent of the total number of lawyers are judges, while the percentage in the United States is three percent."[18] This higher ratio of judges in Germany reflects not so much a preference for large government (as some critics of civil law systems would have it), but rather a belief that litigation should not be a contest of legal gladiators and that justice requires judges to take responsibility for managing litigation. Given especially their preference for "orality," it is not surprising that the economists analyzing the Lex Mundi study found that civil law countries rank higher on the formalism index than common law countries.[19] In short, formalism is just another word to describe the procedures and requirements that are found most often in a civil law system. Whether formalism, as defined in the economists' analysis of the Lex Mundi results, has implications for the rate of economic growth in the developing world is quite a different matter that remains to be analyzed.

High-income countries have less formalism than either African or Latin American countries.[20] If, as suggested above, greater formalism may be associated with greater accuracy (fewer errors of fact and law) and greater justice,

---

16. See Langbein (1985, pp. 830–32).
17. Clark (2002, p. 75).
18. Clark (2002, pp. 75, 81).
19. Djankov and others (2003, p. 510).
20. Djankov and others (2003, p. 510). Moreover, eastern European countries have significantly higher formalism levels than western European countries.

higher-income countries, having more wealth, could be expected to "consume" more formalism. But the opposite is the case. Even within legal families, wealthier common law countries have lower formalism scores than poorer common law countries, and a similar relationship holds for civil law countries.

Considering developing countries as a class, there is little to suggest that formalism is systematically related to the relative level of development of a country. Within some regions, there appears to be no relationship whatever: wealthier Latin American countries have formalism levels similar to poorer Latin American countries. The same is true in Africa. Yet despite similar levels of formalism (actually slightly higher levels of formalism), the wealthier countries in these developing country regions have much shorter average duration times for both check collection and eviction.

Even if one were to conclude that common law is somehow superior to civil law, it does not seem practicable to expect a civil law country to decide to change to a common law system. (In addition to a cultural change in attitudes toward the nature of law and justice, such a change also would require retraining of most lawyers and of all judges.) Therefore, the practical issue is what steps can be taken to deal with simple cases, such as the two cases examined in the Lex Mundi study. Among the options are small claims courts and alternative dispute resolution, such as mediation and arbitration; however, some countries have "various restrictions on alternative dispute resolution mechanisms [that] prevent firms from taking full advantage of them" and many more countries have not taken steps necessary to promote such mechanisms, such as by providing for enforcement of arbitration awards.[21] Another alternative more focused on business activity would be a specialized commercial court.[22]

Judicial Efficiency

The main purpose for the World Bank sponsorship of the Lex Mundi background study in preparation for its annual *World Development Report* (as opposed to the published analysis) appears to have been to analyze judicial efficiency rather than "formalism" or the merits of the various legal origins systems. Although efficiency is only one aspect of the quality of a judiciary, it nonetheless is measurable, unlike some of the other essential qualities.[23] One

---

21. World Bank (2004b, p. 88).
22. Islam (2003).
23. Dakolias (1999, pp. 92–95).

important aspect of efficiency is time to disposition of a case. The study showed that even the simple cases studied can take a long time to resolve. The average duration for all countries in the eviction case was 254 days. For the check collection case, the average was 234 days.

The variance in duration across countries was dramatic. On the high side of the average, Pakistan required 365 days in both cases; Nigeria, 366 days in the eviction case; and Thailand, 630 days in the eviction case.[24] These three countries' systems are based on common law, so delay is not a monopoly of civil law systems. In fact, comparisons within regions show that formalism does not seem to be related to efficiency, at least not in the way the Lex Mundi analysis suggests. For example, the analysis included twenty-two Asian countries, of which half were common law countries and half were civil law countries. Common law countries had lower levels of formalism than civil law countries, but civil law countries were more—not less—efficient: the average duration of the check collection case was 216 days compared with the common law average of 257.

Nor is it simply a question of the stage of economic development of the country (and hence, for example, the resources it can apply to the problem). Certain developed countries with common law systems manifested unusual delay—such as 421 days in Canada and 320 days in Australia in the check collection case (compared with 40 days in Swaziland and 60 days in Belize, also English origin countries). These extreme results within the common law family suggest that much more is involved than just the common-civil law dichotomy. And that much more does not seem to be primarily "formalism," since the formalism indexes for Canada and Australia were much lower than average; indeed, Australia had one of the lowest formalism indexes in the world.[25] Moreover, Swaziland, one of the fastest check collection countries of all, had a formalism index much above the common law average and higher than many civil law countries, including France itself.

In short, the high variance of outcomes within both legal families leads to the conclusion that while it is instructive to look at the regression results from the Lex Mundi studies, sound answers to the policy question of what a particular developing country can do to improve its judicial efficiency require looking at that country's legal system as it exists today. And that is true whether the developing country has a common law or a civil law system.

Still another way of measuring efficiency, reported in the Lex Mundi study, is to use survey evidence to tap into subjective judgments of people with

24. Djankov and others (2003, pp. 494–500, table V).
25. Djankov and others (2003, pp. 494–500, table V; p. 484, table IIb).

some reason to know about a particular country's legal system. The Lex Mundi study, for example, measured "efficiency of a judicial system" of a country by using an assessment of the "efficiency and integrity of the legal environment as it affects business, particularly foreign firms." These ratings were provided by International Country Risk, an international risk assessment company, and were intended "to represent investors' assessment of conditions in the country in question."[26] These perceptions of judicial effectiveness are necessarily based on subjective judgments, but they may be especially valuable where they represent attitudes of local residents in countries that are trying to build market economies and attract more of the population into the market sector. Economic development depends in the long run not only on attracting foreign direct investment, for example, but also on the creation of new local enterprises funded by local savings.

Several further kinds of evidence explain the differing assessments. One is that delays tend to be longer and backlogs greater in African and Latin American countries than in much of the rest of the world. Delays are one important reason for the finding, in a survey conducted in selected Latin American countries, that a "majority of court users are 'not inclined' to bring disputes to court because they perceive the system to be slow, uncertain, and costly, or of 'poor quality.'"[27] Generalization across countries in this respect is misleading, however. For example, one study found that the average commercial case takes almost eight years to verdict in Ecuador but less than a year in Colombia and Peru.[28]

Granted that this kind of assessment is subjective and is not intended to reflect directly the efficiency of various countries' legal systems in dealing with small cases involving domestic parties, it nevertheless provides some insight into the relative ranking of legal systems, including judiciaries. Although English origin countries outscored French origin countries in the Lex Mundi study, the difference is partly based on the fact that Latin American and eastern European countries have the highest duration levels and all of them with the exception of Belize have a civil law origin. Within regions, there appear to be substantial differences based on legal origin, but not necessarily in the direction the Lex Mundi analysis suggests. In Asia, as noted above, civil law countries have shorter durations than common law countries.

A significant difference in efficiency levels exists between developed and developing countries. A World Bank analysis of the data showed, for example,

26. Djankov and others (2001, table 2).
27. Buscaglia and Domingo (1997, p. 296).
28. World Bank (2001b, p. 120).

that "high income countries" scored much higher on efficiency than either African countries or Latin American countries.[29] Another study reached a similar conclusion, finding that a "mean [index] score for the efficiency of the judicial system across developing countries is 6.26, compared with 9.14 in developed countries."[30] Once again the studies point to the need for reform in developing countries but do not help in determining what reforms will work best.

One of the common complaints by developing country judiciaries is lack of resources. More money and especially more judges, other things equal, would presumably lead to faster disposition of cases and perhaps more effective judiciaries. Although budgets are a big problem for developing country judiciaries and some have too few judges, it is reasonably clear that neither budgets nor numbers of judges are the heart of the problem. It is true that Ecuador and Peru have only 1 judge per 100,000 people, but Singapore has less than 1 judge per 100,000 people (compared with 27 per 100,000 in Germany and 10 per 100,000 in France).[31] Indeed, considerable evidence shows that in general the problem is not primarily one of resources. A review of studies in Latin America and the Caribbean showed "no correlation between the overall level of resources and the time to disposition of cases."[32]

So too the size of budgets has to be measured against what the money is actually spent on. Buscaglia and Domingo found that "approximately 70 percent of Argentine judges' time is spent on non-adjudicative tasks."[33] This finding suggests that the problems run more deeply, even insofar as pure efficiency is concerned. In many cases, for example, the judges themselves are opponents of reform measures, a finding that suggests a lack of enthusiasm for actually implementing reforms undertaken.[34] However useful grants may be for computers and case management systems (typical subjects of foreign assistance) where a developing country judiciary is already characterized by independence, competence, and integrity, such grants do not attack the basic problems in some developing countries. In any event, according to a World Bank study, "no correlation between the overall level of resources and times to disposition" was found in a study of data from the United States, Latin America, and the Caribbean.[35]

29. Islam (2003, figures 4 and 6).
30. López-de-Silanes (2002, p. 5).
31. World Bank (2001b, pp. 120–21 and table 6.1).
32. Botero and others (2003, p. 63).
33. Buscaglia and Domingo (1997, p. 297).
34. Santiso (2003, pp. 117, 122); Srinivasan (2004, pp. 95–96).
35. World Bank (2001b, p. 128).

Another possible explanation lies not in the size of judicial budgets but in their composition: What is the money actually spent on? Equally important, what resources go into the legal system beyond judicial budgets? Judiciaries are made up of more than judges and their clerks. Practicing lawyers are also important: according to an Asian Development Bank study, Cambodia, a country of 11 million inhabitants, had only 249 registered members of the bar, of whom only 197 were practicing lawyers.[36] A legal system includes not only lawyers and litigants, but also the government (especially a ministry of justice) and external groups such as bar associations and journalists covering court proceedings.[37] Bar associations and journalists are important if for no other reason than being a judge in civil law countries is a career profession where reputations are likely to count as the judge seeks higher income and more attractive locations through promotion. Hence it would take a thoroughgoing systems approach involving not just judges but the entire environment in which they operate to be sure of the sources of inefficiency and the level of judicial performance.

In some, but by no means all, developing countries, a symptom of dysfunctionality of a judiciary lies in the size of the backlog of cases. Backlogs are of course related to times to disposition and other measures of delays, but backlogs are important in themselves because they lead to a lack of public confidence in a country's judiciary and to a hesitancy to rely on the judiciary in business planning.

Backlogs sometimes result from certain kinds of short-sighted judicial reform. In Brazil, for example, the new constitution of 1988 so expanded the range of constitutional rights, including new social and economic guarantees, and the kinds of plaintiffs entitled to bring constitutional actions, that backlogs multiplied many times over.[38] Moreover, the Brazilian constitution has two hundred and fifty articles, eighty-three transitory provisions, fourteen unnumbered articles, and thirty-seven amendments, with many "specific rules normally found only in codes or regulations."[39] But the Brazilian case illustrates the more general problem that increasing access to the courts (or reducing the cost of access)—which is badly needed in many developing countries—can be expected to lead to heavier workloads. The Brazilian case also points to the need to establish procedures and rules that channel court

36. Asian Development Bank (2003, p. 49).
37. Islam (2003, p. 21).
38. Prillaman (2000, pp. 82–97).
39. Rosenn (2000, pp. 291–92).

use to cases where courts can actually make a contribution; much of the Brazilian constitutional litigation appears to have been motivated by politicians and interest groups.[40] As Prillaman observes, the 1998 constitution was "so prescriptive and detailed that it constitutionalized a staggering range of minor issues and flooded the courts—even the Supreme Court—with the most trivial cases." A decade after its adoption, opinion in Brazil was "unanimous" that "unfettered access for everyone had produced, not surprisingly, access for no one."[41]

Court Decisions as Law

The Brazil case does show one important disadvantage of civil law systems, at least as applied in some developing countries. One of the reasons for the proliferation of constitutional litigation is the notion in many civil law countries that judicial decisions are not a source of law, in contrast to the heavy reliance of common law countries on judicial precedent. Rosenn comments on the consequences for Brazil: "Since Brazil has only a minimal system of binding legal precedent, the courts decide the same constitutional issues many times over." Aside from the waste of resources, the Brazilian approach "leads to conflicting interpretations of constitutional provisions," leading to further litigation. [42] Indeed, the dire consequences of courts not using precedent carries over to lower courts in Brazil. That, according to a *Financial Times* critique, in turn gives rise to a "conviction that every case must be tried on its individual merits," thereby causing multiyear delays even where the outcome should be clear in advance.[43]

This Brazilian experience shows the misleading consequences of taking the French legal system at face value, at least on the issue of precedent.[44] Not all civil law countries ignore precedent (or "jurisprudence," as prior court decisions are called in many civil law countries). Certainly French courts do not do so, as is ably shown in an extraordinary article that uses empirical research to demonstrate in great detail how French courts deal with precedent. In this article Lasser establishes that two key French judicial officials, the advocate general and the reporting judge, "pay extremely close attention to

40. Rosenn (2000, p. 317).
41. Prillaman (2000, pp. 6, 8).
42. Rosenn (2000, p. 291).
43. Wheatley (2005).
44. Merryman (1996).

past judicial decisions. . . . A complete *conclusions* or *rapport* always cites and analyzes relevant case law."[45] This fact is disguised by the form of French judicial decisions, which by tradition are very brief and do not cite case law. These decisions are written in a single run-on sentence, usually with a cascade of "whereas" clauses, that appear to lead powerfully and ineluctably to an inescapable conclusion, like a mighty and irrefutable syllogism machine. This impression is belied, however, by the French reporting judges' practice of preparing for the consideration of their colleagues at least one alternative draft opinion, often coming to a diametrically opposite conclusion.[46]

The Brazil case further illustrates the disadvantage of abstract judicial review. The U.S. requirement that parties raising a constitutional issue must show that it affects them in a direct and legally cognizable way, plus the ability of the U.S. Supreme Court to limit its intake of questions to important issues, has meant that it has been able to keep its actual substantive decisions to well under 200 cases per year, thereby assuring focus and reasoned opinions.[47] The Brazilian Supreme Court, in contrast, was dealing with more than 100,000 cases a year. One has to wonder about the quality of the work product and about the impact on the economy of increasing backlogs and thereby to further attenuation of access to justice. In late 2004 legislation was passed permitting the Brazilian Supreme Court to set binding precedent for lower courts (but presumably not for itself); this and associated measures would cut the flow of cases by only half, leaving a still unwieldy caseload.[48]

Structural Independence

When one turns from efficiency in simple cases to major cases where the government or specific government officials have an interest, broader structural issues are raised. One set of structural issues has to do with issues of judicial review. The two principal kinds of judicial review issues that arise are, first, when legislation is challenged for unconstitutionality and, second, when an administrative act (that is, a decision or regulation issued by a government official or regulatory body) is challenged as being contrary to the constitution or a controlling statute. Each is treated differently.

45. Lasser (1994–95, p. 1376); see also Lasser (2004).

46. Lasser (1994–95, p. 1373); Dawson (1968, pp. 410–11).

47. In its 2003 Term the U.S. Supreme Court disposed of 7,781 cases, but this number included refusals to grant review; only 80 cases were disposed of with full opinions. See *Harvard Law Review* (2004, p. 504, table II, and pp. 507–09, table III).

48. "Not-so-swift Justice: How to Reform Brazil's Justice System," *The Economist*, May 25, 2004.

Not surprisingly, when dealing with judicial review, the question is not whether the abstract power of judicial review exists but rather whether, assuming the availability on the books of such a power, it can be effectively exercised. The answer turns on the independence of the judiciary, including the stature and competence of judges to deal impartially with such high stakes and fundamental litigation. Let us therefore first deal with the question of independence.

In dealing with the independence of the judiciary, it is useful to distinguish structural independence from behavioral independence. The former term, as used here, refers to the way in which government is constitutionally structured: does that structure lend itself to independence? The latter concept is more far-reaching. Are individual judges independent—that is, not just dispassionate and free from bias, but willing to take difficult positions, to resist corruption, and to make truly independent decisions?

In analyzing the structural independence of the judiciary, it is important to dig more deeply into the principle of the separation of powers. While many countries believe that the structure of their government is based on that principle, the content of the principle differs across countries to the point that two fully incompatible versions of that principle exist in the world. One should distinguish the French Revolution concept (bearing in mind that post–World War II developments in France have transformed the French concept in part) from the U.S. concept.

The spirit and the outcome of the French Revolution were to make sure that the people should reign (not the king or the aristocracy), and therefore the Assembly, the legislature, was to be sovereign because it would speak for the people. To achieve that goal, the prerevolutionary French *parlements*— which were more judicial than parliamentary at the national and regional levels—were disbanded because they were viewed as bulwarks of the aristocratic establishment and as having strayed from adjudication into lawmaking.[49] The Assembly would be the sole voice, and to that end the outcome of the French Revolution ensured that courts were given a very minor role of merely interpreting in a narrow, almost mechanical way the meaning of legislation passed by the Assembly.

Under such a structure, there was no judicial review, and the judiciary was not able to act as an independent voice. The separation of powers meant that the power to legislate was in the Assembly, full stop.

In the American sense of the separation of powers (often referred to as a system of "checks and balances"), the U.S. Constitution established three

49. Dawson (1968, pp. 369–71).

independent bodies, the Article I Congress, the Article II presidency, and the Article III judiciary. It is true that the Article III judges were to apply the law, but where the law was a statute contrary to the Constitution the courts were to apply the higher law—the Constitution—and not the statute passed by the Congress. So decided the Supreme Court in the pathbreaking case of *Marbury v. Madison.*[50] Although there were minor precedents of statutes being disregarded or narrowly construed because they were contrary to the common law, this case, decided in 1803, was the first example in the world of judicial review on constitutional grounds.

The *Marbury* decision was widely admired and had great consequences for the rest of the world. The U.S. Constitution—in the sense of a founding document to be enforced by the judiciary—was widely followed in nineteenth century Latin America. A 1974 study found that by the early 1970s nineteen of the twenty Latin American republics had adopted judicial review.[51] In the twentieth century judicial review spread to Europe. After World War II it even arrived in France with the creation in 1958 of a Constitutional Council.

Judicial review was not, however, adopted in Britain. Not only had the British never agreed upon a written constitution in the sense of a single written document, but to the extent that it can be said that the United Kingdom has a constitution, it is to be embodied in a wide variety of sources, some written and some to be found in past customs and events.[52] Thus, although the British Constitution "is based upon a system of tacit understandings, . . . the understandings are not always understood."[53] In short, no agreement exists as to the content of the British Constitution. Indeed, "every author is free to make a personal selection and to affirm that this is the one, even the only one, that embraces all the most important rules and excludes all the unimportant ones—though nobody has ever been so foolish as to assert this."[54]

The British Constitution, if one accepts the position not at all obvious to a foreigner that Britain has a constitution, is quite a different creature from the American Constitution. Indeed, it is much closer in concept to the French revolutionary outcome because the British Parliament, just like the French Assembly of the time, is sovereign. Under long-standing English doctrine, "Parliament has the right to make or unmake any law whatever," and "No

---

50. 5 U.S. 137 (1803).
51. Rosenn (1974, p. 785).
52. For illustrations, see Bradley and Ewing (2003).
53. Finer, Bogdanor, and Rudden (1995, p. 100), quoting Sidney Low.
54. Finer, Bogdanor, and Rudden (1995, p. 41).

person or body is recognized by the law of England as having a right to override or set aside the legislation of Parliament."[55] As Blackstone summarized the matter more than two centuries ago, the competence of Parliament is unlimited in law:

> The power and jurisdiction of parliament . . . is so transcendent and absolute, that it cannot be confined, either for causes or persons, with any bounds. . . . It can change and create afresh even the constitution of the kingdom and of parliaments themselves. . . . It can, in short do everything that is not naturally impossible; and therefore some have not scrupled to call its power, by a figure rather too bold, the omnipotence of parliament.[56]

Unlike written constitutions that have formal requirements (such as special voting provisions or referenda) for their own amendment, British constitutional law can therefore be changed from one day to the next by Parliament in the same way that it enacts statutes.[57]

It has to be said that, with the success of the Glorious Revolution, including the statutes that were adopted by Parliament, the need for a written British Constitution was not apparent.[58] After all, most of the world's constitutions were originally adopted after a major discontinuity in sovereignty or power. Such a discontinuity was the case in the United States, and it was also the case in newly independent countries, notably in Latin America in the nineteenth century and in Africa in the twentieth century, as well as in the countries that sought to transition from communism in the late twentieth century.

Today judicial review of legislation on constitutionality grounds has become common. As noted above, even France introduced judicial review in 1958 in the form of a Constitutional Council.[59] But that council is a very different animal from the U.S. Supreme Court. It can pass on the constitutionality of a legislative measure only before it is finally enacted and then only at the request of designated public officials.[60] Orderly as this may appear, it does little to protect the citizen who may find years later that he is aggrieved,

---

55. Wade (1961, pp. xxxiv–xxxv).

56. Blackstone (2001, vol. 1, book 1, chapter 2, sec. III).

57. Finer, Bogdanor, and Rudden (1995, p. 43).

58. See discussion in chapter 4.

59. For a general discussion on the constitutional council, see Brown and Bell (1998, pp. 14–24).

60. Bell (1992, p. 32).

indeed aggrieved by an "unconstitutional" application of a legislative measure that on its face appears fully constitutional.

Even though the French Constitutional Council cannot be seen as a fully independent and purely judicial body, its role has been greatly enlarged as a result of constitutional changes expanding the class of those who can commence a case coupled with an increasing number of rulings finding unconstitutionality.[61] Still, the limitation on its role to passing on the constitutionality of legislation only before final enactment, limitations on who may bring a case, and the composition of the council itself all make clear that the French concept of separation of powers, even today, is sharply different from the American concept of separation of powers.

Another major difference between the French and American systems of judicial review lies in the fact that the French Constitutional Council is the only tribunal in France that can set aside legislation on constitutional grounds. It is thus an example of judicial review by a specialized court. In the United States, in contrast, any court can set aside a decision on constitutional grounds. Even a state court can exercise judicial review when either a federal or state statute essential to its decision is attacked on constitutional grounds. France is thus an example of "concentrated" judicial review, while the United States is at the other pole of "diffuse" review.

Most European countries concentrate judicial review in a single high-level court, which deals only with constitutional complaints. Some of these cases originate in this single "constitutional court," but many of the cases come to it on reference from some other court where the constitutional issue arises out of nonconstitutional litigation. The result in Europe is that the constitutional issue is often presented as an abstract issue of law, divorced from the facts of any concrete dispute. Even if a case is referred to it, the constitutional court would not normally express an opinion on the nonconstitutional issues, which would remain within the jurisdiction of the court making the reference.

Such "abstract judicial review" decisions reflect an analysis of basic constitutional principles without much consideration in most cases of the impact of the decision on particular persons or particular factual situations.[62] The decision thus normally binds the entire citizenry as well as the government, sustaining the constitutionality of the challenged statutory provision or rendering it entirely inoperative. The French pre-enactment review carries this

---

61. Morton (1988, pp. 89–92). For a general discussion of factors leading to the political character of the Constitutional Council, see Bell (1992, pp. 32–37, 229–34).

62. Favoreu (1990, p. 41).

pattern to an extreme of abstract constitutional decisionmaking because there has been no experience at all with the application of the still unenacted statute.

In the U.S. system where the constitutional issue can be decided by any court, even a state court under U.S. federalism, the constitutional issue is usually presented in the context of a concrete set of facts. This is what is meant by the doctrine that a dispute must present a "case or controversy" to be "justiciable" (that is, for the court to be able to assert jurisdiction of the dispute), however important the constitutional issue may be in the abstract. The result is that the court deciding the case often has the opportunity to see how the challenged statute actually operates. In fact, as a general principle, no U. S. litigant can raise the question of constitutionality of a statute unless directly affected or in imminent danger of being directly affected. As a result U.S. courts often decide whether the statute is unconstitutional on its face or only unconstitutional as applied to the situation of the particular litigant. But the larger point is that although many lawyers and judges consider judicial review an inherently political act, the decentralized system tends to present the issue in terms of a concrete dispute and hence as more judicial in character. That all cases presenting constitutional issues, whether commenced in federal or state court, can be reviewed by the U.S. Supreme Court ensures that fragmentation of constitutional legal principles under U.S. diffuse review rarely occurs.[63]

Behavioral Independence

Judicial independence does not depend solely on the structure of government and the judiciary's formal role within it. It also depends on the judges themselves. That is why analysts speak of behavioral independence. The importance of behavioral independence can be illustrated by reflecting on the constitutional arrangements of the United States and Britain. Although one could easily conclude that the structural arrangements in Britain make judicial independence unlikely, the fact is that the British judiciary, particularly at the highest level, is known for its independence.

Some economic literature speaks of de facto independence in contrast to de jure independence.[64] While this is a valid distinction that has advantages

---

63. Fallon, Meltzer, and Shapiro (2003, pp. 55–267, 1552–620).

64. Stephenson (2003); Feld and Voigt (2004); Ramseyer (1994). One insight of the empirical literature is that courts are likely to be more independent in a functioning democracy with rival parties alternating in office because politicians in power will be aware that another party may soon be in office. This is an important insight but does not afford much useful policy guidance to any particular developing country.

for empirical work, the term *behavioral independence* has advantages for policymaking and public understanding because it recognizes that some—though not all—characteristics that determine how judges act reflect the education, values, and prestige of the judicial profession in a particular country and cannot be traced to legal or formal safeguards. Therefore, the distinction used here is between structural factors of a constitutional nature (such as the separation of powers) and nonconstitutional factors, some of which are based on law, that encourage judges to act independently.

Part of behavioral independence resides in the judge as a person: is a judge able to be dispassionate and free from bias, able to resist political pressures and the temptations of corruption, and so forth? In most societies those are not just questions of upbringing and morality. The answer also depends on the judges' economic security, place in the society, education, and career experience.[65]

In Britain behavioral independence, like the other elements of the rule of law, was acquired after a long struggle in which many English judges were willing to stand up to the English sovereign at great personal risk during the Tudor and Stuart periods (before the Act of Settlement of 1701 gave judges life tenure on good behavior).[66] Behavioral independence was all the more important because the British judiciary was not traditionally structurally independent, as shown by the intermingling of judicial, legislative, and executive functions at the highest level.[67] Until legislation was passed in 2005, the so-called law lords, who formed the highest appellate level in the British judiciary, also sat in the House of Lords, one of the two houses of Parliament. More dramatic was the position of the lord chancellor, who was not only a law lord but also the head of a large government department and thus part of the government of the day, playing a role involving judicial appointments. The lord chancellor was not just a member of the House of Lords, but presided over the law lords and was entitled to chair the House of Lords.[68] The separation of powers objection to this intermingling of roles was not solely conceptual, as shown by the fact that the conduct of the lord chancellor was not always free from controversy.[69]

---

65. See Sajó (2004).
66. Klerman and Mahoney (2005, p. 3).
67. This intermingling is a result of the constitutional settlement of 1689 described in chapter 4.
68. Carroll (2003, p. 36); Bradley and Ewing (2003, pp. 388–91).
69. Bradley and Ewing (2003, pp. 388–91); Oliver (2003, p. 337).

Legislation enacted in March 2005 adopted the thrust of the British government's proposals designed to eliminate the intermingling; the legislation was nonetheless highly controversial in the House of Lords, in some measure over partially symbolic issues. The law lords will be transferred to a newly created Supreme Court (due to take place in 2008).[70] The lord chancellor's role with respect to judicial selection will be in part transferred to an independent judicial appointments commission. The commission will recommend and the lord chancellor will appoint (in his role as the cabinet officer—the Secretary of State—of the Department of Constitutional Affairs).[71] The lord chancellor will no longer be a judge. The chief justice of England and Wales will become head of the judiciary. Thus the judiciary will acquire more formal independence of the government and the legislature.[72] In place of the former lord chancellor with both judicial and nonjudicial roles, there will henceforth be two offices occupied by the same person, the office of the lord chancellor (responsible for the management of the courts) and the office of the secretary of state (responsible for election law, legal aid, human rights, data protection, freedom of information, and regulation of the legal profession). Further, the lord chancellor will continue to be a member of the House of Lords.[73]

Although the independence of British judges was based for so long on behavioral rather than structural considerations, without in practice any notable compromise of the rule of law, it nonetheless does not follow that a developing country can afford to neglect structural independence. Today a developing country, especially where political parties do not regularly alternate in power, would be well advised to adopt procedures and practices, such as life tenure, that encourage judges to be independent.

It is generally thought that lifetime tenure is desirable for judges because it gives them economic security and frees them from undesirable pressures,

---

70. Constitutional Reform Act 2005, chapter 4, p. 12.

71. Constitutional Reform Act 2005, chapter 4, p. 29. The report by the commission will state who has been selected and then the lord chancellor can accept, reject, or require the selection committee to reconsider the selection (p. 33). Until the 2005 change, the lord chancellor simply made the appointments.

72. As a further step toward separation of powers, no member of the Judicial Committee of the Privy Council will be a cabinet minister. On the constitutional changes, see "Trials and Tribulations," *The Economist,* March 26, 2005; "The Constitutional Reform Bill—the Office of Lord Chancellor," House of Commons Library Research Paper 05/005 (January 12, 2005) (www.parliament.uk/commons/lib/research/rp2005/rp05-005.pdf). See entries on lord chancellor and on Constitutional Reform Act 2005 (www.wikipedia.com).

73. That a single person can be a member of both the executive and legislative branches is, of course, normal in a parliamentary system.

whether from government, politicians or private parties. Alexander Hamilton, a "founding father" of the United States, can be said to have sired this concept in the United States, arguing that "nothing can contribute so much to . . . firmness and independence as permanency in office."[74] Hamilton buttressed the argument for permanency by urging a constitutional prohibition on reducing judicial salaries because "a power over a man's subsistence amounts to a power over his will."[75]

Experience has demonstrated that an independent judiciary rests on a permanent corps of judges who can be removed only for cause. Latin America offers examples of the practice, and the effects, of making judges easily removable by the executive. A World Bank report makes the following observations about Peru: "The tenure of judges matters. . . . Peru is frequently rated as the country with the least judicial independence. Former President Fujimori kept more than half of judges on temporary appointments from 1992 to 2000."[76]

Perhaps the most dramatic evidence of the effects of denying judges lifetime tenure is found in the experience of Argentina, where the tenure of Supreme Court justices is one of the shortest in the world.[77] One reason is that those justices have become identified with the party, indeed the president, in power. It started in the 1930s with conservative judges siding with electoral fraud by conservative parties, with the result that public opinion thereafter favored their ouster. When Juan Peron came to power in the 1940s, he arranged for the impeachment of Supreme Court justices from the earlier period. Later presidents followed suit. By 1994 the Argentine Supreme Court had been completely replaced six times since 1946.[78] And Peronist president Carlos Menem in the 1990s expanded the Court from five to nine justices, so that he could "pack" the court with a majority.[79] And so it continued, with a new Peronist president Nestor Kirchner in the first decade of the twenty-first century forcing out Menem-era justices, so that he could gain public support while having his own court.[80] According to a research paper by Alston and Gallo, this populist pattern of attacking the Supreme Court and bringing

74. Federalist Papers No. 78. This was just one of the arguments adduced by Hamilton in support of lifetime tenure on good behavior, including that the "experience of Great Britain affords an illustrious comment on the excellence of the institution."

75. Federalist Papers No. 79.

76. World Bank (2001b, p. 130).

77. Spiller and Tommasi (2003, p. 298).

78. Dakolias (1995, p. 173, n. 18).

79. Miller (2000, p. 373).

80. Valente (2003).

about a situation where new presidents have their own court is a major cause of the continued decline of Argentina from one of the wealthiest ten countries in the world to one of the poorest.[81]

The executive's ability to remove judges has been common in Latin America. Furnish asserts that "by Mexican tradition sitting presidents have dismissed sitting judges whenever it suits their purpose to do so."[82] Wiarda and Kline have explained the consequences: "The court system has not historically been a separate and coequal branch, nor was it intended or generally expected to be. Many Latin American supreme courts would declare a law unconstitutional or defy a determined executive only at the risk of embarrassment and danger to themselves, something the courts have assiduously avoided."[83]

The place in society that a judge enjoys, and feels he has, depends very much on the quality of judges and how the public views them. The practice in the United States and Great Britain of appointing lawyers after they have completed several decades in private practice or in distinguished government service tends to assure judicial independence on this score, at least so long as judges are picked on merit rather than on political criteria, which appears to be the case in Great Britain and has normally been the case in the United States at the federal level. The election of judges in U.S. states probably threatens to compromise the independence of some of them, however. The practice in a few countries of attracting the very best law graduates to a judicial career can also produce an independence of mind and spirit in judges.

Still, although recruitment of judges shortly after law graduation followed by a lifetime judicial career may turn out to be positive for judicial independence, that statement has to be qualified for some judicial tasks and in some countries. With regard to judicial tasks, Mauro Cappelletti, an Italian comparative law scholar, has argued that even in Europe career judges are not suited to deal with judicial review of the constitutionality of statutes:

> The bulk of Europe's judiciary seems psychologically incapable of the value-oriented, quasi-political functions involved in judicial review. It should be borne in mind that continental judges usually are "career judges," who enter the judiciary at a very early age and are promoted to the higher courts largely on the basis of seniority. Their professional training develops skills in technical rather than policy-oriented application of statutes. The exercise of judicial review, however, is rather

81. Alston and Gallo (2005).
82. Furnish (2000, p. 239).
83. Wiarda and Kline (2000, p. 64).

different from the usual judicial function of applying the law. Modern constitutions do not limit themselves to a fixed definition of what the law is, but contain broad programs for future action. Therefore the task of fulfilling the constitution often demands a higher sense of discretion than the task of interpreting ordinary statutes.[84]

The prestige of a judiciary as an institution can play a role in its independence. Questions of prestige, competence, and independence are, of course, interrelated. A judiciary without independence is likely to lack prestige in the legal profession, and law graduates may in turn avoid a career in a judiciary lacking independence. To take an example of how lack of independence degrades both prestige and competence, consider Ukraine: "In Ukraine, where judges' starting salaries are disproportionately low and there is little judicial independence, law students continue to consider a judgeship 'the lowest position available in the legal profession.'"[85]

As the Ukraine example shows, low judicial salaries in some countries lead to less qualified judges. An analysis of the Mexican judiciary reached a similar conclusion:

> Low judicial salaries . . . left the best-trained and most capable young law graduates inclined to pursue careers in private practice. Consequently, lawyers with uncompetitive institutional pedigrees, undistinguished records of professional experience, and/or modest socioeconomic backgrounds tended to pursue careers on the bench. This observation is corroborated, in part, by the findings of 1985 and 1993 judicial surveys that an average of 93.15% of Mexico's federal judges and magistrates graduated from what are generally considered to be inferior quality law programs.[86]

Compensation is a difficult issue in many developing countries, where pay for civil servants is often derisively low, frequently on the assumption that bribes will supplement salaries. Yet quite aside from the corruption issue, compensation levels cannot be ignored if competence is sought. Prime Minister Lee Kwan Yew of Singapore rather indelicately summed up the point: "You pay peanuts, you get monkeys."[87]

---

84. Cappelletti (1971, pp. 62–63).
85. Rekosh (2002, p. 59).
86. Kossick (2004, p. 742).
87. Asian Development Bank (2003, p. 19).

Much depends, however, on how junior judges are trained, managed, and promoted. If promotion is handled by a government agency—the ministry of justice—independence may be compromised. To the extent these functions are in the hands of senior judges, the results will depend on the leadership of the existing judiciary. One outcome may be judges who are reluctant to stand up to the government. For example, younger Japanese judges who too aggressively challenge accepted ideas are likely to find themselves promoted by the judicial secretariat to "a small branch office or a back-mountain family court," meaning that they can expect to spend their career in a backwater without hope of achieving eminent positions in major metropolitan centers.[88] This is an example of how culture—legal culture—can explain how law functions in a society and therefore how it influences economic development. In short, the danger of a career judiciary is that it can produce a bureaucracy that is risk-averse, promotion-minded, and far from manifesting behavioral independence.

Even a noncareer judiciary can act like a bureaucracy. This statement holds true for the judiciary in the United States, as conceded by one of the best-known federal judges below the Supreme Court level in the course of arguing that good judging is more important than substantive law, at least in business litigation. According to Judge Frank Easterbrook:

> [T]he United States relies more on courts and less on law. Good thing, too! For judges are just bureaucrats with general portfolios.... [Judges] can enforce contracts. For then the investors and managers themselves lay down the rules. Judges serve as neutral umpires, enforcing the contracts without regard to who gains and loses in a particular case. The contents of the contracts, however, come from competition in financial markets, rather than from law.[89]

To determine whether a judiciary in a particular country is truly independent is often difficult. Even formal structural independence and uncorrupt judges with adequate legal education, tenure, and compensation do not ensure independence where powerful governmental or political interests are at stake. The Asian Development Bank, which has made illuminating efforts to assess judicial independence and to promote it, has issued thoughtful assessments of

---

88. Ramseyer and Rosenbluth (1993, p. 156).

89. Easterbrook (1997, p. 28). Judge Easterbrook, who serves on the U.S. Court of Appeals for the Seventh Circuit, used the word *law* in this context to refer to statutes. On the bureaucratic role of the judge, see Bell (1987).

member government judiciaries that throw light on how difficult achievement of true judicial independence can be in a developing country.[90]

Administrative Review

Many countries, indeed the majority of civil law countries, have a separate system for review of administrative decisions—that is, decisions by a government official or a governmental agency. The efficacy of that form of review is directly relevant to the rule of law because it provides a principal means of limiting the powers of government to what the legislature provides. Moreover, in the contemporary world, the share of GDP accounted for by state-owned enterprises is quite large, with as much as 30 to 50 percent of the labor force in Latin America in the state sector, at least before privatization efforts in some countries in the 1990s.[91] The huge size of the public sector thus makes review of the action of the state administration of great importance. If in earlier centuries the threat to the rule of law came from a predatory ruler, the contemporary threat is more from a large state administration seeking to control the economy or at least to protect state-owned industries. The review of the bureaucracy's acts is therefore at least as important as judicial review of the constitutionality of legislation.

A separate court for reviewing administrative acts of government is not unusual. Many civil law countries have a separate hierarchy of such courts (on top of tribunals within individual administrative agencies). These special courts are clearly within the judiciary, with judges of the same kind as found in courts dealing with disputes between private parties. This tradition of the regular judiciary reviewing administrative acts contrasts sharply with another tradition of tribunals located outside the judiciary. The leading example of this tradition is the French Conseil d'état (Council of State).

The Conseil d'état is not a court as such. In fact, it was established in Napoleonic times to protect the administration from the courts. It is an administrative body that advises other bodies in the French administration and the government itself. But the conseil has within it a section that is a tribunal deciding cases, called the *section du contentieux*.[92] This tribunal acts as a "court of last resort in public, administrative law."[93] Its members are chosen

90. See Asian Development Bank (2004).
91. Wiarda and Kline (2000, pp. 67–68).
92. There is also a structure of French administrative courts that is not part of the Conseil d'état but for which the tribunal acts as the point of ultimate review. See generally Brown and Bell (1998).
93. Lasser (2004, p. 272).

from among the members of the conseil, and in many instances individual members serve simultaneously in the tribunal and in a purely administrative section of the conseil as the following anecdote from a visitor to the secretive council suggests: "Indeed the author did observe one conseilleur come down in the lift from a judicial hearing to attend part of a meeting of an administrative section and then go back in the lift to return to judicial business."[94] The result appears to be mutual respect and support not just within the council but also between the members of the state bureaucracy and the members of the council, including the tribunal:

> The members of the Conseil are viewed as being themselves part of the administration, with the corresponding attitudes and mentality. They may have been civil servants, or trained as administrators, for example at one of the famous *grandes écoles* specifically established for education of future leaders of the public administration, such as the école Nationale d'Administration. Moreover, the *conseillers d'état* are sometimes made available, on a kind of loan, to one of the ministries, to do temporary jobs requiring experienced trouble-shooters. . . . There is, therefore, a kind of fellow-feeling between the members of the Conseil d'état and the representatives of the administration; their idiosyncracies are not dissimilar. The government bureaucracy knows that the members of the Conseil d'état have acquired a wisdom in matters of administration which can only be beneficial for the management of the public service. As a result, there is mutual confidence. That circumstance may have facilitated the pragmatic way in which the Conseil d'état has always dealt with the problems caused by the discretionary powers of the administration.[95]

Martin Shapiro characterizes the attitudes and values of members of the council as fundamentally different from that of judges:

> Thus the council is not a court staffed by judges but an extremely elite segment of the high civil service designated to supervise the legal behavior of the rest of the civil service. . . . The Conseil d'état and most of the administrative courts of Europe consist of one set of elite administrators watching the rest of the administration. The principal result will be a tighter, more efficient, more disciplined, and more unified civil service and bureaucratic administration. While the form and often the

94. Bell (2001, p. 158).
95. Koopmans (2003, p. 137).

substance are protection of individual legal rights against the state, the ultimate purpose is the improvement and autonomy of the administrative machinery of the state.[96]

The question for developing countries is not, therefore, whether the tribunal within the Conseil d'état is independent and a bulwark against abuse by the state. The council is now two centuries old and has proved its integrity and value.[97] Indeed, it has begun to exercise a form of constitutional judicial review to determine whether executive action is consonant with the constitution.[98] The question is rather, in the spirit of Merryman's question about the French Deviation, whether a system of separate administrative review that is not anchored in the judiciary will work when it is adopted by a developing country without the experience and traditions of the French Conseil.[99] Alexander Hamilton argued for formal independence, now enshrined in Article III of the U.S. Constitution, as well as independence in fact through guaranteed judicial tenure, because the judiciary is in "continual jeopardy of being overpowered, awed, or influenced by its co-ordinate branches."[100] Where administrative courts that are not regarded as part of the judiciary do not have an established "track record" giving them prestige and a sense of independence, it is difficult to conceive of them being able to uphold the rule of law in the face of a determined head of state and a powerful state administration of the kind found in some developing countries.[101]

The position of developing countries that do not permit independent review, even by administrative courts, of administrative acts, has become even more problematic because of the enormous growth of the state apparatus in most countries in the last half century, which in turn has greatly expanded the ambit of governmental impact on the private economy. In Thailand, for example, no administrative courts existed until 2001. Until then, "Thai citizens had almost no recourse to challenge actions of public authorities—even if they were patently illegal or corrupt."[102]

96. Shapiro (1981, pp. 153–54).
97. Brown and Bell (1998, pp. 62–63).
98. Cappelletti (1989, pp. 154–55).
99. Merryman (1996).
100. Federalist Papers No. 78.
101. Dicey raised the same question about France in the nineteenth century, saying that "it is difficult, further, for an Englishman to believe that, at any rate where politics are concerned, the administrative courts can from their very nature give that amount of protection to individual freedom which is secured to every English citizen." See quotation and discussion of the ensuing controversy in Brown and Bell (1998, pp. 4–5). But that was then, and now is more than a century later in France.
102. World Bank (2006b, box 7.4).

Legal Origins and Independence of the Judiciary

The legal origins authors' principal investigation of the judiciary as an institution is an article entitled "Judicial Checks and Balances."[103] The article concludes that judicial independence is particularly important in securing "economic freedom."

The title "Judicial Checks and Balances" leads off what purports to be an analysis of the distinction between French-style "separation of powers," which is concerned with preventing the judiciary from interfering with the sovereignty of the legislature, and U.S.-style "checks and balances," which is concerned with allowing each of the three branches—executive, legislative, and judicial—to check and balance the other two branches. Against that contextual background, the legal origins authors find that common law systems do better than civil law systems in protecting economic freedom (though they find no significant difference in protecting "political freedom"). The authors proceed with their conventional analysis based on the origins of private law, despite the fact that Britain, the original common law country, does not allow judicial review, whereas many civil law systems in Europe and Latin America do indeed allow the judiciary to check and balance the legislature through judicial review.

The advocates of the legal origins hypothesis must deal with another awkwardness: the finding of the Law and Finance authors that the difference between common and civil law systems becomes statistically insignificant for some measures of economic freedom when they include "judicial independence" in their regressions.[104] (In their analysis, judicial independence is an index combining tenure of judges in regular and administrative courts and whether judges consider themselves bound by prior decisions.) The authors' explanation for their statistical result (and for their conclusion) is that judicial independence is the means that explains why common law countries outperform civil law countries.

The legal origins authors fail to note that the separation of powers and judicial independence are phenomena of public law, not private law where legal origin may be a more viable concept. Separation of powers and judicial independence are two different concepts, and they are implemented quite differently in various common law countries, especially the United States and

103. La Porta and others (2004). Note that the authorship of the two articles is slightly different, with Pop-Eleches being a co-author in lieu of Vishny, who participated in the original Law and Finance research (La Porta and others 1998). For a different but related economic study, see Feld and Voigt (2004).

104. La Porta and others (2004, pp. 459, 461, table 7).

the United Kingdom. After carefully comparing parliamentary government where it makes sense to speak of the parliament as sovereign and an American-style separation of powers where it makes no sense to so speak, a well-known scholar with a civil law background perceptively observed: "It is quite possible . . . that the classification of legal systems into 'common law' and 'civil law' families facilitates comparative research in the area of private law. . . . For the study of public law, however, the idea of legal families does not work."[105]

A further reason for doubting the relevance of the legal origins approach to public law is that, certainly in France, public law—at least where the work of administrative departments and agencies is concerned—is almost entirely judge made. A guide to French law written for English language lawyers puts the point directly: "In a loose sense, one might say that French public law looks something like a common-law system in which the basic principles are the work of the courts."[106]

---

105. Koopmans (2003, p. 40).
106. Rudden (1991, p. 9). See also Brown and Bell (1998, pp. 290, 293–95).

6 | Contracts and Property

Commercial bargains are usually carried out without the need for court enforcement. But even though businessmen prefer to work out between themselves any problems with the performance of their contracts, their bargaining about performance takes place in the shadow of the law.[1] The prospect that courts will resolve these disputes impartially if the contracting parties cannot agree often leads to more reasonable bargaining positions and more prompt compromise. Indeed, where the courts are not available for whatever reason, one finds mafia-type enforcement raising its ugly head.[2]

From the standpoint of economic development, perhaps the most unfortunate consequence of the unreliability of court enforcement is that it impedes the effective use of long-term and complex contracts. As economies have evolved, such contracts have become much more important in the developing world than in colonial times. Today such contracts are essential in developing countries, especially for electric generating plants, ports, highways, and many other infrastructure projects.

Similarly, where property rights are not protected, wealth tends to be kept in a more easily safeguarded form rather than being invested in financial instruments that can be fraudulently issued and sold, or even physical objects that can be stolen. The extent of crime in Latin America and Africa must surely be a burden on legitimate business. A survey showed that "more than 50 percent of firms surveyed judged crime a serious obstacle." In Nigeria "37 percent of respondents identify crime as a major or severe constraint on

---

1. Macauley (1985).
2. For various examples, see Gambetta (1993).

their operations," while the numbers increase to 50 percent in Zambia and 70 percent in Kenya. An economic study (as opposed to a survey) concluded that in "Colombia and El Salvador almost one-quarter of national GDP was lost to crime."[3] Moreover, when crime rises rapidly, intimidation and mafia-like protection are apt to proliferate, as the states of the former Soviet Union found in the 1990s. Immediately after the breakdown of the Soviet Union, economic activity had to be carried on in what might be characterized as a law-free space. But even in the much more orderly Japan, Milhaupt and West found organized crime playing just such a mafia-type enforcement role.[4]

The historical and institutional discussion in chapter 4 showed some of the ways that some kinds of bargains can be carried out in law-free space. Transactions at a community market or bazaar almost never give rise to legal disputes because the two parties to the purchase-and-sale transaction perform simultaneously. But when the quid and the quo—say, the goods delivery and the payment—are separated in time, the opportunity for the later-performing party to renege on the deal must be considered. It is more likely to be a problem when the two parties are separated in distance, especially if they are from different communities and cultures. Why is this case different from the situation where the two parties are in the same community and culture? In part it is because social norms sometimes operate to make it unwise for parties in the same community to fail to perform; severe social disapproval, even ostracism, may be the sanction for nonperformance. Analysts often refer to agreements entered into in such circumstances, especially where the parties cannot agree (or fail to agree) on all of the terms of the agreement, as "relational" contracts.[5]

A related reason why such contracts can be entered into and performed, which has been well analyzed in a corner of the social sciences known as the theory of games, is that when two parties conduct frequent transactions with each other, they are likely to perform their sides of a bargain. They recognize that they have more to lose in the future than they could gain by backing out of a particular bargain now. In game theory terms, the current bargain is just one of a series of "repeated games."

Long-Term Contracts

Thus far this discussion has envisioned either simultaneous sale and payment (the bazaar) or a simple credit sale transaction with payment in the future (or

3. World Bank (2004b, p. 89 and figure 4.5).
4. Milhaupt and West (2000, p. 41).
5. Hviid (2000, p. 46).

with payment first and performance later). But many commercial transactions are more complicated. Take a construction contract where the performance of one of the parties takes place over time—for example, a simple construction contract for a house where the buyer pays up front (or at least makes a substantial down payment). Under those circumstances, the house builder may be tempted to engage in what is sometimes called postagreement, or ex post, opportunism. Once the builder has the money, his temptation to do a little less than expected—for example, by cheating on the materials—may be great. Here there may be a relational element that helps to dampen ex post opportunism, say, where both parties live in the same village, even though the repeat game aspect is absent. But even where there is a relational element, the opportunism problem is one reason why construction contracts are often lengthy and complex and why at the end of the day the availability of a court system is important. Court enforcement is all the more important in a contemporary urban society where contractor and client may never have heard of each other before.

Where the parties live in different countries, the relational element may be particularly important in the performance of contracts. Overseas Chinese have traditionally been quite important in commerce in Southeast Asia, for example, in part because they have been willing to make long-term or complex agreements with other Chinese in countries with a weak rule of law. Typically, the two Chinese parties were normally members of the same extended family, or they regularly dealt with each other and hence the repeated game aspect induced them to perform even when the bargain might have turned out to be disadvantageous to one of the parties.

These conceptual tools of social norms, repeat games, and relational contracts help decode some of what would otherwise be puzzles in considering the rule of law in the developing world. When most people in a country lived in tribes or clans, it was not necessary to have independent judiciaries or complex rules of contract and property law. To be sure, traditional or tribal rules existed. But more important, parties performed because the practical social and perhaps economic consequences of not doing so were great. When disputes did arise, traditional or tribal leaders were able to resolve them. But when the flow of people from traditional areas to new frontiers or to cities began, people had to deal with individuals from other tribes or social groups, frequently on a one-shot basis. A commonly agreed law was necessary, and the rule of law became important to economic progress.

Economic development today depends on long-term contracts where relational factors either are not present or cannot suffice. Even the poorest and least-developed countries need, for example, electric power plants, factories, ports, and airports. These infrastructure projects have all the complexity of a house construction multiplied many times over. To build them requires a contract. Not even governments normally attempt to build these facilities themselves. The contract will necessarily be for a long term with many complex provisions. The problems involved go well beyond possible late payment or nonpayment. The parties may negotiate in good faith ex ante, but after the contract is signed, the temptation for ex post opportunistic behavior will be great on both sides.[6] And even if the parties, perhaps because they hope to enter into new contracts in the future, perform in good faith, unforeseen contingencies are bound to arise. Contract law and enforcement help to smooth the way to amicable resolution of the differences that are likely to occur, especially in infrastructure projects.[7]

These kinds of contractual problems are particularly difficult where one of the parties is the government. Then the rule-of-law issues come to the forefront. A country that cannot establish to the satisfaction of the contracting private party that the rule of law will ensure fair treatment can expect to pay more, perhaps much more, just to cover the risk. That is especially the case where no independent enforcement tribunal is available. When the Fujian provincial government of China, for example, "reneged on a 20-year power-purchase contract," the *Far Eastern Economic Review* opined that contracts in China "might not be worth the paper they are printed on."[8]

Private contractors have traditionally tried to deal with these kinds of rule-of-law problems in two ways: arbitration and corruption. Arbitration is often used by foreign contractors, especially when dealing with governments; arbitration clauses calling for arbitration in London or New York are found in many such contracts. In effect, an arbitration clause involves the parties agreeing that, in event of a dispute, they will "rent" an independent tribunal located in a country where the rule of law prevails.

Local contractors, however, are often unable to use arbitration in a third country, at least in contracts with their own government. Furthermore, local construction firms run the risk that the party they are contracting with can rely on political or crony contacts with the government or with powerful political leaders. Thus corruption is often resorted to, not just to obtain the contract but to smooth over differences that arise from unforeseen contingencies.

6. On opportunistic behavior in contracting, see Masten (1996, pp. 6–10).
7. On infrastructure contracts, see a series of articles on concessions in EBRD (2001a, pp. 19–60).
8. Dolven and Lawrence (2002, p. 52).

The likelihood of bribery rises to the extent that, in either purely private contracts or contracts with the government, government permits are required at various stages of the construction process. After all, corruption has both a supply and a demand side. And of course even in long-term complex contracts between private parties, it may pay to have taken the political or other steps necessary to make sure that the government is on one's side. Simply put, the absence of a reliable contracting law and an independent judicial enforcement system is a barrier to economic development.[9]

Ex post opportunism is not the only problem in long-term contracts. Such contracts can almost never be "complete." It is not just a question of unforeseen contingencies, which, of course, being unforeseen cannot be dealt with in writing. Even when contingencies can be foreseen, they may not be dealt with in the written contract because it would be too time-consuming or too costly to the relations between the parties to negotiate on all contingencies; after all, there are a multitude of things that might or might not occur in a long-term construction or supply contract.

American lawyers are notorious for the length and complexity of the agreements they draft, but in much of the world the written agreement is merely intended to memorialize the main points of the outcome of the negotiations, either because lawyers are not part of the negotiations or because the parties place greater emphasis on good personal relations. And sometimes the weaker party to the negotiations may simply want to "get the order," hoping to work out any contractual problems later.

Where trust is high and is highly valued by the parties, the parties may be able to work out new problems as they arise. But as economies become more complex in the process of economic development, trust is rarely enough. Almost by definition it is unwise for an individual or private firm to trust a government not to change its mind; turnover of officials and political changes can be anticipated during the performance of a long-term contract.

The problems in long-term contracts arise not just from postagreement opportunism but from the fact that one of the parties may have to make specific investments to be in a position to perform. Depending on the nature of the contracts, these specific investments may range from buying specialized equipment to training employees. But whatever the nature of the specific investments, they are made up front, meaning that the firm is even more exposed to the counterpart's ex post opportunism.[10]

9. For a general discussion on the role of arbitration in overcoming these kinds of problems, see a series of articles on contract enforcement in EBRD (2001b, pp. 16–53).

10. On what is often called the "asset specificity" problem, see Masten (1996, pp. 13–14).

Another kind of problem arises where a long-term contract involves a natural resource. Natural resource exploitation is, of course, important in many developing countries. Because the prices of natural resources fluctuate—indeed, typically fluctuate greatly over the period of a long-term contract—it is not uncommon for the price term to be left open or to be based on some standard that requires interpretation. (A cost-plus contract is conceptually of the latter type because cost is an accounting concept, often open to some quibbling if not outright disagreement, especially with regard to overhead items.) Even a price based on some index is not in practice a completely definite price term because of the need for quality adjustments—involving, for example, the level of impurities at different times in an extracted resource. Other kinds of indefinite terms that can make long-term resource contracts prone to ex post disagreement include "best efforts" and "substantial performance" provisions.[11] Here again impartial third-party enforcement by the judiciary helps to deal with ex post opportunism.

Contracts have also become increasingly important for developing countries with the worldwide movement from vertically integrated firms to new patterns involving "breaking up the value chain" by having components made in low-cost locations, especially developing countries. Another example is the growth of networking relationships between firms in high-tech industries, which are becoming increasingly important to developing country communities with a cadre of highly educated engineers and technicians, such as Bangalore and similar cities in India. Here local investments in plant and equipment depend in part on the ability of local firms to commit themselves credibly to downstream firms in more developed countries. Credibility depends in at least some measure on the ability to enforce these contracts in local courts.

The Relation of Contracts to Property

As the foregoing discussion suggests, contracts are often about things—buildings or natural resources. That is why important issues in economic development may have both contractual and property elements. This becomes even more obvious when intangible property, such as intellectual property (patents or copyrights), or corporations are involved. For example, the owner of a patent may exploit that patent through patent licenses; both protection of the patent and enforcement of the patent license agreements are dependent on the state of the rule of law in a country.

11. Masten (2000, p. 37) and sources cited therein.

Corporations provide another example. In today's developing world, the corporate form of enterprise has taken on great importance. Shareholders own shares, which are a form of property.[12] The shareholders are thereby conceptually the ultimate owners of the corporation. The corporation owns physical property, say, offices and factories. But the relationships within the corporate entity are contractual. The corporate officers' relationship to the corporation is essentially contractual, even though governed by corporate law. In fact, the officers are essentially agents of the corporation. Just as a person may not be able to carry out some business transactions without hiring an agent, so too the corporation can act only through officers and employees.

Economists analyze the problem of corporate governance as one of agency. Agency is essentially a contractual relationship. The principal acts through an agent, and the agent can legally commit the principal. But how can one be sure that the agent—the corporate officer—is acting faithfully in the interest of the corporation (and thereby in the interest of the ultimate owners, the shareholders)? That question and the analogous issue with respect to members of the governing board (such as the board of directors in the United States) are the central issues in corporate governance, even though they are attenuated in some countries to the extent that local law demands that the corporation, and thereby corporate officers and directors, owe duties to other stakeholders, such as the community and the labor force.[13]

Finance often involves both contracts and property. Most countries, certainly in the developing world, rely much more on bank loans than on equity finance. Yet a loan is nothing but a contract. A large portion of these loans involve collateral; the collateral is property, and the ability of the lender to reach the collateral in the event of nonpayment is as much a question of property law as of contract law. Here again the financial system works best with reliable third-party enforcement provided by the judiciary.

Property

The central ideas of property are easiest to grasp if one thinks of physical things—land and movable objects (of any kind, whether autos or materials or jewels). Yet intangibles can be property as well—think of shares of stock or patents or copyrights. In all cases there is a fundamental difference between

---

12. After some hesitation, English court decisions rejected the notion that shares merely represent the property of the corporation and chose the view that the shares themselves are property (Ireland 1996, pp. 48–62).

13. Issues of corporate governance are discussed at length in chapter 8.

the legal rights derived from property ownership and those derived from a contract; as Friedman put it, "the most striking difference between contract law and property law is that while a contract right is good only against the other party to the contract, a property right is good against the world."[14] This straightforward concept of property led William Blackstone to write in his famous eighteenth treatise on English law, "there is nothing which so generally strikes the imagination, and engages the affections of mankind, as the right of property; or that sole and despotic dominion which one man claims and exercises over the external things of the world, in total exclusion of the right of any other individual in the universe."[15]

This concept of property as a right against the whole world has become somewhat muddied in advanced economies because of an increasing emphasis on the harmful impact that the use by one person of his property may have on another's property. These spillover effects (termed "externalities" in economics), especially environmental harms not just to another's property but also to people and even resources owned by nobody (such as the atmosphere), have become of great concern in the most developed countries. Increasingly the focus has been on exactly what rights an owner should have in his property, leading to the sophisticated view that property ownership is just a "bundle of rights" versus others and the society at large. That in turn raises the question: What may a person *not* do with respect to his own property?

The "bundle of rights" view, however analytically useful, especially in highly developed economies, puts the emphasis on the wrong points for most developing countries where the economic development problem is precisely the lack of security of property ownership.[16] If ownership is insecure, investment in the property and its intelligent use will be circumscribed, and economic growth in the economy will be suboptimal.

Much literature on property in developing countries has been inspired by the writings of Hernando de Soto, who stresses the importance of owners having titles to their property, an issue that will be discussed at length in the next chapter on land.[17] The growing interest in titles sometimes unfortunately obscures the question of who the owner is. In the developing world the owner is often not a person or a legal entity (such as a corporation) but a tribe or other communal group. When two or more people own a piece of

---

14. Friedman (2000, p. 109).

15. Blackstone (2001, vol. 2, book 2, chapter 1, ¶ III). See discussion in Merrill and Smith (2001).

16. Merrill and Smith (2001, pp. 383–84).

17. See de Soto (2000, 2002).

land, Western law knows how to handle the situation conceptually, as well as how to handle titling issues. Under U.S. law, for example, two or more owners are either tenants-in-common or joint tenants, with fully predictable consequences flowing from each of the two possible characterizations. In tribal societies the community typically owns the property, and the rights of individuals and families within the tribe, even with respect to land they till and houses in which they live, depend on the law of the particular tribe—referred to generally as communal law.

The colonial powers, in imposing their own law on their colonies, did not bother to take into account communal law for this purpose since, as discussed in chapter 4, they applied their own Western law only to relations among Westerners and to relations between Westerners and the indigenous population. Because relationships between members of the indigenous society, including their property relationships, were of no concern to the colonial powers, they were ignored.

When independence came, the newly independent governments tended to continue with Western law—hence the legal origins issue discussed in earlier chapters—and often failed to incorporate communal land law into the inherited legal structure.[18] If that failure was an oversight, it need not have been harmful since the tribes could continue to govern themselves, including governing property relations within tribal areas. But resulting intellectual confusion of two types has produced some unfortunate consequences.

The first confusion came about in countries with governments that wanted to manage the economy directly. Some of these governments decided to start by nationalizing all land (and water resources) that were not publicly registered as private property. The effect, which may in some cases have been intentional, was to dispossess native populations of their communal property; this communal property simply did not appear on public land registries and therefore it became government land.

To understand why this change was unfortunate, it is essential to consider the second confusion—that between communal property and open-access property. Communal property, sometimes called common property, is property held outright by a community, notably by a tribe that internally allocates obligations and benefits regarding the property among its members. But the tribal community has the same right to exclude nonmembers of the tribe from its communal land as a private individual has with regard to privately owned land. In short, the community has rights against the world outside

18. Ostrom (2000, p. 337).

the community and thus is a property owner in the same sense as any property owner who has rights in land against the world.

Open-access property, in some circumstances called "common pool" property, is something else entirely. No one has the right to exclude anyone from such property. The whole world has equal rights. The open seas are an example, and the way in which such unlimited access to all fishermen leads to overfishing is well known. A similar phenomenon, also well known, is overgrazing on public lands. In 1968 Garrett Hardin published an article entitled "The Tragedy of the Commons."[19] That article was so compelling in drawing attention to the overuse phenomenon and so well titled that the "tragedy of the commons" entered popular speech, at least among those aspiring to intellectual reputation, and has dominated discussion of land and resource use in recent decades. But the use of the word "commons" in the title has sown massive confusion because the evils against which Hardin inveighed occur only where there is open access. Common property in the communal law sense need have no such unfortunate overuse effect, so long as the community can exclude nonmembers and has the power, as tribal communities have usually had, to regulate use by the members of the community.

When some newly independent governments, however, nationalized all land (at least all property not registered as private property), they converted the communal land thus nationalized into open-access property, at least so far as the nonmembers of the tribal community were concerned. Although the tribal community might still be able to control use by its members, it lost any power to exclude nonmembers because so far as the national legal system was concerned, the land was government land, not communal land. A city dweller, for example, could simply go into tribal areas and fell trees and shoot animals in communal forests, fish in communal lakes, and even start a farm or ranch without fear of the national government or the courts (whatever the risk of violence from members of the tribal community might have been).[20]

The entire question of property titles and communal land is investigated in the next chapter. The main points, however, go well beyond the question of developing country agricultural land to include policy issues involving the exploitation of natural resources generally. Lakes, forests, irrigation systems, and many other resources also run the risk of being overused when governments lack the ability to allocate those resources to individual owners or even to put them off-limits to the public at large. Such risk is the result of a failure

19. Hardin (1968).
20. Ostrom (2000, p. 337).

of governments to act appropriately. Arrangements for dealing with overuse and overexploitation, often called common property arrangements, are well known in many countries, from the mountain grazing areas of Iceland, Norway, and Switzerland to nineteenth century ocean whaling to the gold fields of the California gold rush.[21] In some of these cases where there was no government to regulate use, private parties joined together for collective action to work out solutions.[22]

Even where a government decides, and is able, to take charge of the exploitation of these kinds of resources, it sometimes merely trades one set of problems for another. To take a modern example, Britain and Norway decided to promote drilling for natural gas and oil in the North Sea in the 1960s and 1970s. These governments had no technological or organizational capability to carry out those goals directly and had to use contracts with private firms to do so. But they also decided not to give the private firms property rights. Rather they used contracts and economic regulation, particularly in the case of Britain, in an attempt to retain control over the pace of activity, quantities, and eventually prices. The problems of allocating resources and of deciding how fast to carry out the exploitation (with Britain deciding to hasten it and Norway to moderate it) produced a multitude of economic development problems and inconsistencies, which were further complicated in Britain by disputes over pricing strategies after oil production began. The story of the development of the North Sea shows that even when there is a single unchallenged owner, the state, and when no "tragedy of the commons" is threatened, the practical contract problems can still be profound.[23]

21. Ostrom (2000, pp. 334–45); Ellickson (1993); Clay and Wright (2003). The California gold field example can be interpreted either as private property rights evolving spontaneously or as a collective effort to allocate the individual right to exploit open access land in a way that maximizes total product.
22. See generally Ostrom (1990) and various articles in Anderson and McChesney (2003).
23. For a general discussion on the North Sea experience, see Dam (1976).

7 | *Land*

Real estate is a major source of value in both developed and developing countries. In the United States households have $9.6 trillion, or 16 percent of their wealth, in real estate.[1] Farmers have another $1.3 trillion of equity in their farms, bringing total household wealth in real estate to nearly 20 percent of household assets.[2] Hernando de Soto, writing in 1993, said that some 70 percent of Peruvian wealth was in real estate.[3] One study found that in Uganda "between 50 and 60 percent of the asset endowment of the poorest households" was land.[4] The World Bank confirms that the proportion of real property is between one-half and three-quarters of wealth in most economies.[5]

In some countries, of course, agricultural production may be less important because mining or fishing or village enterprise takes precedence over agriculture, but urban living is still the exception in most of the developing world. In the United States, in contrast, despite its vast expanse, 79.0 percent of residents live in urban areas. But in highly populated India, only 27.8 percent of people lived in urban areas in 2000. And in some African countries the

1. This is a net figure after deducting mortgages on property; see Federal Reserve, *Flow of Funds Accounts of the United States: Flows and Outstandings Fourth Quarter 2004.* Release Z.1. p. 102, Table B.100 (March 10, 2005).

2. 2005 estimate; see Economic Research Service, U.S. Department of Agriculture. *Balance Sheet of the U.S. Farming Sector, 2001-2005F* (February 11, 2005).

3. de Soto (1993, p. 8).

4. Deininger (2003, p. xx). This reference is a book-length review of research on land ownership and transactions in developing countries and incorporates results of previous World Bank and academic research. The reader is therefore referred to the original studies cited and reviewed in the Deininger book.

5. World Bank (2006a, p. 32). These results appear to be based on 1985 data.

urban population is an even smaller proportion; for Ethiopia the proportion of urban dwellers is only 15.9 percent.[6]

Legal Uncertainty

To simplify, it is useful to think of agricultural land as the most important development topic so far as real estate is concerned. Yet, in the developing world, agricultural land ownership is often shrouded in legal uncertainty. As Deininger wrote: "In many countries, especially in Africa, . . . often more than 90 percent of land remains outside the existing legal system."[7] In cities the legal situation is often even more uncertain and problematic because social norms and bonds of tradition are much looser than in the less rapidly changing countryside. De Soto's study of Peru led him to conclude that "more than 90 percent of rural and half of urban property rights in Peru are not protected by formalized titles—that is, they are 'informal.'"[8] Deininger noted that African and Asian developing countries present a similar problem: "More than 50 percent of the peri-urban population in Africa and more than 40 percent in Asia live under informal tenure and therefore have highly insecure land rights."[9]

In rural areas, it is not just the livelihood of those who work the land that is at risk. Legal insecurity has broader costs to the economy. For example, where land ownership is not recorded in a land registry, farmers often have to pay for fences, trees, and other boundary markers because there is no other way of knowing where land boundaries begin and end. These capital investments involve costs not just to the farmer but to the economy as a whole. But without them, disputes over ownership and boundaries are more frequent. Of course, neighbors, especially when they are members of the same extended family or tribe, may be able to avoid disputes. But often, as de Soto famously observed, the only way for a stranger to know when he steps from one person's land to another's is that a different dog barks.[10] Disputes resulting in litigation consume real resources of the disputants and of the state.

The economic and financial consequences of legal uncertainty are profound. The farmer cannot mortgage his property where no legal infrastructure protects it or describes its metes and bounds. And if he cannot mortgage his property, he cannot borrow to improve his property, or to buy more land,

6. *Britannica Almanac 2003* (pp. 292, 431, 602).
7. Deininger (2003, p. xxiii).
8. De Soto (1993, p. 8).
9. Deininger (2003, p. xxv).
10. De Soto (1993, p. 12).

or to start a new business. Of course, even with title, he may still be unable to borrow against the land if his property is so small that formal sector lenders have no incentive to lend the commensurately small sums involved. Moreover, social norms in indigenous areas may work against putting land up as collateral because nonpayment may result in transfer of the land to outsiders.[11]

Investment in improving land, whether in drainage, irrigation, or new types of crops, is important to output, productivity, and the environment. Increasing legal certainty through titling also increases investment in improving the land, leading to higher agricultural production. A World Bank report gave examples:

> Farmers in Thailand with title invested so much more in their land that their output was 14–25 percent higher than those working untitled land of the same quality. In Vietnam rural households with a document assigning clear rights of control and disposition commit 7.5 percent more land to crops requiring a greater initial outlay and yielding returns after several years than households without documentation. In Peru almost half those with title to their property in Lima's squatter settlements have invested in improvements, compared with 13 percent of those without title."[12]

Moreover, where greater legal certainty has been created in developing country land markets, prices for land increase. According to the same World Bank report, the "value of rural land in Brazil, Indonesia, the Philippines, and Thailand increases by anywhere from 43 percent to 81 percent after being titled."[13] Although higher land prices may be thought to create fairness issues, these higher prices are a good measure of the value of legal certainty created by titling. And the higher prices in turn create the collateral base for obtaining credit to improve the land, in turn leading to even higher prices.[14]

Creating security of title thus has a two-part reinforcing effect. Not only does it reinforce the incentive to invest in land, but it also creates the wherewithal to be able to do so by increasing the ability to borrow the requisite funds. Again, the World Bank reports: "Farmers with secure title in Costa Rica, Ecuador, Honduras, Jamaica, Paraguay, and Thailand obtain larger loans on better terms than those without it. In Thailand farmers with title borrowed anywhere from 50 percent to five times more from banks and other

11. Migot-Adholla and others (1991).
12. World Bank (2004b, pp. 80–81); Feder and others (1998).
13. World Bank (2004b, p. 80).
14. Deininger (2003, pp. 42–51).

institutional lenders than did farmers with land identical but without title."[15] Similarly, the ability to start a business with funds obtained from mortgaging real estate is especially important, as de Soto observed for the developed country experience: "In the United States, up to 70% of the credit that new businesses receive comes from using formal titles as collateral for mortgages."[16] Without legal certainty as to ownership, transferability of land is equally uncertain. Without legal certainty as to transferability, a market in land is difficult to create. And hence the normal function of land markets in moving land into more efficient and productive hands is likely to be slow or nonexistent.

Lack of legal certainty also makes it difficult for an ambitious farm worker to become a farm owner. The result is that much land in developing countries is farmed by rental tenants. These tenants often enter into sharecropping agreements, in which the owner—who may be a distant city dweller—and the tenant share the crops (or their proceeds). Although such sharecropping agreements need not be notably inefficient from an economic viewpoint, studies show that farms let under such sharing arrangements are not usually as efficient as farms operated by a resident owner.[17] Thus lack of legal certainty is not only a barrier to social and economic progress for the poor, but it also results in less than optimal agricultural production, a particularly serious economic problem in a developing economy still heavily focused on agriculture.

Finally, legal uncertainty is not good for the environment (contrary to the primitive notion that measures taken to increase agricultural output necessarily harm the environment). For example, a major cause of deforestation in the Brazilian Amazon is the absence of property rights, which leads to short-term strategies for rapid exploitation of land.[18] A study of fifty-three countries concluded that "a modest improvement in the protection of property rights could reduce the rate of deforestation by as much as one-third."[19] The correlation between greater security for property rights and sounder environmental practices is not limited to the deforestation example. Another study showed that "Ethiopian farmers are less likely to plant trees and build terraces to protect against erosion—and more likely to increase the use of fertilizer and herbicides—if their rights to land are insecure."[20]

---

15. World Bank (2004b, p. 81).
16. De Soto (1993, p. 11).
17. See studies and references in Deininger (2003, pp. 90–93).
18. Deininger (2003, p. 41); Alston, Libecap, and Mueller (1999).
19. World Bank (2004b, p. 81, box 4.3).
20. World Bank (2004b, p. 81, box 4.3).

In short, steady and sustainable economic development in the rural sector depends upon creating legal certainty with respect to ownership and transferability of land.

Urban Real Estate

Legal uncertainty as to ownership in cities is even more serious for economic development. This is true not just for business premises but also for house and apartment ownership. It is difficult for people living in developed countries with excellent legal certainty to appreciate what urban life, especially for the poor, can be where legal uncertainty prevails. Yet more than 50 percent of the peri-urban population in Africa and more than 40 percent in Asia live under informal tenure systems and have no protection from the formal legal system.[21]

Just as security of tenure adds to property values of land, so too with urban residences: "For urban land, titling increases the value by 14 percent in Manila, by almost 25 percent in both Guayaquil, Ecuador, and Lima, Peru, and by 58 percent in Davao, Philippines," the World Bank reported. And here too titling leads to investment, although not just in the premises; in Lima, Peru, the World Bank found, residents who received title to urban property used that property as "collateral to buy microbuses, build small factories, and start other types of small businesses."[22]

City dwellers with uncertain ownership not only may have the same problems as rural dwellers when they try to borrow against their property or buy or sell it, but other economic activities may also be circumscribed. For example, the ever-present possibility of seizure or dispossession that arises when a householder cannot assert legal rights of ownership leads to the need for at least one family member to remain at home to protect the residence. Many city dwellers are therefore forced to find some way of earning money at home.[23] Often, of course, this means that women cannot enter the mainstream labor force and improve their economic position. Beyond the social effects, the economic result is that a large portion of the population is not able to make a reasonable economic contribution through their work. Moreover, the lack of opportunity for the improvement of skills through on-the-job experience and training restricts the economic development of the community. Titling of residential property leads to greater work outside the home with favorable long-term results for the economy.[24]

21. Deininger (2003, p. xxv).
22. World Bank (2004b, pp. 80–81).
23. Field (2004, p. 839); Lanjouw and Levy (2004, pp. 918–21).
24. World Bank (2004b, p. 81).

Sources of Legal Uncertainty

What are the sources of legal uncertainty? The short answer is that legal uncertainty arises because the question of ownership often lies outside the legal system. Ownership may be safeguarded by custom or social norms within a tribe or an extended family or even by customary legal systems operating without reference to, or support from, the formal legal system established by the state. Customary legal systems may dominate within vast tracts of territory. But the formal legal system, meaning the courts and administrative bodies of the state, often is not available to provide legal certainty—or, in common parlance, to protect property rights.

In particular, legal uncertainty starts with the absence of property titles. One's farm or house becomes, so far as the law is concerned, like an article of clothing or a personal computer to a resident of a developed country. Social norms against stealing and misappropriation may operate. But one's ability to use the legal system to assert ownership and keep possession is minimal. One is best advised to keep one's hands on the clothing and the computer, or lock them away. Unlike clothing and computers, real estate cannot be moved, yet an owner without legal title may be dispossessed simply by someone more influential or stronger taking possession.

In the case of land, the situation may not be a problem in a traditional community untroubled by outsiders. But rising population in many developing countries has strained even these communities as more and more people seek to survive and better themselves economically on the same amount of land. But even more disturbing to certainty than the multiplying of the local population is the intrusion of outsiders, whether they be wealthy merchants who seek land as an investment or entrepreneurial land companies or even urban and foreign settlers. An illustration is the case of Kenya in the 1930s, where "land hunger" sparked by white settlement led to a demand for, and the introduction of, modern land legal systems, even though titling and land registration did not become systematic until the 1950s.[25]

Economists studying the evolution from traditional communal land arrangements to legal protection have explained the protection as "endogenously" created by the interaction of supply and demand. In other words, the new legal system for land was not created because some domestic or international civil servant thought it would be a good idea. Rather the demand from ordinary people for protection and certainty increased as land pressure and resulting disputes grew. In turn, the state (meaning politicians seeking votes

25. Platteau (2000, pp. 124, 134).

or authoritarian rulers seeking popular support) invested in a legal system for land.

Titling is a mechanism to promote legal certainty. When does demand for titles arise? North and Thomas trace the transition in northern Europe from communal ownership to legally protected individual ownership to population increases.[26] The use of titling often occurs in the second stage of development. In China thirty-year use rights have recently been created and given at least some legal protection, but outright ownership and especially titling, along with their economic development advantages, remain only future possibilities. Sometimes, as the Kenya example shows, the demand for titles arises either from, or because of, new groups that enter the previously communal space. Of course, the demand for titles sometimes creates disputes between different population groups.

An interesting example of the combination of population increase, new groups entering, and disputes between groups can be found in U.S. history. A major feature of the nineteenth century saga of westward expansion in the United States was conflict between ranchers and farmers. Most of the United States between the Great Plains and the Pacific coastal region is relatively arid, more appropriate in the pre-irrigation era for ranching than farming. But U.S. public land policy, including the famous Homestead Act of 1862 (allowing those who improved land over a five-year period to obtain title), was patterned on the idea that land sales and homestead grants by the U.S. government should be for 160 acres (one-fourth of a "section" measuring one mile square) per family since 160 acres was large enough for one farm family's economic success in the part of the country already settled. Since plenty of good farming land remained available in the eastern half of the country in the early part of the nineteenth century, the ranchers were the first to arrive in the western United States. But 160 acres was not enough for profitable ranching and so the ranchers, being unable to acquire government-owned land, simply made informal claims to much larger areas. By a combination of local agreement and social mores coupled with violence against those, especially newcomers, who did not recognize the informal claims, an informal land system of ranch-size claims arose.[27]

As the better farmland in the eastern United States grew scarce and the growing population of landless farmers, fed in part by immigration from Europe, pushed westward, conflict—sometimes violent—was inevitable.

---

26. North and Thomas (1973, pp. 59–64).
27. Anderson and Hill (2004, pp. 160–66).

Naturally the farmers sought to homestead the land or buy from the U.S. government, thereby obtaining titles to the same land that the ranchers were exploiting without titles.[28] The ranchers—considering the farmers mere squatters—acted, first, by illegally fencing their claimed lands, and then by taking their cause to the U.S. Congress, where various compromises resulted over a period of decades.[29]

Issues in Titling

The most common issues concerning titling involve finding a way to give existing "owners" actual titles. De Soto popularized the idea of titling in his 1989 and 2000 books.[30] But titling was a government response, even in the developing world, before de Soto wrote his two books. Titling was introduced successfully in the 1980s in Thailand.[31] A major titling effort in Ecuador beginning in 1993 was directed at urban areas.[32]

One of the problems in titling, especially in urban areas, is determining the identity of the actual owner who should be awarded the title. In the massive movement of people off the land into cities in the latter part of the twentieth century in the developing world, vast informal urban agglomerations grew up without effective governance and law. In Peru, de Soto's home country, a massive titling effort ran into difficulties in these informal areas because of conflicting claims to the same parcel of land.[33]

Titling is only half of the battle if the objective is to create economic development. The elimination of existing restrictions on free transferability of land is equally important. Unless land, even if it is titled, can be mortgaged, it cannot be used as a means of raising money for investment in the land, whether for improved productivity or for side commercial ventures. And mortgages will not be available unless foreclosure is possible, which means that the lender must be able to assume title to the land. One study of Thailand found that the major benefit of titling was precisely the ability to borrow from formal financial institutions rather than security of ownership as such. Access to credit was more than three times greater on titled than on untitled land.[34] Hence the

---

28. Anderson and Hill (2004, p. 23).
29. Libecap (1981, pp. 3, 20–23, 31–36); Gates (1968, pp. 466–68).
30. De Soto (1989, 2000).
31. World Bank (2001b, p. 36).
32. Lanjouw and Levy (2004, p. 912).
33. Payne (2002, p. 17).
34. Deininger (2003, p. 49, figure 2.5).

benefit of titling comes in large measure, at least in Thailand, from legal transferability.[35]

A political, and sometimes ideological, issue that can arise in developing countries is that free transferability of land evokes an image of landless rural poor. The notion is that small farm owners will be duped or coerced into selling out. Indeed, market-oriented land reform involving free transferability is at odds with the ideology of land reform once prevalent in many countries that supported the breaking up of large estates in favor of landless peasants. At the same time, it must be recognized that these early land reform efforts not only broke up large estates but sometimes increased output and productivity through transfer of ownership to individual farmers.[36] In more policy-oriented terms, the fear is simply that transferability will lead to greater income inequality. Yet lack of transferability is likely to limit the economic development promise of titling efforts in the countryside. Moreover, transferability was shown, in a World Bank study of Colombia, to "make a significant contribution to greater equalization of the operational structure of land holdings and, to a more limited extent, the ownership structure." In short, "rental and sales markets were more effective in transferring land to poor but productive producers than was administrative land reform." [37]

A different kind of problem arises from the hard-to-escape condition that titling involving free transferability must be based on the existence of a land registry.[38] It is only by land registration that a buyer can be sure to be dealing with the legal owner, that the land is free of legal encumbrances such as mortgages, and that the boundaries of the plot of land correspond to the seller's representations. A registration system must not only be created, but the existing owner has to know about the land registration process and be motivated

---

35. Feder and Feeney (1991).

36. Deininger (2003, pp. 16–17) and sources cited therein.

37. Deininger, Castagnini, and González (2004).

38. The United States does not use a land registration system but rather a system for the recordation of deeds and encumbrances such as mortgages. A Torrens land registration system was partially adopted in some states in the twentieth century, but even in those states land registration has not been a successful competitor with an already well-established recording system (supplemented by title insurance); see Casner and others (2000, pp. 783–820) and Miceli and others (2002). Britain made a major move to a land registration system in 1925 (Bostick 1987). The reason land registration has not been successful in the United States has little relevance for developing countries, which would most probably find it even more difficult to introduce an American deed and mortgage recording system, which in practice requires not just qualified civil servants but also private lawyers (to interpret the result of title searches) and a title insurance system.

to register. The result in Kenya has been that it is the larger farms with better access to markets that turn out to be the farms that are registered.[39]

Titling costs money. It cannot function properly without the rest of the legal infrastructure that goes with it: a cadastral survey showing property boundaries and landmarks is indispensable. So too land registries are expensive to create and maintain.[40]

More than just the mechanics of surveys and registries is involved. A competent administration of the system is needed. Accuracy and promptness are important. A World Bank study found:

> In Mozambique there is a backlog of about 10,000 applications for land rights, which means long delays between receipt of an investment plan and eventual granting of the land right. In Cameroon the minimum amount of time it takes to register a plot is 15 months, and registration commonly takes between 2 and 7 years. In Peru the official adjudication process takes 43 months and 207 steps in 48 offices, although an expedited process is now being implemented in selected areas.[41]

Obviously middle-income countries are more likely than poorer countries to be able to afford the infrastructure and perhaps also to field a sufficiently competent bureaucracy to make land registration work smoothly. A further important factor is that the judiciary has to be educated in the new system and be ready to enforce these newly created formal rights. Land registration is thus an example of a situation where some economic development is required to generate the resources necessary for legal solutions that create the basis for further economic development. In short, legal development and economic development in such instances must necessarily advance hand in hand.

If the advantages of a developed legal system for land titling, registration, and transferability are to be realized, especially with regard to enabling mortgage borrowing through the use of land as security, appropriate laws on mortgage security are necessary, though by no means sufficient. The judiciary must be prepared to foreclose in accordance with the statute. Otherwise, banks and other financial institutions will not lend. Among the problems that can arise, aside from corruption, is that judges may be reluctant to throw the poor off their land or out of their houses. Still another problem is that financial institutions may be unwilling to lend for other reasons. In Brazil, India, and Russia, macroeconomic instability and the resulting rampant inflation

39. Platteau (2000, pp. 134–35).
40. Deininger (2003, pp. 70–71).
41. World Bank (2001b, p. 35, box 2.4).

made the development of a mortgage market difficult.[42] In any case banks may be unwilling to lend to borrowers of small sums; capacity to pay and the costs of servicing small bank loans remain crucial to bank lending decisions.[43]

Transferability: Precedents and Problems

Titling and land registration, even with all the administrative and legal infrastructure, will fail to deliver the full economic benefits if transferability is limited by statutory restrictions. One common restriction limits transfer to the transferor's kinship line. Alternatively, transfer may be subject to approval by some specified authority.[44]

Similar restraints on transferability of land were common in early English history. These restraints contrast with the ancient world of Greece and Rome, where free transferability was more common. "Plato bought a farm. Cicero sold his house."[45] In England restraints arose mainly as part of feudal land relationships established in the Middle Ages and modified over time in the ensuing struggle between the Crown and nobles. Under the early feudal system all land was, in principle, owned by the Crown and held in a chain of dependent ownership through the high nobility and down to the actual tenant owner. Furthermore, all transfers required, in principle, the approval of the Crown or an intervening noble in the feudal chain.[46]

Even after the 1290 statute *Quia Emptores* simplified the feudal system by prohibiting "subinfeudation," and thereby restricting chains of dependent ownership, problems arose that would not have arisen under a system where each plot of land was owned outright by a single person. Over the centuries the English aristocracy and later the rising gentry class sought to ensure that their landed estates would remain within the family generation after generation by using various legal devices, especially strict settlement and common recovery.[47]

These legal techniques were restraints on transferability that kept land off the market. Eventually, in an evolution that lasted some centuries, *entail*, an

42. Lewis (2004, pp. 155, 240).
43. Kagawa and Turksta (2002, p. 68).
44. Ellickson (1993, p. 1375).
45. Ellickson (1993, p. 1377).
46. Casner and others (2000. pp. 253–58).
47. For a general discussion on the gentry, see Tawney (1941). For a nontechnical explanation of strict settlement, see English and Saville (1983) and Spring (1993, pp. 123–47). On common recovery, see the example in the definition for "common recovery" in Garner (2004, p. 295) and Simpson (1986, pp. 129–32). For further details, see Biancalana (2001).

interest in land normally created, for example, in the use of strict settlement, was abolished.[48] (In Virginia entail was abolished by statute under the leadership of the thirty-three-year-old Thomas Jefferson.)[49] The abolition of entail constituted a rejection of the aristocratic desire to keep land permanently within a family and a transition to the principle that land, in a modern economy, should be freely transferable. But even under modern Anglo-American land law, it is possible for an owner to find alternatives to entail so long as the conveyed interest vests in some person within, under one formulation of the Rule Against Perpetuities, "a life in being plus 21 years." The policy of this rule is that "a man of property . . . [may] provide for all of those in his family whom he personally knew and the first generation after them upon attaining majority."[50] Legislation in some U.S. states has recently amended the Rule Against Perpetuities to allow so-called perpetual trusts and other devices for tax avoidance in the transfer of property from one generation to another.[51] But, in general, contemporary policy in developed countries, certainly in Anglo-Saxon law countries, treats land as a commodity in a market economy, subject to land use restrictions imposed by public regulation.

The gradual elimination of restraints on transferability in the developed world was accompanied by more rapid economic growth and ensured that such growth was enjoyed in the agricultural as well as in the commercial and emerging industrial economies. Some economic studies substantiate the importance of removing restraints on transferability. "Several studies of China, one of the few countries that has experimented with allowing different systems of transfer rights across different provinces, have confirmed that higher levels of transferability were positively correlated with higher levels of farm investment," a World Bank study reported.[52]

Restrictions on, and regulation of, land markets can have major economic effects for the entire economy. Another World Bank analysis pointed out that "high transactions costs in land markets can also either increase the cost of providing credit or require the costly development of collateral substitutes, in both cases constraining private sector development. . . . [A] recent study . . . estimates that taking both direct and indirect effects together, land market distortions reduce the annual rate of gross domestic product growth in India by 1.3 percent."[53]

48. See Leach and Tudor (1952, § 24.16) and Reid (1995) and sources cited therein.
49. "Entail." *Encyclopædia Britannica.* 1970. 607–08.
50. Quoted in Dukeminier and Krier (1993, pp. 299–300).
51. See Sitkoff and Schanzenbach (2005).
52. World Bank (2001b, p. 35).
53. Deininger (2003, p. 2).

A poorly functioning land registry system is a de facto restriction on land markets and thereby on both financial markets and on entrepreneurship in creating new enterprises. Property registration need take no more than a week, but it takes on average 274 days in Nigeria, 363 days in Bangladesh, and 683 days in Haiti. Costs can be much less than 1 percent of the property value, but they range as high as 18 percent in Senegal, 22 percent in Zimbabwe, and 30 percent in Syria.[54]

One particularly pernicious restraint involves restrictions on land rentals. Such restrictions can have profound effects in view of the popularity of rentals as a dominant form of farmland exploitation. Even where communal holdings are not a factor, the family-owned farm is not necessarily the model followed. In developed countries a large percentage of all farmland is rented; percentages range from 71 percent in Belgium to 43 percent in the United States, where in certain regions the family-owned farm has iconic importance. [55] A variety of economic factors lead to the conclusion that the owner-operated farm is not always the optimal form of farm enterprise.[56] Land rental has the social advantage of allowing people who would otherwise be farm employees or even unemployed to become independent farm operators. In fact, where the objective is to provide the poor with their own land, land rental has been shown to be more effective than land reform.[57]

From a rule-of-law perspective, restrictions on land sales and rentals are restrictions on enforcement of contracts as well as limitations on property rights. However, restrictions on land sales are usually by-products of national real property systems. To take just one example, if land is legally held in communal form, then individual farmers—whatever their rights within the community—have no governmentally protected right to transfer their particular parcel to nonmembers of the community. Restrictions on rentals, however, take many forms, some having little to do with the underlying property rights system. A prime example involves rent controls, which make illegal any rental contract exceeding the ceiling rental amount. Such rent controls have seriously discouraged land rentals.[58]

A number of countries do not recognize land rental contracts at all. Often these prohibitions are part of a land reform program involving the breakup of large estates, and the prohibition is motivated by a desire to ensure that the

---

54. World Bank (2006a, pp. 27–32 and table 5.2).
55. Deininger (2003, p. 99).
56. Bierlen and others (2000).
57. Deininger, Castagnini, and González (2004); Deininger and Jin (2002).
58. Deininger (2003, pp. 116–18).

recipients of the redistributed land actually farm them. This is no doubt the motivation for the purported prohibition on rental tenancy in India's land reform regulations; this prohibition led to a much lower rate of even informal land tenancy.[59]

Some countries prohibit certain forms of rental contract; the most common is a prohibition on sharecropping.[60] One motive for such prohibitions may be to protect those who work the fields. Despite a long tradition even among economists of viewing sharecropping as an inefficient substitute for cash rentals, restraints on sharecropping are today generally considered unfortunate from an economic viewpoint; sharecropping allows the poor, who do not have the resources to acquire land, to benefit nevertheless from their energy and skill as farmers without having to limit themselves to being simply farm laborers. Thus, although as previously noted, sharecropping may not be as efficient as owner-operated farming, it is often the most efficient form of rental contract available.

Recent decades have seen the developing world gradually shed restraints on land sale and rental that were imposed by earlier governments of a revolutionary or socialist ideology and that sought thereby to reduce inequality in income and wealth. The gradual lifting of these restraints appears to result in part from greater understanding that these restraints limit economic growth and do not necessarily lead to greater equality. An interesting historical parallel can thus be drawn to the gradual elimination of restraints on alienation in traditional English (and early American) land law, again as the pernicious impact of the restraints came to be understood. The difference between the recent developing country experience and the earlier experience is, of course, that the English-origin restraints on alienation were originally intended to preserve inequality of income and wealth by keeping land within aristocratic families generation after generation.

Implementation Problems

If titling and registration are so important, why don't developing countries adopt the appropriate measures immediately? Aside from the cost and the absence of a trained bureaucracy, titling and registration are sometimes resisted by the very people who could benefit. Their objections may be rational from their individual point of view, at least in part, but as in so many issues

---

59. Deininger (2003, pp. 108 , 117–18); see also Ray (1996).
60. Deininger (2003, p. 119).

of economic policy, individual preferences do not necessarily add up to an optimum result for the economy as a whole. Still, one reason why optimism about the economic development effects of titling should be tempered is that in many countries, land constitutes a combination of insurance and pension fund. According to Platteau:

> Land continues to be perceived as a crucial asset for the present and/or future subsistence of the family, all the more so as it is a secure form of holding wealth and a good hedge against inflation. ('It is our bank and we will not part with it', said the member of a founding lineage in a village close to Matam, Senegal.) That considerations of social insurance determine attitudes of deep attachment to land is understandable in a context of scarce alternative employment opportunities and risky labour markets.[61]

One of the transition problems in moving from the traditional concept is that the patriarch of an extended family may very well be the person who would register the land on behalf of the family. However, social norms and family pressures may work against registration. For example, other members of the family may feel dispossessed by the movement to a market economy concept of ownership if they lose the implicit right to be supported in their old age, or if they become disabled or seriously ill. For a lawyer trained in the common law system, the situation is analogous to one where a trustee of a trust on behalf of a widow and minor children decides to transfer the property held as trustee into the trustee's own name; the trustee may still feel responsible to the beneficiaries, but they cannot count on it.

Even if a family patriarch or clan leader might want to recognize the rights and expectations of the rest of the members of the extended family or clan through the land registration process itself, it is almost impossible to see how that could be done without losing many of the benefits of land registration. If members of the extended family were to be listed as co-owners, the written agreement of all would be necessary to mortgage the property or to sell the land. The upshot is that for some people in the developing world, land registration creates more legal and economic uncertainty than it eliminates. An Anglo-American type of trust (or its civil law equivalents) might work, but the trust—which arose over the centuries in the evolution of English law—may not be available and in any event the institution of the

---

61. Platteau (2000, p. 152).

trust evokes a culture distant from most traditional societies in the developing world.[62]

Another kind of problem involves fraud in the land registration process. Lawyers in developed countries might classify this problem as a law enforcement matter, but in the field it is more often classified as "land grabbing." Platteau summarizes documented examples in Kenya where "clever, well-informed or powerful (and usually educated) individuals . . . often successfully jockey to have parcels not previously theirs registered in their own name while the mass of rural people are generally unaware of the new land provisions or do not grasp the implications of registration." He also refers to a "few well-connected Kenyans who succeeded in having pasture lands registered in their own names on the ground that they would bring them into cultivation" whereas "their intent was not to exploit the land in question but just to use it as collateral in order to obtain loans from banks in Nairobi" for personal purposes; the borrowers intended from the outset not to repay the loans but to allow the land to be foreclosed.[63] In peri-urban areas where wealthy city dwellers are intent on real estate development in nearby formerly agricultural areas, fraud and corruption in the titling process may lead the farm population to perceive titling as more of a threat than a benefit.

In a developed country with the rule of law, a few well-publicized criminal prosecutions might stamp out such unfortunate practices. But such frauds are more likely in poor rural areas of the developing world where the rule of law itself is still in question and where neither the legal and administrative infrastructure nor the countryside literacy required to build confidence in the intention and integrity of the new system has yet been developed. At least in Africa, feelings of resentment and jealousy toward groups that benefited from land registration led to social tensions and a reassertion of tribal and clan rights, even to the extent of rewriting history to reinforce those rights. These feelings have been exacerbated by ethnic tensions where one ethnic group sees itself losing by land registration to a stronger, wealthier ethnic group.[64]

In sum, registration of agricultural land may be an important stimulus to economic development, but its adoption is likely to be resisted by many peo-

62. According to Johnston (1988), the trust was available under Roman law, and Helmholz and Zimmermann (1998) find that equivalents of the trust have been worked out in some civil law countries.

63. Platteau (2000, p. 166).

64. Platteau (2000, pp. 164–77) and sources cited therein.

ple in the developing world who would ultimately benefit by the economic advantages it could bring over time. Resistance to registration may also stem from tribal traditions and social mores demanding that land that belonged to ancestors should be kept. At least in earlier decades local violence and more subtle forms of resistance were used to keep ancestral land in some African countries out of the hands of outsiders, particularly foreigners.[65]

Communal Land

Land titling and transferability apply to land that is already in private hands (what is often called freehold tenure). But what of land that remains owned by tribes or other group entities?

The question of communal (often called customary tenure) land is extremely important. In many developing countries, communal land, operating under traditional institutions, predates not just independence but colonization itself. With few exceptions, issues involving communal land are outside the formal legal system. In Africa, for example, only 2–10 percent of the total land area is covered under the formal legal system. Disputes that arise, therefore, have to be dealt with by customary institutions—say, within the tribe or clan—and no effective resort to the regular courts is possible because the national substantive land law simply does not apply. In general, colonial powers applied their own law to their citizens and often to disputes between citizens and the native population, but the native population was left to its own customary law. Until such time as land is titled and registered, a developing country may have no way of applying national rules concerning land. As a result, Deininger found, "in Africa, customary institutions administer virtually all of the land area, including some peri-urban areas with high land values where demand for land transactions and more formal property rights is increasing."[66]

In some cases, past and present, communal ownership has stood in the way of efficient economic development. U.S. history is rife with examples. The two most famous American settlements, Jamestown and Plymouth, started off with communal ownership, but both soon switched to individual ownership. The results for productivity were positive, and in both cases, the switch may have been just in time for survival.[67]

---

65. Platteau (2000, pp. 152, 154–55).
66. Deininger (2003, p. 62).
67. Ellickson (1993, pp. 1335–41).

It would be a mistake, however, to conclude that all communal ownership is so inefficient that it is an obstacle to economic development. The most common communal arrangement involves plots controlled by individuals with, say, pasture and perhaps hunting areas subject to open access for members of the community—but not open to access by outsiders. In many cases, the strips are scattered. But where the tribe or clan is sufficiently close-knit, with local governance and social norms ensuring compliance with the strip boundaries, there is no problem of a tragedy of the commons because the communal property is not truly open access property. Indeed, an advantage is that only the land of the community as a whole has to be fenced to keep out animals and perhaps strangers.

The communal property arrangements are under a special legal system—communal law administered by the tribe or clan. Often the individual plots can be bought and sold, albeit within the tribe or clan. And they often can be inherited. Thus a good deal of legal certainty obtains, but as the foregoing discussion of titling and land registration indicates, these arrangements are not optimum for economic development of the kind enjoyed in the developed world. That does not necessarily mean that communal property arrangements are not efficient within the communal land area itself, at least where exchange and sale among members of the community can occur and rights are inheritable.

Larger questions arise where population pressures, encroachment of urban life, and discontinuities cause communal systems to break down. Certainly the unorganized squalor on the outskirts of some developing country cities (which is presumably what de Soto had in mind in the Lima area that he researched) is not an example of communal property at all. Here the new residents often have no property rights, either individually or through their membership in a communal property group. A confusion between communal property and "unofficial" settlements simply clouds understanding and analysis.

As already discussed, communal pasture and hunting areas are normally open-access land, but only to members of the community. If outsiders can be kept out, then it is up to local governance and social norms to prevent the "overgrazing" that the tragedy of the commons postulates. In effect, some kind of quota system has to be worked out, explicitly or implicitly, if pasture and hunting land proves scarce. Here again one can see that private ownership would in principle be better for economic development. Nonetheless, even the common areas have something to be said for them, again so long as nonmembers of the community can be kept out. Not only are fences dividing pasture and hunting areas of the community unnecessary, but it is possible to take advantage of certain efficiencies; for example, one part of the common pasture area may be better in certain seasons than other parts and hence the ability of herds of all farmers to move with the season may be an efficiency consideration that offsets any tendency toward overgrazing.

Another Look at History

The discussion thus far suggests that the process of moving to a market economy in land is likely to be evolutionary rather than purely technocratic. Legal transplants can help, but only if the supporting legal infrastructure is in place, and even then results in most countries are likely to be measured in years, if not decades. This conclusion is all the more important for the process of moving from communal to individual ownership. Again the lessons of northern Europe some centuries ago, especially the conflict involved in the enclosure movement, suggest that attitudes and practices involving something as fundamental as land are likely to take at least one or two generations to change.

Although communal land systems today unquestionably differ greatly from country to country, even within a region such as sub-Saharan Africa, the resemblance of the economic aspects of traditional communal tenure arrangements to the historical situation in northern Europe before the enclosure movement is nevertheless remarkable. Although the details in northern Europe differed from country to country, the well-documented system in England conveys the strengths and weaknesses of communal ownership. It also shows that a country's land system can evolve successfully, though not without controversy, from communal to individual ownership over a period of time.

Beginning at least as far back as the fifteenth century and continuing until parliamentary legislation became the standard method in the mid-eighteenth century, the enclosure movement in the English Midlands involved converting communal land to private ownership through mutually agreed transactions among all members of the community (the "proprietors") or bilaterally between two of them, such as by purchase or exchange.[68] As land became less plentiful and population increased, controversy arose as to the impact of enclosures on the poor. Finally, beginning in the mid-eighteenth century enclosures pursuant to private acts of parliament increased, and in 1801 a General Enclosure Act created a procedure for enclosure.[69]

68. Allen (1992, pp. 27–28).
69. "Enclosure," *Encyclopædia Britannica 2003*.

The structure of "open fields" in England resembles communal property in much of today's developing world. Individual farmers had strips within a community, and there was a common pasture. The strips could be sold or exchanged, the common pasture was available to all members of the community, and even the strips were open to pasture when no crops were being grown on them.

Strip farming had its disadvantages. The strips were often so small that plows could be used only in the lengthwise direction of a given strip, and even if a given farmer's lands might be more rectangular in shape, a farmer's separate plots might be too widely spaced to permit efficient use. As McCloskey described, "A moderately prosperous peasant would hold his 20 acres in 20 plots scattered over the face of a village the size of Central Park."[70] But many villages did not even have plots of that one-acre average size, and in many cases a farmer's lands would be spread over many more plots. Turner points to a village in Lincolnshire where a 105-acre farm was separated into 162 separate plots and to a farm in Buckinghamshire where a Mr. Yates, though he had 78.5 acres, had to farm them in 218 separate plots.[71]

But there were advantages to the open fields system as well. One was that fences were not necessary, except perhaps around the village as a whole, although, of course, a shepherding or other arrangement had to be used to keep the sheep and cattle out of the crops during part of the year. The absence of fences was a substantial cost saving to the agricultural economy. Other advantages were that the separate strips might have had diversification or insurance payoffs since the quality of land and even the temperatures might vary from one plot to another; hence the farmer could specialize within his own acreage by matching plants to soil and frost conditions, while at the same time not putting "all of his eggs in one basket."[72]

From Communal Property to Individual Property

Given the advantages of communal property arrangements and the political sensitivity of any changes that might threaten individual economic well-being and even survival, one policy implication is that the transition from communal ownership to individual ownership has to be handled carefully. The history of Côte d'Ivoire, which committed itself to a transition to full

70. McCloskey (1991, p. 344).
71. Turner (1986, pp. 671–72).
72. McCloskey (1989, pp. 34–46); see also H. Smith (2000).

nationwide individual ownership within ten years, is instructive. The task (which, remember, includes surveys, demarcation of boundaries, a registration process involving a large governmental staff, and more) was simply too much for an inadequate bureaucracy. It has been suggested that the recent civil war in that country is not unrelated to the difficulties created by the land tenure conversion effort. Fortunately, alternatives exist permitting the upgrading of tenure security over time as opposed to a one-shot conversion from communal to pure individual ownership. An experiment along such gradualist lines was carried out in Namibia. Similarly, Botswana has successfully used gradualism to make the transitions.[73]

Certainly a move from communal ownership, however much tempered by individual use rights, to full-fledged individual titles and land registration is likely to meet some resistance. One constraint that has sometimes stood in the way of thoroughgoing titling and registration reforms is a set of social norms that conflict with the individualistic philosophy of the reforms. One particular problem, for example, has been the difficulty of assuring women the right to participate in ownership and registration upon the death of a spouse, especially where the prior communal systems subordinated their rights to those of their husband or extended family.[74]

A different kind of problem arises in those countries such as China, Ethiopia, and Mexico in which collective ownership was imposed in the wake of revolutions. The consequence was that neither local governance nor social norms worked to ameliorate the negative economic effects of the resulting "communal" system. The negative consequences of such forced communalization can be found in the Mexican *ejido* system introduced in the 1920s and 1930s, and not comprehensively reformed until 1992.[75] Under the *ejido* system, investment fell, the work became more labor intensive, and even crop choice was biased toward short-term payoffs.[76] The reformed system provides for full privatization, including land registration, and the ability to mortgage land. In some parts of Mexico, however, farmers have been reluctant to take advantage of such titling, in part because taxes on privatized land rise sharply, surely a counterproductive approach to improving productivity and farm incomes.[77]

China has used a gradualist approach by implementing, through the household responsibility system, individual use rights in the early 1980s. This

73. Deininger (2003, pp. 64, 65, 52).
74. Deininger (2003, pp. 57–62).
75. Deininger (2003, pp. 121–22).
76. De Alessi (2003, p. 103).
77. Brown (2004, p. 2).

approach has ameliorated the effects of collectivization and has had a good effect on productivity and output. China, however, has had neither local governance nor the social norms that give effective rights to individual farmers under traditional communal systems to cushion the transition. For example, corruption and abuses of power by village authorities were reasons why the degree of tenure security varied greatly from village to village and why the Chinese government moved more recently to deal with those problems.[78] In 2003 a rural land contracting law became effective, giving farmers thirty-year use rights to their land, subject to some limitations. Abuses by local government and party officials remain a problem, however.[79]

Similarly, urban property owners have found little protection of their land use rights. Four million residents in Shanghai and Beijing were evicted without compensation between 1991 and 2003.[80] Although some cities have acted to allow mortgages, the legal basis for mortgages is not uniformly available across China. Moreover, as the 2005 prospectus for a Hong Kong offering of shares of China Construction Bank, one of China's largest banks, makes clear:

> The procedures for liquidating or otherwise realizing the value of collateral of borrowers in China may be protracted, and the enforcement process in China may be difficult. As a result, it may be difficult and time-consuming for banks to take control of or liquidate the collateral securing non-performing loans. Furthermore, according to a judicial interpretation issued by the Supreme Court of the PRC . . . courts may not foreclose on, auction off, or otherwise liquidate collateral if such collateral is the borrower's essential residence. Accordingly, we may be unable to realize the expected value on collateral in a timely manner or at all.[81]

Nevertheless, the reforms show that the central government has attempted to guide the evolution of land holdings toward a more efficient system despite the reluctance of local authorities who fear loss of flexibility and, no doubt in some cases, of opportunities for personal gain.

78. Deininger (2003, p. 55, box 2.2).
79. Ping Li (2003). The 2003 law followed on a 1993 decision by the Communist Party to the same effect; see Lubman (1999, p. 184). According to a World Bank survey, at about the turn of the century some 55 percent of farmers had signed a thirty-year contract but only 12 percent felt it would "definitely prevent [administrative] reallocations, and 46 percent felt that reallocations will definitely continue despite the new policy" (Lohman Somwaru, and Wiebe 2002).
80. Wilhelm (2004, p. 231).
81. China Construction Bank Corporation (2005, p. 23).

Another approach involves starting by giving official legal status to existing communal institutions. Colombia, for example, has introduced collective land titling for particular indigenous groups.[82] In Mozambique a 1997 statute recognized customary rights of individuals but gave communities what amounts to titles and registration. At the time, some twenty different customary systems were operating (which was one reason why giving land titles to individuals was beyond the fiscal and bureaucratic capacity of the country). And while the system does not provide the credit advantages of individual titling and registration, it does provide a system by which individuals can transfer their land, and it also allows the community to negotiate with outsiders for the exploitation of natural resources.[83]

An increasing number of countries simply recognize in their formal legal systems the validity of individual rights under existing communal systems. This approach, which bows to the fiscal and bureaucratic difficulties of full-scale individual titling and registration, is only a small step in the direction of a market economy approach to economic development.

Nonetheless, formal legal recognition of individual rights to a plot in a larger tract of communal land may have some economic value. Indeed, as suggested earlier in this chapter, such recognition of individual rights already exists in many communal systems. However, traditional communal law frequently gives elders or chiefs the power to reallocate some or all of a plot, where, for example, they conclude that the owners are not properly working the plot. Since naturally at least some neighbors want more land, the resulting pressures for reallocation cause current owners to be cautious, especially about taking part-time jobs off the farm because they fear it may lead to land being reallocated away from them. Since "greater involvement by rural households in the off-farm economy is widely recognized as a critical pre-condition for broad-based rural development," protecting farmers against reallocation through the formal legal system can assist national economic development.[84] Although the quantitative effect on labor supply of threatened land reallocation is difficult to isolate, comprehensive titling and registration have on average increased labor supply by households in Peru substantially.[85]

In sum, communal land systems need not be inefficient and therefore automatically in need of conversion to individual ownership. But that conclusion may be irrelevant where the forces of economic and population

82. Plant and Hvalkof (2001, pp. 33–34).
83. Tanner (2002).
84. Deininger and others (2003).
85. Field (2004, pp. 860–61).

expansion encroach upon communal land. Expansion of cities, new mining and logging ventures, and discovery of oil resources are examples of the kinds of economic changes that can undermine communal systems when the changes encroach on the boundaries of communal land. Then property arrangements will have to be modified, and the tactical issue for the country is whether to attempt to safeguard the communal land system or to adjust to the encroaching reality by a transition to individual freehold ownership.

In any event, for countries with substantial indigenous populations, a change in substantive land law is clearly a major economic development decision. Titling is important, but the implementation of a titling program is fraught with administrative, financial, and even human capital issues involving surveys and registration systems. And, as in so many other areas of substantive law, even a successful implementation of a titling program will run into longer-term difficulties if the judiciary does not possess integrity and competence.

The Financial Sector

Any study of the role of law and legal institutions in economic development must pay particular attention to the financial sector. The reasons are many.

The importance of the financial sector is well established. The link between financial development and growth of per capita gross domestic product has been the subject of extensive studies, which have established that banking and stock market development are good predictors of economic growth.[1] Some studies directly address the issue of whether financial development actually causes growth and conclude that it does, despite the fact that causation is always a difficult question in cross-country econometric studies showing a correlation between variables.[2] Finally, some recent research establishes that a strong financial sector not only tends to cause economic growth but, somewhat contrary to political fashion that associates finance with the wealthy, financial development actually lessens inequality and thereby reduces poverty.[3]

The link between the strength of a country's legal system and the development of its financial sector has also been well studied. Most of the legal origins articles involve the financial sector of the economy. And even those who are skeptical of the thesis that some legal origins (say, common law) promote economic development better than others (say, civil law, especially French

1. Levine and Zervos (1998); Rajan and Zingales (1998); Beck and Levine (2004); Beck, Demirgüç-Kunt, and Levine (2004b); Levine (2004); Demirgüç-Kunt (2006).
2. Levine, Loayza, and Beck (2000). See survey of research in Levine (2004). For an economic history perspective, see Sylla (2002).
3. Beck, Demirgüç-Kunt, and Levine (2004a).

law) are nonetheless left with the conclusion that law plays a vital role, at least in financial sector development.

From a historical point of view, the development of the financial sector created the most severe problems of separating the quid and the quo, as discussed in chapter 4. The very definition of a financial transaction is that the time of performance of the two parties to a financial contract is different. In a credit transaction, the borrower receives the money up front and the creditor is paid only later. Even in equity transactions, as in the issuance of stock in a corporation, the payment for the stock may take place at the same time as the issuance, but in the absence of a secondary market for corporate stock, the value of the investment to the stockholder will be determined only by cash flow and control rights as they work out in practice. Hence the reasons that a creditor might distrust a debtor corporation could equally cause a stockholder to distrust the management of the corporation. In the absence of an effective legal system, trust has not proved sufficient to support the development of a broad-based financial sector. Just as long-distance trade developed only slowly, so too financial transactions and the financial sector of the economy developed slowly in an evolutionary process.

From a legal point of view, finance is mostly about contracts. This is the case for a simple extension of credit (since a loan involves a contractual obligation to pay interest and repay the principal) but also for bank loans, which typically involve complicated written contracts. In the United States, for example, these contracts typically contain numerous conditions and covenants concerning the creditor's right to exercise control rights or to accelerate the due date in the event of certain contingencies.[4]

The point applies even to equity finance. Certainly the pooling of assets by partners in an enterprise is based on a partnership contract. The same is true of an agreement among investors to create a corporation. Once formed, the corporation and the shares themselves are types of property. And so both of the main economic strands of the rule of law—the enforcement of contracts and the protection of property—come into play.

On the question of corporations, one encounters some other strands of the rule-of-law concept. As we have seen, one of the great historical problems was how property owners were to be protected from a predatory ruler. The analogy here, and it is remarkably close, is how minority shareholders in a corporation are to be protected from efforts by a predatory controlling

---

4. Baird and Rasmussen (2005).

shareholder to take away the value of the holdings of the minority by expropriating corporate assets. A comparable problem arises, especially with widely held corporations, where the managers of the corporation seek to appropriate to their own use and ownership the assets or cash flow of the corporation. Just as control of the state is a question of governance, it is no accident that this last question is normally discussed today as a question of corporate governance.

The discussion in part III is divided into two chapters, roughly comparable to the difference between equity and debt. In the first chapter, questions involving corporations, shareholders, and managers are discussed. The second chapter focuses on debtor-creditor relations. Note that borrowers are sometimes individuals and sometimes corporations. Corporations sometimes borrow from banks but other times issue bonds. When they issue bonds to the public, the problems are analogous in some respects to issuing stock to the public.

It is, admittedly, somewhat artificial to separate the discussion of equity and debt, at least in the context of particular countries. For one thing, countries differ with respect to their institutional and legal characteristics. In some countries corporations are typically more heavily indebted than in other countries. That is often the case where public issuance of equity securities is difficult for legal or other reasons. But it is also the case that in most countries bank loans and retained earnings are the main source of capital for the corporate world.

Even in countries where equity capital plays a major role, only two countries—the United States and the United Kingdom—have corporate sectors primarily based on widespread ownership of stock, dispersed broadly among both individuals and financial institutions. In most other countries, including Western European countries and Japan but especially in developing countries, the role of the dominant shareholders is crucial. Even in the United States and the United Kingdom, publicly held corporations typically have debt in their capital structure, either loans—usually from banks—or debt securities. Much attention has been paid to the optimal financial structure, referring to the relative use of different kinds of equity—common stock and various forms of preferred stock—and of various forms of debt. Research has shown that legal characteristics of different countries can affect those choices.[5]

---

5. Kaplan, Martel, and Strömberg (2003); Lerner and Schoar (2004); Doidge, Karolyi, and Stulz (2004); Bottazzi, Da Rin, and Hellman (2005).

In addition, different investors have different objectives, depending on their relative appetite for risk versus return. Because in most countries it is possible to go beyond "plain vanilla" equity and debt to create special corporate securities having different mixes of equity and debt characteristics, investors can achieve their special objectives by selecting a security having the appropriate mix. For example, an investor preferring a regular guaranteed income and anxious to have priority in bankruptcy ahead of common stockholders, but also hoping to benefit from the upside of especially strong corporate performance, might seek to buy a convertible bond (an instrument that pays interest but is convertible to common stock at an agreed price). In short, such a security protects against the downside while still permitting participation on the upside.

The legal characteristics of the country and the preferences of the investor interact. Where bankruptcy law is defective and a creditor cannot count on priority access to a failing corporation's assets, the investor may choose to invest in senior equity instead—say, a convertible preferred stock. Such a security would ensure that so long as any dividends are paid, the investor would be paid dividends before common stockholders were paid, but would also assure an upside opportunity to convert into common stock at an agreed price.

These examples of different kinds of securities could be multiplied; the main point is simply that the dichotomy between equity and debt can be overemphasized if the focus is on any specific investment opportunity. But for the purpose of analyzing the protection of property and the enforcement of contracts in different developing countries, the equity-debt distinction is useful.

Equity Markets and the Corporation

Modern economies are heavily dependent on the corporate form of doing business. The sheer scale of modern commercial activity, once it goes beyond the individual store and workshop, increasingly demands capital beyond the resources of most individual entrepreneurs. Although the capital needs could in some cases be met by partnership, the partnership form has proved rather inflexible and is used primarily by very small enterprises and by the professions.[1] The use of companies to pool large sums of capital and therefore to raise capital for large new commercial ventures has been increasingly common since the Dutch and English East India companies were organized at the beginning of the seventeenth century.[2] By the twentieth century corporations had become the dominant organizational vehicle for commercial ventures almost without exception throughout the world.

The Corporation in Historical Perspective

The corporation was an institution that helped to solve the long-distance trade problem of early Europe, just as were the various enforcement institutions

1. In the United States, some professional organizations using the partnership form—such as accounting and law firms—have taken advantage of various special statutory entity forms, such as limited liability partnerships and limited liability corporations, that grant limited liability but cannot be easily used as a source of large-scale capital from public investors. Allen and Kraakman (2003, pp. 76–79); Hansmann, Kraakman, and Squire (2006, pp. 53–54). The choice of these limited liability organizational forms is often dictated by tax considerations.

2. See "East India Company and Dutch East India Company," *Encyclopedia Britannica Online*. There were precedents for the English East India Company, the first of which was perhaps the Russia Company of 1553 (Scott 1912, p. 18).

(surveyed in an earlier chapter) that helped to bridge the problems created when goods and payment—the quid and the quo—were not exchanged at the same time.[3] At least in England the corporation was much more important in long-distance trade than it was in domestic commerce. The English East India Company received a charter from the Crown in 1600.[4] But companies had existed for centuries before they were used for economic ends. In England they had been "regulated companies" limited to nonprofit purposes.[5] Only after regulated companies began to be chartered by the Crown for trading purposes were they gradually superseded by joint stock companies.[6] Those joint stock companies were not chartered by the state but rather represented a private sector contractual arrangement.[7] Over time transferability of shares of joint stock companies became common de facto if not de jure, and only later did limited liability become common. That shareholders could not be held liable for the debts of the company was not fully established until Parliament enacted the limited liability acts of 1855 and 1856.[8]

Even in the early days of the trading company, these predecessors of the modern corporation provided a means for assembling capital from a large number of merchants sufficient to finance the especially large ships that, sailing beyond the protection of the Royal Navy, had to be armed. Capital was also needed to pay the crew and cover provisioning costs for the two to three years required to sail to the Indian subcontinent and beyond to the Spice Islands and Java and return with valuable and exotic cargo.[9] To undertake such ventures through partnerships would have had a number of disadvantages. With several hundred partners, the legal mechanics would have been unwieldy.[10] Partnership law would probably have required a new partnership

3. Kindleberger (1984, p. 196). See chapter 4 on the separation of the quid and the quo.

4. A historical issue is whether the English or the Dutch East India Company was first. It appears that the Dutch were the first to send regular sea voyages to East Asia but the English were the first to charter a company, the Dutch East India Company (VOC) having received a charter only in 1602 (Harris 2005).

5. See J. Davis (1905) for a survey of the use of corporations, which stresses their use for ecclesiastical, municipal, guild, educational, and eleemosynary purposes in feudal and early modern Europe. Davis's second volume continues the survey, including a discussion of the transition to the use of regulated companies and then joint stock companies.

6. See generally Evans (1908, pp. 339–45).

7. Hansmann, Kraakman, and Squire (2006, p. 45).

8. Scott (1912, pp. 442–43) states that "from an early period in England, shares were bought and sold with a considerable degree of freedom." Scott refers to a sixteenth century example, that is, before the East India Company was organized. See discussion in Harris (2000, pp. 17–132) and Blumberg (1986, pp. 577–86).

9. Harris (2004, pp. 10–11).

10. Harris (2000, p. 21).

agreement each time a particular partner died; one or more of the London-based merchants backing the voyage almost certainly would have died during the lengthy voyages, requiring a new partnership agreement. Kuran has made a powerful case that the failure of Islamic law to permit business in corporate form was a major impediment to economic development, especially in Arab countries, at least until the corporate form was added to those countries' menu of legal choices under the influence of colonial powers.[11]

In the case of the East India Company ventures, the pattern of creating a separate company for each voyage or group of voyages developed, diversifying the risk across multiple ventures.[12] After all, sailing to and from Asia was risky at the beginning of the seventeenth century, and in the early years not all safely completed voyages yielded net profits.[13] The East India Company was an early example of drawing capital not just from entrepreneurs themselves (and their families) but also from passive investors.[14] Although the East India entrepreneurs at first used the regulated company form with separate accounts for each voyage, they later turned to separate joint stock companies that apparently did not have either a royal or a parliamentary charter; their legal characteristics were murky. Later, however, the East India Company itself was given a longer-term monopoly of England-India trade and with it a charter, by this time as a permanent joint stock company.[15]

Parliament later became the source of the privilege of incorporation in England, while in the United States, the legislatures of the several states began to grant corporate charters. Inevitably the practice of granting individual charters led to a merger of politics and business. The problem was not so much that a businessman might bribe politicians to obtain a charter, but that politics would drive business activity to the advantage of particular politicians. In other words, "venal corruption" was not the problem but rather, in the useful dichotomy of Wallis, "systematic corruption." The latter term, according to Wallis, embodies "the idea that political actors manipulated the economic system to create economic rents that politicians could use to secure control of the government."[16] This merger of politics and business thus created a serious rule-of-law problem from both the political and the economic

11. Kuran (2003, 2004b).
12. Baskin and Miranti (1997, p. 64); Chaudhuri (1965, pp. 208–09).
13. Chaudhuri (1965, p. 212); Baskin and Miranti (1997, p. 72).
14. Chaudhuri (1965, p. 33).
15. Harris (2004, p. 31); Evans (1908, pp. 349–50). The sequence of the different forms in which the East India enterprise functioned in the early years is not entirely clear. See also Scott (1912, pp. 150–65) and Chaudhuri (1965).
16. Wallis (2004).

perspectives. Consequently, the move to free incorporation in England in 1844, calling for articles of incorporation to be issued under administrative procedures to all entrepreneurs meeting statutorily prescribed standards, was a major step toward a rule of law.[17]

Even though the joint stock company was the predecessor of the modern corporation, it did not acquire all at once the hallmarks of the modern corporation, such as limited liability, legal personality, and transferable shares. As in so many aspects of economic development, the legal framework evolved. Before limited liability was enacted for all corporate entities in England in 1855 and 1856, it was used only for large-scale undertakings such as canals and railroads and had to be approved by an act of Parliament.[18] In the United States limited liability had become available slightly earlier, in the 1830s, in some leading commercial states.[19] But limited liability in its entirety did not reach California until 1931.[20]

Whatever the validity of the legal origins hypothesis in the contemporary world, it does not mean that common law countries were more progressive in legal evolution than continental countries, especially France. Take, for instance, the example of limited partnership. American lawyers and businessmen strongly approve of the concept of limited partnerships (in which some partners invest but, not being managers, are not responsible for the partnership's debts beyond the value of their investment). Napoleon introduced limited partnerships in 1807 in his commercial code, but the English judiciary held that limited partnerships could not be recognized without a parliamentary statute. Supporting this ruling was the simple-minded notion that such partnerships had always been contrary to the common law—an interesting reason given the widespread idea that the common law is more flexible and more keyed to commercial needs than is continental code writing.[21] (Harris observes that British judges were from the tight-knit rank of barristers, who were overwhelmingly from the landed classes, had few acquaintances among the merchant class, and even dealt with their merchant clients through intermediary solicitors; his observation suggests that the common law of the time was truly autonomous and that any flexibility in it was strictly intellectual, not a response to economic changes.[22]) In any case, the French economy benefited

17. On free incorporation, see Lamoreaux and Rosenthal (2005) and Harris (2000, pp. 282–86).

18. Blumberg (1986, pp. 583–85).

19. Baskin and Miranti (1997, p. 141).

20. Blumberg (1986, pp. 597–99).

21. Harris (2000, p. 30); see also Lamoreaux and Rosenthal (2005, p. 33).

22. Harris (2000, pp. 230–49, especially pp. 231–32).

from limited partnerships for half a century before England got around to confirming the availability of limited liability for corporations in 1856 and for a century before Parliament passed the Limited Partnership Act of 1907.[23]

Turning from legal rules to financial development, a problem with the legal origins hypothesis is that it appears to apply among developed countries only to the post–World War II world. Rajan and Zingales find that "financial markets in countries with a Civil Law system were not less developed than those in countries with Common Law in 1913 and in 1929 but only after World War II." Their data show that France had 13.29 listed companies per million people in 1913 whereas the United States had only 4.75. As late as 1960 France had twice as many listed companies per million people as the United States. The United States surpassed France only during the 1970s, long after—it might be noted—nearly all French law countries in today's developing world had become independent. Similarly, the data show that in 1913 the percentage of gross fixed capital raised in public equity offers was roughly the same in France and Britain and more than three times greater than in the United States.[24] Thus the notion that French law condemned French law countries to inferior equity markets seems poorly supported historically within the developed world.

Advantages of the Corporation Today

The corporate form spread because it had several advantages beyond the pooling of capital. One of those advantages, as previously noted, is limited liability of the shareholders, which simply means that the corporation is liable for its debts but its shareholders are not; shareholders are liable only for their own debts and can lose only what they have already invested in the corporation. Limited liability tends to promote risk-taking (though founders of new enterprises find that they may have to guarantee the corporation's debts to induce creditors to provide loans).

Another advantage is that the corporation has a legal personality, meaning that it can enter into contracts without requiring the signature of its shareholder owners or indeed without even consulting them, at least for contracts in the ordinary course of business. But legal personality also has advantages from the standpoint of property rights and liability. The protection of the corporation's assets from the creditors of the shareholders has been called "entity shielding" (or alternatively "affirmative asset partitioning") because it

23. Harris (2000, p. 30).
24. Rajan and Zingales (2003a, pp. 42; 17, table 5; 16, table 4).

permits a corporation to own assets and thereby to borrow on the strength of its asset position or even to pledge the assets directly as collateral.[25] Limited liability and entity shielding are thus mutually reinforcing effects from the standpoint of the economy for they create what Hansmann and Kraakman call "a default regime whereby a shareholder's personal assets are pledged as security to his personal creditors, while corporation assets are reserved for corporation creditors":

> In an enterprise of any substantial magnitude, this allocation generally increases the value of both types of assets as security for debt. It permits creditors of the corporation to have first claim on the corporation's assets, which those creditors have a comparative advantage in evaluating and monitoring. Conversely, it permits an individual's personal creditors to have first claim on personal assets, which those creditors are in a good position to evaluate and monitor and which creditors of the corporation, conversely, are not in a good position to check. As a consequence, legal personality and limited liability together can reduce the overall cost of capital to the firm and its owners.[26]

Although this explanation may appear rather abstract, it makes especially good sense when applied to large corporations with widely diversified ownership and many individual equity investors. In these circumstances, the sources of credit for the corporation are likely to be completely different financial institutions from those that finance the individual investors. Whether those advantages of the corporate form are as great in developing countries may depend on the development and diversity of finance-providing institutions.

These advantages of the corporate form are intimately tied up with a legal characteristic that puts the individual shareholder in a different situation from an individual creditor and therefore is at the root of the difference between equity and debt as a source of capital for the corporation. The corporation is in principle perpetual and therefore the shareholder cannot demand that the corporation cash out his shares. A share of stock does not mature and become payable (though it is true that so-called preferred shares are sometimes callable by the corporation).[27] A creditor, whether a bond-holder or an ordinary creditor, is, of course, tied up for the agreed term of the

---

25. Hansmann, Kraakman, and Squire (2006).
26. Hansmann and Kraakman (2004c, p. 9).
27. For a general discussion of lock-in, see Stout (2004); see also Blair (2003).

bond or debt. But a creditor, unlike a shareholder, can agree on a short term or can even insist that the debt be payable on demand. The lock-in effect of shareholding is satisfactory to large numbers of shareholders, of course, only in conjunction with the transferable share, a circumstance that is usually considered a further advantage of the corporation.[28] But the key is the lock-in effect because it means that the corporation is not dissolvable, as in the case of a partnership, when one of the owners dies or simply wants out.

The transferability of shares, in contrast to the partnership, underpins the perpetual life characteristic of corporations and is thus another advantage of the corporate form. Transferability also provides liquidity to shareholders, and it supports savings and investment by individuals by providing opportunities, through investment in many companies, to build a diversified portfolio, thereby reducing risk. Finally, in the twentieth century the advantage of the corporation in the hiring of professional management began to be important in many developed countries, although even in publicly held corporations dominant shareholders still often hold management positions, especially in the developing world.[29]

All of these advantages of the corporation add up to a great strength for an economy. A prime function of a financial system is channeling funds from the ultimate savers in a society to enterprises that will invest those funds in productive uses, and the corporation has proved to be efficient for gathering funds for such uses. Although the corporation can borrow, it is particularly attractive for those investors who are willing to be last in priority in the case of corporate insolvency in order to be entitled to a potentially greater return in the event of corporate profitability—which is from the investor's viewpoint the fundamental distinction between equity and debt.

Legal Origins Analysis of Equity Markets

The characteristics of the corporation and the status of shareholders are defined by law. Some of the underlying rules of corporate law have proved better for economic development than others. But as in the other legal fields surveyed in other chapters, the greater difference among countries lies in the enforcement of the rules rather than in their exact content. Nonetheless, the legal origins literature places great emphasis on the substantive rules of corporate law.

---

28. Hansmann and Kraakman (2001, pp. 439–40).
29. Hansmann and Kraakman (2001, pp. 450–51, 453).

A close look at the methodology of the LLSV study on law and finance shows how the legal origins approach works in practice. The six substantive law rules that were characterized by LLSV as "anti-director rights" were "proxy by mail allowed," which makes it possible for shareholders to vote without physically showing up at shareholder meetings; "shares not blocked before meeting," which precludes companies from requiring deposit of shares as a prerequisite to shareholder voting and thereby limiting sales and purchases for a period before and even after shareholder meetings; "cumulative voting" or "proportional representation," which allows a minority to obtain representation on the board; "oppressed minorities mechanism," which allows minority shareholders one or more of several remedies in the case of fundamental transactions such as mergers; "preemptive rights," which make it more difficult for controlling shareholders to dilute the voting power or value of minority shareholders' interests; and "percentage of share capital to call an extraordinary shareholder meeting," which if kept low gives minority shareholders the power to appeal to shareholders as a group.[30]

With respect to the first five antidirector rights, which have a binary character, each of the countries in the LLSV survey were given a one if the right was accorded by substantive law, and a zero if the right was not accorded. The sixth antidirector right, not being binary, was scaled to give a one where the percentage was at or below the world median of 10 percent and a zero otherwise. The sums of these scores were then added, with the possible antidirector rights score ranging from 0.0 to 6.0. (Other substantive law provisions that might bear on shareholder rights included "one-share, one-vote," which preclude dual class shares, and "mandatory dividend." These were also scored, but they can be ignored for present purposes because they played little role in subsequent legal origins analyses.)

The country scores were averaged across legal family (English, French, German, and Scandinavian origin) to give a score for each legal origin. The higher the score, the greater the protection to minority shareholders the legal family was credited with giving. In racing terms, one can observe from these averages that English origin came in far ahead with 4.00 compared with French origin and German origin in a dead heat for last at 2.33, with Scandinavian origin in between at 3.00. Statistical tests showed that differences between English origin and the three civil law origins were significant, indeed significant at a high level (the 1 percent level) for the difference between common law and French and German law.

---

30. La Porta and others (1998, pp. 1122–25, table 6, and 1126–28).

These kinds of cross-country statistical tests often evoke quite different responses from economists and lawyers. For most economists and many social scientists, such statistical analyses are necessary to come up with valid general propositions that are more than impressions. For many lawyers, in contrast, general propositions are inherently suspect, especially if they are based on giving legal rules ones and zeros or otherwise simplifying the richness of detail that one finds in any legal field. In large part this difference lies in the training and perspective of economists and lawyers; economists are trained to find general principles that lie beneath the churning and discontinuous surface of life, while lawyers are trained to distinguish factually between cases that for most people seem to be much the same.

Even from a lawyer's perspective, the results in the legal origins literature are rather powerful. But on further examination (and putting to one side the kind of discrepancies in the classification of countries discussed in chapter 2), some anomalies can be perceived in the investor protection results.

In the first place, one can question the choice of antidirector rights. Preemptive rights, for example, under which existing shareholders have the right to participate in any new issuance of equity by subscribing to the offer, have long since virtually disappeared from the scene in the United States.[31] And they have disappeared for the good reason that they have costs to the corporation and to the economy. Preemptive rights, wrote Rock, Kanda, and Kraakman,

> delay new issues of shares by forcing companies to solicit their own shareholders before turning to the market. They also limit management's ability to issue blocks of shares with significant voting power. Both constraints reduce a company's ability to raise equity capital, which may explain why the EU's Second Company Directive permits those Member states that allow authorized but unissued shares to also allow shareholders to waive pre-emption rights. These constraints may also explain why both Japan and the U.S. states have abandoned preemptive rights as the statutory default, and why Japanese and U.S. shareholders almost never attempt to override this default by writing preemptive rights into their corporate charters.[32]

All U.S. states now make preemptive rights only an optional term in corporate charters.[33] This is in fact one of the examples of the movement of

---

31. Allen and Kraakman (2003).
32. Rock, Kanda, and Kraakman (2004, p. 148).
33. Cox, Hazen, and O'Neal (1997, p. 474).

American corporate law toward a default-term concept of corporate law, which allows shareholders either to opt in or to opt out of certain terms. The default term usually chosen is the term that parties forming corporations would normally choose. Thus, in most if not all states of the United States, preemptive rights do not apply unless they are chosen in the articles of incorporation; in other words, they are opt-in rather than opt-out provisions (that is, preemptive rights are permissible but not mandatory, and they must be affirmatively chosen to be applicable).[34] In Delaware, which is the state LLSV chose to represent all U.S. corporate law, preemptive rights are opt-in provisions. It is, to say the least, rather odd that the LLSV test of preemptive rights accords a zero where preemptive rights are available only on an opt-in basis when they chose a different approach for proportional representation, according one point where proportional representation is allowed, though not required.[35] Three of the original Law and Finance authors belatedly acknowledged the weaknesses of their methodology in this regard in an unpublished paper drafted in 2005.[36]

Whatever the pros and cons of the default-term approach, it seems obvious that preemptive rights have a smaller role in countries where there is a vigorous market for new stock issues among widely dispersed shareholders, compared with countries with primarily concentrated share ownership. In the absence of a vigorous market for new issues, preemptive rights reflect in part an assumption that new equity capital for an existing corporation will most usually have to come from existing shareholders. Preemptive rights also are a recognition that where share ownership is concentrated, the relative position of such owners is a major issue. In the absence of preemptive rights, a controlling shareholder could, for example, gradually squeeze out or otherwise disadvantage existing minority shareholders, including those who had major stakes but who, in the absence of a liquid stock market for the company, had little prospect of selling those stakes to anyone other than the controlling shareholder. Thus the use of preemptive rights is a sign of a weak, not a strong, market for corporate equities.

34. The dominant theory of American corporate law that has emerged in recent decades is that a corporation is essentially a contractual arrangement in the sense that a corporation is a bundle of rights; see Easterbrook and Fischel (1991). In this vision of the corporation, corporate law is to a substantial degree a set of default rules, which can be varied if the shareholders agree; see Ayres and Gertner (1989).

35. La Porta and others (1998, pp. 1128, n. 6, 1122).

36. In a December 2005 working paper, Djankov and three of the LLSV authors proposed dealing with the opt-in, opt-out inconsistency by revising the antidirector index (Djankov and others 2005). See also Spamann (2006), recoding the antidirector index to deal with other inconsistencies and omissions.

Some important protections for minority shareholders do not find themselves on LLSV's list. At least in the United States, the concept of directors' fiduciary obligations, particularly the duty of loyalty, is generally regarded as the most important safeguard for minority shareholders.[37] Yet it finds no place in the LLSV list of antidirector investor protection provisions.

An important perspective on the LLSV approach is gained by observing that the adoption of the LLSV antidirector rights is not systematic within legal families. Cumulative voting (or proportional representation) is possible in only five of the eighteen common law countries (and with respect to the United States, only in some states), whereas it is found in roughly the same proportion of French law countries. More important, preemptive rights are required in only 44 percent of common law countries in contrast to 62 percent of French law countries (thereby suggesting that, at least if one were to take the LLSV view of preemptive rights, French law origin in this respect is more protective, not less protective, of minority shareholders than common law origin). The comparisons suggest that the relative scores for legal families may be more a construct of the choice of rights deemed to protect minority shareholders than a systematic difference in shareholder protection among legal families.

Third, because LLSV looked at statutory law and apparently failed to consider case law, they have scored certain continental countries too low, according to commentators from civil law countries. This is certainly an oddity in view of declarations in LLSV articles about the supposed superiority of judge-made law (that is, of the common law method).[38] According to Cools, LLSV also failed to look at functional equivalents of substantive rules they scored.[39] Taking these two and related points together, Cools claims that LLSV got their conclusions backward: France, according to Cools, should have gotten a 4 or 5 (or, accounting for recent changes in French law, a 6) rather than a 3, Belgium a 4 rather than a 0, and the United States a 4 rather than a 5. In other words, according to Cools, French and French-origin law is at least equal to Anglo-American law, particularly of the U.S. variety.

Similarly, Berndt has criticized as inconsistent the scores on preemptive rights for Germany compared with the United Kingdom.[40] After a detailed analysis of the actual state of corporate law and practice with regard to the LLSV antidirector rights in Germany, Vagts came to the conclusion that the

37. Hertig and Kanda (2004, pp. 114–18).
38. For a review of the LLSV articles on this point, see Beck and Levine (2004).
39. Cools (2005, pp. 734–35). See La Porta and others (1998, pp. 1130–31, table 2).
40. Berndt (2002, pp. 17–18).

difference in national scores between Germany and common law countries "is not such as to concern an internationally sophisticated lawyer advising a client where to invest." In his view, "It is hard to agree with LLS & V that 'the evidence points to a relatively stronger stance favoring all investors in common-law countries.'"[41] And Spamann completely reworked the LLSV coding, based on a more thorough analysis of individual country law, arriving at results that were much more favorable to civil law countries and less favorable to common law countries than LLSV had found.[42]

In sum, the LLSV method of selecting certain statutory rights and scoring them, sometimes on an opt-in basis and sometimes on an opt-out basis, is deficient—according to some critics—because LLSV have the wrong values for the variables, in part by ignoring what courts actually do (as opposed to only what statutes explicitly provide) and in part by ignoring functional substitutes. These shortcomings lead to the observation that the devil in the LLSV method is definitely in the details. Econometrics unquestionably has the virtue that it helps to highlight regularities by abstracting from details. But one cannot ignore the obvious fact that a failure to use the right values for the variables or to use consistent methods of assigning those values can produce misleading, even erroneous, conclusions.

Fourth, even if the variables—that is, the chosen antidirector rights—are roughly the right ones, the variance among countries within any legal family is remarkably high if indeed the origin of a country's law makes a decisive difference, especially for economic growth in developing countries. India and Pakistan rank at the top of the list in total antidirector rights with a score of 5 out of 6 (along with Canada, the United Kingdom, and the United States), but others like Sri Lanka and Thailand receive only a 3 and a 2, respectively.[43] And in the French law family, Chile achieves a 5 out of 6, whereas many French law countries receive only a 1. Most striking of all, Germany ranks lowest of all among German law families with a 1 out of 6, whereas Japan— a German-law country—achieves a 4. Perhaps this oddity can be traced to Japan's corporate law being based, thanks to the post–World War II occupation under General MacArthur, on Illinois law, not German law.[44] Mattei observes that "Japanese law . . . is as much influenced by American legal culture as by German or French. . . . In corporation law American legal culture

---

41. Vagts (2002, pp. 595, 602, 606).

42. Spamann (2006).

43. La Porta and others (1998, pp. 1130–31, table 2). The reader should be aware that the LLSV classification of Thailand as a common law country is not free from doubt.

44. West (2001, p. 529).

has the lead."[45] Still, a poll of international corporate lawyers might easily come to the conclusion that minority shareholders are at least as well protected de facto in Germany as in Japan.

If the purpose of considering the utility of the LLSV-preferred corporate law rules is to look for policy implications and to give advice to developing countries, one should focus on the pros and cons of specific shareholder rights, given the nature of particular countries' economies and existing equity markets, as well as the prevailing social norms and other informal constraints. In that light, the LLSV studies are merely an introduction to a series of issues that each developing country needs to resolve against this local background. The influence of legal history and path dependence may be great in many fields of law, but it is likely to be less so with regard to legal provisions applying to publicly held corporations and particularly to rules governing the issuance and trading of securities. Reform, especially in the securities field, occurs frequently even in developed countries. Here the dead hand of the past is less likely to be a constraint than in more traditional legal fields.[46]

Several other considerations bear on the proper evaluation of the LLSV antidirector rights approach. First, the LLSV authors claim that enforcement of corporate law works better in common law than in French law countries.[47] Their conclusion raises the immediate question of whether enforcement is not a dominant consideration. This point is of particular relevance to issues of corporate governance, at least in a country such as the United States recognizing fiduciary duties of directors and officers and holding them responsible for violations of such duties.[48]

The Japanese adoption of Illinois corporate law illustrates the critical role of enforcement in determining the workability of transplanted law. When Japan adopted a U.S.-style fiduciary "duty of loyalty" as a substantive standard, it failed to provide a U.S.-style remedy in the form of disgorgement of profits derived by the officer or director. The oversight is understandable; whereas common law judiciaries are accustomed to fashioning remedies to effectuate the policy behind a substantive rule, Japanese courts are not

45. Mattei (1997, p. 128).
46. Zweigert and Kötz (1998, pp. 388–99).
47. La Porta and others (1998, pp. 1140–43, including table 5).
48. See generally Hansmann and Kraakman (2004a). Financial responsibility of directors and officers for breach of fiduciary duty has been greatly tempered in the United States by the corporate use of insurance to cover this risk. Indeed, at least until very recently, officers and directors were rarely forced to pay out of their own pocket damages to investors for violation of their fiduciary duties, but the recent Sarbanes-Oxley statute may lead to a change in this respect.

comfortable in giving any remedy not specified by statute. Hence a substantive rule that works in one legal system may not fit the legal infrastructure and culture of another system.[49] As a review of countries in transition from communism to capitalism (especially Russia) shows, a country can enact a modern world-class corporate law without enjoying the expected benefits if the country fails to consider the enforcement infrastructure.[50]

Fiduciary duties, such as the duty of loyalty, are examples of standards. As Hansmann and Kraakman put it, "*Rules* . . . require or prohibit specific behaviors, [but] *standards* . . . leave the precise determination of compliance to adjudicators after the fact."[51] In contrast to well-defined "bright-line" rules (which call on the judge to make a binary decision—yes or no—whether the rule has been violated), legal standards require a judge to use mature and trained judgment to determine whether the standard has been met, taking into account all of the factual circumstances of the case (often in complicated factual situations, say, under the "duty of loyalty" in a corporate self-dealing case). Hansmann and Kraakman list "dividend restrictions, minimum capitalization requirements, or capital maintenance requirements" as common examples of corporate law rules, which can be thought of as ex ante prohibitions or prescriptions.[52] Those requirements and restrictions are either met or not, and the kinds of fact-weighing judgments required for standards are usually not necessary for rules.

The economic development issue is whether standards, which are a key to corporate governance litigation in the United States, make sense for a developing country. Richard Posner, a well-respected U.S. federal appellate judge, thinks not:

> The relative simplicity of rules has two consequences for the kind of weak judiciary one is apt to find in a poor country. The first is that the application of rules places fewer demands on the time and the competence of the judges and is therefore both cheaper and more likely to be accurate. The accuracy is a little illusory, because it is a property of governance by rules that they never quite fit the complex reality that they govern. But this observation is consistent with their being more efficient than standards if administered by a judiciary that has a limited capability for the kind of nuanced and flexible decisionmaking that

49. Kanda and Milhaupt (2003).
50. Black and Tarassova (2002, pp. 253–261); see also Berglöf and Claessens (2004).
51. Hansmann and Kraakman (2004a, p. 23).
52. Hansmann and Kraakman (2004a. p. 24).

standards require. Second, rules facilitate monitoring of the judges and so reduce the likelihood of bribery and the influence of politics in the judicial process. The less discretion a judge has in making decisions, the easier it will be to determine whether a case has been decided contrary to law or whether there is a pattern of favoring one class or group of litigants over another.[53]

Standards are, of course, not at all unknown to the civil law; concepts such as "good faith" are common in the German Civil Code, for example.[54] But it is also true that standards are less used in corporate law in civil law countries than in common law countries, at least the United States.[55] It is curious that the opposite is true in corporate accounting. There the United States relies on a rulebook based on U.S. generally accepted accounting principles, whereas Britain and continental countries rely more on "principles-based" accounting.[56] It was precisely the tendency of U.S. companies to use a "check-the-box" approach to U.S. accounting rules that led to some of the corporate scandals in the early 2000s. But if bright-line rules are unlikely to deal effectively with self-dealing by controlling shareholders, standards are likely to be difficult for developing country judiciaries to apply effectively.

Corporate Governance

Despite the great benefits the corporate form brings to an economy, it also produces rule-of-law problems. A useful perspective on these problems that may be particularly relevant in developing countries because of the prevalence of concentrated share ownership in those countries is based on the concept of agency.[57] As noted earlier, agency exists whenever one person acts on behalf of another. The phenomenon is ubiquitous in the modern economy; common examples would be a stockbroker buying or selling securities for a customer and a lawyer acting for a client. The customer and client are the principals, and the stockbroker and lawyer are agents. The general shape of the legal problem in any agency relationship is to ensure that the agent acts in the interest of the principal rather than in his own interest or, failing

53. Posner (1998, p. 5).
54. See the discussion of Section 242 of the German Civil Code in Zweigert and Kötz (1998, p. 150).
55. See the discussion of the "standards strategy" and the "trusteeship strategy" in Hansmann and Kraakman (2004b).
56. Benston and others (2006, pp. 215–16).
57. See generally Hansmann and Kraakman (2004a).

that, to ensure that the principal will be able to remove the agent and select a new one.

The relationship between a corporation's shareholders, directors, and management means that at its base, corporate governance is fundamentally about agency. The directors and management (in American parlance, the "officers") act for the owners, namely, the shareholders. In some countries (though not so much in the United States), there is legal support for the notion that directors and management are to act for other stakeholders (the community, labor, the environment, and so on) and not just for the shareholders. These communitarian notions all too often allow directors and management (who in some countries tend to be the same people) to act in their own interest by purporting to act for a constituent of convenience of the moment. Thus this ambiguity as to the responsibility of the owner's agents creates its own rule-of-law problems.

In addition, a second agency problem arises when a controlling shareholder or block of shareholders takes action to the detriment of minority shareholders, say, by self-dealing. Hansmann and Kraakman explain: "The second agency problem involves the conflict between, on the one hand, owners who possess the majority or controlling interest in the firm and, on the other hand, the minority or noncontrolling owners. Here the noncontrolling owners are the principals and the controlling owners are the agents, and the difficulty lies in assuring that the former are not expropriated by the latter."[58]

The resulting corporate governance problem is exacerbated by the permanence of a corporation, which is a prime characteristic from which many of its economic advantages flow. As noted above, an individual shareholder cannot ask for his money back, and under most corporate charters more than a simple majority of shares is needed to dissolve the corporation. But therein lies one of the great issues of corporate law and some of the major choices that countries must make in creating and regulating a corporate sector. These issues, commonly referred to under the heading of corporate governance, have proved to be of the greatest importance not just for developing countries but also for the most developed countries.

The permanence of a corporation creates a central dilemma for legal policy. If the shareholder cannot get his money back, then why should he invest in the first place? Of course, where there is an efficient secondary market for stock, the shareholder can always simply sell when dissatisfied. But that is not

---

58. Hansmann and Kraakman (2004a, p. 22). A third agency problem in the corporation lies in its relations with third parties, especially creditors; this issue is discussed in chapter 9.

much of an answer for the poorer developing countries because an adequate secondary market may itself be difficult to develop. Even in developed countries, the sale option for individual shareholders does not work well for corporations that have not "gone public." Thus the fact that the management controls the assets of the corporation and the shareholders have at most whatever residual rights over the corporation that corporate law and the corporate charter give them leads to the much-discussed problem of the separation of management and control—or to put it another way, the relative absence of the ultimate owners' control over management.

The essence of the corporate governance issue in most developing countries, in contrast, arises from the fact that the great majority of even the largest corporations do not have widely diversified shareholdings. Instead, they are controlled by a single shareholder or by a family or other block. On the positive side, this means that controlling shareholders are in a far better position to monitor management than is the case for widely diversified shareholders. But when ownership is concentrated, the risk is that a minority shareholder may find himself at the mercy of a controlling shareholder who may seek to transfer the value of the minority shareholding to himself by some form of self-dealing. Of course, sometimes control is in a group or in a family, but the problem is the same.

The means of making this transfer of value takes many forms, sometimes by outright self-dealing, sometimes by seizing an opportunity that belongs to the corporation, and sometimes by high salaries, extravagant expenses, and other techniques for private enjoyment of corporate assets. Other means involve transactions between the controlled public corporation and a company solely owned by the control person or group; in such a situation, a below-arms-length price of a sale of corporate assets to the latter (or an above-arms-length price of a purchase) will suffice. In short, the key is the ability of the control person or group to select transfer prices on transactions with, in effect, themselves. These methods are often referred to, depending on the context, in pejorative terms ranging from the private benefits of control to expropriation of minority shareholding interests.[59]

The failure to solve the private benefits–expropriation problem adequately inevitably leads to scandals and setbacks that are a threat to public

---

59. Although corporate governance issues in the United States are normally discussed in the light of the prevailing pattern of widely held publicly traded corporations, it is useful to note that U.S. law is less demanding in a small, family-owned corporation situation where there are no public shareholders (referred to as "close corporations"), which is the usual situation in many developing countries.

and corporate confidence and therefore may impede economic development. In any event, the dominance of dispersed shareholding free of control by a single shareholder or group is by and large a phenomenon limited to the United States and the United Kingdom.[60] Elsewhere in the world, even though stock markets may exist, a substantial proportion (often a majority) of listed corporations are controlled by a single shareholder or group of shareholders. Indeed, even in the United States several hundred publicly traded firms have one shareholder with more than 50 percent of the shares.[61] Obviously in an otherwise widely held corporation, ownership of 20 percent or even 10 percent of the shares may be enough for de facto control, enabling a de facto controlling shareholder to select directors and thereby indirectly determine corporate policy. The controlling shareholders often also manage the corporation (which is, of course, a solution, though a less than satisfactory solution, to the much-discussed separation of management and control); indeed, this pattern of owner-managers is often found in family companies—that is, companies where the controlling owners are members of the same family.

The pattern of concentrated ownership, often family ownership, is widespread in continental Europe. A recent study of the French corporate world characterized the ownership structure as having three salient features: "(1) concentration of ownership; (2) extensive family ownership; and (3) the role of holding companies."[62] In Germany two-thirds of all listed companies in the mid-1990s had a single shareholder or blockholder that owned at least one-fourth of the corporation's shares.[63] In Italy a history of interwar nationalizations and subsequent partial privatizations, coupled with several large, family-controlled companies, initially led in the postwar period to the dominance of concentrated ownership; a series of legal changes in the 1990s has since led to a somewhat more diversified ownership structure.[64]

Concentrated ownership is no doubt even more common in some countries, particularly in the developing world. In a survey of the twenty largest publicly held corporations in twenty-seven countries, La Porta, López-de-Silanes, and Shleifer found that only about one-third were widely held. In their survey "widely held" was narrowly construed to mean that no person or family held directly or indirectly more than 20 percent of the shares. Among

---

60. La Porta, López-de-Silanes, and Shleifer (1999).
61. Holderness and Sheehan (1988).
62. Murphy (2004, p. 5).
63. Schmidt (2004, p. 394).
64. Rajan and Zingales (2003b, pp. 212–16).

a sample of medium-size corporations, the proportion of those widely held was less than one-quarter. [65]

From the standpoint of economic development, the striking feature of this research can be deduced from the few developing countries found among the twenty-seven countries examined in the survey (Argentina, Israel, Mexico, and South Korea). All of those developing countries were middle-income countries, and the percentage of concentrated ownership (at the 20 percent control level) among both the twenty largest and the sample of medium-size corporations within those countries was well above average for the twenty-seven countries as a whole. Of these four countries, Argentina and Mexico had no widely held companies among either the twenty largest or the medium-size corporations. South Korea, however, counted 55 percent widely held companies in the first category and 30 percent in the second category, and hence was more like continental Europe than the other developing countries in the survey or the United States. Israel's ownership patterns were closer to those in Argentina and Mexico than to those in South Korea.[66]

This survey of corporate ownership developed some further data indicating that in many countries more than one-third of large, publicly held corporations were family controlled (at the 20 percent share level), as were almost one-half of the sample of medium-size publicly traded companies.[67] Many of these family-controlled corporations accounted for a large percentage of publicly traded corporations within their countries: more than one-quarter, on average, of the twenty largest firms in the study's twenty-seven countries; more than one-half in Argentina; and 100 percent in Mexico.

Perhaps the most important point about family control is that in at least seven out of every ten cases, families that controlled the firms also participated in their management.[68] This figure was 95 percent in Mexico, 75 percent in South Korea, and 62 percent in Argentina. Further, participation in management was narrowly defined to ensure that the survey was looking only at participation at the top of the company. The significance of family control with management participation is apparent when one considers minority shareholders who run the risk of expropriation both by controlling

---

65. La Porta, López-de-Silanes, and Shleifer (1999, pp. 492–95, tables II and III).

66. La Porta, López-de-Silanes, and Shleifer (1999, pp. 492–95, tables II and III). An earlier study by LLSV suggests that countries less developed than the four just listed show results not sharply different from Argentina and Mexico (La Porta and others 1998, pp. 1147–48, table 7).

67. La Porta, López-de-Silanes, and Shleifer (1999, pp. 492–95, tables II and III).

68. La Porta, López-de-Silanes, and Shleifer (1999, p. 500).

shareholders and by management separately. The experience in Russia, for example, was that the combined efforts of controlling shareholders and management were devastating for minority shareholders.[69]

Dual Class Shares and Pyramids

Controlling shareholders are perhaps a fact of life, but corporate law itself in most countries permits controlling shareholders to magnify their ability to control a corporation. Among the legal means at their disposal are two widely used techniques. One creates two (or more) classes of shares, one without voting rights and the other with voting rights, the latter issued to the controlling shareholder (or the controlling group of shareholders). A second technique involves pyramiding, in which control is magnified by holding shares through a series of controlled corporations. To take one simple, albeit atypical, example of pyramiding, an individual or a family might hold 20 percent of an otherwise widely held corporation, which in turn held 20 percent of the target, also an otherwise widely held corporation. In effect, the ultimate shareholder could achieve de facto control with only 4 percent of the total investment (or, put differently, with only 20 percent of what would be required to achieve de facto control by direct ownership of shares in the target). In this light, the primary purpose of pyramiding appears to be to gain control of the corporation with a lesser investment. This achievement of de facto control in turn facilitates self-dealing by the controlling group.

The use of dual class shares is tailor-made for self-dealing. A cross-country study by Nenova involving all dual class firms in the eighteen countries (among the twenty largest national capital markets) that allow dual classes of shares differing in voting rights found substantial private benefits of control. Under the methodology used and assuming that the two classes of stock have similar attributes (for example, the same dividend rates) other than the right to vote, the private benefits of control can be measured by the difference between the market value of the voteless shares and the price commanded by the voting shares in a sale of control. The private benefits of control in the dual class share situation can be interpreted as the percentage of the value of the firm that controlling shareholders can expropriate from minority shareholders. Remarkably the potential expropriation ranged as high as 28 percent of the value of the firm in South Korea and 36 percent in Mexico.[70] The most

---

69. Black, Kraakman, and Tarassova (2000); Goldman (2003, pp. 210–11, 240–44).
70. Nenova (2003, p. 334, table 3).

important factor in determining the extent of expropriation, however, was not the nature of substantive legal protections or of takeover rules, but rather the quality of enforcement—showing again the crucial role of an independent and effective judiciary.[71]

To see, however, the point about the control of the corporation's cash flow, an example involving the practice of pyramiding is useful. Assume the ultimate shareholder owns 50 percent of a first-tier public company that in turns owns 50 percent of another public company—the second-tier company—so that control is not at risk in either tier. Then, with only a 25 percent indirect ownership (50 percent of 50 percent), the ultimate shareholder can easily direct speculation in new ventures by the second-tier company. Take speculation in high-risk ventures (by definition, ventures that involve a small chance of a big payoff and a large chance of loss): The ultimate shareholder's proportion of wins versus losses does not change, but he is able to control the decisions with a much smaller personal investment. This kind of pyramiding is sometimes used, for example, in the domestic U.S. real estate industry to allow promoters to diversify their investment across more real estate ventures than their personal funds would otherwise permit. Pyramids, however, also allow the ultimate shareholder to engage in self-dealing by transactions between himself (or a corporation he controls) and a company in the pyramid that he controls only by reason of the pyramid. From this possibility arises the corporate governance challenge of pyramiding.

An alternative explanation, raising further corporate governance issues, is that pyramiding allows controlling shareholders to economize on capital transactions involving assets they own outright, thereby facilitating the transfer of wealth out of publicly held companies to themselves.

The corporate ownership research previously analyzed gives some examples of pyramiding from Canada, Hong Kong, Japan, and Korea. The Hong Kong example involves its most prominent company, Hutchison Whampoa, where the Li family held 35 percent of Cheung Kong Holdings, which in turn owned 43.9 percent of Hutchison Whampoa. The authors also give a more dramatic example in the South Korean firm, Samsung Electronics, whose chairman controlled Samsung with only a 14.1 percent ownership of two companies that in turn held Samsung stock.[72]

---

71. These types of measures of the extent of expropriation may underestimate the loss attributable to self-dealing because they arguably fail to account for the loss in revenues due to waste and mismanagement where controlling shareholders devote their energy to diverting resources from minority shareholders rather than to managing the enterprise.

72. La Porta, López-de-Silanes, and Shleifer (1999, pp. 482–83, 485, figure 5).

The Blockholder Phenomenon

Much scholarly literature concludes that well-dispersed shareholding can be expected to develop only in countries where corporate law reaches adequate solutions to the corporate governance problem. Put differently, concentration of ownership—at least to the extent of a group of so-called blockholders being able to act on behalf of the shareholders as a group—is an inevitable consequence of inadequate corporate governance rules. The blockholders can, acting together, control the management. Of course, in many cases— especially with family firms—the blockholders are the management, and in those cases minority shareholders are potentially doubly vulnerable. In short, concentrated ownership involving control by a few individuals, especially by a family, may turn out to be desirable for minority shareholders when the controlling owner monitors the management and keeps it focused on the success of the company (as opposed to the managers' own perquisites and incomes). Consider, for example, the outstanding stock market performance of the family-controlled Wal-Mart over recent decades in the United States. But concentrated ownership coupled with deficient legal protections for minority shareholders can be another matter entirely.

Consequently, even where there are neither dual class shares nor pyramidal arrangements, controlling shareholders can be in a position in some countries to take pecuniary advantage of minority shareholders. Dyck and Zingales found that control premiums (the excess of the price per share when control was sold over the price in ordinary share trading) ranged, on average, as high as 27 percent in Argentina, 65 percent in Brazil, 37 percent in Turkey, and 58 percent in the Czech Republic.[73]

Legal institutions thus play a vital role in the development of equity capital markets. An earlier chapter addressed a central problem of governance of countries, namely, the difficulty of constructing a political and legal system strong enough to assure citizens that a predatory ruler would not expropriate their property. The issue of corporate governance is a close analogue. As the foregoing discussion makes clear, corporate governance problems come in two parts in many developing countries. First, if shareholders, certainly small shareholders, cannot control the management, how can they be protected against expropriation of the value of their economic interest by management? Second, in the case of the blockholder solution to the first problem

---

73. Dyck and Zingales (2004, p. 551, table II). Some of the countries, such as Brazil, allowed dual class shares.

(a solution to the extent that the blockholders, at least collectively, can discharge the management), the minority shareholders find themselves at risk of being expropriated by the blockholders. This second version of the expropriation issue is especially severe when the blockholders and the management are the same people, because then the first and second problems merge to the disadvantage of minority shareholders. And where the two problems merge, it is likely to be very difficult to raise money from small shareholders; the economy, therefore, has a more difficult challenge in channeling savings from ultimate savers to productive uses.

Legal Protection

In the context of legal protection of minority investors, three kinds of protection should be distinguished: corporate law, securities law, and stock exchange listing requirements. Most of the focus in the development literature has been on corporate law. Thus the original article by LLSV addressed substantive rules of corporate law.[74] The legal origins approach was partially validated in the Nenova study of expropriation potential, reviewed above, with the median value of controlling block votes highest in French civil law countries (22.6 percent), followed by German civil law countries (11.0 percent), and then by common law and Scandinavian civil law countries (only 1.6 percent and 0.5 percent, respectively).[75] Dyck and Zingales found, however, that any supposed advantage of common law over French law with regard to control premiums disappeared once certain nonlegal factors such as newspaper circulation and tax compliance affecting corporate behavior were included in their regressions.[76] This finding, particularly with respect to newspaper circulation, is not the kind of thing that the legal origins approach takes into account, but rather is in the spirit of the World Bank Institute governance approach.[77]

An approach to economic development in the equity capital area that would be primarily focused on bringing best practice to developing countries

---

74. In 2005 the LLSV successor authors reformulated the original Law and Finance work to focus more directly on the conflict between dominant shareholders and minority shareholders in an "anti-self-dealing index." See Djankov and others (2005). This index focused not just on legal rules but also on private enforcement mechanisms, such as disclosure, approval, and litigation.

75. Nenova (2003, pp. 334–35, table 3).

76. Dyck and Zingales (2004, pp. 588–89, table XI).

77. See the discussion in chapter 2 of "voice and external accountability" in connection with the governance approach.

through the process of legal transplantation would run into several kinds of hurdles—the nature of the substantive rules and the ways in which the courts deal with those rules. Even accepting that the LLSV list of corporate law provisions was not optimum and that a better set of rules could be devised, the nature of the enforcement of the rules must be taken into account.

The lack of enforcement led to serious problems in Russia and in other transition countries in the early days of the 1990s after the demise of the Soviet Union, and similar problems can be seen more recently in several Latin American cases involving abuse by controlling shareholders.[78] The first Latin American case became public only because the firm and people involved were charged by the U.S. Securities and Exchange Commission with U.S. securities violations involving a major Mexican entrepreneur, Ricardo Salinas Pliego, in which Salinas Pliego personally profited by $109 million. Salinas Pliego is alleged to have used his control of the holding company of TV Azteca, a major Mexican television chain, to enter into a complex transaction involving two related companies. The purchase of the debt of one related company for one-third of its face value was followed by the payment by that company of the debt at the full face value to net a profit of more than $200 million for insiders. In this Mexican corporate governance debacle, enforcement was in the hands of the U.S. Securities and Exchange Commission because of an SEC filing by TV Azteca.[79]

The second such case involved the CEO and six executives of a Chilean electricity utility. After the privatization of the formerly state-owned company, a Spanish utility holding company acquired stock in Chilean holding companies that in turn held stock in the Chilean utility. These Chilean holding companies had two classes of stock: Class A, which held most of the equity of the Chilean utility but no voting rights, and Class B with little equity but majority voting power. Class A shares were held by small shareholders and pension funds, and Class B shares by the executives. The price paid to the executives, whose class B shares controlled the utility, was 1,000 percent greater than the price paid for the Class A shares of the small shareholders and the pension funds. While the case may illustrate the value of control, it also shows a great corporate governance problem that became a scandal in Chile. In this case the problem seems to have arisen because of both deficient substantive law and the absence of any effective enforcement mechanism.[80]

---

78. On Russia, see Pistor, Raiser, and Gelfer (2000).
79. Securities and Exchange Commission. "SEC Charges TV Azteca and Its Chairman—Ricardo Pliego—with Fraudulent Scheme To Conceal Salinas' $109 Million Windfall Through Related Party Transaction." Press Release 2005-1 (January 4, 2005). See also Dempsey (2005).
80. A. Clarke (2003, p. 40).

Securities Laws

A second reason why legal differences play a large role in the corporate area has to do with the securities laws. With widely dispersed shareholders, the availability of remedies with regard to disclosure of information to such shareholders is particularly important. As Black has observed, it is hard to envision strong securities markets without a strong legal foundation: "Creating strong public securities markets is hard. That securities markets exist at all is magical, in a way. Investors pay enormous amounts of money to strangers for completely intangible rights, whose value depends entirely on the quality of information that the investors receive and on the sellers' honesty."[81]

In a 2006 study using cross-country regression methodology, La Porta, López-de-Silanes, and Shleifer found that securities laws are particularly important to the development of a strong financial sector and especially to achieving a large stock market capitalization as a percentage of gross domestic product. Indeed, they found that their measure of corporate law effectiveness loses most of its explanatory power for stock market development when securities law variables concerning disclosure and standard of liability for failure to disclose adequately are included in their regressions.[82] In short, corporate law may be primarily important for protection of minority shareholders in closely held corporations, where stock is not sold to the public, but stock market development depends considerably more on the quality of securities laws than on the quality of corporate law, at least as the original legal origins articles measured corporate law quality.

What is particularly striking about the 2006 study is the finding that the existence of securities laws mattered but that the most important factor was private enforcement allowing financial recovery by injured investors for securities law violations. In contrast, the authors found that enforcement by a government agency was of relatively little importance. Specifically, they found that public enforcement plays a modest role at best in the development of the stock market. Mandatory disclosure was important, however, in part because it made it easier for investors to recover damages in private litigation.[83] These findings suggest that good substantive law and a competent, independent judiciary go hand in hand in this legal area as well as others.

An interesting aspect of the study's finding that private enforcement is more important than public enforcement is that the United States, while relying to a

81. Black (2001, p. 782).
82. La Porta, López-de-Silanes, and Shleifer (2006).
83. La Porta, López-de-Silanes, and Shleifer (2006, pp. 14, 20).

very large and growing extent on private securities actions, also relies heavily on public enforcement. The U.S. authorities, including administrative agencies and self-regulatory organizations, expend far greater resources, not just in money but also in numbers of actions (even adjusted for market size) than do either the United Kingdom or Germany. This result is part of a greater effort by U.S. authorities across the entire range of financial regulation, including regulation of banks and insurance companies.[84] If it is true, as concluded earlier in this book, that enforcement is more important to the rule of law than the details of substantive law, then the United States is not just a public exponent of the rule of law but actually relies internally on the rule of law, at least in the financial sector.

Securities regulation is a recent phenomenon. Although it first came to England in primitive form in 1848 and 1869 in the form of statutory prospectus requirements, modern securities regulation in England dates only to the end of the 1920s and began in the United States with the Securities Act of 1933.[85] Both countries relied on legislation, not the common law nor general corporate law. This fact necessarily raises some doubts about what it means to say that legal origin has much to do with the efficacy of securities laws in different countries. Moreover, the rules on securities regulation are almost entirely statutory and regulatory even in common law countries. Indeed, as Roe has pointed out, common law countries regulate securities through dense and complex laws and regulations that resemble civil law codes far more than they do the common law or even traditional statutes found in earlier times in common law countries.[86] To be sure, common law countries, particularly the United States, using the concept of fiduciary duty, rely much more heavily on private litigation to recover losses experienced by investors. Once again, enforcement is at least as important as the content of substantive law.

Important as securities regulation is today to the continued expansion of securities markets, it is certainly true that extensive securities markets can form without such regulation. In fact, securities markets blossomed in the United States and Britain in the nineteenth and early twentieth centuries before modern securities regulation was introduced. But unregulated securities markets are vulnerable to various forms of manipulation and abuse.[87] The very growth of securities markets thus gave rise to a constituency of stockholders and securities-related firms that supported or even sought

---

84. Jackson (2005, pp. 18–19, 29, including figure 11).
85. For early English regulation, see Coffee (2001, p. 42, n. 135).
86. Roe (2006).
87. Coffee (2001).

regulation to protect their acquired wealth and business interests in a well-functioning market.

In Europe securities markets also developed before securities regulation. Not only did the French market have more listed countries in 1914 per million people than the U.S. and British markets, as noted earlier, but Germany also had more listed companies than the United States, and this continued to be true through 1960.[88] The same European superiority was present when stock market capitalization is measured relative to GDP for Germany and France versus the United States, but the United States moved ahead as Europe suffered the devastation of two world wars.[89] It is generally acknowledged that shareholding is more diversified in the United States and Britain, and this was probably true before World War I, although there are apparently no confirming statistics available. Coffee has argued that the greater concentration of ownership in France can be attributed to French government action favoring a monopoly for the Paris Bourse, and in Germany, to statist intervention that stunted the market.[90]

The importance of enforcement, including public enforcement, to the success of securities regulation was brought home with force in the development of stock markets in the transition countries of Eastern Europe. Glaeser, Johnson, and Shleifer studied the experiences of Poland and the Czech Republic. They found that Poland "created an independent and highly motivated regulator to enforce the rules" but that the Czech Republic, in contrast, left enforcement to "an unmotivated office in the finance ministry." The result in Poland was "rapid development of securities markets," enabling "a number of firms to raise external funds," whereas the Czech securities scene was characterized by "delistings and a notable absence of equity finance through a public market by either new or existing firms."[91] Thus, where private litigation is not available as an enforcement tool, vigorous public enforcement is especially important.

The difference in the size of the equity markets in the two countries shows the significance of the difference in enforcement. Although the Czech stock market was twice as big as the Polish stock market in 1995—$9.2 billion compared with $4.6 billion—the situation was more than reversed by 2001, with the Czech market size essentially unchanged and the Polish market having increased over fivefold to $26 billion.[92]

88. Rajan and Zingales (2003a, table 5).

89. Rajan and Zingales (2003a, table 3).

90. Coffee (2001, pp. 45–58).

91. Glaeser, Johnson, and Shleifer (2001, pp. 855–56). See also Coffee (1999); Rajan and Zingales (2003a).

92. Berglöf and Pajuste (2003).

9 | Credit Markets, Banks, and Bankruptcy

Credit markets are just as important as equity markets to financial development. In most countries far more finance is generated in credit markets than in public equity markets. This is true even in the United States, which is usually thought to be the country with the most pronounced equity culture.[1]

In equity markets, the legal issues revolve around questions of corporate law and securities regulation. In debt markets, the bank—the central institution for large-scale lending—is the point of departure. Some countries, especially the more developed ones, do have corporate debt markets, but even the countries of Southeast Asia that have been successful in developing stock markets are still at an early stage of developing corporate debt markets.[2] Hence the first part of this chapter focuses on banks. The discussion then turns to special problems that creditors—not just banks but all creditors—face when the borrower cannot pay or fails to pay. The core of the legal issues turns on creditors rights law and bankruptcy law.

The Role of Banks

Banks play an especially important role in developing countries. The fundamental economic role of a bank is to be an intermediary between savers and

1. Rajan and Zingales (2003a, table 4).
2. Dickie and Fan (2005). In this respect, some developed countries, such as the United States, have through "disintermediation" reached the point where debt securities far exceed borrowing from banks (Rajan and Zingales 2003b, p. 248).

the ultimate users of savings, who invest those savings in nonfinancial assets. (Of course, in some countries the public sector deficit is large and financial intermediaries use the flow of savings to increase their holdings of government bonds, which from the standpoint of the real economy is normally not investment but rather a dissipation of savings.) The efficiency of the transmission of savings to those ultimate users is essential to economic development. To the extent that banks are the principal channel of that transmission, as is the case in most developing countries, banks play a crucial role in the development process.

For several reasons, however, banks may not play that role with efficiency. The banks may themselves be state-owned; over 42 percent of the equity in the ten largest banks in the average country was owned by the state as late as 1995.[3] For all kinds of political and personal reasons, it is difficult for managers of state-owned banks to make purely business decisions. Perhaps not surprisingly (though the direction of causation may be an issue), Barth, Caprio, and Levine found that greater government ownership of banks is associated with less-well-developed financial systems.[4] And La Porta, López-de-Silanes, and Shleifer found that "higher government ownership of banks is associated with slower subsequent development of the financial system, lower economic growth, and, in particular, lower growth of productivity."[5] For one reason, as Sapienza shows with respect to Italy, the "lending behavior of state-owned banks is affected by the electoral results of the party affiliated with the bank." In particular, she found that "the stronger the political party in the area where the firm is borrowing, the lower the interest rates charged."[6]

Directed Lending, Crony Capitalism, and Related Lending

Privately owned banks may not be in a position to operate solely on a commercial basis. On the one hand, the government itself may direct the flow of savings. This is particularly the case where much of the economy is in the hands of state-owned industries and therefore the government chooses to use the savings of citizens to provide financing (often to cover losses) for state-owned industries. A mechanism for doing so is *directed lending,* in which political influence is used to allocate bank loans to favored sectors and companies. Even where the government chooses to use directed lending to

3. La Porta, López-de-Silanes, and Shleifer (2002, p. 267).
4. Barth, Caprio, and Levine (2001, p. 47).
5. La Porta, López-de-Silanes, and Shleifer (2002, p. 267).
6. Sapienza (2004, p. 357).

assist sectors of the private economy that it considers of strategic importance, as was a central tenet of South Korean development policy for several decades, one can question whether directed lending interferes over the long run with the development process by undermining the vitality of the banking sector and by misallocating resources.[7]

Even where a developing country government does not consciously use directed lending as a development policy, it may not have available the normal tools of monetary policy and therefore may actively encourage or discourage certain types of lending in order to stabilize the macroeconomy. For example, in 2004 China tried to fight off an overheating of the economy by directing banks to reduce certain kinds of lending. But since local governments were themselves directing lending to locally popular "prestige projects," the discouragement of that lending by the central authorities is a further illustration of the perils and complexities of a system based on directed lending.[8]

Governments, of course, find it difficult to avoid having some influence on bank lending. For example, prudential regulation, which is generally regarded as an essential responsibility of governmental banking regulators in both developed and developing countries, may steer banks away from what the regulators regard as overly risky loans. The intent of prudential regulation is to ensure the safety and soundness of the banking system, but it may also affect development outcomes, especially where there are few other channels for savings to reach the ultimate users of those savings.

Another distortion of bank lending lies in what has been termed *crony capitalism*. In many countries controlling shareholders of banks tend to have broad interests, including politics if only because political influence is good for their bank's success. As a result those controlling shareholders may be motivated to lend to friends of the government or of the party in power. Such crony capitalism lending played a considerable role in the Asian financial crisis of the late 1990s. A particularly egregious combination of directed lending and crony capitalism was experienced in Indonesia leading up to that crisis. Dwight Perkins of Harvard University pointed to the contrast between pre-crisis efforts to strengthen the Indonesian banking system and what actually happened in the crisis:

> The Harvard Institute for International Development, among others, was involved in [a bank-strengthening] effort in Indonesia over many

7. Cole and Park (1983, p. 284).
8. Kynge (2004).

years. The laws were rewritten, bankers were trained, private banks were authorized and proceeded to grow rapidly, and the commercial banks were given substantial autonomy from the central bank. And yet, as of 1999, all of Indonesia's banks were technically bankrupt. . . . Indonesia's banking problems . . . were [in part] a result of a decade in which many of the banks had been the toys of the ruling elite and could not have withstood even a mild crisis without government support . . . . To prevent the recurrence of a similar crisis at some later date, the banks must stop being subject to the discretionary interventions of high officials in support of pet projects.[9]

Moving banks away from directed lending and crony capitalism is only partly a task for substantive law and the legal system. More competition in banking would help to drive bank management toward greater efficiency. And a hands-off policy by the government would equally help. But even if directed lending and crony capitalism were eliminated, corporate governance issues concerning self-dealing take on a central importance in the banking sector because of banks' central role in the economy of most developing countries.

Banks are, of course, corporations and some of the problems in the banking industry parallel those of corporations generally. Problems related to controlling and minority shareholders discussed in chapter 8 are directly relevant to banks. In addition to the ways in which controlling shareholders can gain financially at the expense of minority shareholders in nonfinancial corporations, they have even more options for doing so in banks. A survey of forty-four countries showed that only about 25 percent of banks are widely held (having no shareholder with more than a 10 percent interest); among the remaining 75 percent, a family is in control of more than half.[10] Hence the opportunities for controlling shareholders to engage in self-dealing are abundant. One of the more common practices is known as *related lending*, that is, lending to parties related to the controlling shareholders. La Porta, López-de-Silanes, and Zamarripa listed twenty-four developing countries where "prominent" banks were "controlled by persons or entities with substantial nonfinancial interests." To study the incidence and effect of such related lending by banks, the authors picked a random sample of loans from the top 300 loans of all banks in Mexico outstanding at the end of 1995 and followed the loans' performance through the end of 1999. Among their many findings were that

9. Perkins (2000, p. 242).
10. Caprio, Laeven, and Levine (2004, p. 16).

compared with loans to unrelated parties, interest rates for loans to related parties were 4.15 percentage points lower; moreover, loans to related parties were 30 percent less likely to be made against collateral; were less likely to be backed by personal guarantees (such as by an officer of the borrower); and were made for longer maturities and with longer grace periods. Their findings on outcomes were even more dramatic. The default rate was 66.4 percent for related borrowers compared with 37 percent for unrelated borrowers. And the recovery rates for bad loans were 27 percent for related borrowers versus 46 percent for unrelated borrowers. These two findings on outcomes are mutually reinforcing; loans to related borrowers not only produced more defaults but also led, after default on a particular loan, to a lower recovery rate.[11]

The problem is by no means limited to Mexico or even Latin America. Faccio, Lang, and Young reported that "effectively all (96.91%) Asian loosely-affiliated non-financial corporations are affiliated to a group that also controls a bank at the 10% level."[12]

The conclusion is clear that banks present not just special corporate governance problems, but, in view of the centrality of banks in the economies of many developing countries, a special challenge to prudential regulation of banking activities. The corporate governance issues are essentially legal problems, but the prudential regulation issues are largely beyond the scope of this book.[13]

The Relationship of Creditors Rights and Bankruptcy

Two related fields of law heavily influence the strength of a financial sector in the credit arena. One is the law of creditors rights, and the other is bankruptcy law. Both legal fields are underdeveloped in the developing world. Being closely related, the two fields are sometimes confused in the eyes of policymakers who focus on the inability of debtors to pay and therefore on the rights of creditors in the event of bankruptcy.

Short of bankruptcy, there is a problem of debtors who are solvent but who simply find it more convenient not to pay interest and principal when

---

11. La Porta, López-de-Silanes, and Zamarripa (2003, pp. 233, 253–54, 256). In interpreting these outcomes, it is important to know that Mexico experienced a financial crisis in the wake of a December 1994 devaluation of the Mexican peso, and so during the 1995–99 period the overall incidence of nonperforming loans was quite high and indeed many banks became bankrupt or were rescued by the government.

12. Faccio, Lang, and Young (2003, p. 25).

13. On prudential regulation, see Barth, Caprio, and Levine (2004) and related articles in Mishkin (2001).

they believe they can avoid doing so. Economic development will be compromised if debtors can get by with procrastination. The size and growth of credit, which is the lifeblood of business, will be suboptimal. An adequate law on secured credit helps to deter procrastination by allowing creditors to foreclose on property provided by debtors to secure their repayment. In many countries, well-meaning but misconceived legislation designed to protect debtors has become a deterrent to the use of secured credit and hence a barrier to economic development. The World Bank has estimated "annual welfare losses caused by barriers to secured transactions . . . at 5 to 10 percent of GDP in Argentina and Bolivia."[14]

The importance of bankruptcy law lies in part in making the resolution of multiple creditors' conflicting claims more orderly and thereby enlarging the amount of their joint recovery. Efficient bankruptcy procedures can thereby enhance the willingness of creditors to lend in the first place and hence strengthen financial markets.

Efficient bankruptcy procedures have an economic function as well in markets for goods and services. Just as entry, free of unnecessary governmentally imposed barriers, is important to competition and hence to economic growth, exit is also important to economic progress. Inefficient firms need to exit the economy to make room for more efficient firms. To be sure, failing firms may eventually close their doors when they run out of money, fail to pay existing creditors, and can obtain no further credits.[15] But a large firm may have many creditors, and a legal fight among creditors over the assets may delay the actual exit of the firm, especially if the firm still has some value as a going concern that could justify a sale to a more able entrepreneur. The continued presence of doomed firms is not just an unnecessary barrier to the entry of more efficient firms but also impedes economic development. An efficient bankruptcy system may make their exit faster and less damaging to third parties, particularly creditors. The World Bank found a correlation between creditors' recoveries and the level of private credit (measured as a percentage of GDP): the industry from which the inefficient firm exits achieves higher productivity, and productivity in the economy as a whole correspondingly increases. According to the report's findings, "Exit of unviable businesses contributed 19% to productivity growth in Taiwan (China), 23% in Korea and 39% in Indonesia in the 1990s."[16]

14. World Bank (2001b, p. 93).
15. World Bank (2005, p. 67).
16. World Bank (2005, p. 73, figure 9.7).

The temptation of governments to intervene in or to preempt the judicial machinery of bankruptcy, particularly for big companies with large numbers of employees, is well known, even in developed countries. In earlier periods when state ownership of industry was more popular than it is today, nationalization of failing companies and industries was a favorite technique. Experience shows that much state ownership of industry arises from just such bailouts. Italy created large, state-owned, conglomerate holding companies (such as IRI) in the 1930s, not out of ideology but rather to protect existing industrial and utility companies against creditors' threats to dismember the companies by selling their assets in bankruptcy.[17] With nationalization having fallen from favor, governments still attempt to fend off bankruptcy with state credits or state credit guarantees, moves that simply ensure bankruptcy cannot carry out its economic function of facilitating exit.

Although bankruptcy may facilitate exit for a firm with many creditors, it is not necessary where there are few creditors. In that simpler situation, secured credit can substitute for bankruptcy; the secured creditor can foreclose, enforcing his secured interest, without any need for a bankruptcy court. Indeed, especially in a case where the debtor is solvent but simply unwilling to pay, even an unsecured creditor can bring an action in court, obtain a judgment, and then proceed to levy on the debtor's property in satisfaction of his judgment. Of course, insolvent firms often simply close down voluntarily. In 2003 there were some 57,000 bankruptcies in the United States, but the remainder of the 600,000 business closures that year took place outside of bankruptcy.[18]

Quite aside from governmental influence and corporate governance issues, there is a further set of legal issues about the rights of creditors when borrowers face financial difficulties. Insofar as corporate bond markets and other forms of securitization of credit have not been developed, banks are likely to be the principal creditors. But at this more general level of analysis, it makes little difference whether creditors are banks or groups of bondholders or other kinds of lenders, or even trade creditors who supply goods and services on credit. The important contribution that law reform can make in this area of economic development is in the legal fields of secured credit and of bankruptcy law.

Much of the literature on economic development fails to distinguish between creditors rights law and bankruptcy law. The result, for example in

17. Rajan and Zingales (2003b, pp. 212–16).
18. World Bank (2005, p. 67).

the legal origins literature, is considerable confusion. And the distinction is not an easy one because the two areas of law interact whenever bankruptcy is declared.

Two legal points are crucial. First, the rights of creditors are established by commercial law, not by bankruptcy law (although those rights can be affected once bankruptcy is declared). In particular, secured creditors have enforcement rights against a nonpaying debtor; the most important of those rights have to do with collateral. Secured creditors can enforce those rights even though the debtor is not in bankruptcy. And the priority (that is, which class of creditors gets paid first out of available assets) among different classes of creditors is normally the same in both creditors rights law and bankruptcy law, at least in principle. Secured credit rights are of great importance in everyday life. To take a simple example, repossession of automobiles by lenders is an everyday occurrence on the streets of U.S. cities. This is an instance of a self-help creditor remedy. But court actions are also common.

Second, once bankruptcy has commenced, a new legal situation is created. The rights of creditors, including secured creditors, and the priorities of different classes of creditors normally carry over to the new bankruptcy context. The question of absolute priority, when raised in the bankruptcy context, refers to the enforcement of those prebankruptcy priorities in the bankruptcy context. However, bankruptcy law controls this issue.

Most economists believe that the best system for economic development is one that gives the strongest protection to creditors. The theory is that such protection maximizes the willingness to lend and hence leads to greater financial development. But there are different kinds of creditors whose rights potentially conflict: lenders who contract for security (such as a mortgage); unsecured creditors, including trade creditors (who sell under a contract calling for future payment); workers who normally are paid only after labor is performed; and governments that are owed taxes.

A World Bank study finds a correlation between country per capita income levels and what kinds of claims have priority: "Lower-income countries are less likely to give priority to secured lenders" and more likely to give priority either to claims of labor or to government claims.[19] The law in many countries, including developed countries, makes tax claims of governments and certain rights of workers, normally the right to unpaid wages, senior even to secured creditors. According to a World Bank survey, labor claims have top priority in France and in many French legal origins countries as well as in

19. World Bank (2004a, p. 76).

India (a common law country), while taxes have top priority in several countries of French, German, and common law legal origin.[20] (The United States also gives tax claims of the federal government priority over private secured creditors, but the impact is limited by the rule that the government claim has to be manifested in the filing of a tax lien in the appropriate registry—which normally takes place a few years after the tax becomes due; even when filed the U.S. tax lien does not take priority over creditors acquiring their secured interest before the filing of the lien.[21])

Secured Credit

In view of this complex relationship between secured credit and bankruptcy, it is best to start with the prebankruptcy rights of creditors. And the most important of those rights have to do with secured credit. A secured loan involves collateral. Where the debt is secured by real estate, a mortgage is involved. When the debt is secured by movable property, several terms are used (among them, security interest, pledge, charge, and lien), causing considerable confusion. But the terminology is less important than the existence of an effective mechanism to enable secured credit. It is in this area that legal reform is especially important in the developing world, as the European Bank for Reconstruction and Development (EBRD) learned in its work with the transition countries, where initially "none of the EBRD's 26 countries of operations had any workable laws permitting non-possessory security over movable assets."[22]

The greatest barrier to greater use of credit in some developing countries has to do with the difficulties of making collateral legally available for secured lending. A World Bank task force found that where secured credit was limited to real estate, "the extension of credit and the development of the national economy have been seriously impeded. This has been found to be the case, for example, throughout most of Latin America and in Central and Eastern Europe."[23] Some secured credit systems provide only for a "pawn shop" type of security arrangement, where the debtor deposits the collateral with the lender, thereby defeating the value of secured credit to expansion of economic activity. For example, as Walker notes, "Thai law does not recognize security interests in property that remains in the debtor's possession."[24]

20. World Bank (2004a, p. 76, table 6.3).
21. Picker, Baird, and Jackson (2002, pp. 429–33).
22. Simpson and Menze (2000, p. 21); see also Dahan and Simpson (2004).
23. World Bank (2004a, pp. 63–64; 2001a, p. 19, ¶49).
24. Walker (2000, p. 37).

Few large-scale loans of the type necessary to finance companies and projects are likely to be forthcoming in many developing countries without the borrower providing collateral. To some extent this is true in developed countries as well. According to an IMF paper: "About half the credit offered in the United States is secured by some kind of movable property: about two-thirds of bank loans are secured by either movable property or real estate, and nonbank institutions that lend against movable property—such as leasing and finance companies—do almost as much lending as banks."[25] Indeed, collateral is also normally needed by small individual borrowers. That was illustrated in chapter 7 on land, where the inability to obtain mortgages turned out to be in substantial part a legal problem regarding farmers' and homeowners' inability to establish title to their property—an essential precondition for real estate to function as collateral for a loan. In the commercial sector of the economy, a healthy financial sector requires legal rules that allow businesses to pledge machinery, inventories, accounts receivable, and other nonrealty assets.[26]

The advantage of going beyond a reliance on mortgages for real estate to facilitating pledges of movable property is illustrated in a World Bank document:

> Uruguay and Kansas have similar typographies and well-educated populations interested in advanced technologies and able to apply them, and both are world-class exporters of beef cattle. In Kansas, private banks view cattle as one of the best forms of loan collateral; this is also the view of the bank examiners at the Federal Reserve Bank of Kansas City. Banks with 'cattle paper' are seen as solid whereas banks with 'exposure to farm real estate' are seen as risky. By contrast, in Uruguay, because of flaws in the legal framework governing secured transactions, private banks and bank examiners prefer real estate as collateral for loans; they consider a pledge on cattle as worthless as collateral. The unacceptability of cattle as collateral applies to all types of transactions, including sales of cattle on credit, sales of cattle finance by third-party lenders like banks or finance companies, or working capital loans for other purposes that might be secured by cattle.[27]

Facilitating greater use of secured credit is not just a question of establishing substantive law supporting such pledges of movable property (including not just cattle but also vehicles, inventories, and intangibles, such as accounts

25. Fleisig (1996, p. 44).
26. World Bank (2004a, pp. 68–69).
27. Fleisig (1996, p. 45).

receivable). It is also a question of establishing collateral registries. Without such a registry system, so that lenders do not have to worry that the assets have already been pledged to earlier lenders, credit is less likely to be forthcoming. The essence of a registry is that pledges registered earlier in time have priority over subsequently registered pledges and all unregistered pledges. Many countries do not yet have such registries for movables, even if they have them for land.[28] The creation of registries was a special problem in the transition countries of Central Europe and the former Soviet Union after the collapse of communism. The EBRD reported that, even after a number of years and despite secured credit legislation in most countries where EBRD operated, "the issue of the existence of an effective system for publicising non-possessory charges gave rise to very mixed results across the region."[29]

Some countries maintain registries but put formidable obstacles in the way of their use. In many countries it takes more than a month to complete registration. To take an extreme example, in Poland a requisite to registration of a security interest is a court certification of the legality of the underlying credit agreement, which can take as long as six months.[30]

Sometimes small borrowers have no property to serve as collateral. Then the doors of the financial community are usually closed to them, at least in much of the developing world (unlike developed countries such as the United States where credit cards and other forms of unsecured credit are more freely available). The popularity of microfinance arises in large measure because very small firms, especially individual entrepreneurs (such as women engaged in home production), are unable to borrow from the formal banking sector because they have no collateral to pledge. Hence, by relying on their personal reputation among individuals or nongovernmental organizations who know them, they are able to borrow small amounts. Within this context, reputation can serve as a substitute for collateral.[31] But, as its name implies, microfinance is not designed to meet the borrowing needs of large firms and therefore cannot suffice to power an economy as a whole, even in a poor country. And it is precisely in the case of large loans that reputation alone is unlikely to be a substitute for collateral.

Where the collateral is movable property, the rights of creditors to seize collateral and then sell it as a "self-help" measure in the event of nonpayment is an important issue. Only one-quarter of the 130 countries surveyed in a

28. World Bank (2004a, p. 68).
29. Fairgrieve and Andenas (2000, p. 35).
30. World Bank (2005, p. 44).
31. World Bank (2001b, p. 92). See also Barr (2001).

study for the World Bank permit the sale of collateral by the creditor without court involvement.[32] The extent to which creditors must first establish in court their right to seize movable collateral is one issue. In some countries self-help seizure of collateral by the creditor is permitted where expressly agreed in writing. Where court action is required, enforcement is often illusory. For example, the World Bank described this situation: "In Chile, the creditor files a claim with the court, and the court must declare default and order a bailiff to seize assets, before there is a public auction. The debtor may appeal the process at every stage. In Argentina, enforcing collateral in the hypothetical good-case scenario takes 148 days and costs an amount equal to 42 percent of the country's average per capita income.[33]

In some countries the delays are even more startling. While it "takes a week for a creditor to seize and sell collateral in Germany, Ireland, Tunisia, and the United States," according to the World Bank report, "it can take five years in Bosnia and Herzegovina, Brazil, and Chile."[34] In fact, in some forty countries "enforcing collateral requires the same long court trial as for unsecured debt."[35] Brazil illustrates the difficulties of requiring court proceedings: "Long proceedings ensue before the judge decides to enforce and orders bailiffs to seize the assets. After appraisal, a public auction is scheduled and advertised. The court determines a minimum price. If met, sale proceeds are deposited in a public agency and distributed through settlement procedures. Debtors have unlimited opportunities to drag the process by appeal. Enforcement takes more than 7 years."[36]

A related and possibly offsetting consideration to speed (and its benefit in making credit more easily available) is, of course, the extent to which borrowers can protect themselves against wrongful seizure where prior judicial determination is not required. The U.S. rule, which attempts to balance the interests of the creditor, debtor, and the economy, is that out-of-court seizure (often called repossession) of collateral is permissible if it can be done without breaching the peace, which de facto means that things that are kept behind locked doors cannot be taken.[37] When one considers, of course, the overall interests of debtors as a class, debtors have the same interests as creditors insofar as expanded credit markets favor debtors. Nevertheless, the occasional

---

32. World Bank (2004a, p. 62).
33. World Bank (2004a, p. 62).
34. World Bank (2004a, p. 63).
35. World Bank (2005, p. 44).
36. World Bank (2005, p. 44).
37. Picker, Baird, and Jackson (2002, pp. 309–28).

scandal created by unscrupulous creditors may sometimes make it difficult politically to introduce out-of-court enforcement of collateral.

The case of India, described in a World Bank report, illustrates the difficulties in finding a politically sustainable balance:

> Ten years ago it was almost impossible to enforce collateral in India. The process could easily take 25 years. In 1998 the government established Debt Recovery Tribunals, with expedited enforcement proceedings. Expected time to enforce was cut to around 10 years. More reforms were introduced in May 2004. State-owned banks, which account for 90% of lending, were permitted to enforce out of court. On default the bank must notify the debtor. After a 60 day grace period the bank can seize the assets directly and sell by public auction. Introducing the reform was difficult—it had to survive a Supreme Court challenge. But the new procedure is widely used. Creditors can expect to enforce within 9 months.[38]

The fact that only state-owned banks can enforce out of court discriminates against private sector banks and nonbank lenders and hence limits the long-term strength of India's financial system.

Even if out-of-court enforcement by seizure of collateral is not permitted, court reform can be a partial substitute by making delay by the debtor difficult. Estonia, for example, has introduced summary procedures that limit the grounds on which debtors can defend and appeal.[39]

However, where out-of-court enforcement is not possible, weaknesses in the judiciary translate to weak credit markets. The finance minister of Mexico made the point clearly and in detail:

> Judicial processes [in Latin America] are unpredictable, riddled with corruption, long, and expensive. Their costs are reflected, among other effects, in high bank intermediation margins. Excessively high credit rates discourage demand for credit, and poor credit demand is, in turn, reflected in a scant supply of deposits and of other banking services. Intermediation margins are, after all, the "price" or cost of the financial sector which, when expensive, result[s] in a flabby banking sector. Such immature and insufficient financial sectors often mean insuperable entry barriers for small firms and a dearth of housing mortgages.[40]

38. World Bank (2005, p. 47).
39. World Bank (2005, p. 47).
40. Gil Diaz (2003, p. 8). On the impact of judicial inefficiency on credit spreads, see also Laeven and Majoni (2003),

Court delays are costly not just to creditors but also to the development of credit markets. Jappelli, Pagano, and Bianco put the key point succinctly: "The key function of courts in credit relationships is to force solvent borrowers to repay when they fail to do so spontaneously. Hence poor judicial enforcement will increase opportunistic behavior on the part of borrowers: anticipating that creditors will be unable to recover their loans easily and cheaply via the courts, borrowers will be tempted to default. Lenders respond by reducing the availability of credit."[41]

Using Italian data on mortgage markets, these authors found that "in Italian provinces with longer trials or large backlogs of pending trials, credit is less widely available." They also found that "judicial performance is important to the performance of credit markets [as evidenced by their] findings . . . that judicial efficiency correlates positively with the volume of lending and negatively with proxies for credit constraints."[42]

Delays and costs are relevant even where secured credit is available. Where enforcement is weak, creditors often demand "overcollateralization." A World Bank report found that "banks in Malawi, Moldova, and Mozambique typically secure more than 150 percent of a loan's value" because the "prospects of recovering [the collateral] are dim."[43]

An important issue for the creation of a strong financial sector involves the kinds of property in which a creditor can obtain a security interest. Although virtually every country has some provision for security interests in movable property, the kind of movables and particularly the kind of intangibles that are available make an enormous difference. Only forty countries, counting both developed and developing countries, allow the debtor to pledge "a changing pool of assets (such as inventory or receivables), future assets (such as crops) and the entire business as collateral."[44] Many countries require the specific property to be listed, which effectively eliminates pledges of many kinds of movable property, both tangible and intangible. For example, a manufacturer of products cannot as a practical matter pledge inventory if every time a new item comes off an assembly line the credit agreement must be amended (and the credit registry updated). A similar problem confronts any firm selling a product in using receivables financing.

---

41. Jappelli, Pagano, and Bianco (2005, p. 225).

42. Jappelli, Pagano, and Bianco (2005, pp. 223–24). But see Padilla and Requejo (2000, p. 6), who state that they found "no conclusive evidence on the sign and magnitude of the effect of creditor rights on credit market efficiency, [but found evidence of] the great importance of macroeconomic stability for credit market performance."

43. World Bank (2004a, p. 61).

44. World Bank (2005, p. 43).

The Relevance of Legal Origin

The entire notion behind the legal origins approach—namely, systematic differences between common law and civil law, and in particular between common law and French law—is seriously misleading as applied to secured credit, according to the EBRD research undertaken in connection with bringing secured transactions law to the transition countries of Central Europe and the former Soviet Union. The reason is that "there are very few common rules or standards in western legal systems [and] the full extent of this lack of commonality is rarely recognised."[45] U.S. law and U.K. law differ not just in terminology but also in the principles of secured transactions law; for example, a "floating charge" over current and future assets of a debtor is possible under English law but not under U.S. law.[46] U.S. law was revolutionized by the adoption in the mid-twentieth century of the Uniform Commercial Code, which created the "concept of a unitary security device, which takes the place of the former variety of devices (for example, pledge, chattel mortgage and conditional sale), each of which had been governed by its own law."[47] While the concept of a unitary security device has been adopted in a few common law countries, no uniform approach, even as to basic concepts, exists in the common law world. Civil law systems also show great diversity, according to the EBRD research. Even within the French law family, countries as close in legal history and approach as Belgium and France—the commercial law of both being rooted in the Napoleonic Commercial Code—reflect "differences . . . that have major practical effects on the validity and availability of secured transactions."[48]

The relationship of creditors rights to bankruptcy was approached in the seminal LLSV Law and Finance study discussed in connection with shareholder rights in chapter 8. One of the shortcomings of the LLSV legal origins literature insofar as credit markets are concerned is its focus on bankruptcy rules, as opposed to secured credit law. Of the four rules LLSV chose, all assume bankruptcy and at least two are specifically applicable only in reorganization proceedings. LLSV do not look at secured credit outside of bankruptcy, even though in many developing countries the bankruptcy system is

45. Dahan (2000, p. 38).
46. While the blanket security interest is a movement in U.S. law in the direction of the British floating charge, the latter—once it crystallizes—extends to all assets of the debtor. In addition, the floating charge mechanism gives creditors procedural rights not available under U.S. law. For a description of the floating charge, see Davydenko and Franks (2004, p. 23).
47. Dahan (2000, p. 41).
48. Dahan (2000, p. 40).

rarely used, except for "state-owned enterprises or subsidiaries of foreign firms." To take a specific example, a World Bank study found that "the five largest banks in Mozambique, which account for about 90 percent of bank loans to enterprises, . . . never use formal bankruptcy." And even where the bankruptcy system is used, reorganization procedures may not be used.[49]

Their study is somewhat confusing from a legal point of view because it does not clearly distinguish between creditors rights when the debtor is in bankruptcy and when bankruptcy has not been declared and perhaps is not even in prospect because the debtor is just procrastinating. For example, it does not consider the right of a secured creditor to self-help seizure.

The difference in the two situations is important. First, secured credit law can be thought of as a substitute for bankruptcy law. Collection of an unpaid debt may be much faster and cheaper if bankruptcy proceedings are not necessary. This is particularly the case where self-help is permitted. Second, many countries have totally inadequate bankruptcy laws. Often it is not the law itself that is inadequate but the bankruptcy system, which does not function properly due to a shortage of bankruptcy judges or their lack of training. The inadequacy of the bankruptcy system in Southeast Asia became painfully clear in the Asian financial crisis of the late 1990s, especially for situations where financial distress was systemic.[50]

Although bankruptcy proceedings can be brought with respect to all kinds of debtors, including individuals and even nonprofit institutions, LLSV focused on corporate enterprises. Such corporate enterprise bankruptcies fall into two major classes: "bankruptcy" in the narrow sense of leading to liquidation of the corporation; and "reorganization," referring to a proceeding in which the corporation survives in a new form, usually with new management and new shareholders (in the typical reorganization the old creditors become the new shareholders). The LLSV analysis does not crisply distinguish between bankruptcy in the narrow sense and reorganization. To be sure, in view of the authors' disposition toward maximizing the rights of creditors, ignoring the boundary between the two types of proceedings is perhaps understandable. (However, in the United States, the two types are statutorily separate, with bankruptcy in the sense of liquidation being in Chapter 7 and

---

49. World Bank (2004a, pp. 74–75, 78, 80).

50. Three important developments reflecting this lesson of the Asian financial crisis were the publication of Claessens, Djankov, and Mody (2001) by the World Bank; the development by the World Bank of *Principles and Guidelines for Effective Insolvency and Creditor Rights Systems* in 2001; and the widespread enactment and updating of bankruptcy codes throughout the developing world (World Bank 2004a, p. 71).

reorganization being in Chapter 11 of the Bankruptcy Code; the LLSV analysis pertains to Chapter 11.)

Four substantive law rules characterized by LLSV as "creditor rights" were "no automatic stay on assets," meaning that secured creditors could seize collateral even though bankruptcy proceedings had commenced; "secured creditors first paid," which established the rule of absolute priority among creditors, ensuring that secured creditors would be paid in bankruptcy proceedings before unsecured creditors; "restrictions on going into reorganization," which referred to statutory provisions ensuring that management could not start reorganization proceedings without the consent of creditors; and "management does not stay in reorganization," which refers to a rule automatically ousting management from their positions upon the commencement of the proceedings.[51]

The methodology was the same as in their study of shareholder rights: each country was given a binary 1 or 0 score for each rule, and so each country would, by simple addition, end up with a score from 0 to 4. Here again the common law countries won the competition with an average score of 3.11, with the French law countries achieving the lowest average score, 1.58, German law and Scandinavian law countries scored in between, with 2.33 and 2.00, respectively. The relative relationship between the common law score and the average of the three civil law scores was significant at the 1 percent level, as was the relationship between the common law and French origin score, thus strongly supporting the view that the common law countries accord stronger rights to creditors than do civil law countries in general and French law countries in particular.

An examination of the details, however, reveals a number of anomalies that may raise questions about the results, particularly if one is concerned with policy implications for developing countries. The first and most startling result is that the United States, the economy that has grown the most rapidly in the developed world in recent years, came up with the low score among common law countries—a mere 1 out of a possible 4 (though admittedly higher than the 0 scored by such diverse countries as France and Peru).

Moreover, there was wide dispersion within each of the four legal families. Just to take the common law family: Australia, Canada, and Ireland shared the

---

51. La Porta and others (1998, p. 1136, table 4). LLSV also include a "remedial" measure—the existence of a legal reserve requirement—that is found in only one English-origin country (England itself) and only at a relatively low level. Since even LLSV did not include the legal reserve requirement in summing their rankings of the four substantive rules to arrive at a composite "creditor rights" score, the legal reserve remedial right is ignored here.

same low ranking as the United States, falling short of a number of weak economies within the common law family that nevertheless achieved the maximum score of 4, such as Kenya, Pakistan, and Zimbabwe (none of which is renowned, to say the least, for its credit markets). To be sure, quite a number of countries, many of them strong successful economies, also achieved a 4—notably the United Kingdom itself. Nonetheless, common law countries certainly showed wide disparity in their willingness to follow the mother country, which again raises the question of the value of the concept of legal origin for policymakers.

The French law countries showed equally startling divergences. France led, if that is the right word, with a 0 score, but such countries as Ecuador, Egypt, and Indonesia—despite being in the French law family—achieved the same 4 as the United Kingdom.

One final discrepancy, though of a somewhat different kind, is found in the German law countries. Since the rights of creditors are of the greatest interest to the main credit providers, namely, the banks, it is interesting that the lowest ranking among German-law countries went to Switzerland, where banks historically have played a leading role in the economy.

Economic Development, Law and Finance, and Legal Origin

The LLSV results in their seminal 1998 article highlight three major issues about the usefulness of cross-country regression results, one that LLSV address, but two that they ignore. The issue they address is that enforcement may be more important than substantive law in protecting shareholders and creditors. The two issues they do not address are, first, that their cross-country regressions may not provide results that are relevant to economic development in developing countries and, second, that the need imposed by the use of cross-country regression techniques may lead to an oversimplification of key rules, even a misassessment of the extent to which their selected substantive rules accurately describe legal rights of shareholders and creditors in practice.

With regard to the results for developing countries, it is interesting that LLSV were not particularly focused on the issue of economic development and therefore dealt only in passing with whether the results were as strong for developing countries as for developed countries. Nonetheless, they did note that "creditor rights are, if anything, stronger in poorer than in richer countries." In fact, their own analysis reveals an inverse relationship between stronger creditors rights (as they select and measure them) and income levels, with the bottom 25 percent of countries (sorted by gross national product per capita) ranking stronger than the mid-50 percent, which in turn rank stronger than the highest 25 percent. The authors speculate that this surprising relationship may exist because "poor countries adapt their laws to facilitate secured lending for lack of other financing opportunities." [52] But if secured lending is important to a stronger financial sector and hence to economic development, then one would expect countries well along in the development process to have stronger laws, not weaker laws, in the secured transaction area. Here, as in the case of shareholder rights, the LLSV discussion of the relation of legal origin to economic development is so sparse that one should be cautious as to the legal implications for developing countries.

Furthermore, when Djankov, McLiesh, and Shleifer later did a regression study based on newer data that included 129 countries (not 49 countries as in the original LLSV paper), they found that the "statistical significance of [the creditors rights] variables disappears," suggesting that what is important is the level of development of legal systems, not their legal origins or the substantive law of creditors rights. [53] Hence the fundamental driver for economic development purposes in the creditors rights area is likely to be the quality and effectiveness of enforcement.

Per capita income levels are not, of course, the same thing as economic development (the latter being a process of rising incomes), but LLSV look at per capita income levels, not growth in those levels. In the course of an interesting study proposing that the real difference between legal systems is not the actual substantive law rules but rather the philosophies of the respective legal families regarding the role of the state, Mahoney ran regressions to examine the relation between legal origin and per capita income growth. Because Latin American and African countries performed poorly during the period he was investigating, he used dummy variables for those two continents in an attempt to test whether unidentified omitted variables rather than legal origin might account for that poor performance. He found that common law origin pointed to higher growth than civil law origin, but at a lower level than without the dummy variables and at a lower statistical significance level (5 percent rather than 1 percent). [54]

Even more striking, as pointed out in chapter 2, Kaufmann and the World Bank Institute found "evidence of a small but significant correlation between

52. La Porta and others (1998, pp. 1133, table 3, 1139).
53. Djankov, McLiesh, and Schleifer (2005, pp. 15, 21–22).
54. Mahoney (2001, p. 517).

legal origins and governance performance" for common law countries over countries with civil law origins, but when they looked just at "the set of 75 lower-income countries, the differences between common and civil law essentially disappear."[55] (This large-scale study examined various dimensions of governance that included a legal origins component.) These last three studies suggest that cross-country legal origins regressions do not necessarily carry strong policy implications for financial markets in developing countries even though legal origin may be important in the developed world, at least for common law and French origin countries.

Culture and Religion

In assessing the policy implications of the original LLSV results with regard to credit markets, it is useful to consider what the root causes are for differences in the size and strength of credit markets and the posture of legal institutions toward those markets. A fundamental characteristic of all credit markets is the charging of interest, explicitly or implicitly. Two broad societal attitudes are therefore in question in considering credit markets. Is the charging of interest frowned upon, or even prohibited? And what is the attitude toward rates of interest so high that they are considered to constitute usury? Perhaps these attitudes influence a country's legal rules on creditors rights and bankruptcy.

The leading cultural factor involved is probably religion, although social attitudes toward the poor within a society may lead to usury laws designed to protect them from exploitation by money lenders. Muslim law—that is, the Sharia—forbids the charging of interest, although in modern times so-called Islamic finance involves finding ways to structure transactions to obviate the explicit charging of interest.[56] Catholic doctrine has traditionally condemned usury. Since every French law country in the LLSV data is a Catholic or Muslim country, one has to ask whether the LLSV results concerning French law countries are not a consequence of the reflection in law of attitudes toward money lending rather than something inherent in the legal system as a whole. English common law countries, on the other hand, are both Protestant and Catholic and therefore present an interesting focus for further research. Nordic countries, it should be noted, are Protestant.

---

55. Kaufmann (2004a, p. 147).
56. Kuran (2004b, pp. 7–19).

Stulz and Williamson found that "Catholic countries have . . . significantly fewer long-term debt issues than Protestant countries [and] significantly less bank credit than non-Catholic countries." In other words, financial development is weaker in Catholic countries. They also found that "Catholic countries have significantly weaker creditor rights than other countries [even] when [they] control for the origin of the country's legal system as well as for GNP per capita."[57] This conclusion and the Sharia example suggest that reforming legal institutions in the creditors rights arena faces substantial cultural headwinds, not—or not only—a lack of legal understanding or interest group opposition.

What Is Meant by a Common Law Legal Origin in Creditors Rights?

The legal origins approach depends on the premise that legal families exist with respect to the legal field under discussion. For creditors rights and bankruptcy, however, the notion of legal families is none too solidly based. There are two reasons for caution. First, at least within the "common law family," the commonality of law is debatable. Second, the law on creditors rights and especially bankruptcy in most common law countries is relatively new and is almost entirely statutory, not judge made.

An easy way to assess the assumption of commonality within legal families in this substantive legal field is to compare the law in the United States and the United Kingdom. One would expect U.S. corporate bankruptcy law to resemble U.K. bankruptcy law. However, the United States is accorded a particularly low score of 1 and the United Kingdom the top score of 4, based on the four criteria that LLSV consider crucial in determining the nature of a bankruptcy system. But it is not just that the rules differ. Although U.K. bankruptcy law and even its procedure were indeed created in a common law case-by-case manner (with statutes enacted on particular points only), U.S. bankruptcy law is laid down in a comprehensive Bankruptcy Code. Even the U.S. Constitution has provided, since its inception in 1787, for Congress to legislate on bankruptcy, and the first U.S. statute was passed in 1800; bankruptcy legislation has been continuously in effect since 1898.[58] (It is true that the U.S. concept of corporate reorganization evolved in the nineteenth

---

57. Stulz and Williamson (2003, pp. 343, 346).

58. Kathleen A. Bussart, "Authority of Congress under Bankruptcy Clause of Federal Constitution . . . to Legislate on the Subject of Bankruptcy," 71 L.Ed. 2d 905 (2004).

century to meet widespread railroad insolvency by courts applying equitable principles and was not fully captured in legislation until 1978.[59])

Today the principal lender to a U.K. corporation, having a "floating charge" representing a secured interest in corporate property as a whole (including property acquired after the secured interest agreement was entered into), is entitled upon the debtor's default to appoint a receiver (normally outside any court action). The receiver then proceeds to liquidate the debtor company or its assets, including sale of the enterprise as a going concern. The management of the now defaulting company normally leaves office immediately.[60]

In the United States, in contrast, once the debtor corporation files for bankruptcy (or is put into bankruptcy involuntarily by a creditor), the management of the defaulting corporation normally becomes the "debtor in possession" and continues to manage the company, while creditors organize themselves in a creditor committee (often more than one committee if there are different classes of creditors). Although the rule of absolute priority constitutes the "black letter law" of bankruptcy, it is also true that junior creditors are entitled to procedural protections so that the system in practice involves negotiations among all classes of creditors of the bankrupt corporation. The normal right of secured creditors to seize collateral is subject to an "automatic stay" once bankruptcy is declared, and all creditors, including unsecured ("general") creditors, have a procedural right to participate and be heard in the formulation of the "bankruptcy plan," which determines who gets what. The creditors, therefore, bargain "in the shadow" of the rule of absolute priority.[61] The outcome of the bargaining need not be entirely in the interest of the secured creditors. Unsecured creditors may receive something as a "price" for resolution of the dispute, even though the secured creditors receive less than payment in full. And it happens sometimes that the equity holders receive something as part of side deals or other arrangements to finalize the agreement. At the end of the day, if the reorganization is successful, the corporation emerges from bankruptcy and goes on to live as a legal person another day. Under U.S. law, therefore, the existing equity holders may occasionally emerge from last-minute bargaining with some equity even if all creditors are not paid in full and indeed the old management may sometimes remain in office.

59. Franks and Sussman (1999).
60. Westbrook (2004, pp. 818–20). As Westbrook points out, the floating charge does not necessarily entitle its holder to absolute priority over all assets.
61. Baird (2001, pp. 77–78).

Because of these differences, it is often said that the British system is "creditor friendly" and the U.S. system is "debtor friendly" or "management friendly." Yet absolute priority is the substantive rule in both countries. Some economists believe that the U.K. system is obviously superior because it grants creditors, especially secured creditors, the strongest possible tactical position. Conversely, Stiglitz argues that, especially in developing countries facing the prospect of systemic bankruptcy (as in the Asian financial crisis), a rule that compromises absolute priority by giving existing management and shareholders some prospect of a surviving interest would be desirable because it would discourage them from delaying the commencement of bankruptcy and from engaging in value-destroying actions such as asset stripping.[62]

U.S. Corporate Reorganization Practices

Under the LLSV scoring, the United States has only one of the four creditor rights counted in the study, the rule that secured creditors get paid first (that is, the rule of absolute priority). According to the LLSV reading of the U.S. law, which is accurate so far as it goes, U.S. law does not prohibit management from remaining in place during reorganization. Moreover, U.S. law does impose an automatic stay on enforcement action by creditors, and it allows management to take the corporation into bankruptcy (or reorganization) without the consent of creditors. So far so good for a cross-country regression study, but the facts as to what happens in the United States on the first point are actually quite different from what one might infer from LLSV's understanding of the substantive rules. And whether the other two criteria are actually desirable for developing countries in drafting a new statute is a question that is addressed later in this chapter.

The actual results in the United States on the issue of management remaining in place can be derived from a study by Baird and Rasmussen of every reorganization completed in the United States in 2002.[63] The analysis makes clear that the creditors call the tune for the management in reorganizations under Chapter 11. Creditors have regularly changed management when they have felt it to their advantage to do so. Management rarely remains in place at the end of the reorganization. (Of course, when Chapter 7 liquidation is chosen, then there is no longer a business to manage.) Perhaps the

---

62. Stiglitz (2001, p. 19).
63. Baird and Rasmussen (2005).

largest point to be drawn from the Baird and Rasmussen research is that competent and specialized bankruptcy judges and a strong bankruptcy bar are of great importance. Indeed, when those factors are present, the formal substantive rules of bankruptcy law are less important.

A Survey of Developing Countries

Although the experience in large developed country economies, such as England and the United States, remains relevant, a more typical case was one studied by the World Bank and the International Bar Association. In this study a hypothetical set of detailed facts was prepared, and a survey was taken of bankruptcy lawyers and judges in developing countries to determine how the assumed bankruptcy would be handled.[64]

The essence of the hypothetical concerned a hotel company with revenues equal to 1,000 times the per capita income of the developing country in question (for comparison, if the country were the United States, the revenues would have been $34 million). This medium-size hotel had 201 employees and 50 creditors. The principal creditor was a bank with a mortgage on the hotel property; the amount of the mortgage principal still payable was equal to the market value of the hotel, with ten years remaining in the payment schedule. The bank had one majority shareholder, and its shares were not publicly listed. Of the total claims against the hotel, unsecured creditors held 26 percent in value, and the bank's secured claim constituted the remaining 74 percent. The bank preferred liquidation in the fastest and cheapest way, while the management and the majority shareholder preferred to keep the company in operation. On the legal side, it was assumed that there were three options: reorganization; liquidation by sale of the hotel, either as a going concern or piecemeal; and reorganization involving continuation of the company and management. It was postulated in the facts that the hotel would be worth more as a going concern than in piecemeal liquidation.

Against this stipulated factual background, the questionnaire contained questions about how the case would be handled in the particular country in question. The questions of greatest significance concerned the speed and cost of the proceedings and whether the case would lead to an "efficient outcome." Efficiency in this instance was defined as the realization of the value of the company as a going concern, either by sale as a going concern or through

---

64. World Bank (2004a, pp. 72–74). The questionnaire is available on the World Bank's *Doing Business* website (www.doingbusiness.org/default.aspx).

"successful rehabilitation with management dismissed."[65] It was stipulated that the financial distress was the fault of the management. The results of the survey supported the legal origins research in the sense that common law origin countries did better, on average, than French legal origin countries on the speed dimension, 2.7 years compared with 3.7 years. But the costs were roughly the same, indeed slightly higher in the common law countries.[66] With regard to achievement of the efficient outcome—realization of the going concern value—the common law origin countries again bested the French origin countries, 48 percent to 23 percent of the time.[67]

The policy relevance of the legal origins literature is thrown into some doubt by the wide variance in outcomes within particular legal families. India, an English common law country, was the slowest, followed by Chad (French), Brazil (French), and the Czech Republic (German). The most expensive were Macedonia (German), Israel (English), Venezuela (French), the United Arab Emirates (English), and Uganda (English), a considerable mixture of legal traditions. Moreover, regional differences were pronounced. On the time dimension, South Asia, which has both common law and civil law countries, averaged five years, more than the developing country average of three to four years and well behind the high-income countries, where bankruptcies were resolved in less than two years on average.[68]

As for cost, the high-income countries had the best record, with the average cost of the process consuming well under 10 percent of the value of the assets. South Asia, in contrast to its record on time, had nearly as good a performance as the high-income countries, with an average cost of about 10 percent. The Latin American, African, Middle Eastern, and Eastern European averages all clustered near 15 percent. And in East Asia, the average cost was about 20 percent.[69]

The third dimension (in addition to time and cost) was the ability to achieve an efficient outcome. Here again regional variation was pronounced. Although 77 percent of the high-income countries achieved the efficient outcome, not one South Asian country did so (even though South Asia contains both common law and French law countries). East Asian countries (which are mostly civil law countries), in contrast, achieved the efficient outcome in 42 percent of the countries.

65. World Bank (2004a, p. 75).
66. World Bank (2004a, p. 74, and figure 6.2).
67. World Bank (2004a, p. 76, figure 6.3).
68. World Bank (2004a, p. 74, figure 6.2).
69. World Bank (2004a, p. 74, figure 6.2).

Policy Implications

What are the policy implications of a legal origins approach in view of the difference in outcomes in the World Bank study? A preliminary point is that the transplanting of best-practice or state-of-the-art legislation should be easier and more successful in corporate bankruptcy than in many other legal fields. There are two primary reasons. First, the direct effects of corporate bankruptcy are focused on a relatively small number of people, and hence social norms and other informal constraints are less likely to be a constraint (the possibility of corruption aside). Second, corporate bankruptcy is a highly specialized field with relatively few (albeit knowledgeable) legal practitioners involved, and therefore the general level of the legal profession as a whole is not likely to be a concern. In any event, corporate bankruptcy, even in common law countries, has progressively become a subject of legislation and hence any postulated advantages of a common law case-by-case approach have become attenuated.

Still, at the time of the Asian financial crisis, bankruptcy laws in the region were antiquated and often unused. Indonesia had never translated the 1905 Dutch law into the local language, and as a result judges and lawyers had little or no bankruptcy knowledge or experience. Korea, in contrast, had a modern bankruptcy law, but it was seldom used until the 1990s.[70] Bankruptcy systems may have existed for some time in the rest of the world, but they often are so inefficient that they do not serve the needs of creditors or of the economy for swift exit of inefficient firms. This is particularly the case where the statute provides for reorganization of ailing firms; these procedures often simply provide a mechanism for delay, allowing debtors to be protected from creditors. As the World Bank reported: "Reorganization lasts nearly 6 years in the Philippines and about 4 years in Costa Rica and Romania. Brazil takes the longest: creditors can start foreclosure but there are many opportunities for appeal, each time suspending the process. It typically takes 10 years."[71]

The Russian experience illustrates the difficulty of transplanting "world class" bankruptcy law in a developing country with a weak judiciary. Black and Tarassova outline the problems:

> [The Russian bankruptcy statute] was drafted with extensive assistance from Manfred Balz, a top German scholar and the principal drafter of

---

70. See generally Walker (2000); see also Lim (2002).
71. World Bank (2005, p. 70).

the highly regarded German bankruptcy law. Quibbles aside, the Russian bankruptcy law is internally consistent, has no major inconsistencies with other laws, and mostly makes sensible policy tradeoffs. But it assumes that judges and bankruptcy administrators are honest; the procedure for creditors to choose trustees will not be rigged by false claims; judges can distinguish valid from invalid claims; and insiders will not collude with sham creditors to put solvent firms into bankruptcy. These assumptions are fine in Germany, but fatally flawed for Russia.[72]

At the same time, as the World Bank Consultation Draft on Effective Insolvency Systems suggests, a bankruptcy procedure is not absolutely necessary if an effective informal private sector workout process can be established. If so, as is the case in some developed countries under the "London rules," a workout would at least avoid problems involving weak judiciaries and corruption.[73] Nonetheless, the facts are that bankruptcy laws are being introduced or updated throughout the world.[74] The World Bank study found that Latvia, which (against a nonmarket socialist background) adopted its first bankruptcy law in 1996 and updated it in 2001, ranked among the top ten countries in achieving an efficient outcome.[75]

In such new legislation and updates, choices must be made. If judicial corruption is a problem, then adoption of a system that maximizes the role of creditors and minimizes the role of courts is to be preferred. As shown earlier, the British system allows the principal creditor to administer essentially the entire process. In an intermediate solution, the U.S. system allows a specialized bankruptcy judge to supervise what amounts to a private negotiation among creditors. In light of the British and U.S. practice, the World Bank study assessing the relationship between the powers of the court and the likelihood of achieving an efficient outcome is worth keeping in mind. Constructing a "court powers index," the researchers found a direct correlation: the greater the power of the court, the less likely bankruptcy was to secure the efficient outcome.[76] In short, if a principal objective of bankruptcy is to ensure an efficient outcome, too great a role for courts may in many countries be counterproductive.

---

72. Black and Tarassova (2002, p. 257).
73. World Bank (2001a, p. 78).
74. World Bank (2005, p. 67).
75. World Bank (2004a, p. 77).
76. World Bank (2004a, p. 78, figure 6.5). To see the court powers indexes of sample countries, see World Bank (2004a, pp. 130–32).

Another conclusion is that the less financially developed an economy, the more important is the improvement in secured transaction law, as opposed to bankruptcy law, if for no other reason than that bankruptcy procedures are unlikely to be used very often. The focus on secured transaction law is particularly called for where large-scale lenders predominate and they are able to use informal workouts.[77] The researchers in the World Bank study came to the conclusion not only that bankruptcy is not necessary to the enforcement of secured creditors rights but also that "bankruptcy is one example where the establishment of a sophisticated bankruptcy regime in a developing country generally results in inefficiency and even corruption. . . . In the poorest countries, it is better not to develop a sophisticated bankruptcy system and to rely instead on existing contract-enforcement mechanisms or negotiations between private parties. . . . Countries with ill-functioning judiciaries are better off without sophisticated bankruptcy systems [because such] laws usually exacerbate legal uncertainty and delays in developing countries."[78]

Assuming, however, that a bankruptcy law is to be adopted or updated, then the choices made are important. For example, it is not at all clear that the four LLSV criteria either are the most important provisions or even necessarily point in the right direction for a developing country. Consider LLSV's view that an automatic stay against creditor actions upon the commencement of bankruptcy proceedings is undesirable because it prevents creditors from pursuing other remedies and therefore infringes on creditors rights. Three points can be made. First, it is hard to see how a multicreditor reorganization can proceed efficiently without a stay. The World Bank task force on effective insolvency systems saw a stay as necessary in reorganization proceedings because a "business cannot be reorganized if it has no assets left to reorganize."[79] More generally, a business cannot continue in operation if key assets are awarded to creditors and hence the going concern value (assuming it is higher than the piecemeal liquidation value) will not be realized in the reorganization, even through sale of the enterprise if it has already been dismembered. Second, the reason that U.K. bankruptcy law needs no stay on creditor actions is that the bankruptcy proceedings are, as previously explained, normally in the control of the principal creditor with a floating charge on corporate assets. And third, it is always possible to provide for a lifting of the stay by court order, as is the case in U.S. law, when a creditor's

---

77. World Bank (2004a, pp. 79–81).
78. World Bank (2004a, pp. xvi, 72).
79. World Bank (2001a, p. 42).

action will not interfere with the reorganization.[80] This solution is what the World Bank task force recommended.[81]

Credit Registries

An important issue in credit markets involves the role of credit registries (sometimes called credit bureaus) that facilitate the sharing among creditors of information concerning borrowers with regard to repayment and related information. It is essentially an organized way to build on reputation, which normally works only among people who know each other or who live in a small community. Through credit registries, information with regard to the borrower's reputation can be shared on a nationwide or even larger scale.

The credit registry question is only peripherally a legal issue. It would not be worth addressing if it were not for some discussion in the economic literature to the effect that credit registries may perhaps be a substitute for stronger rights for creditors. According to a World Bank study, such private institutions sprang up to fill a business need in Paris and Amsterdam in the seventeenth century and in the United States in the eighteenth century.[82] Public credit registries are found in even more countries than private registries, particularly in the developing world. The World Bank found that private registries generally contribute more to promoting credit markets than do public registries. [83] However, one study suggests an association between legal origin and the decision whether to permit private registries, with "common law emphasizing ex post private dispute resolution, and civil law (particularly of the French variety) emphasizing public ownership and ex ante regulation."[84] Still, every developed country (except France) has at least one private sector registry.[85]

The principal legal issue that arises in some countries is whether private credit registries should be prohibited. Some countries do so.[86] Certainly from the standpoint of economic development, there is every reason for governments to permit, even promote, private registries. They have been found to be associated with larger credit markets in cross-country regressions.[87] Hence it

80. Baird (2001, p. 169).
81. World Bank (2001a, p. 31).
82. World Bank (2004a, pp. 56, 59).
83. See Djankov, McLiesh, and Shleifer (2005).
84. Djankov, McLiesh, and Shleifer (2005, p. 22).
85. World Bank (2004a, p. 57).
86. World Bank (2004a, p. 60).
87. Djankov, McLiesh, and Shleifer (2005, pp. 17–18).

may make sense for a poor country to support a public registry so long as it does not prohibit private registries.

Important issues of privacy may, of course, arise in the sharing of information about borrowers. Regulation, not prohibition, seems the obvious solution to the problem, even though regulation may turn into a covert form of prohibition, especially if used to protect a dominant firm or a state-owned public registry. The details of such regulation—like every other form of economic regulation—count, but the subject of economic regulation is beyond the scope of this book's inquiry.

A Review of
Some Key Themes

In a wide-ranging book it is a convenience to readers to offer conclusions. In this particular instance I would like to suggest that themes are more appropriate than hard-and-fast conclusions. Economic development is a grand but uncertain goal. Nobody can claim to grasp fully and with confidence what makes some countries develop rapidly and other countries develop hardly at all. Certainly we can say that institutions count and that legal institutions in particular count. But much else counts as well, as I outline.

An academic tradition, especially in economics, involves trying to prove that one particular factor is decisive in explaining any phenomenon. Some criticize this approach as reductionist. But it is a healthy academic instinct that builds on the principle of Occam's Razor—that simpler explanations are to be preferred to complex ones and often the simplest explanation is the best. Yet this kind of academic rigor can be misleading—even a trap—for the policymaker. Economic decisions have to be executed in a political world inhabited with people who care little for economics as an intellectual discipline but a great deal about certain social norms, cultural values, and, often, religious precepts.

In chapter 10 a number of themes are reviewed. But that is not the end of the inquiry. I have set myself, and the reader, a challenge for the final chapter. If the rule of law is vital to sustained economic development, then how is the case of China to be explained? China is the fastest-growing country in the world, and it is showing comparable progress in many fields. Yet few people would claim that China today has the rule of law.

Does that mean that the rule of law and indeed legal institutions are not important? Or is there another way to look at China? That is the question that I address, and I hope the reader addresses as well, in chapter 11, "China as a Test Case."

10 | The Implications of a Rule-of-Law Approach to Economic Development

The importance of institutions to economic development is well established. By the end of the 1990s, the theory that institutions were the most important determinant of the pace of economic development in any given country became a dominant view in much of academia and in the research departments of various international financial institutions. Other views remain important. One competing view emphasizes the role of geographical factors in explaining differing rates of economic growth. Another school of thought emphasizes social factors (social norms, culture, religion) in a country's population. Still another advocates increased emphasis on particular kinds of developing country programs, especially for health, education, and infrastructure.

From the standpoint of a particular country, the debate over institutions versus geography versus social factors makes little difference. Whatever the causes of its low incomes, a country wants economic development. If a country is disadvantaged by its geographical situation, it still will want to develop as rapidly as its circumstances permit. As for social factors, the country's policymakers would probably be unwise to think that public measures could alter social norms, much less culture and religion. But they should nonetheless take these factors into account in adopting new policies. There is little point, for example, in enacting new legislation that citizens will ignore because it runs contrary to social norms or dominant religious precepts.

And while policymakers concerned with development issues in both rich and poor countries will certainly want to understand the new emphasis on institutions, especially legal institutions, they should not think of the institutional approach as rendering irrelevant more traditional policies and concerns. The flow of public resources through multilateral and bilateral assistance is going to continue, and the point is that this flow of resources should be configured to support institutions, not undermine them. Education programs remain important because human capital is a form of capital, which no institutionalist would deny is a crucial factor of production and hence of growth. So too a sound health system and physical infrastructure are necessary to development, even if they are not sufficient without sound institutions, including legal institutions.

Implementing an Institutional Approach

The purpose of this book is to analyze the institutional approach with regard to law and legal institutions. Assuming the institutional hypothesis (rather than trying to add to the large literature assessing its validity), the question is what kinds of legal issues arise in trying to implement a reform program based on an institutional approach.

For that purpose, the alternative explanations will be taken into account insofar as they may modify what might otherwise seem the first-best solutions to the problems countries face. A leading illustration is the transplant issue. A developing country embarking on legal reform will be wise to look at a menu of reform possibilities and undertake a serious review of what has worked and not worked in other countries, developed and developing alike. But not even world best-practice solutions will work if the society will resist them or ignore them. That is why an understanding of local social norms, culture, and religion is so important.

In analyzing the issues that arise in pursuing an institutional approach to legal reform, I have chosen to focus on a narrow set of issues having to do with the oft-heard slogan that developing countries have to enforce contracts and protect property rights. Although Douglass North in his influential work preferred to limit the definition of institutions to rules of the game and to exclude organizations, the two concepts flow together in practice. In the legal area, for example, the judiciary has to be considered. And in considering other reforms beyond the law area, a broader definition is warranted as well; for those who think that education is the most important factor, for example, it is surely important to understand the rules of the game by which education is required of, and made available to, the youth of a country. Just as I have argued that the quality of the judiciary is crucial to the enforcement of law, so too the quality of educational organizations is important. The same may be said of health care rules and organizations.

In focusing on enforcing contracts and protecting property rights, I have emphasized two principal sectors of the economy. The first involves land, which includes both agricultural land and city real estate. Agricultural land is a vital economic resource in almost every developing country, and many legal problems arise, especially in connection with legal title to land. With legal title can come economic security for the owner, the ability to finance improvement of the land, and the ability to sell or buy land. In the case of city real estate, the inability to acquire title to apartments and real estate has profound implications for the society, particularly the ability of women to participate in economic life.

The second sector is the financial sector. A large body of research establishes the vital importance of this sector to economic development. The sector is best analyzed by looking at its two crucial markets—the market for equity securities and the credit market. The credit market is by far the more important in the developing world, where commercial banks are the dominant providers of credit for economic activity. But stock markets much like those in the most developed economies now operate in all middle-income developing countries, and some kind of market for equities exists in nearly every developing country with a sizable nonagricultural sector. In the case of China, a test case discussed in the concluding chapter, the stock market has been a vital tool for more than a decade in trying to finance state-owned industry, and many financial observers expect it to become more important in the future for private enterprises.

Law and Finance: A Reprise

Throughout the book I have looked at substantive law, even though I believe that the exact content of substantive law is less important than its enforcement. In looking at substantive law issues, I have given considerable attention to a body of research generally known as Law and Finance; those who developed the field were economists who investigated primarily financial issues. I have also referred to this research as the legal origins literature because it has been taken by many writers to show the superiority of common law over civil law, at least in financial markets.

The finance field has an advantage for empirical research because there is a great deal of data. The Law and Finance literature has been seminal in focusing research on institutions involving law and their role in development. It is, however, an example of important academic research that has few direct policy implications for developing countries. Its importance lies in underscoring the point that substantive law involves many choices that make a difference in the financial sector, a sector that other research shows is crucial for economic development. The inferred conclusion, often drawn by commentators but rarely explicit in the Law and Finance literature itself, is that legal origin is an important determinant of the rate of economic development in developing countries. Even if the conclusion that common law is superior to civil law, especially French law, were to be accepted, it would not provide significant guidance to policymakers. A country's legal origin cannot be changed. Indeed, its inalterability for a given country was the very reason the original authors in this field chose it; its choice enabled them to address issues of causality in their econometric studies.

In any event, the original Law and Finance authors do not concern themselves greatly with development issues. They lump together the forty-nine countries (later sixty countries), developed and developing, in their data in order to present their results. When they do break out developing countries in presenting their results, it turns out that the poorer countries tend to have better legal rules than the richer countries, according to LLSV criteria. Moreover, the usefulness of their insights with regard to particular kinds of developing countries is limited. For example, their data set for Africa is heavily weighted toward common law countries. Only one country in the data set is a civil law country (Egypt), despite the large number of former French colonies in Africa.

A problem with the LLSV research is that the authors specify what the characteristics of good law are without much consideration of the options available. Indeed, it is hard to escape the conclusion that they assume their answer with respect to the crucial subjects and preferred rules. This is most clearly seen in their study of credit markets where they assume that corporate reorganization rules are crucial for financial development. In doing so, they ignore three major factors. First, secured finance law, especially with regard to enforcing security interests outside of court, is at least as important as bankruptcy rules (although the two are related with respect to rules of priority). Second, LLSV focus on corporate reorganization rules even though liquidation is far more frequent than reorganization. Third, they fail to ask how reorganization works in practice, whatever the formal rules.

A further problem with the Law and Finance work is the quality of the data. Having chosen their rules, the authors then score the performance of a country as a one or a zero with regard to a particular rule based on someone's reading of the country's legislation. As discussed in an earlier chapter, they have failed to ask such questions as whether the country has an alternative rule that accomplishes the same purpose and whether the courts have supplied a rule that cannot be found in the legislation. Such a deeper inquiry could result in a reversal of the ranking of key countries with regard to corporate law. These are not small quibbles because econometric results can be only as reliable as the underlying data.

The legal origins literature seems, however, to have convinced a great many people, including some policymakers, that Anglo-Saxon common law is superior to civil law in general, and French law in particular. American legal scholars seem the most ready, perhaps for understandable reasons, to embrace that conclusion! Yet even they cannot agree on the reasons.

I find little basis, for the reasons set out in various chapters and briefly summarized in this chapter, to conclude that the superiority of the common law system has been established. This is certainly true with respect to substantive law. Indeed, I think it is wrong to conclude that one system is inherently better than others. After all, what counts the most in most legal fields is the quality of enforcement. Yet there are so many differences between English and American procedural law that it is hard to know what one means by common law (or Anglo-American) enforcement. Consider, for example, that the United States is almost alone in the world in using juries in noncriminal cases, that the United States uses contingent fees but few other common law countries permit them, and that the United States has not adopted the English loser-pays principle to deter frivolous litigation and cases commenced for the purpose of extracting a quick settlement from the defendant. And as the chapter on the judiciary shows, the notion that the common law countries are inherently more efficient in disposing of cases is undermined, whatever the averages are, by the great variance in disposition times across countries within a legal family. In short, hardly any conclusions as to the inherent superiority of one legal origin over another can be made. One is drawn ineluctably to the twin conclusions that no legal origin stands in the way of high-quality rule of law and that no legal origin guarantees it.

Though LLSV deserve credit for bringing the attention of the research community to legal institutional issues, Kaufmann and his World Bank associates offer a more policy-oriented set of insights. This is in part because they have more than 200 countries in their data set and they gather fresh data every two years, thereby having a better basis for cross-country comparisons and for tracking trends over time.[1] The principal reservation one must have about

---

1. Recently some of the original Law and Finance authors, together with Simeon Djankov (working with the World Bank), have begun to use many more countries than used in the original Law and Finance work (Djankov and others 2005). But they have not revisited in any systematic way the early landmark Law and Finance studies, which remain widely cited for their conclusions.

the Kaufmann research is that, being based on surveys, issues of subjectivity and choice of questions must play a role in the assessment of their results. At the same time, the Law and Finance literature—though appearing to be objective—is based on judgments as to what the most important rules are and, apparently without any particularized legal analysis, as to whether or not any given country has that rule in actual practice. These judgments are increasingly challenged by legal commentators. Moreover, to be able to come up with numbers for their regressions, the Law and Finance authors answer the latter question in binary fashion, affirmative or negative. Compared with the Law and Finance authors' mechanistic methodology for gathering their data, it is hard to be highly critical of Kaufmann's survey research methodology.

FROM THE STANDPOINT of policymakers, the most relevant chapters of this book are, aside from the chapter on land to which I have already alluded, those on the judiciary, on equity markets, and on credit markets. The main themes of those chapters can be summarized rather briefly.

The Judiciary

Substantive law is important, but it is likely that enforcement is even more important, and the judiciary is a main vehicle for enforcement of substantive law. Three useful ways to look at the judiciary are to investigate the operational details of the court system, the quality of the judiciary, and the relation of the judiciary to the rest of the government. Most bilateral and international economic assistance programs have focused on the first perspective—the operational aspects (with financial support going, for example, to computerization). While efficiency is surely important, the problems facing the judiciary in many developing countries go much deeper, which leads to the second perspective: the quality of the judiciary and, not least, the judges themselves. The weaknesses of legal education and the nature of legal careers are at least as important for the quality of the judiciary as the operational details of its functioning.

From a rule-of-law viewpoint, the third perspective—the relationship of the judiciary to the rest of the government—is crucial, both in enforcing law and in dealing with the problem of the predatory state. The independence of the judiciary from the rest of government is not only of fundamental importance, but also a matter on which outside assistance is unlikely to be of much benefit. This is particularly true of structural independence, which is a fundamental constitutional issue that can be addressed only internally at a constitutional level. The behavioral independence of judges is equally important but may benefit from greater resources, particularly for higher judicial salaries, from improvement in legal education, and perhaps from specialized judicial training.

Equity Markets

A strong corporate sector is vital to development. The private corporation is, for many of the reasons reviewed earlier in this book, the ideal vehicle for attracting and deploying the financial and managerial resources required for large-scale economic activity. But the governance of corporations creates significant problems in developing countries, where concentrated shareholding is the rule. The United States and the United Kingdom are the two countries in which the corporate sector is dominated by firms with widely dispersed shareholdings. In most countries, one shareholder or a block of a very few shareholders—often a family—controls a large proportion of corporations. Often these few shareholders also participate in management. The problem is that such a structure presents a tailor-made formula for expropriation of the value of minority shareholdings. The ways in which a dominant shareholder can, through self-dealing, dispossess the minority are legion. So long as that is the case, the ability of the economy to mobilize capital through broad-based equity markets is inevitably limited, and the role of the corporate sector in spurring economic development is correspondingly limited. The solution to these problems lies in improved corporate law, and especially its enforcement by a strong, independent judiciary.

Credit Markets

Credit markets are larger than equity markets, even in the most advanced economies but especially in the developing world. Although loans within families and microfinance can fund many family and individual enterprises, banks are central to the financial support of larger companies and hence to economic development. Corporate bond markets are still small or nonexistent in many developing countries.

Banks are corporations, and so all of the problems of corporate governance apply to banks and are especially important because the centrality of banks in a developing economy means that they often do not operate on a purely commercial basis. Three kinds of lending can present governance problems: directed lending, in which governments and powerful politicians use their influence to direct bank loans to favored sectors and companies; crony capitalism, in which a bank's controlling shareholders and executives— often the same people—may lend to politicians or others who can protect and promote the bank; and related lending, in which banks lend to enterprises owned by the bank or its executives (or both).

These and other governance issues can be addressed by law reform and prudential regulation. But laws on secured credit and bankruptcy are crucial to building a strong financial sector. Credit markets are thus prime candidates for law reform, on both the substantive side and the enforcement side, where judges and bankruptcy courts have demanding roles that go well beyond what is required in run-of-the-mill contract and property cases.

A Personal Caveat

When all is said and done, this book should be seen as drawing conclusions as to the policy areas that are raised by a major premise that has gained ascendancy in the development community, especially in academia and in multilateral agencies, namely, that institutions matter and that, in particular, legal institutions matter.

I believe that premise—let us call it the "law matters" premise—is correct. But I do not attempt in this book to prove it, much as I am convinced that it is correct. My comparative advantage as a legal scholar and as a former economic policymaker is to unpack the premise into fields of law and the principal economic sectors involved.

Proof of the correctness of the law matters premise would be an entirely different exercise, more appropriate for economists and perhaps other social scientists than for lawyers and policymakers. Nonetheless, the efforts to show that institutions in general matter to economic development are well advanced. But efforts to show that law itself matters are less far along. Historical evidence from the securities field tends to show that strong securities regulation (at least in the United States) followed, not led, the growth of dispersed ownership of equity securities.[2] From this kind of evidence, one can hypothesize that healthy economic growth can create a constituency for legal protection of the gains achieved, and hence to that extent, law can both cement gains already achieved and build a base for further strengthening through legal means.[3] That has been the record in the United States in the decades since federal regulation of securities was instituted in the 1930s.

2. Coffee (2001).
3. Johnson, Ostry, and Subramanian (2006).

But proof that economic growth and stronger law can go hand in hand does not prove that law reform can actually cause economic growth in the first place. After all, law tends to reflect a society as a whole—its history, its values, its culture, and its politics. Although illustrations exist of situations where law was truly autonomous,[4] some evidence (which I will not attempt to expand upon) does tend to show that law can accelerate economic growth. To take equity markets as an example, recent research shows that sound securities regulation can significantly reduce the cost of capital.[5] Similarly, one can compare how different legal structures affect outcomes in comparable countries, such as differences in securities regulation in Poland and the Czech Republic.[6]

A reader might ask whether one should not wait for better proof that law itself truly matters before focusing on the policy implications. My background as an academic tends to make me sympathetic to such an approach. But my experience as a policymaker makes me reject it emphatically. Policy decisions on economic development issues are being made every day in every developing country and in bilateral and multilateral agencies in the developed world as well. Economy policymaking is necessarily carried out under conditions of uncertainty—uncertainty about the facts and about underlying principles and causes. So decisions whether to change legal institutions and substantive law will be taken—if only by inaction—in substantive fields, such as land, equity markets, and credit markets as well as in enforcement, including the role and nature of the judiciary. Since policymakers know that institutions matter to economic development, it would be foolish for them to assume that legal institutions—both the rules of the game and law's organizations, especially the judiciary—do not matter.

A Parting Challenge

To round out an appreciation of the relationship between legal institutions and economic growth, it is worth taking up a final subject that raises in "real time" the role of law, and especially the rule of law, in economic development. That subject is presented by contemporary China, whose rapid growth presents that question as a challenge to our understanding of the entire subject. A reader may well ask whether the rule of law is truly necessary to economic

4. See discussion in chapter 8 on the role of the English judiciary in rejecting the growth of new forms of business enterprise on the ground of incompatibility with the common law.
5. Hail and Leuz (2005). See also some recent work by legal origins authors LaPorta, López-de-Silanes, and Shleifer (2006).
6. See discussion in chapter 8; Glaeser, Johnson, and Shleifer (2001); and Coffee (1999).

development in view of China's rapid growth over the past few decades and its well-known rule-of-law weaknesses. The China case thus raises squarely the question whether, as asserted, the rule of law must precede economic development. An alternative view is that China's rapid economic development from its current low absolute level may be enough to create the resources and the public constituency for better rule-of-law institutions that will support further growth toward developed country status.

The subject of China, addressed in the final chapter, provides the further advantage of illustrating a number of the themes of this book, especially the difficulty of building a strong, independent judiciary and a first-class financial sector, both of which have been thought essential to sustainable economic development.

11

China as a Test Case

China is the fastest-growing country in the world. Moreover, its economy has already become one of the most important. Some commentators predict that China's economy will surpass the size of the U.S. economy some time in the second decade of this century (albeit at a much lower per capita income level). For most purposes, these predictions are quite misleading.[1] Yet China's prowess in manufacturing is already a challenge to the manufacturing sectors of the most advanced economies, at least in labor-intensive industries. Moreover, China is going beyond low-wage manufacturing and entering the high-technology arena (from the top down, so to speak) through high-level research backed by a growing army of highly educated scientists and engineers and through the outsourcing to China of research and development activities from some of the world's most accomplished high-technology firms.

1. The predictions of total Chinese GDP soon surpassing U.S. GDP are based on purchasing power parity comparisons. Whatever their value for certain purposes, these comparisons are almost surely unjustified for any inference about China's influence on global national security and foreign policy issues. Cooper (2004), for example, finds that under a market exchange rate comparison, China's GDP in 2020 would still be only 24 percent as large as U.S. GDP and significantly lower than Japanese GDP (see also Cooper 2002). Green (2003, p. 2) also points out that under current growth trends, China's GDP in 2025 would be $5 trillion, about 40 percent as large as the U.S. economy was in 2005. In October 2005 Hu Jintao stated at a G-20 meeting that China intended to "bring our GDP up to around 4 trillion U.S. dollars and per capita GDP to around 3,000 U.S. dollars within the next 15 years" (www.gov.cn/english/2005-10/16/conntent_78589.htm). That Chinese GDP figure for 2020 would still be equal to only about one-third of 2005 U.S. GDP and obviously much smaller still on a 2005 U.S. per capita GDP basis. (The estimates cited in this note should be adjusted to reflect the one-time upward adjustment of Chinese GDP by about one-sixth announced by the Chinese government at the end of 2005. See note 15.)

Yet the level of China's adherence to the rule of law is frequently criticized.[2]

How does China's growth rate fit with its rule-of-law profile? Does the coexistence of high economic growth and lax adherence to the rule of law mean that institutions are not important to economic growth after all? Does it mean, at the very least, that legal institutions, and the rule of law in particular, are not important?[3] One group of scholars, Allen, Qian, and Qian, has reached more than half way to that conclusion. "China is an important counterexample to the findings in the law, institutions, finance, and growth literature: Neither its legal nor financial system is well developed by existing standards, yet it has one of the fastest growing economies," they write.[4]

China's Ranking on a Law and Finance Scale

In arguing that China is a counterexample to the legal institutional approach, Allen, Qian, and Qian gave China scores on corporate and creditors rights law following the methodology developed by La Porta and his colleagues in their seminal 1998 Law and Finance article.[5] In corporate law China earned a shareholder rights score of 3 (out of 6) and a creditors rights score of 2 (out of 4). In both cases China's shareholder rights score fell below the average for countries whose law originated in English common law but above the average for those whose law originated in French civil law. If China had been in the LLSV list of countries, it would have ranked right at the average of all LLSV countries (developed and developing) for shareholder rights. China's creditors rights score, while higher than the 1 scored by Australia, Canada, and the United States, was nonetheless far below many of its neighbors: Hong Kong, India, Indonesia, and Malaysia all scored a 4.

Though one might think that these comparisons leave China in a reasonably strong position, Allen, Qian, and Qian decided on a different comparison (based on the number of countries above and below a given sample mean) that made China's results appear weaker than the LLSV methodology would have. Abandoning LLSV averages, Allen, Qian, and Qian emphasized that "almost half of the countries in the French-origin subsample . . . have

---

2. For a detailed and balanced, if optimistic, view of the rule of law in the Chinese context, see generally Peerenboom (2002).

3. Peerenboom (2002, pp. 462–63).

4. Allen, Qian, and Qian (2005a, p. 57).

5. Allen, Qian, and Qian scores are found at Allen, Qian, and Qian (2005a, p. 65, table 2A, and p. 66, table 2B). The LLSV scores are found at La Porta and others (1998, pp. 1130–31, table 2, and 1136–37, table 4). The LLSV methodology on shareholder and creditors rights is discussed in chapters 8 and 9. See also chapter 2.

equal or better measures of creditor and shareholder rights" and that the "overall evidence . . . suggests that the majority of LLSV-sample countries have better creditor and shareholder protections than China."[6] Although China's shareholder rights score of 3 was exactly the same as the average score of the forty-nine countries in the LLSV sample, Allen, Qian, and Qian chose to emphasize that 65 percent of the LLSV countries had a score "higher or equal to three."[7]

Nonetheless, if one takes the LLSV analysis as giving a reliable insight into corporate and creditors rights law (despite the skepticism expressed in earlier chapters about their choice of substantive law provisions), the bottom line is surely that China's substantive law is not hopelessly weak. Indeed, looking at the LLSV sorting of countries by per capita income, China would rank somewhere in the middle of the pack—slightly below the midpoint of the middle 50 percent of countries for both shareholder and creditors rights.[8] Nonetheless, the real question is how well the substantive law is enforced.[9] According to a report from the Organization for Economic Cooperation and Development (OECD), surveys show that "China is still seen as comparing unfavourably to its Asian competitors" with regard to "actual corporate governance practices."[10]

World Bank Rankings

A second way to rank China is to use the World Bank's *Doing Business* studies. Some of their categories are analogous to rule-of-law indicators and correspond roughly to legal areas studied in earlier chapters of this book. For example, for "contract enforcement," a measure of the performance of the

6. Allen, Qian, and Qian (2005a, p. 64).

7. Allen, Qian, and Qian (2005a, p. 66, table 2B). The authors do not state what percentage of the LLSV countries had a score "lower or equal" to 3, a category obviously overlapping with "higher or equal."

8. See La Porta and others (1998). Pistor and Xu (2005, p. 191, table 2) find China somewhat below average for "legal shareholder protection" both as a matter of formal law and in regulatory quality among transition countries.

9. Allen, Qian, and Qian (2005a, p. 68, table 2C) not only make the same point about enforcement but also attempt to measure enforcement in China. However, their measures, taken from La Porta and others (1998), are mostly about issues such as risk of expropriation, risk of contract repudiation, and accounting standards, matters that do not bear on judicial enforcement of substantive law, or about issues such as corruption and the rule of law, matters that are much too general to be able to measure judicial enforcement. In any case, Allen, Qian, and Qian do not attempt to rate China on most of their enforcement measures.

10. OECD (2002, p. 36).

judiciary in contract litigation between private parties, the World Bank ranks China as 47th best out of the 155 countries ranked. China ranks higher than the average country in both the East Asian and South Asian regions, though well below the average of OECD member countries.[11]

"Registering property" shows that China's land registration system is especially strong, even though the nature and quality of China's protection of real property are still limited (since land belongs to the state and occupants normally have only user rights).[12] Despite this substantive shortcoming, all three of the procedural aspects of registration—the number of procedures, the time in days, and the cost of registration as a percentage of property value—rank above the OECD average. In fact, whatever the substantive land property rights (which are not measured or ranked in the study), China's procedures are efficient, allowing China to rank 24th of the 155 countries.

"Protecting investors" is a different story, however. China ranks 100th. The main reason for this poor showing lies not on the substantive law side, where China ranks high, but rather on the enforcement side: China ranks 1 on a scale of 1 to 10 with regard to director liability for self-dealing and 2 on the same scale for shareholder's ability to sue officers and directors for misconduct. (On this scale a ranking of 1 is the worst score; 10 the best.)

"Getting credit" is concerned with both legal rights and credit information registries. On a legal rights index, which measures the degree to which collateral and bankruptcy laws facilitate lending,[13] China scores 2 on a scale of 10, well below the East Asia and the South Asia average scores of 5.3 and 3.8, respectively, and even further below the OECD average score (6.3). Nor does China make up for legal deficiencies through credit information registries, where its score is 3. This score is higher than the two surrounding regions' rankings, but that is only because the credit information index refers to formal rules; in fact, only 0.4 percent of adults in China are covered by a public registry and none (0.0 percent) are covered by a private registry.

For "closing a business," the World Bank study uses a methodology based on law firm responses to a hypothetical case to assess the time and cost of

11. The discussion of China in the World Bank *Doing Business* studies is to be found online in a substantial number of different (and changing) documents (last accessed by this author on May 11, 2006), which are best accessed through the following web address (from which one can click on individual topics or countries): (doingbusiness.org/ExploreEconomies/).

12. See discussion of China's land system in chapter 7 and later in this chapter. For the World Bank *Doing Business* view of Chinese substantive land law, see (doingbusiness. org/Documents/Registering-Property/42.pdf).

13. This legal rights index with respect to facilitating lending is based on Djankov and others (2005).

bankruptcy.[14] Here China ranks 59th, with scores on time, cost, and recovery rate being better than the average of East Asian countries but well below the average of South Asian countries (even though China's procedures take less time). And China ranks far below the OECD average on all three dimensions.

From these various World Bank *Doing Business* rankings it is apparent that China's rule-of-law profile, much as in the Allen, Qian, and Qian study, is somewhere in the middle range of developing countries as a group. It is noteworthy that China is well below the average, however, in a few crucial financial sectors, notably in equity markets where, despite reasonable substantive corporate law, China's enforcement measures for protecting investors, as noted above, rank quite low.

The Chinese Economy: Is a Slowdown in Growth Ahead?

The absolute size of the Chinese economy and the penchant among journalists and economic pundits for mechanical extrapolation into a distant future of current trends lead many a credulous reader and television viewer to believe that China is well on its way to becoming a developed country. Nothing could be further from the truth!

The Chinese economy is well down the list of developing countries in per capita income. In 2004 per capita income (according to official Chinese statistics) was $1,500 (U.S.) at current exchange rates. (This figure received a one-time upward adjustment for 2004 of about one-sixth simply by adding services to the GDP account.[15]) Using purchasing power parity (PPP), per capita GDP was $7,634 in that year. For North American readers, it may be helpful to compare China with Mexico, since those readers will probably be at least somewhat aware of Mexican life, where one can encounter great wealth (often behind high walls) but also millions upon millions of impoverished citizens. At current exchange rates Mexican per capita income in 2004 was $6,790, four times as great as per capita income in China; and Mexico's per capita income on a PPP basis was $9,168, substantially greater than China's.[16]

---

14. See discussion of this case in chapter 9 on credit markets.

15. "Revised GDP for 2004 Up by 16.8%," *China Daily*, December 21, 2005. See also Giles and Guerrera (2005).

16. World Bank (2006b) (data in current international dollars). However, according to the Economist Intelligence Unit (2006b, pp. 22–23), the newly discovered services output came largely from price increases in services and did not change the fact that "China's economy remains centered on manufacturing, and is relatively energy-inefficient and increasingly unequal in terms of the distribution of wealth."

One can argue about the right measure to use for comparisons—purchasing power parity or current exchange rates. PPP numbers reflect the buying power of a resident in the local economy at local prices, where money purchases of services and locally produced goods in poor countries are often at prices well below international levels calculated at market exchange rates. In a village in a developing country a local resident can acquire haircuts and the services of domestics at a tiny fraction of what they would cost in a highly developed country (compared at market exchange rates).

In any event and even if one can trust Chinese economic statistics for GDP in Chinese currency, there is every reason to be skeptical of the PPP figures for Chinese GDP. Albert Keidel, who prepared a 1994 World Bank report casting doubt on the technical basis for PPP estimates of Chinese GDP, reaffirmed the inadequacy of those approximations in 2004, stating: "China's PPP is really unknown. We have no statistics on what the purchasing power parity measure of China's GDP should be . . . . And so we're looking at a Chinese economy that in PPP terms is much smaller, in my mind, than the numbers that are usually used."[17]

Similarly, Richard Cooper argues: "Even if one were inclined to a purchasing power parity . . . [measure], the PPP data that we have for China can only be described as flaky. That is to say, even if one preferred a PPP measure, we have a terrible time measuring an accurate PPP, and it is subject to all kinds of judgments by the analysts, not least the weights that one attaches to different components of output."[18] Two Washington think tanks concluded that they "did not believe that World Bank estimates of China's GDP measured in terms of PPP should be taken seriously."[19]

A reason for being cautious about past Chinese growth rates is that, as Alwyn Young points out, China has used a different method from most countries for arriving at national GDP; it adds up local production reports to reach a national total, with predictable incentives for local overreporting when actual growth is weak and underreporting in periods of overheating in the economy.[20] Young also cautions that even assuming the correctness of Chinese nominal national income statistics, inflation was underestimated by

17. Statement of Albert Keidel at an IMF Economic Forum on China in the Global Economy: Prospects and Challenges. Washington, October 19, 2004 (imf.org/external/np/tr/2004/tr041019.htm).

18. Cooper (2002, p. 788).

19. Bergsten and others (2006, p. 163, n. 2).

20. Young (2003, p. 1224, n. 5). See also Holz (2006). On the weaknesses of the Chinese statistical system, see OECD (2005a, pp. 169–96).

Chinese authorities so that real GDP growth in the 1986–98 period was overstated by 3.0 percentage points a year.[21] Using Young's analysis, the real growth in GDP during that period was 6.2 percent rather than 9.2 percent. Annual growth of more than 6 percent is still, of course, an extraordinary achievement but would not lead to the kind of assumptions about the future that underpin so much contemporary discussion. Over twenty-four years, the compounding of 9 percent growth yields an eightfold increase in total growth; compounding of 6 percent growth would yield only a fourfold increase—resulting in a Chinese economy only half as much larger than the base year.

The policy question is not what the exact Chinese growth rate is, but whether it can be sustained. One reason for doubt derives from the recent history of China's neighbors. The uncontroversial fact that China is currently at a much lower level of per capita GDP than those neighbors is key. Japan, South Korea, Taiwan, and several other neighbors grew at least as fast as China when their per capita GDP levels were at the current Chinese level. In that sense China is no outlier in East Asian growth statistics. Moreover, the enthusiasm about future growth now so apparent in the case of China was widespread with regard to China's Asian neighbors in the early 1990s. A highly popular 1997 book titled *Megatrends Asia* carried the excitement right up to the 1997 Asia financial crisis, celebrating "Asia's rapid ascent to global economic dominance."[22]

Martin Wolf, using data from Angus Maddison's most recent work, summarizes the comparison with the growth rate of China:

> China's gross domestic product per head at purchasing power parity rose by 370 per cent between 1978 and 2004, a trend rate of 6.1 percent a year. Yet between 1950 and 1973, Japan's GDP per head had increased by 460 percent, a trend rate of 8.2 percent. Between 1962 and 1990, South Korea's GDP per head rose by 680 percent, a trend rate of 7.6 percent, while Taiwan's rose by 600 percent, between 1958 and 1987, a trend rate of 7.1 percent.[23]

The important point about the comparison with China's neighbors is that the spurts of growth Wolf refers to (lasting from twenty-three years for Japan to twenty-nine years for Taiwan) are comparable to the period between the

---

21. Young (2003, p. 1232). See also World Bank (1997, p. 3, box 1.1).

22. Naisbitt (1997, p. 14).

23. Wolf (2005). To be sure, China's growth rate has been in the 9–10 percent range recently, but China produced considerably lower growth in some earlier reform periods.

announcement by the Chinese Communist Party (CCP) under the new leadership of Deng Xiaoping in 1978 that its focus would shift to economic development and the first decade of the twenty-first century. And shortly after the end of their surge of growth, most of the neighbors experienced a substantial slowdown in growth. In Japan, the economic downturn was longer even though Japan's rule-of-law record is stronger than the other neighbors.

The slowdown among China's neighbors such as Indonesia, Malaysia, South Korea, and Thailand was quite pronounced. A careful study using data up to mid-2001 found that the loss from the slowdown beginning in 1997 was never made up, resulting in a permanent loss in cumulative GDP.[24] Data for later years show, moreover, that after the turn of the millennium, the growth rate continued to be substantially below that of the period leading up to 1997. Those countries have recently grown more rapidly than in the 2001–03 postcrisis period, but this is a period in which the world economy as a whole has been growing at a higher rate than in the period before the onset of the Asian crisis; in 2004, *The Economist* noted that the world economy was "growing at its fastest rate for almost 30 years."[25]

Thailand grew at rates between 6.8 and 11.2 percent from 1990 to 1996, with 1997 marking the beginning of a recession. But between 2000 and 2004, Thailand managed only 5.4 percent average growth and is expected to grow by only 5.0 percent in 2006. Indonesia grew at rates between 7.2 and 9.0 percent between 1990 and 1996, but averaged only 4.6 percent average growth from 2000 to 2004 and is predicted to grow by 5.0 percent in 2006. Some pundits claimed Malaysia did not suffer much from the Asian financial crisis because it fenced off its financial sector with capital controls. It nevertheless was unable to replicate its 8.9 to 10.0 percent growth of the 1990–96 period, achieving only an average of 4.4 percent during the 2000–04 period, with the 2006 prediction being 5.5 percent.[26]

The reasons for this marked slowdown, especially after the recession, among China's neighbors are controversial and multiple. One reason is that as a country reaches a GDP per capita level closer to that of the developed world, the opportunities for "catch-up" with first world technology and business methods become more difficult and expensive to realize. This was particularly the case with Japan, which reached West European levels several

24. Cerra and Saxena (2005).
25. "Dancing in Step." *The Economist* (U.S. Edition, November 11, 2004).
26. World Bank (2006b, table 4.1). The predictions were released by the International Monetary Fund in April 2006 (in other words, well into the year in question, 2006); see IMF (2006, p. 35, table 1.6).

decades ago. Moreover, some of the slowdown was the result of economic policy errors. It is certainly true that the region was affected during the rest of the 1990s by the 1997–98 Asian financial crisis, which some analysts blame for the subsequent slowdown, and which might have been avoided or lessened by different economic policies. Some analysts attribute the financial crisis, for example, to purely macroeconomic factors.

A strong case—indeed, a surprisingly strong case—can be made that the trigger for the Asian financial crisis was a series of institutional failings. These failings were particularly striking in the financial sector—poor corporate governance, directed and related lending, and the absence of effective bankruptcy laws, as well as a perceived implicit government guarantee to banks and poor banking supervision facilitating "crony capitalism." [27] An important study by Simon Johnson and colleagues showed that although poor macroeconomic management may have triggered the Asian financial crisis, the extent of exchange rate depreciation and of stock market declines among the Asian crisis countries was closely related to their respective weaknesses in legal institutions regarding corporate governance, particularly lack of protection for minority shareholders.[28] A statistical study found significant results for Thailand and Indonesia (the two countries perhaps worst hit by the Asian crisis), suggesting a high degree of expropriation of minority shareholders.[29]

In Indonesia much of the banking system proved to be insolvent, in large part because of connected and directed lending. As one study put it: "The main cause of private banks' nonperforming loans was connected lending, with these banks being used to channel credits to bank owners. In the case of state-owned banks, the main cause was state-directed lending."[30] According to *The Economist*, crony capitalism was remarkably blatant in Indonesia during the Suharto period: "President Suharto's family dominates the economy, owning huge chunks of business, including power generation, an airline, construction, telecoms, toll roads, newspapers, property and cars. Family members and their cronies get first pick of government contracts and licenses, so it helps to have one of their names on the company letterhead. Paying off

27. For a journalistic review of corporate governance failings and abuse of minority shareholders leading to the Asian financial crisis, see Vines (2000, pp. 141–60). See also "Six Deadly Sins," *The Economist*, March 5, 1998; and "On the Rocks," *The Economist*, March 5, 1998. On implicit guarantees, see Bai and Wang (1999, pp. 436–37) and Krugman (1998). On bank supervision, see Pomerleano (1999).

28. See Johnson and others (2000) and Claessens, Djankov, and Lang (2000) on the shareholding structure that made minority shareholders vulnerable.

29. Claessens and others (1999).

30. Srinivas and Sitorus (2004, pp. 153–55).

family members or well-connected officials can add up to 30% to the cost of a deal."[31]

In the case of Japan, it is now apparent that its inability to resume consistent growth has been partly related to its weak banking sector, which in turn was related to the insistence of the government, especially the ruling Liberal Democratic Party, that Japanese banks support sectors and regions important to the government of the day. Lending by banks quickly turned into several decades of nonperforming loans that continue to some extent today.

The question for the future, therefore, is whether China can avoid the slowdown experienced by its neighbors. Will its institutional weaknesses, especially in the financial sector, endanger continued Chinese growth rates just as similar weaknesses reduced the growth rates of its Asian neighbors? The World Bank Country Director for China recently laid out the risks:

> While China has grown well since 1990, it is remarkable how much savings and investment this has required . . . . On the one hand, the need for such a large amount of investment for China's level of growth reflects the inefficiency of the financial system and the preference of local governments for large amounts of investment. A lot of bad investments are financed which ultimately produce little value. This is wasteful for China in real terms, and also creates the financial sector problem of a large volume of non-performing loans. This situation creates a systemic risk for China, in which some kind of internal or external shock could set off a costly financial crisis.
>
> It also seems clear that this pattern of growth cannot be sustained indefinitely. Investment cannot just keep rising as a share of GDP and it will be increasingly difficult for China to keep increasing its share of world trade at the same rate.[32]

In short, according to this line of analysis, the weak and inefficient financial sector will lead to either a crisis similar to the Asian financial crisis or a less rapidly growing China. Either way, a weak financial sector is likely to create a slowdown in growth.[33]

---

31. "Six Deadly Sins," *The Economist,* March 5, 1998.

32. Slide presentation by David Dollar: "Improving the Efficiency of China's Growth Is Important for the Whole World" (cgdev.org/docs/DDollarslides.pdf [undated but presented in June 2005]).

33. This analysis involves a short-term slowdown in Chinese per capita growth. Over the longer term a slowdown in the growth of total GDP seems inevitable given the demographic structure of China, created in large part by the one-child policy. China's population profile is aging more rapidly than most other Asian countries, notably India.

A Closer Look at the Chinese Growth Record

Before looking more closely at China's rule-of-law weaknesses, it is worth examining the nature of Chinese growth in recent decades and comparing it with the growth of China's neighbors during their period of rapid growth. This examination can be conducted using growth accounting, an approach that involves breaking down the sources of growth into capital and labor inputs. Both of these inputs can be adjusted for quality—labor, for example, can be adjusted for the levels of growth in human capital (represented, say, by increasing years of education of the labor force). The residual of the overall growth, which is that portion that cannot be explained by adjusted capital and labor inputs, is usually called total factor productivity (TFP) and is usually taken as a measure of the portion of growth attributable to added efficiency from, say, innovation. TFP, as Alwyn Young puts it, "represents the proportional increase in output that would have occurred in the absence of any input changes."[34]

Young has explored Chinese statistics to determine whether Chinese growth, like the growth of the Asian Tigers in the precrisis period, can be explained primarily by China's ability to mobilize labor resources and by China's high rate of investment. He noted that, in the context of increased labor force participation rates and disproportionately large increases in the working age population, a change in the proportion of the population employed in agricultural labor relative to nonagricultural labor had taken place. While the agricultural labor force had hardly grown (less than 1 percent a year from 1978 to 1988), the nonagricultural labor force grew rapidly: 4.5 percent a year.[35] In a lengthy, complex analysis, which cannot be adequately summarized in a few sentences, he concluded that the disproportionate increase in the nonagricultural labor force coupled with its increased educational attainment and the increased labor force participation accounted for most of the well-publicized high growth rate. (Put in laymen's terms, Young was analyzing primarily the economic result of the shift in the relative proportion of Chinese workers from farm to factory and from the rural west to the more dynamic eastern and southern coastal areas.)

A possible conclusion is that while China is currently growing rapidly, its growth is much like that of the Asian Tigers and therefore at some point a Chinese slowdown should be expected. Of course, over the very long run, as

34. Young (2003, p. 1223).
35. Young (2003, p. 1235, table 6; p. 1237, table 8).

China approaches a per capita income level similar to that of the developed world, its growth likely would gradually decline to that of the developed world. The opportunities to catch up with the capital depth and technological know-how of the developed world will have been exhausted, and in that case China is no different from any developing country and at some point its rate of growth must naturally slow.[36] The question now, however, is whether there will be an unnatural slowdown such as that experienced by the Asian Tigers.

China is far from reaching that point of natural slowdown. With tens of millions of unemployed and underutilized workers, especially in rural western China, the period before slowdown may well be longer than in the Asian crisis countries. [37] Further, tens of millions of underutilized workers in China's state-owned enterprises (SOEs) have been laid off, and the shift of the workforce out of SOEs is apparently continuing.[38] Finally, Chinese emphasis on education, including higher education, may enable continued growth through what Robert Fogel calls "factor enhancement."[39] At the same time, China has a rapidly aging labor force because of its one-child policy and therefore there is not a massive army of young adults (relative to its 1.3 billion population) ready to join the labor force. In fact, China's population is one of the oldest on average in Asia.[40]

The influx of rural workers into the modern commercial and industrial economy is not the only significant factor in China's economic growth. An extremely high investment rate in China has led to speculation that an investment bubble is occurring.[41] Investment rates have grown to 45 percent of GDP, leaving consumers with less than half of GDP (the remainder going to government noninvestment expenditures).[42] Since the very word *bubble* suggests an unfortunate ending, the question whether one exists not only is important, but also raises the further question whether legal institutions are

---

36. See the same point as applied to the Asian Tigers in Radelet and Sachs (1997).

37. Wu (2005, pp. 133–38).

38. According to Fishman (2005, p. 74), 53 million people working in China's state sector lost their jobs between 1996 and 2001. See also Qian (2000a) and Wu (2005, p. 198).

39. Fogel (2006).

40. According to Qian (2003, p. 301), "at the outset of reform in the late 1970s, over 70 percent of China's labor force was employed in agriculture. By 2000, China's agriculture labor force had already declined to below the 50 percent mark, which is impossible without successful development outside the agricultural sector."

41. "Struggling to Keep the Lid On," *The Economist*, April 27, 2006.

42. IMF (2005b, pp. 96–97, box. 2.1); Kuijs (2005). The Economist Intelligence Unit (2006c, p. 5) reports that private consumption has been growing more slowly than GDP. Meanwhile, investment in fixed assets has been growing much faster than GDP, increasing by 27 percent, year over year, in the first quarter of 2006.

implicated. After all, the use of the word in this sense dates back in England to a speculative mania leading to the collapse of the South Sea Company in 1719–20. The collapse was followed by enactment of the Bubble Act of 1720 (prohibiting the formation of joint stock companies without royal charters), giving rise to the notion that changes in law may arrest the formation of bubbles.[43]

The South Sea incident involved financial investment, as opposed to real investment— say, in plant and equipment—and that has been true of nearly all bubble incidents, including the tech stock bubble in the United States and the rapid growth and then collapse of Germany's Neuer Markt at the dawn of the twenty-first century.[44] Not only has there been relatively little financial speculation in China since 2000 (even though the Chinese stock market began to rise rapidly in the first half of 2006), but investment in China has been heavily in physical infrastructure—roads, airports, and the like. Still, there has been a great deal of investment in real estate, some taking on speculative dimensions analogous to stock market speculation.[45] One worrisome aspect of the investment surge in real estate (and to some extent in physical infrastructure) is the involvement of political officials for their private gain, a key feature of the South Sea bubble.[46] The involvement of local governments with private housing contractors led a prominent Chinese business columnist to attack government "manipulation" of the property market, observing that a "profit-driven local government cannot ensure the stable development of the sector."[47] Nonetheless, the bubble question will not be addressed here because, corruption aside, any speculative element does not appear closely related to institutional failings in China of the kind examined in this book. In any event, even if the bursting of an investment bubble were to derail Chinese growth, the slowdown would likely prove temporary if one is to judge by U.S. experience where panics leading to sharp recessions were experienced five times in the nineteenth century. Indeed, the panic of 1873 was set off by an investment bubble in Chicago following the great Chicago Fire in 1871. An investment boom took place in which, according to

43. The classic descriptions of the South Sea incident, as well as of the contemporaneous bubble involving John Law's Mississippi Company in France, are Mackay (1841, pp. 1–88) and the successive editions of Kindleberger's *Manias, Panics, and Crashes*. See Kindleberger and Aliber (2005). See also Garber (2000).

44. On the Neuer Markt, see Burghof and Hunger (2003).

45. For a view on whether a real estate bubble exists in China, see Lau (2006).

46. Garber (2000, pp. 111–12), on what he calls "The Purchase of Parliament."

47. McGregor (2006), quoting Hu Shuli.

a contemporary observer, "every other man and every fourth woman had an investment in house lots."[48]

In addition to its high investment rate and its ability to mobilize labor resources for some time to come, China has also shown an ability thus far to increase total factor productivity. Heytens and Zebregs, surveying the literature, found that Chinese "TFP growth was . . . particularly high following the liberalization of the agricultural sector in the early 1980s, and in the early 1990s after market-oriented reforms were accelerated, and [was] well above that of the prereform period (1952–78)."[49] Thus, even when capital and labor resources are plentiful, rapid growth is at least partly dependent on TFP growth, and institutional reform has fed TFP growth in China in the past. An OECD study found that the growing private sector in China had a higher rate of TFP increase than the state-owned sector, and this was true even though the state sector had higher labor productivity because it was able to apply three times the capital that was used by the private sector (as shown below, the private sector has relatively little access to bank lending or a corporate bond market in the current stage of Chinese institutional reform).[50]

The pressure on the Chinese leadership to force rapid growth in overall Chinese GDP growth may have been based on the need to provide jobs for an expanding population, especially migrants to the cities, and an increase in the number of university graduates. But this need is expected to decline somewhat, in part because the one-child policy has led to a decline in the rate of population growth and therefore in the need to provide additional jobs. The result is that the leadership may be able in the coming decades to devote increased resources to institutional reform, including legal reforms such as an expanded and better-trained judiciary.

The leadership can, if it so chooses, turn to foreign borrowing to finance institutional reform. Not only does it have massive foreign exchange reserves, but governmental external debt is remarkably low.[51] Moreover, domestic debt is also low, even though there are huge implicit liabilities for future cleaning up of nonperforming loans of banks and other nonperforming obligations of state-owned enterprises. Further financial flexibility is provided by a fiscal

48. On the five panics, see Kindleberger and Aliber (2005, pp. 259–62). The quotation regarding the Chicago investment boom is a paraphrase of an earlier source; see Kindleberger and Aliber (2005, p. 101).

49. Heytens and Zebregs (2003, p. 12).

50. OECD (2005b, pp. 86–87).

51. The Economist Intelligence Unit (2006b, p. 5) has estimated total external debt at $263 billion in U.S. dollars with a debt service ratio (debt service to current account surplus) of only 5.2 percent.

deficit that is relatively modest compared with other countries; China's budget deficit was only 1.5 percent of GDP in 2005.[52] Despite its financial flexibility, though, China's ability to avoid a growth slowdown depends in substantial measure, as the experience of China's Asian neighbors suggests, on whether it can successfully address institutional issues, including rule-of-law issues.

Enforcement and the Chinese Judiciary

The Chinese government and society have been placing increasing importance on law. According to Potter:

> Judicial caseloads are averaging nearly 5 million per year nationwide, while the number of additional disputes resolved through mediation and arbitration is burgeoning. Bookstores in Beijing, Shanghai, and other major cities are well stocked with books on law, and crowded with prospective purchasers. Law faculties are filled to capacity with many of China's best students, driven by the prospect of lucrative employment to study a field that for all intents and purposes did not exist 25 years ago. Law firms have multiplied—more than 5,000 have been established since 1990, bringing the total to more than 9,000.[53]

An interest in, and even an emphasis on, law does not, however, mean that enforcement is of high quality. It is useful to break the issue of enforcement quality into two parts: the relationship of the state to the actors in the economy, and the quality of the judiciary.

Despite the explosion in the size of the Chinese private sector, the remaining size of the state-owned and collective enterprise sectors, coupled with the influence of the government, the Chinese Communist Party, and those allied with government and the party, suggests that the central issues are likely to involve the problem discussed in earlier chapters—the predatory ruler. In China the potential problem is much greater than a sixteenth or seventeenth century Tudor or Stuart King seizing property or reneging on his debts; as powerful as the Crown might have been, most of England was untouched by what was a tiny government and public sector.[54] In China the issues arise from the large role of government and the influence of the Chinese Communist Party.

52. Economist Intelligence Unit (2006c, p. 3).
53. Potter (2004, p. 466).
54. See discussion of the conflicts involving the Crown in England, chapter 4.

As for the role and quality of the Chinese judiciary and, more broadly, the legal system as a whole, a few striking aspects of Chinese history play an important role. China had essentially no legal system when the economic reforms began in 1978. With the creation in 1949 of the People's Republic of China, even the notion of law was in flux, and with the onset of the Cultural Revolution under Mao's leadership, law was subordinated to party policies.[55] As Donald Clarke points out, a "legal vacuum" was created that "ultimately had to be filled by whatever authoritative materials decisionmakers had at hand, including Party newspaper editorials, policy documents, and leaders' speeches."[56]

Even during the Imperial period (ending in 1911) the legal system was largely a penal system, and although a good deal of academic controversy exists on the point, the use of law to settle private disputes was less common than in other countries.[57] Chow summarizes the traditional Western view of Imperial law:

> Citizens viewed law as being administered vertically, from the state upon the individual, as opposed to being used horizontally to resolve disputes between actors with one another . . . . [T]he use of law as a form of state administered power upon individuals also struck fear in most of the general population with good reason. Ordinary subjects who had disputes resolved them through informal means and mediation by various customary and unofficial channels such as through the use of craft or merchant guilds or through the intervention of village elders. The aversion to using the legal system among the general populace meant that China did not develop a civil law system useful in resolving civil disputes. Formal law only served the public interests of the state and was not viewed by ordinary Chinese as a tool to resolve private disputes.[58]

Nonetheless, in 1904, near the end of the Imperial period, a company law was passed, but it had few favorable economic consequences and did not provide for private dispute settlement.[59]

---

55. Peerenboom (2002, pp. 44–46).

56. D. Clarke (2005).

57. Diamant, Lubman, and O'Brien (2005, p. 4); Scoggins (1990). For a general discussion on the rule of law during the Imperial period, see Peerenboom (2002, pp. 36–43).

58. Chow (2003, pp. 52–53). Between the Imperial and Mao periods, attempts were made to adopt Western-type codes, but according to Lubman (1999, p. 31), these codes "had little effect on Chinese life, especially outside the cities," in part because the codes "were often too complex and irrelevant to Chinese conditions and were adopted and studied in an abstract and mechanical spirit."

59. Wei (2003, pp. 27–29).

In the first half of the Republic of China period (which ran from the end of the Empire in 1911 to the creation of the People's Republic of China, or PRC, in 1949), various attempts to introduce statutory law to govern disputes between private parties were made. But the technique of using legal transplants from Western systems did not find fertile soil, and private disputes continued to be dealt with primarily through customary mediation techniques.[60] Perhaps one reason that the transplants did not take root is that China, never having been a colony, did not have a foreign legal system as a base of departure. Indeed, the modern idea of a court had been foreign to Chinese Imperial law, which, Clarke reported, had "no special, differentiated institution ('court') before which disputing parties advance legal claims."[61] In any event, legal reform efforts were cut short by civil war and the Japanese invasion, and Western laws and institutions evaporated with the 1949 creation of the PRC and especially the Cultural Revolution.

Beginning in 1978, with Deng Xiaoping's ascent to party leadership, a legal reform effort was launched. Its purpose was an announced shift "from class struggle and political campaigns to economic development and modernization."[62] The 1982 constitution struck a rule-of-law theme by stating that the constitution "is the fundamental law of the state and has supreme legal authority . . . . No organization or individual is privileged to be beyond the Constitution or the law." That theme was generalized in the 1999 amendments to the constitution, which called for the country to "be built into a socialist country based upon the rule of law."[63] In 2004 the constitution was further amended to protect property; the amendment provided that "citizens' lawful private property is inviolable," that the state, "in accordance with law, protects the rights of citizens to private property and to its inheritance," and that the state "shall make compensation for the private property expropriated or requisitioned."[64]

If enforcement, even more than substantive law, is the key to the rule of law, then the first place to focus is on the Chinese judiciary. What is striking is how few of the requisites discussed in chapter 5 on the judiciary are to be found in China, even today. The judiciary has no power to review the constitutionality of statutes. Moreover, there is little evidence that the constitution

60. Lubman (1999, pp. 31–32).
61. D. Clarke (2005).
62. Chow (2003, p. 75).
63. Quoted in Chow (2003, pp. 77–78).
64. Constitution of the People's Republic of China, as amended in 2004, Article 13. A follow-on proposal to unify Chinese law on property rights, however, failed to pass in 2006; see Kahn (2006).

has any direct effect at all in litigation; legislation determines the law, and the legislature is thus sovereign (the role of the party aside).[65] One can object that British courts have no power of judicial review either. But of course the British have no single written document known as a constitution (and Chinese judges occupy a completely different role and societal position than British judges do).

Even more important than the absence of judicial review is the lack of judicial independence in the Western sense. One Chinese view of independence is that it is the judiciary as a whole that is to be independent, not the individual judge.[66] Hence judges may and often do consult with other judges, especially higher-level judges, in reaching decisions—just as a bureaucrat would naturally consult with superiors before reaching important decisions.[67] This practice reflects a bureaucratic culture pervading the Chinese judicial system.

Bureaucratic consultation leads to unusual judicial practices. Higher courts sometimes act on their own initiative, without hearing parties or counsel, to instruct lower courts how to decide cases.[68] Another bureaucratic practice is the use of adjudicative committees, which sometimes discuss cases before trial, leading to the assertion that "those who try the case do not decide it, and those who decide the case do not try it."[69] The bureaucratic culture results in a situation, according to the president of the highest Chinese court, where "courts have often been taken as branches of the government, and judges viewed as civil servants who have to follow orders from superiors, which prevents them from exercising mandated legal duties."[70] The 2005 Supreme People's Court Five-Year Plan for court reform called attention to the need for reform of adjudication committees, but the nature of that reform remained under consideration.[71]

Corresponding to the lack of judicial independence is the absence of any doctrine of separation of powers. As Clarke described it:

65. Lin (2003, pp. 275–76); Gewirtz (2001, p. 208).
66. Lubman (1999, p. 262).
67. Hung (2004, pp. 99–104); Lubman (1999, p. 263).
68. Chow (2003, p. 219).
69. Quoted in Lubman (1999, p. 261); see also Peerenboom (2002, pp. 323–25).
70. Quoted in Hung (2004, p. 52).
71. Congressional-Executive Commission on China (2005, pp. 85-86). See also the March 2006 report by Xiao Yang, president of the Supreme People's Court, who simply states on this point that "we must perfect the adjudication committee system" (X. Yang 2006).

The PRC also rejects the notion of horizontal separation of powers between different branches of the government (for example, the traditional troika of legislative, executive, and judicial branches). A necessary separation of functions is acknowledged, but constitutionally speaking the National People's Congress (in form, a legislature) sits at the apex of China's political power structure. In reality, that position is occupied by the Standing Committee of the Politburo of the Chinese Communist Party, but both form and reality share the rejection of multiple power centers.[72]

That judges are regarded as bureaucrats leads to unusual consequences when the litigation involves the government. Some government offices of equal or higher bureaucratic rank than that of a judge see no reason to consider themselves bound by that judge's orders; on the contrary, government officeholders tend to consider themselves bound only by orders issued by their superiors.[73] And judgments can be reopened long after they are rendered, just as a government bureaucracy can always change its mind; in short, the concept of finality plays much less of a role in litigation in China than in most Western systems.[74]

The interaction between the courts and the government bureaucracies is also affected by "local protectionism."[75] Federalism has been carried, especially on a de facto basis, much further in China than in most countries. As is discussed later, this has beneficial aspects, but it is not an unmitigated blessing where the legal system is concerned, especially given that the court system is supposedly national. Trial courts and judges are heavily dependent on local governments (and local people's congresses) for funding, salaries, and even continued employment. Courts are thus often unsympathetic to plaintiffs from other provinces, especially where the defendant is a locally based state-owned enterprise. Civil judgments rendered in other provinces are often refused enforcement.[76]

Perhaps the largest question of judicial independence involves the role of the Communist Party.[77] Interference by party members is probably more

---

72. D. Clarke (2005).

73. Chow (2003, pp. 223–24).

74. D. Clarke (1996, pp. 41–49); Chow (2003, pp. 213–15).

75. Peerenboom (2002, pp. 311–12).

76. Peerenboom (2002, pp. 311–12, 472); Chow (2003, pp. 221–24).

77. For a general discussion on the party's influence on the judiciary, see Peerenboom (2002, pp. 302–09, 319–20). For a Chinese reform view, see Wu (2005, pp. 427–28).

common in administrative rather than judicial bodies. Although judicial review of abstract rule-making by administrative bodies for compliance with the constitution and with legislation is not available, judicial review of administrative decisions to determine whether legislation has been complied with in particular cases involving particular parties (sometimes called legality review) is in principle available. But it is generally conceded that judicial control of administrative decisions leaves a good deal to be desired.[78]

The early practice under which courts would ask for instructions from the party's political-legal committee at the court's level has become less common, except perhaps in exceptional cases involving politically sensitive or controversial litigation.[79] Because the role of the party is not set out clearly in law, the techniques of interference take many forms. Hung recounts that in the 1989–2000 period, a basic court in Jiangxi province handled 200 first-instance administrative cases, but the administrative defendants simply failed to appear in 95 percent of the cases. Hung also states that lawyers are reluctant to take cases challenging administrative acts for fear of losing their license to practice law.[80] She observes that the party tries to propagate the notion that judges should rely on party leadership in administrative litigation; as evidence Hung points to an article published on the official web site of Chinese courts: "The handling of many [administrative] cases involves the overall working situation of the party and the state and involves social stability and economic development [and] therefore, [judges] must tightly rely on the party committee's leadership . . . to ensure the orderly development of administrative litigations . . . ."[81] She notes that courts even "boast in their annual reports about their efforts in 'taking the initiative' to get support from the party" in connection with administrative cases.[82] Hung also notes other kinds of interference by administrative bodies, such as harassing witnesses, pressuring plaintiffs to withdraw cases, and ex parte approaches to judges to "inquire" about cases and to "exchange" views, something which may be initiated by both administrative and party officials.[83]

In 2004 the president of the Supreme People's Court conceded that the "difficulty of executing civil and commercial judgments has become a major

78. For a detailed review, see Peerenboom (2001).
79. Chow (2003, pp. 198–99).
80. Hung (2004, pp. 88–89, 91).
81. Quoted in Hung (2005, p. 10).
82 .Hung (2005, p. 11).
83. Hung (2004, pp. 92–93). See Hung (2005, p. 12) for an example of ex parte communications by an administrative official.

'chronic ailment' often leading to chaos in the enforcement process." According to his statement, "China's courts lack the authority and stature to command obedience to their decisions, especially where such decisions affect other government branches and officials."[84]

Lawyers from common law countries, where judges often make law, should perhaps be reminded that the influence of the party in legislation has traditionally been so dominant that the party can simply change legislation to achieve its ends. As Chow notes, the National People's Congress, which is the legislature, and its standing committee "have generally been viewed as docile, rubber-stamp bodies that routinely approve by unanimous or near unanimous vote legislation already approved by the [party]."[85] Hence direct influence on courts is not always essential for shaping the way that substantive law develops; influence does become important, however, in actual enforcement of the law.

The party's influence on enforcement can thus take various forms. Where adjudication committees are used, for example, they "usually make their decisions after consultation with the CCP's political-legal committees at corresponding levels."[86] In addition, party influence is partly exercised through the power of local people's congresses over judicial budgets, salaries, and tenure. Moreover, as Alford reports, "virtually all significant legal personnel are Party members or have been closely vetted by the Party prior to assuming office [and] this is particularly the case with regard to the judiciary."[87] Judges, especially at the trial level, are thus not necessarily behaviorally independent, especially because they frequently lack the education and competence necessary to command societal prestige and because administrative officials (who are often party members) tend to lack respect for legal knowledge and law. [88]

Moreover, party influence can be said to be partly structural because of the particular type of federalism in China where the trial-level judiciary is not in practice shielded by the prestige of higher-level appellate courts; trial courts in that sense, not having independence and not benefiting from a notion of

84. China Law and Governance Review (2004).

85. Chow (2003, p. 178). Chow (2003, pp. 179–84) acknowledges some attenuation in the unanimity of legislative voting but points to only two instances where a party-backed proposal was blocked.

86. Hung (2005, p. 10).

87. Alford (2003, pp. 134–35).

88. Hung (2004, pp. 93, 100–01). Z. Chen (2003, p. 454) points out that "a large number of judges, especially in less developed provinces, are former military officers who had no formal legal training prior to being a judge." See also Peerenboom (2002, p. 14).

separation of powers, are forced to show some deference to local government and hence to the party. Clarke describes the situation:

> Bifurcation between a people's congress on the one hand and a day-to-day government on the other hand is replicated several layers down into local government. In each case, the government organization is responsible not to the government organization the next level up, but rather to the people's congress at the same level. Again this is the formal structure. In practice, the Communist Party organization at any given level of government has a monopoly on political power. This monopoly, of course, does not mean absolute power to do whatever the Party organization wishes. There are always constraints on capacity, whether economic, political, or social.[89]

Efforts to meet this structural problem by creation of intermediate appellate courts with jurisdiction over more than one province have failed; hence China has no equivalent of U.S. courts of appeal that normally have federal trial courts located in several U.S. states within their territorial jurisdiction.[90]

As noted in chapter 5 on the judiciary, behavioral independence depends heavily on the tenure of judges and their salaries. Since the adoption of an amendment to the Judges Law, China has had a version of life tenure on good behavior; the grounds for dismissal are limited, but they involve such broad criteria as "unqualified for the present post and decline to accept other assignments."[91] Also, the appointment and removal of chief judges of particular courts can be made by the corresponding legislative body.[92] Judicial salaries are comparatively low. Judges' education and training leave much to be desired, although educational attainment is improving; in 2003 some 40 percent of Chinese judges had earned a four-year university degree, a 21 percent increase since 1998.[93] Corruption appears to be common.[94] Finally, a 1998 rule issued by the highest court made judges liable for intentional or negligent violation of any law or regulation; some 2,000 judges were held to have violated the rule in the 1999–2000 period, and the consequences of

---

89. D. Clarke (2005).

90. Peerenboom (2002, p. 328); Wu (2005, p. 428).

91. Article 40, Judges Law of the People's Republic of China, 2001.

92. Lubman (1999, p. 256).

93. Peerenboom (2002, pp. 320–22); Congressional-Executive Commission on China (2005, p. 88).

94. Peerenboom (2002, pp. 322–23); Hung (2004, pp. 105–08); OECD (2005a, p. 107 box 3.1).

violation were potentially substantial.[95] Behavioral independence is thus questionable, despite the limitations on dismissal in the Judges Law. Lack of independence is most likely a problem largely in the review of administrative acts, where the interests of both the party and the bureaucracy are more likely to be directly engaged than in ordinary civil litigation.

The Transition in China's Economic and Legal Structure

Although enforcement may be as important as substantive law and poor enforcement is more likely than weak substantive law to be a hindrance to growth in developing countries, Chinese officials have begun to recognize publicly that the substantive legal system presents a major risk to the Chinese financial system.[96]

China faced a particular challenge during the reform era at the end of the Cultural Revolution. All property having a function in the economic system belonged to the state. Agricultural land belonged directly to the state. Non-agricultural economic activities, especially in industry, were carried on within companies, but these companies were not legal persons but rather were more like units of the government, often local government. State-owned corporations in the sense of legal persons with the legal qualities of Western corporations did not yet exist.[97] In fact, the transfer of such activities from the earlier companies to distinct legal entities with shares owned by the state—a process sometimes called corporatization—was considered a major reform at the time.[98] The separation of management from control was regarded as a step forward because it made possible, at least in theory, professional management that could respond to economic considerations rather than to bureaucratic whim or fashion. The executives of state enterprises were still bureaucrats at heart, however, even to the extent of retaining their rank as state or provincial officials.[99]

The enactment of a company law made the corporate form (and hence limited liability) available to private enterprises as well and led in time to a

95. Hung (2004, pp. 104–05). Efforts have been made by the Supreme People's Court to limit the application of such court responsibility systems; see Congressional-Executive Commission on China (2004, pp. 78–79).

96. See speech by Junbo Xiang, Deputy Governor of the People's Bank of China, "Improve the Legal System to Prevent Financial Risk," at the 2005 High-level Forum of China's Financial Reform, Shanghai, April 26, 2005 (www.pbc.gov.cn/english//detail.asp?col=6500&ID=75).

97. Wu (2005, pp. 154–56).

98. D. Clarke (2003, p. 496); Osgathorpe (1995–96).

99. Tenev and Zhang (2002, p. 82).

decline in the market share of SOEs.[100] In any event, the move to SOEs was far from a solution and did not give China a market economy. An SOE was still prone to bureaucratic interference. The ultimate owner—the Chinese people—could not act as an ultimate owner, exercising residual control rights; in fact, even if one is prepared to say that the state is the agent of the people with respect to governance of an SOE, the state itself was not able to fulfill that function.[101] Legislation passed in 2003, creating a State Assets Supervision and Administration Commission to monitor and supervise SOEs controlled by the central government, was intended to concentrate the state's ownership responsibilities.[102] Parallel institutions were formed at provincial and local levels. Despite this legislation, SOEs may nonetheless remain subject to conflicting demands and preferences, particularly of local party and local government officials. And the party often appoints the managers.[103]

These problems are particularly acute in the financial sector where government allocations of capital to enterprises were replaced in the 1980s by loans from four state-owned commercial banks (SCBs).[104] These SCBs tended to use government and party criteria to allocate loans and at the very least were sensitive to government and party priorities for the promotion of particular industries and regions.[105] Local governments were likely to heavily influence local bank branches in making their credit allocation decisions. As a result of these pressures, as much as 90 percent of SCB loans went to SOEs.[106] The SCBs were further handicapped in pursuing purely market considerations in lending decisions by what the *Financial Times* editorially called "large-scale fraud, embezzlement and other misdeeds, from branch offices all the way up to the boardroom."[107]

Given the role of the government and the party, it is little wonder that SOEs acted, initially at least, more like government agencies than true private sector enterprises. Even after various reforms, the state-dominated financial system did not produce satisfactory mobility of capital across China. To the extent capital was mobile, there was a tendency "to allocate capital systematically

100. L-Y. Zhang (2004, p. 2032, including table 1).

101. D. Clarke (2003).

102. OECD (2005a, pp. 301–22). This change took the Ministry of Finance largely out of the line of responsibility for nonfinancial SOEs.

103. Tenev and Zhang (2002, pp. 20–28).

104. Naughton (1995, pp. 255–57); Wu (2005, p. 219).

105. McGregor (2005a); Tenev and Zhang (2002, pp. 55–65).

106. Cull and Xu (2000, pp. 2, 8, figure 1). See also Dyer (2005d).

107. "Chinese Corruption: Deeper Reforms Are Needed to Stop the Rot," *Financial Times*, March 28, 2005. For details on the banking scandals, see Barboza (2005); "Personal Banking, China Construction Bank," *The Economist*, March 26, 2005; and Lague (2005).

away from the more productive regions towards less productive ones," in part because the SCBs concentrated on funding SOEs.[108]

Meanwhile, the SCBs were supplemented by other state-owned financial institutions such as joint-stock banks, although at the end of 2004 SCBs still accounted for nearly 60 percent of banking system assets.[109] Unlike the original four SCBs, whose operations reflected the national perspective of their origin in a central planning period, the eleven joint-stock banks have been more focused on the business of banking.[110] In addition, some 1,000 or more "city" banks owned by municipalities have emerged. Still other publicly owned banks have been created for agricultural and nonbusiness purposes.[111] Only in 1995 was the first private sector bank licensed, and the few private banks in operation have a tiny percentage of the commercial-industrial market.[112] According to the Economist Intelligence Unit, "entrepreneurs in various parts of China have tried for years to establish private banks, although the pace has been glacial, [reflecting] government's disposition for private investment in existing state-controlled banks rather than the emergence of newcomers that will add to the pressure piled on the state-owned banking sector."[113] Most state-owned financial institutions continue to focus their lending on keeping afloat SOEs, many of which are in parlous financial conditions. As Aziz and Duenwald report:

> Bank loans appear to have been channeled to provinces with heavy concentrations of SOEs. These provinces have, at the same time, also been the ones that have tended to grow relatively slowly, suggesting that the productivity of lending was relatively low . . . . The banking system has been used to keep inefficient state enterprises afloat so as not to produce excessive layoffs and raise the cost of transition to levels where social stability might be threatened.[114]

---

108. Boyreau-Debray and Wei (2004); Cull and Xu (2000, p. 2); Lardy (1998, p. 83).

109. Wu (2005, p. 233); Podpiera (2006, p. 3).

110. OECD (2005a, p. 384).

111. Cull and Xu (2000, pp. 6, 7, table 1); Lardy (1998, pp. 61–76, 80).

112. Cull and Xu (2000, pp. 6, 7, table 1).

113. Economist Intelligence Unit (2005, pp. 6–24). According to this report, China's first private bank, China Minsheng Banking Corp., became a listed company on the Shanghai stock exchange in 2000 and was the ninth largest bank in China in 2004. This bank, however, has many "state owned" shareholders and therefore "strictly speaking" is "not a private bank." The report counts only two private banks in China but notes that more than ten foreign private banks operate in the country.

114. Aziz and Duenwald (2002). On foreign direct investment in the form of minority interests in SOEs, see Wu (2005, p. 302).

More generally, as a 2006 IMF report states, "The pricing of credit risk [by SCBs] remains rather undifferentiated, and bank lending does not appear to take enterprise profitability into account when making lending decisions."[115]

The dominance of state banks results in the private commercial and industrial sector in China having had relatively little access to formal credit.[116] Yet private sector enterprises outperform public sector enterprises.[117] But, as Aziz and Duenwald note, retained earnings and private savings are the dominant sources of private sector financing, although informal credit markets do exist:

> Between 1990 and 1997, the new jobs created in the private sector accounted for 56 percent of new formal employment in urban areas. This rapid growth has occurred with relatively few resources from the financial sector: in the period 1991–97, the share of private investment in the national total was in the range of 15–27 percent, with little recourse to formal bank loans (less than 1 percent of working capital loans went to the private sector).[118]

Foreign direct investment has been a supplementary source of capital for private sector enterprises.[119] Moreover, China has increasingly turned to foreign investment to stimulate reform in state-owned enterprises. Recently the Chinese government has encouraged minority investment (so-called strategic investment) by foreign banks in state-owned banks. The rationale for this foreign investment reflects the Chinese economic leadership's frustration with the SCBs. As the China Banking Regulatory Commission explained:

> It should be recognized that transforming the Chinese state-owned commercial banks into real commercial ones would be an arduous task . . . . Such an ownership structure makes it easy for banks to depart from market principles, but difficult for them to set up a sound corporate governance structure or an efficient operation mechanism. Consequently, it makes it hard for the banking supervisor to implement scientific and sound standards, resulting in both the high and accumulating impaired assets and low business performance. Such circumstances could not only block the banks from achieving sustainable

115. Podpiera (2006, p. 3).
116. Wu (2005, pp. 232–34).
117. D. Clarke (2003, pp. 494–95, n. 2 and sources cited therein).
118. Aziz and Duenwald (2002). It appears that city-controlled and other local banks have begun to make loans to local private companies in order to promote local economic activities.
119. Aziz and Duenwald (2002).

development, but also have a direct impact on the control and mitigation of risks as well as the efficient allocation and safety of the funds in the whole society. Therefore, it has long been imperative for China to carry out in-depth banking reform, so as to be better adapted to the development of the socialist market economy and in particular to meet the urgent needs of all-round opening up of the Chinese financial sector after the WTO entry. To this end, the purpose of introducing experienced and qualified overseas strategic investors is an effective method to promote as well as enhance the reform.[120]

The willingness, indeed apparent eagerness, to bring in strategic bank investors was apparently linked in Chinese leadership thinking to making initial public offerings (IPOs) in the Hong Kong market of minority interests in state-owned banks.[121] Neither the interest in strategic investors nor the IPOs were necessarily driven by the need for more capital. In a revealing statement, the chairman of the State Assets Supervision and Administration Commission asserted in December 2005 that IPOs in overseas markets (in which he apparently included Hong Kong) were justified because "overseas markets are more regulated and Chinese companies can benefit and learn to fine-tune corporate structure and governance."[122]

The SCBs, which were carrying out government (and party) policies in extending loans to the SOEs, not only had massive holdings of nonperforming loans but also tended to earn negative returns on assets.[123] Wu reported that "according to Chinese government statistics, as of the end of 2002, China's four major state-owned commercial banks collectively had recorded a bad asset ratio of 25 percent."[124] This figure does not include nonfinancial institutions; state-owned corporations, for example, had nonperforming loans equal to half of their total assets as of 1996.[125]

Although official figures for SCB nonperforming loans more recently began to decline as a percentage of assets, the decline was apparently caused in part by a rapid increase in the volume of lending (the base for calculating that ratio).[126] Moreover, it is likely that nonperforming loans would have

---

120. China Bank Regulatory Commission (2005).
121. China Bank Regulatory Commission (2005). See Dolven, Winn, and Murphy (2004).
122. Dyer (2005c).
123. Lardy (2003, p. 67).
124. Wu (2005, p. 382). See also Lardy (2004, pp. 108–09, table 5-2).
125. Lardy (2003, p. 71).
126. García Herrero and Santabárbara (2004, pp. 22–24); OECD (2005b, p. 149). Economist Intelligence Unit (2005, p. 20) cites the Chinese central bank as giving a nonperforming

risen since 2003, not fallen, were it not for the infusion of capital from the state.[127] This infusion continued with the contribution in 2005 of $60 billion in capital by the central bank (taken from foreign currency reserves) through the Huijin Investment Company, which thereby became a major stockholder of several SCBs.[128] A Bank of Spain study estimated that total injections of governmental capital into the Chinese banking system from 1998 to 2005 were equal to 20 to 25 percent of China's 2004 GDP, a truly huge subsidy that could easily account for the decline in the nonperforming loan ratio.[129]

The Rise of Stock Exchanges and Securities Regulation

A transformed corporate landscape was created by the reforms of the 1980s and 1990s in which loans by state-owned commercial banks and later by other state-owned financial institutions replaced capital allocations from the state coupled with the conversion of state enterprises into corporations owned by the state—that is, SOEs. These two changes soon led to further changes, in large measure because the SOEs were no longer able to generate enough profits to fund their own growth, even when coupled with bank loans from SCBs. Indeed, additional loans from the SCBs to the SOEs seemed to generate steadily increasing portfolios of nonperforming loans for the SCBs.[130]

A partial answer to this financing quandary was to create stock exchanges in Shanghai and Shenzhen in 1990, thereby generating a climate that would induce Chinese citizens to use some of their savings to purchase stock of the SOEs in IPOs. One important effect, and perhaps a prime purpose, of the move to public issuance of securities was to tap private savings to finance the

---

loan figure of 15 percent in March 2005 but states that in the past "official statements suggested that 20-25% of all loans were non-performing, with 6-7% being unrecoverable."

127. According to Jinglian Wu, Standard and Poor's reported in September 2003 that even with the "substantial increase in total outstanding loans," the nonperforming loan ratio was 40 to 45 percent (Wu 2005, p. 382). See also "A Muffled Report," *The Economist*, May 20, 2006.

128. Browne (2005).

129. García Herrero, Gavilá, and Santabárbara (2005). To illustrate the costs to the Chinese government of cleaning up nonperforming loans, a proportionately large series of bank bailouts in the United States would cost between $2 trillion and $3 trillion in total.

130. Allen, Qian, and Qian (2005b, p. 35, table 2). As noted earlier in the text, nonperforming loans for SCBs declined later, because state bodies, including asset management companies, bought loans in default or otherwise put additional funds into SCBs (García Herrero and Santabárbara 2004, p. 15, table 5).

SOEs.[131] Private savings were going to the same ultimate use before through the intermediation of state-owned financial institutions, but expansion of that route was plagued by the steady rise of nonperforming loans and by the low interest rates paid on savings deposits.

In retrospect, one can see that the creation of the stock exchanges was designed not just to support the issuance of stock to the public by providing venues for secondary trading but also to stimulate the desire to invest by implicitly promising greater returns to savers. What resulted was an enthusiastic search by the public for riches and indeed a new kind of gambling for many Chinese citizens; Jinglian Wu, a leading Chinese economist who served as an adviser to the State Council, observes that "the government boosting the stock market and SOEs grabbing the money" created a "casino without rules."[132] Between 1990 and 2001, the Shanghai stock market composite index went up approximately twentyfold, although the rate of increase slowed after 1996.[133] As the market rose (with price-earnings ratios reaching, in Wu's words, a "ridiculously high level of 100 to 200 in the early 1990s)," the amount of money raised by the SOEs through IPOs and further stock issuances (seasoned equity offerings) increased, reaching 1.7 percent of GDP in 2000.[134] This was almost as high a percentage as in the United States during the Internet bubble and a far higher percentage than Japan ever reached.[135]

The popularity of stock issuance created a new set of rule-of-law problems. The SOEs' demand for new capital continued to grow and with it all kinds of stratagems to convince savers to buy what in many cases were financially weak companies. Market manipulation and even outright fraud became a path for that purpose—"creating fake receipts and fake contracts to make up whatever profits that are needed to meet IPO requirements."[136] Zhiwu Chen gives the illustration of splitting an SOE into a "good" entity and a "bad" entity, selling shares to the public in the good entity but arranging for the bad entity to end up with the controlling interest in the now public company.

131. L.-Y. Zhang (2004, p. 2044) reports that the "stock market has failed to . . . improve resource allocation. Rather it provided SOEs with unprecedented access to cheap direct finance." See also Green (2004, p. 11) and Green (2003, pp. 22–24, 26).

132. Wu (2005, pp. 243–44). Similarly, the head of the China State Council's Development Research Council called the stock market "worse than a casino" because at least in a casino there were rules (Green 2003, p. 165).

133. Z. Chen (2003, pp. 459, 460, figure 1); Gao (2002, p. 7, chart 1).

134. Wu (2005, p. 244); Z. Chen (2003, p. 458).

135. Z. Chen (2003, p. 459, Table 2).

136. Wu (2005, p. 242); Z. Chen (2003, p. 457). On fraud, see also Wu (2005, p. 251); Green (2003, pp. 24, 135–39).

Efforts of regulatory authorities to ensure that only healthy companies issued stock by imposing minimum profit regulations simply led, in Chen's words, to companies adapting their "accounting manipulation schemes" to the new regulations.[137]

Efforts to commence shareholder securities cases to attack such fraud and manipulation were quite a strain for the Chinese judicial system, which had no idea how to manage mass tort litigation—that is, how to handle a massive number of individual claims against the same defendant for exactly the same alleged wrongdoing. The Supreme People's Court, apparently panicking at the prospect, issued a notice in 2001 directing lower courts not to accept private securities lawsuits for the time being, despite the existence of the underlying 1999 securities act providing supporting substantive legal standards.[138] Subsequently, in a complex and rapid evolution, rules were worked out in consultation with many private sector experts, interpreting the underlying statute and creating the basis for actions by shareholders acting jointly.[139] However, class actions (in which one or more shareholders sue jointly on behalf of shareholders as a class) are apparently still not feasible in China.[140] Moreover, private class actions apparently require, as a predicate, a prior adjudication in favor of the government with respect to the underlying violation.[141] As a result of the sale of shares in SOEs to the public and their listing on exchanges, a structure resulted in which, very roughly, an average of one-third of SOE shares ("A shares" for Chinese citizens buying with local currency, plus "B shares" for foreign currency purchasers) are held by the public with about another third held by the state (state shares) and the last third (legal person shares) held by a variety of institutions, in many instances state-related entities including provinces and municipalities.[142] State shares

137. Z. Chen (2003, pp. 457–58).

138. Z. Chen (2003, p. 464).

139. For a general discussion, see Hutchens (2003) and Z. Chen (2003, pp. 464–67).

140. Lu (2003, pp. 798–801) and Hutchens (2003, pp. 640–45). Hutchens surmises that class actions were seen as a threat to SOEs and perhaps as a threat to the party by fomenting class struggle. But see IIF Equity Advisory Group (2004, p. 4), which refers to the first class-action shareholder lawsuit pending in a Beijing Court.

141. Hutchens (2003, pp. 634, 640).

142. Li and An (2004); L.-Y. Zhang (2004, p. 2035). The one-third, one-third, one-third breakdown conventionally used for expository purposes ignores an underlying variation among industries and companies. See, for example, Li and An (2004, p. 385, table 1), showing that many listed companies have more than 50 percent of their stock in state share form. For details on different kinds of shares, see Schipani and Liu (2002, p. 65, table 1). H shares, which are traded in Hong Kong, composed about 5 percent of all Chinese shares in 1998. See also Tenev and Zhang (2002, pp. 76–77).

and legal person shares, unlike shares held by the public, are in principle not tradable on exchanges. However, many nontradable shares have in fact been bought and sold off the exchanges for a variety of reasons.[143]

At the turn of the millennium, Chinese leaders broached their interest in selling state shares to the public—a policy known as "reduction of state-owned shares." In 2001 the China Securities Regulatory Commission issued a notice to that effect.[144] Although the notice was thought by many to have been a move toward making SOEs true private sector enterprises, a more powerful motive may have been to raise still more funds to finance SOEs, which were consuming vast amounts of capital for expansion and for covering losses. These demands for capital could not be entirely met by SCBs and other state-owned financial enterprises, which were weighed down with large quantities of nonperforming loans and hence were not well placed or strongly motivated to meet these demands.

The news of these intentions coincided with a downturn in the Chinese stock market and, while perhaps not causing the downturn, certainly exacerbated it.[145] This development might not have surprised a more sophisticated financial community. Shareholdings (including shares held indirectly through SOEs) by government—state, provincial, and local—were larger than shareholdings in the hands of the public and therefore constituted a huge overhang of potential supply, leading potentially to at least a doubling (or if legal person shares were also sold, a tripling) of the number of tradable shares outstanding.[146] (At the end of 2002, only 34.7 percent of shares in listed companies were tradable on Chinese stock markets.[147]) By mid-2005 the Shanghai stock exchange index, which once traded above 2200, was at a five-year low, trading near 1000.[148] In August 2005 the China Securities Regulatory Commission announced that all listed companies' shares would be made tradable, though at the discretion of the companies. To encourage the change, holders of domestic shares (A shares) were promised compensation; this policy discriminated against foreigners who hold other classes of shares and against even Chinese who later acquired B shares originally issued to foreigners against foreign currency.[149]

---

143. The complexity of motives for such transactions is explored in Green (2005).
144. Li and An (2004, p. 378).
145. Dyer (2005d).
146. "Hangover Cure," *The Economist,* May 5, 2005; Dyer (2005b).
147. Wu (2005, p. 165).
148. Wu (2005, p. 250); Areddy (2005); Dyer (2005a).
149. Dyer and Guerrera (2005a).

Coexisting with these issues involving SOE shareholdings is an absence of ready securities market financing. Outstanding corporate domestic currency bonds constitute less than 1 percent of GDP (in contrast to Malaysia at 50 percent, South Korea at 28 percent, and emerging markets as a whole at more than 5 percent).[150] As for primary markets in equities, public issuance and listing of non-SOE shares (that is, shares of purely private sector companies) are far from the norm. According to Le-Yin Zhang, "The chance for nonstate firms becoming listed is extremely slim. Indeed, the first public company with a private background did not appear until 1998, on the Shanghai Stock Exchange."[151] In 2005 the *Financial Times* reported that "only between 30 and 130 of the 1,300 companies listed on the Chinese market have a private-sector background—and even some of those are in reality controlled by branches of the state."[152]

Moreover, private sector firms are not always able to borrow money because state-owned financial firms may not always be willing or able to lend. Chinese businesses, including SOEs, relied in the first quarter of 2005 on banks for 99 percent of their funding, but, according to the *Financial Times*, "private companies—the motors of growth in the modern Chinese economy—borrow money for start-up finance from 'underground' banks that charge high interest rates."[153] According to one review of the evidence: "There is a wealth of data illustrating the extreme financial constraints facing the domestic private firms. A number of international surveys show that [China's] private firms are more financially constrained than private firms in other countries.[154]

Under conditions that so favor the financing of SOEs over private companies, how can one explain the declining SOE share of GDP? In 2002 SOEs accounted for only 44 percent of Chinese GDP and only 41 percent of gross industrial output?[155] One possible answer is that state-owned industry is

150. Eichengreen and Luengnaruemitchai (2004, table 1). See also Barnett (2004). Even government enterprises find difficulties in issuing bonds; see Mingli and Liu (2001).

151. L.-Y. Zhang (2004, p. 2035). However, Zhang also states somewhat contradictorily that "80% of the listed companies were state-controlled," implying that as much as 20 percent of the companies were not state-controlled. However, some companies are controlled by provincial and local governments.

152. Dyer and Guerrera (2005b); J. Zhang (2005).

153. Guerrera and McGregor (2005). See also Tsai (2002); OECD (2005b, pp. 159–60). Some mainland private firms also borrow through Hong Kong affiliates. For an example of the obstacles to bank borrowing, see Huang (2005, p. 31).

154. Huang (2005, p. 27).

155. L.-Y. Zhang (2004, p. 2036). Wu (2005, p. 29, table 2.5) shows that the combined share of the nonstate and noncollective sector (that is, the private or nonpublic sector) has

highly inefficient and wasteful of capital. For China as a whole, an important measure of capital efficiency is the incremental capital-output ratio, or the ratio of investment (as a percentage of GDP) to real economic growth (as a percentage of GDP). At 5 to 1, this ratio "was comparatively higher than that for Japan, South Korea, or Taiwan when they were experiencing high economic growth."[156] Because of the very high Chinese savings rate and the high level of foreign direct investment, China is apparently able to waste capital, but an inefficient and inadequately reformed financial sector could prove to be a barrier to continued rapid growth if a crisis of the nature, say, of the Asian financial crisis should erupt.[157]

Corporate Governance

The existing SOE shareholding structure with the state retaining control is not just inefficient; it also creates a built-in corporate governance problem, leaving the public shareholders locked in the position of minority shareholders. The public shareholders are thus vulnerable to expropriation by management or by state bureaucrats responsible for the firm or the industry in question.[158] The risk of such expropriation is heightened by the weaknesses of the Chinese judiciary. As Clarke has observed, "Chinese courts are not politically powerful and are hence reluctant to take cases involving large sums of money and politically powerful defendants."[159]

The abuse by the majority is not just a theoretical possibility. A report by a task force of the Institute of International Finance found, based on data from the China Securities Regulatory Commission, that "about 75 percent of listed companies have seen their IPO proceeds channeled back to the parent company and/or have experienced other forms of asset stripping via transfer pricing following the IPO."[160] Individual accounts of outright fraud and asset stripping by majority shareholders abound. Schipani and Liu cite one example: "The 1999 annual report of Daqing Liyani Co. revealed that the largest

---

been above 40 percent since 1998. Similarly, the share of urban employment of the private sector has been above 50 percent since 1999, and above 60 percent since 2001 (Wu 2005, p. 199, table 5.1).

156. Kwan (2004). See also comment on ICOR in Wu (2005) and Wolf (2003).

157. See the analysis of savings and investment in Rawski (2005).

158. A corollary is that no market for corporate control exists (J. Zhang 2005, p. 2035).

159. D. Clarke (2003, p. 503).

160. IIF Equity Advisory Group (2004, p. 3). The data apparently became available because the China Securities Regulatory Commission adopted additional requirements to attempt to deal with these problems.

majority shareholder stole RMB 620 million Yuan from this corporation, accounting for 50% of its total corporate assets."[161] In 2001, Bai and colleagues reported, "Sanjiu Pharma's largest shareholder extracted US $301.9 million, 96% of the listed company's total equity."[162]

Two new regulatory provisions imposed in recent years indicate that Chinese leaders recognize the need for corporate governance reforms. One provision requires independent directors; the other imposes a fiduciary duty upon directors.[163] The real question, of course, is how these requirements are to be given specific content and actually enforced in view of the weakness of the Chinese judiciary and the elusiveness of the legal concepts involved. In the Chinese context, where the state owns, directly or indirectly, the majority of the shares, controls senior personnel appointments, and supports the actions taken, what does independence of directors mean, what exactly is a fiduciary duty, and to whom is it owed?[164]

One common practice is to steer SOE business into transactions with private sector companies under their own control or influence. Tenev and Zhang describe the situation:

> With the rapid development of the nonstate sector, managers or their relatives and friends often have their own businesses, which provides opportunities for diverting state assets to private benefits. A large body of anecdotal evidence indicates that asset stripping, or siphoning resources into structures where the controller has both majority control and income rights, is widespread. Furthermore, the "grafting" of nonstate property onto the state sector also offers opportunities for asset stripping, for instance, by using the appraisal and valuation process to form joint ventures . . . .[165]

Similarly, Tenev and Zhang write, managers of SOEs with subsidiaries that are listed and hence have many small shareholders can use their SOE's control of listed companies to transfer wealth through "soft loans from listed companies on a long-term basis; the use of listed companies as guarantors to borrow money from banks; and the sale of assets to listed companies at unfair

---

161. Schipani and Liu (2002, p. 61).

162. Bai and others (2003). For examples of self-dealing by SOE managers, see Wu (2005, pp. 395–96).

163. On fiduciary duties (or the lack thereof) in China, see Wu (2005, pp. 169–70). On the independent director requirement, see Wu (2005, pp. 174–75), Shen and Jia (2005), and D. Clarke (2006).

164. On senior personnel appointments, see McGregor (2005a).

165. Tenev and Zhang (2002, p. 22).

prices, usually without an appraisal by an independent evaluator."[166] Even bankruptcy has become a convenient occasion for self-dealing by corporate groups: a "common practice was to move most of the productive assets to other firms before bankruptcy," Ma, Mok, and Cheung write.[167]

Credit Markets

In contrast to capital markets, credit markets provide the great majority of funds for enterprise. In fact, China has the dubious distinction of having the largest banking sector relative to GDP of any big economy in the world.[168] But the credit system has its own weaknesses. Aside from the poor financial condition of the banking system, which has required state bailout subsidies of state-owned commercial banks and the use of asset management companies to take nonperforming loans off the banks' books, the credit system has legal problems. [169]

The core of these problems lies in the uncertainty about secured debt. This uncertainty is tied to the absence of a bankruptcy system appropriate to an economy so dependent on a large financial sector. In the early reform years, the very concept of bankruptcy was resisted, Shirk explains, because officials thought it "unfair to punish enterprises that could not make profits because of external, 'objective' . . . causes beyond their control (prices, demands of planners, fixed assets, etc.) [and] because the burden would fall mostly on a few actors (coal, steel, heavy machinery) and the inland provinces where these sectors were concentrated."[170] Nonetheless, a bankruptcy law for SOEs became effective in 1988, and the 1991 Law of Civil Procedure "introduced rudimentary provisions for the bankruptcy of legal persons."[171] A more adequate bankruptcy law has been under consideration for some years.[172] The

166. Tenev and Zhang (2002, p. 101).

167. Ma, Mok, and Cheung (2001, p. 60, n. 15). See Wu (2005, p. 160).

168. "A Great Big Banking Gamble," *The Economist,* October 27, 2005. China has a particularly large financial sector compared with most other countries at its present stage of development (OECD 2005b, p. 138, figure 3.1).

169. "A $45 Billion Shot in the Arm," *The Economist,* January 6, 2004; "Failing to Perform," *The Standard,* June 20, 2005.

170. Shirk (1993, p. 132).

171. Tenev and Zhang (2002, p. 15).

172. OECD (2005b, pp. 91–93); Booth (2004, p. 95); World Bank Office Beijing (2005). See speech by Junbo Xiang, deputy governor of the People's Bank of China, "Improve the Legal System to Prevent Financial Risk," at the 2005 High-level Forum of China's Financial Reform, Shanghai, April 26, 2005 (www.pbc.gov.cn/english//detail.asp?col=6500&ID=75). See also Rogoff, Bag, and Wang (2004).

biggest stumbling block has apparently been the question of absolute priority for secured creditors. The principal issue has been the relative priority of secured creditors versus employee claims for past wages, pensions, and social welfare payments. This issue has had to be addressed in every country, but in China it appears to have been a question of ideology favoring workers' rights versus the needs of the economy for putting secured creditors first in priority to assure a steady flow of secured credit to key enterprises.[173] Another bankruptcy issue has been the uncertain status of assets pledged as security, particularly land that has been "allocated" by administrative authorities.[174]

Meanwhile, the great preponderance of all credit continues to be provided by advances from state-sector banks. The corporate bond market has remained small, with outstanding bonds constituting only 0.7 percent of GDP in China in 2004, compared with 11.8 percent in Thailand, 21.1 percent in Korea, and 38.2 percent in Malaysia.[175]

Legal and Institutional Reform

This review of China's financial sector points to deep flaws in equity and credit markets and especially in corporate governance. Yet in the business and financial communities abroad attitudes toward China's economic future remain optimistic, especially compared with attitudes toward much of the rest of the developing world. Is this unjustified euphoria derived from

173. Lardy (2003, pp. 72–73). See speech by Junbo Xiang, deputy governor of the People's Bank of China, "Improve the Legal System to Prevent Financial Risk," at the 2005 High-level Forum of China's Financial Reform, Shanghai, April 26, 2005 (www.pbc.gov.cn/english// detail.asp?col=6500&ID=75). While this book was in press, the Chinese legislature in August 2006 passed a bankruptcy law that favors creditors over employees, except for bankruptcies of state-owned enterprises.

174. Barale (2005). Traditionally, and certainly in the Mao period, all land was owned by the state, and the status of land remains a major economic issue going far beyond the question of bankruptcy law. In the Chinese countryside the land issue has been so important, particularly when cities expand over agricultural land, that it has produced violent conflicts. See "Turning Ploughshares into Staves," *The Economist*, June 25, 2005 (U.S. edition). See also Peerenboom (2002, p. 482) and McGregor (2005b) concerning land disputes as a major source of unrest. For a general discussion on land in China, see Ho (2001) and Brandt and others (2002). In 2003, a change of law granted farmers thirty-year land use rights, but still did not give them legal title or the power to mortgage the land for farm improvements or other uses. As many as 40 million to 50 million farmers have lost land through expropriation (UNDP 2005, p. 4). See chapter 7 for a general discussion of the role of land rights in economic development, including a brief description of the evolution of Chinese land law.

175. IMF (2005a, p. 107, table 4.2). See Green (2003, pp. 41–44). Corporate bonds of more than one-year maturity apparently cannot legally be issued; see Kuo (2006).

extrapolation of past growth? Or can one find in Chinese institutional reform a basis for optimism?

Certainly China has not pursued the same strategy of reform as the Eurasian transition countries of Central Europe and the former Soviet Union. Reform in those countries tended to involve two strategies, the first to make large and quick changes—a Big Bang approach of moving from a past of state dominance, state planning, and comprehensive price control to a Western-style market economy. The idea, particularly for removing price controls, was to act quickly before political opposition could arise.[176] The second strategy was to adopt the best Western substantive statutes—world "best-practice" legislation. For the reasons reviewed generically in earlier chapters of this book (notably a failure to improve enforcement commensurately and societal resistance to legal transplants), the record in those transition countries, especially in the former Soviet Union (aside from the Baltic states), has not been encouraging.

China adopted a different reform strategy—one that can be characterized as incremental, selectively adaptive, or more perceptive.[177] (Deng Xiaoping called it "crossing the river by feeling for stones.") However it is characterized, China's approach was certainly different and arguably more intelligent. Because legal reform was needed to enable economic reform, legal reform had to take on some of the same incremental characteristics. Lichtenstein mentions "gradualism, experimentation, regional differences" and "piecemeal and sometimes unconnected approaches and early vagueness supplemented by later detail."[178] Most of all, both economic and legal reforms were evolutionary in character. Although the Chinese reform was more centrally directed and had a fundamental impact in only a few decades, it is nonetheless reminiscent of the evolutionary developments over centuries in the English legal and political system that culminated in the Glorious Revolution.[179]

Why was China able, or perhaps forced, to carry out a different strategy from the Eurasian transition countries? One explanation is the considerable continuity in Chinese leadership, despite changes in leadership after Mao's death. No post-Mao revolution of the type that could permit a completely new leadership to assume power occurred, in contrast to the experience in most of the Eurasian transition countries. In China the old leadership, below the very top, was still partially in power but knew that change was necessary. Yingyi Qian explains one reason the leadership did not opt for a Big Bang

176. Hoffman (2002, p. 183).
177. See Wu (2005, pp. 43, 57–74) on a strategy of incrementalism.
178. Lichtenstein (2003, pp. 275, 287).
179. See discussion in chapter 4.

transformation: China had had two of them before—the Great Leap Forward of 1958 and the Cultural Revolution from 1966 to 1976—and both had ended disastrously. No appetite was left for messianic transformations.[180]

Three early reforms illustrate the Chinese approach: the dual track, the township-village enterprises (TVEs), and fiscal federalism.[181] All three involved the necessity of taking into account the predictable opposition of established economic power centers. As a corollary, the reforms were based on a political recognition that not everything could be reformed at once— that it was hopeless to attempt to change from a totally socialist society to a market economy in just a few years. In addition, all three reforms were an intelligent harnessing of a key insight of both neoinstitutional economics and classical microeconomics—the importance of incentives. To be sure, this explanation is a backward-looking rationale of the Chinese reforms. At the beginning, there was no leadership announcement of a market economy goal. Even after the market economy goal came into clear sight, ideology and politics required the goal to be articulated as a "socialist market economy." In sum, Chinese reforms recognized that in a political world the fastest route between two points is not necessarily a straight line. Recognition of a goal does not automatically make clear the means for achieving the goal, as experienced policymakers throughout the world are well aware.

THE DUAL TRACK SYSTEM

The dual track reform of the mid-1980s was the path chosen to exit both from state planning (in the mandatory socialist sense) and from its concomitant comprehensive price control. This control system had powerful proponents: the bureaucrats who administered it and the producers that enjoyed a guaranteed margin, buying their inputs and selling their product at designated prices. The dual track system effectively bought off both sets of beneficiaries because plan quantities remained the same as under past rules and the beneficiaries were able, as economists would say, to enjoy the "rents" from this noncompetitive system. In this instance, existing firms and political power centers were "grandfathered" as part of a consensus decision system. But the rules were different for additional production, either by expansion of existing firms or by entry of new firms. For additional production, firms were allowed to buy inputs at whatever price they could and to sell their outputs at whatever price they could.[182]

180. Qian (2000b, p. 169).
181. The discussion of Chinese reform draws heavily on Wu (2005) and Qian (2003).
182. See generally Shirk (1993); on the dual track reform, see Wu (2005, pp. 68–71) and Lau, Qian, and Roland (2000).

Not only were the incentives to expand production and to establish new firms strong, but the new inputs and outputs would be traded in what was a market economy. The reform was economically efficient because it harnessed the economic insight that what counts for efficiency is marginal prices, not average prices. GDP in China's industrial sector, for example, began expanding at double digit rates in 1983 and (except for 1989 and 1990) continued at those higher rates. The evolutionary character of the dual track is best seen in the steel industry. By 1988, with economic expansion being stimulated by the market as opposed to the plan, production in the steel industry was far greater than the plan quota.[183] At the consumer level, retail level transactions at plan prices "declined from 97 percent in 1978 to only 30 percent in 1990" and the decline continued thereafter.[184]

TOWNSHIP-VILLAGE ENTERPRISES

TVEs were an adaptation of the commune and brigade enterprises of the Mao period. The leadership used them because they already existed "on the fringe of the central planning" system, but renamed them TVEs, and harnessed them to provide additional production.[185] One way of looking at TVEs is to think of them as being a de facto alliance of local government and small collective enterprises.[186] In the absence of any system of private property, the prime predator for local firms to fear would have been the local government (since Beijing was far away, and the central government was in no position to exercise direct power in the country as a whole).[187] Putting the local government in business as the owner of the TVEs was a way of protecting entrepreneurial firms in the face of insecure and ill-defined property rights.[188] As owners, local governments had a stake in making the TVEs successful because if their profits grew, there would be more money available to local government owners for their own function—the provision of local public goods. Moreover, these public goods—such as law enforcement, public health services, and infrastructure—were beneficial to the central government, and hence the center was disinclined to intervene. The TVE reform thus worked because of its effect on the incentives of the firm, the local government, and the central government.

183. Qian (2003, p. 302, table 11.2; p. 309, table 11.3).
184. Lau, Qian, and Roland (2000, pp. 139, 140, table 4).
185. Qian (2003, p. 314).
186. H. Chen (2000, p. 7).
187. A Chinese proverb "The mountains are high and the emperor is far away" thus has a contemporary meaning.
188. McDonnell (2004).

Over time the TVEs began to compete with each other both in the product market and in the market for capital. By 1993 these local government-owned firms were providing 27 percent of all industrial output.[189] In a further evolution, the government began privatizing TVEs, usually by management buyouts.[190] Meanwhile, many TVEs, especially older ones in rural areas, are being displaced by private firms, and TVEs no longer appear to be a favored part of China's economic reform.[191]

FISCAL FEDERALISM

Reform of intergovernmental fiscal relationships started in 1980 with a fiscal contracting system that, although varying regionally and evolving over time, had the characteristic of a compact between lower and higher levels of government within China's decentralized system.[192] Each province, for example, divided its tax and other revenue into several categories, normally budgetary and extra-budgetary funds. Budgetary funds were to be shared between central and provincial governments according to a previously set formula.[193] A formula might, in the case of provincially raised revenues, for example, call for a fixed proportion to be remitted upward—perhaps with an annual adjustment—and the rest retained by the provincial government. A preset formula had the advantage that the more revenue a government was able to collect, the more it could devote to its own purposes. Extra-budgetary funds, which were derived from such special sources as locally owned SOE retained profits, were to be entirely retained by the level of government that raised them.

The system, to the extent it worked as planned, provided a strong incentive to lower levels of government to maximize revenues by promoting rather than preying on local business since they no longer had as much reason to fear that any increases would be taken away by a higher level organ of government.[194] Thus, to use the Chinese slogan of the time, the center and the local

189. Roland (2000, p. 281).

190. Laixiang (2005, p.102). Moreover, in the 1990s the growth of TVEs began to give way to the growth of private firms; see McDonnell (2004, pp. 977–82).

191. Fishman (2005, pp. 74–75); Peerenboom (2002, p. 486).

192. The description of the fiscal contracting system draws heavily on Wu (2005, pp. 259–81) and Montinola, Qian, and Weingast (1995). Details vary from province to province (Wu 2005, pp. 258–63), and no attempt is made here to describe the fiscal contracting system in any detail.

193. The central government also collects revenues, such as tariffs and taxes on enterprises subject to central control; see Wu (2005, p. 260).

194. Qian and Weingast (1997). Compare the experience in China with that in Russia where annual negotiations were necessary between the provinces and the center; see Roland (2000, p. 280).

governments were to "eat in separate kitchens."[195] The segregation of extra-budgetary funds was a particular success in the sense that by the early 1990s these revenues had grown to be about equal to budgetary revenues.[196]

In the mid-1990s Weingast popularized the notion that Chinese fiscal federalism, as a form of "market-preserving federalism," promoted economic growth.[197] It should not be thought, however, that the federalism was of a constitutional kind. As Dali Yang has explained, "unlike federalist systems in developed Western economies," Chinese federalism does "not rest on any form of constitutional protection or explicit binding agreement," but rather, "again and again, local authorities are reminded that the Center calls the shots and can rewrite the rules in its own favor."[198] Moreover, the fiscal system proved unstable and had to be revised frequently to specify taxes the central government and the provincial governments each would be responsible for collecting. The fiscal arrangements illustrate the recurring phenomenon that each stage of reform created its own perverse incentive and roadblocks, which required adjustments introduced by the leadership.[199]

Guided Evolution?

Much of the economic research on the institutional determinants of economic development has wrestled with the econometric problem of showing causation. One of the reasons has been that many opponents of the thesis that institutions (and particularly legal institutions) have to precede faster economic development have argued that such institutions are expensive and that only a wealthier society can afford them. The economists' response has been that their econometric studies ran from institutions to development, rather than the other way around; in this view, to wait for development to generate the wealth necessary for better institutions would simply mean that, at best, economic development would be slow.

The Chinese experience suggests, however, that China's leaders, beginning with Deng Xiaoping, have been following what might be called a "guided" evolutionary approach. Thoroughgoing reform, especially of the Big Bang

195. Shirk (1993, pp. 149–78). Sometimes the Chinese slogan is translated as "eating from separate pots."

196. Montinola, Qian, and Weingast (1995, p. 64).

197. Weingast (1995). In 1994 the fiscal federalism system was reformed so that the provinces separately collected taxes for the central government and for themselves, with the center deciding on forms and rates of taxation; see Lieberthal (2004, pp. 253–54).

198. D. Yang (2006, pp. 146–47).

199. Wu (2005, pp. 269–90); D. Yang (2006).

type, was not an available option for Deng. He evidently felt that he had to feel his way (feeling for stones on the way across the river to development). Political, ideological, and especially bureaucratic obstacles had to be overcome, circumvented, or sometimes perhaps simply outwaited. Many of the steps taken in the early reform years correspond to this interpretation.[200]

Such a hand-in-hand relationship in the progress of economies and law can be found, as John Coffee has documented, in the growth of the U.S. securities markets. Those markets developed rapidly in the United States in the nineteenth century without an adequate legal structure for deterring fraud and self-dealing (although the New York Stock Exchange listing standards constituted a self-regulatory approach to investor protection). But it was not until after the 1929 crash that the Securities Act of 1933 and the Securities Exchange Act of 1934 were enacted, creating the legal structure for today's U.S. securities markets. Coffee, reviewing the U.S. experience and a comparable U.K. experience, observes that the political constituency necessary for the legal reforms was not in place earlier but resulted from the desire to support and safeguard the expansion of already existing markets:

> Although there is little evidence that strong legal rules encouraged the development of either the New York or London Stock Exchanges . . . , the reverse does seem to be true: Strong markets do create a demand for stronger legal rules. Both in the United States and the United Kingdom, as liquid securities markets developed and dispersed ownership became prevalent, a new political constituency developed that desired legal rules capable of filling in the inevitable enforcement gaps that self-regulation left.[201]

This is a comforting notion and does seem to describe how Chinese leaders unleashed rapid growth in the post-Mao period, filling in the chinks and gaps in the legal infrastructure to support further development as they went forward. In fact, unlike Coffee's securities markets example, the Chinese experience seems to be less purely reactive to scandal than the U.S. Depression-period legislative reform. Chinese reform seems to be more thought out and even guided by the leadership of the CCP.[202]

200. For an excellent review of early Chinese reform consistent with this interpretation, see Shirk (1993). See also Baum (1994, pp. 15–18) for a critical view of the Deng Xiaoping reform approach, noting that "some of Deng's stepping stones became millstones."

201. Coffee (2001, p. 80).

202. Shirk (2003, pp. 123–24) makes the point that reform was slowed down when the CCP leadership was divided or at least perceived as divided by the bureaucracy.

However, although this kind of "feeling for stones" evolution put China on the path to rapid economic development, the momentum of reform appears to have slowed over the last decade, at least in the financial sector. Stock exchanges were well accepted when they helped finance SOEs, but the SOEs themselves seem to have resisted further reform.[203] (However, SOEs have been able to downsize by shedding almost 40 percent of employees between 1998 and 2003.[204]) The shareholding structure of SOEs has seriously delayed further expansion of securities markets and has discouraged investors (if one is to judge by market averages). The Chinese leadership can apparently manage political and ideological barriers, but not always and not indefinitely.

Still, it is noteworthy that each generation of Chinese leaders appears increasingly comfortable with the notions that market influences should determine the direction of the economy, that the rule of law deserves at least verbal support as an objective, and that incentives play a crucial role in economic growth. A key problem facing the current Chinese leadership has been created in large measure by recent Chinese political, economic, and ideological history, which has left the leadership to deal with a multitude of stumbling blocks, ranging from underperforming state-owned industrial and financial enterprises to state bureaucracies and local governments that enjoy de facto autonomy in many spheres and that therefore have strong incentives to resist change.

The fact that Chinese leaders and thinkers have expressed an interest in Douglass North and his work suggests that they know that their institutions are not sufficiently strong for indefinite sustained growth.[205] The Chinese have no doubt been wise to avoid a legal transplantation strategy in view of the distinctive social norms and culture that China's long history, its relative isolation from outside influences, and its internal twentieth century

203. One chronicle of Chinese reform calls SOE reform a "miserable failure"; see Qian (2003, p. 306).

204. Fishman (2005, p. 74) reports that "from 1996 to 2001, 53 million people working in China's state sector lost their jobs. That is 7 million more people than the total employment rolls of 46 of the five hundred largest corporations in the world. Or, to state the numbers another way: in the four years beginning in 1998, state-owned companies fired 21 million. That's more than all the Americans who work in manufacturing." According to other data, employment in the state-controlled industrial sector fell by 40 percent from 1998 to 2003; see OECD (2005b, p. 95).

205. In his Internet autobiography Douglass North notes that after his Nobel Prize, he had been asked to elaborate his views, "particularly in China, where there is much enthusiasm about the implications of the new institutional economics applied to solving problems of the Chinese political economic future." See Douglass C. North—Autobiography (nobelprize.org/nobel_prizes/economics/laureates/1993/north-autobio.html).

upheavals have produced. In that light, such adaptations as TVEs and the dual track system can be interpreted as wise efforts to adapt existing Chinese institutions rather than to attempt to transplant alien institutions. But evolution has its limits too. Evolution toward the rule of law in Western Europe, including England, took centuries. In China the evolution is more controlled from the center than anyone could claim about the earlier evolution in Europe, but there may be limits to how fast and successfully evolution can be force-fed.

In a book edited by Dani Rodrik and devoted to a review of the economic growth history of several developing countries, Rodrik drew the following two overall conclusions. First, he concluded that "the onset of economic growth does not require deep and extensive institutional reform." China certainly presents powerful evidence in support of that conclusion. But Rodrik's second conclusion raises squarely the China case: "Sustaining high growth in the face of adverse circumstances requires ever stronger institutions."[206] This is a precept that the Chinese leadership seems to understand. What is not yet known is whether they will be able to continue to implement the necessary institutional reforms.

The econometric evidence examined in earlier chapters showing that causation runs from institutions to growth rather than vice versa may be interpreted to say that *on balance* the causation runs from institutions to growth but that to some extent increasing wealth helps to build institutions. This more nuanced interpretation of institutions and economic growth makes practical sense. If, for example, low pay for judges makes for a weak, even corrupt, judiciary, then a willingness to use new revenues derived from economic growth to strengthen the judiciary can help to create the institutional basis for further economic growth. In that light, it is significant that while the first ten years of transition in Eastern Europe were marked by poor institutions, by the end of the 1990s institutional improvement was becoming relatively rapid—more rapid than could have been predicted by the absolute level of economic development at the outset of reforms.[207] More generally, Johnson, Ostry, and Subramanian studied developing countries with initially weak institutions that experienced an acceleration in growth—usually through a surge in exports of manufactures—and were able to sustain that growth for fifteen or more years. They found that a "preponderance" of those countries "saw the quality of their broad economic institutions improve during growth

---

206. Rodrik (2003, pp. 15, 16).
207. Murrell (2005).

episodes." This result suggests, they say, "the potential for a virtuous circle through which growth and the policy levers used to achieve growth lead to positive institutional change." The authors hypothesize that "growth in manufactured exports benefits a cross-section of the population (in a way that natural resource growth does not), creating a constituency for improving institutions more broadly."[208]

One interpretation, therefore, is that economic growth can lead eventually to a surprisingly strong improvement in institutions when supported by strong political leadership intent on achieving institutional reform and where a constituency for reform is engendered by the initial growth. Indeed, one view of the Asian Tigers' rapid growth followed by crisis is precisely that those countries achieved very rapid growth despite weak institutions so long as they were still at a relatively low level of economic development, but that they failed to invest their growing incomes in improvement of institutions and eventually the failure to do so led to the Asian financial crisis.

That is why it is crucial to understand that China is still a poor country, well below the per capita income of the Asian (former) Tigers when their growth slowdown began. China is still short of the point where it has to overcome the types of challenges, institutional and macroeconomic, that led to the Asian crisis. In China the current difficulties and dilemmas in the financial sector illustrate the complexities resulting from earlier compromises and half measures. And the leadership's inability thus far in the strictly legal arena to overcome such challenges as local protectionism and lack of judicial independence illustrates the heights still to be scaled.

All of these circumstances recall Zhou Enlai's famous answer to a question about the consequences of the French Revolution, "It is too early to tell." It is certainly too early to accept the notion that recent Chinese experience is a counterexample to the need for a focus on institutions in the developing world and, indeed, for a rule of law in China itself. Rather the Chinese experience is consistent with Rodrik's view that considerable development is possible without strong legal institutions but sustainable growth to higher per capita levels requires considerable development of legal institutions.[209] While a definitive conclusion will not be able to be drawn for several decades, it is nonetheless clear that little thus far in the Chinese experience leads to the conclusion that rule-of-law issues are not important in economic development.

208. Johnson, Ostry, and Subramanian (2006).
209. Rodrik (2003, pp. 15–16).

References

Acemoglu, Daron. 2003. "Root Causes: A Historical Approach to Assessing the Role of Institutions in Economic Development." *Finance and Development* (June): 27–30.

Acemoglu, Daron, Simon Johnson, and James A. Robinson. 2001. "The Colonial Origins of Comparative Development: An Empirical Investigation." *American Economic Review* 91 (5): 1369–401.

———. 2002. "Reversal of Fortune: Geography and Institutions in the Making of the Modern World Income Distribution." *Quarterly Journal of Economics* 117 (4): 1231–94.

———. 2004. "Institutions as the Fundamental Cause of Long-Run Growth." Working Paper 10481. Cambridge, Mass.: National Bureau of Economic Research (May).

———. 2005. "The Rise of Europe: Atlantic Trade, Institutional Changes, and Economic Growth." *American Economic Review* 95 (2): 546–79.

Alford, William P. 2003. "The More Law, the More . . . ? Measuring Legal Reform in the People's Republic of China." In *How Far Across the River? Chinese Policy Reform at the Millennium*, edited by Nicholas C. Hope, Dennis Tao Yang, and Mu Yang Li, pp. 122–49. Stanford University Press.

Allen, Franklin, Jun Qian, and Meijun Qian. 2005a. "Law, Finance, and Economic Growth in China." *Journal of Financial Economics* 77: 57–116.

———. 2005b. "Will China's Financial System Stimulate or Impede the Growth of Its Economy?" In *Asia Program Special Report No. 129: China's Economy Retrospect and Prospect*, edited by Loren Brandt, Thomas O. Rawski, and Gang Lin, pp. 33–41. Washington: Woodrow Wilson International Center for Scholars.

Allen, Robert C. 1992. *Enclosure and the Yeoman*. Oxford: Clarendon Press.

Allen, William T., and Reinier Kraakman. 2003. *Commentaries and Cases on the Law of Business Organization*. New York: Aspen Publishers.

Alston, Lee J., and Andrés A. Gallo. 2005. "The Erosion of Checks and Balances in Argentina and the Rise of Populism in Argentina: An Explanation for Argentina's Economic Slide from the Top Ten." Working Paper PEC2005-0001. University of Colorado Institute of Behavioral Science, Research Program on Political and Economic Change.

Alston, Lee J., Gary D. Libecap, and Bernardo Mueller. 1999. *Titles, Conflict, and Land Use: The Development of Property Rights and Land Reform on the Brazilian Amazon Frontier*. University of Michigan Press.

American Law Institute. 2003. "International Statement of Mexican Bankruptcy Law." In *Transnational Insolvency: Cooperation among the NAFTA Countries*. Huntington, N.Y.: Juris Publishing Inc.

Anderson, Terry L., and Peter J. Hill. 2004. *The Not So Wild, Wild West: Property Rights on the Frontier*. Stanford University Press.

Anderson, Terry L., and Fred S. McChesney. 2003. *Property Rights: Cooperation, Conflict, and Law*. Princeton University Press.

Aoki, Masohiko. 2000. *Information, Corporate Governance, and Institutional Diversity*. Oxford University Press.

———. 2001. *Toward a Comparative Institutional Analysis*. MIT Press.

Areddy, James T. 2005. "China to Relax Foreign Quotas; Overseas Investors Will Get Chance to Buy $6 Billion More in Shares." *Wall Street Journal*, July 12, 2005, p. C12.

Asian Development Bank. 2003. "Judicial Independence Overview and Country-Level Summaries." Judicial Independence Project RETA 5987 (www.adb.org/Documents/Events/2003/RETA5987/Final_Overview_Report.pdf).

———. 2004. *Law and Policy Reform at the Asian Development Bank, 2003 Edition*. Manila.

Aucoin, Louis. 2002. "Judicial Independence in France." In *Guidance for Promoting Independence and Impartiality*, rev. ed. U.S. Agency for International Development, 72–82.

Ayres, Ian, and Robert Gertner. 1989. "Filling Gaps in Incomplete Contracts: An Economic Theory of Default Rules." *Yale Law Journal* 99: 87–130.

Aziz, Jahangir, and Christoph Duenwald. 2002. "Growth-Financial Intermediation Nexus in China." Working Paper WP/02/194. Washington: International Monetary Fund (November).

Bai, Chong-En, Qiao Liu, Joe Lu, Frank M. Song, and Junxi Zhang. 2003. "Corporate Governance and Market Valuation in China." Paper 564. University of Michigan Business School, William Davidson Institute (April).

Bai, Chong-En, and Yijiang Wang. 1999. "The Myth of the East Asian Miracle: The Macroeconomic Implications of Soft Budgets." *American Economic Review* 89 (2): 432–37.

Baird, Douglas G. 2001. *The Elements of Bankruptcy*, 3d ed. New York: Foundation Press.

Baird, Douglas G., Robert H. Gertner, and Randall C. Picker. 1994. *Game Theory and the Law*. Harvard University Press.

Baird, Douglas G., and Robert K. Rasmussen. 2005. "Private Debt and the Missing Lever of Corporate Governance." Vanderbilt Law and Economics Research Paper 05-08; University of Chicago Law and Economics, John M. Olin Working Paper 247 (March).

Baker, Leonard P. 1976. "The Circuit Riding Justices." In *Yearbook,* pp. 63–69. Washington: Supreme Court Historical Society.

Baker, Richard D. 1971. *Judicial Review in Mexico.* University of Texas Press.

Barale, Lucille. 2005. "A Law Built on Shaky Foundations." *Financial Times,* September 28, 2005.

Barboza, David. 2005. "Inside Jobs Hit Chinese Banking, Frauds Hinder Financial Modernization." *International Herald Tribune,* March 23, 2005, p. 1.

Bardhan, Pranab K. 2000. "Understanding Underdevelopment: Challenges for Institutional Economics from the Point of View of Poor Countries." *Journal of Institutional and Theoretical Economics* 156: 216–35.

Barnett, Steven. 2004. "Banking Sector Developments." In *China's Growth and Integration into the World Economy: Prospects and Challenges (IMF Occasional Paper 232),* edited by Eswar Prasad, pp. 43–50. Washington: International Monetary Fund.

Barr, Michael S. 2001. "Microfinance and Financial Development." *Michigan Journal of International Law* 26: 271–96.

Barro, Robert J., and Rachel M. McCleary. 2003. "Religion and Economic Growth." Working Paper 9682. Cambridge: National Bureau of Economic Research.

Barth, James R., Gerard Caprio, Jr., and Ross Levine. 2001. "Banking Systems around the Globe: Do Regulation and Ownership Affect Performance and Stability?" In *Prudential Supervision: What Works and What Doesn't,* edited by Frederic S. Mishkin, pp. 31–95. University of Chicago Press.

———. 2004. "Bank Regulation and Supervision: What Works Best?" *Journal of Financial Intermediation* 13: 205–48.

Bartlett, John. 2002. *Bartlett's Familiar Quotations,* 17th ed. Boston: Little, Brown.

Barton, J. L. 1993. "The Mystery of Bracton." *Journal of Legal History* 14 (3): 1–142.

Baskin, Jonathan Barron, and Paul J. Miranti, Jr. 1997. *A History of Corporate Finance.* Cambridge University Press.

Baum, Richard. 1994. *Burying Mao: Chinese Politics in the Age of Deng Xiaoping.* Princeton University Press.

Beck, Thorsten, Asli Demirgüç-Kunt, and Ross Levine. 2003. "Law, Endowments, and Finance." *Journal of Financial Economics* 70: 137–81.

———. 2004a. "Finance, Inequality and Poverty: Cross-Country Evidence." Working Paper 10979. Cambridge: National Bureau of Economic Research (December).

———. 2004b. "Law and Firms' Access to Finance." Working Paper 10687. Cambridge: National Bureau of Economic Research (August).

Beck, Thorsten, and Ross Levine. 2004. "Legal Institutions and Financial Development." Working Paper 10417. Cambridge: National Bureau of Economic Research (April).

Bell, John. 1987. "The Judge as Bureaucrat." In *Oxford Essays in Jurisprudence,* edited by John Eekelaar and John Bell, 3d Series, pp. 33–56. Oxford: Clarendon Press.

———. 1992. *French Constitutional Law*. Oxford: Clarendon Press.

———. 2001. *French Legal Cultures*. London: Butterworths.

Benston, George J., Michael Bromwich, Robert E. Litan, and Alfred Wagenhofer. 2006. *Worldwide Financial Reporting: The Development and Future of Accounting Standards*. New York: Oxford University Press.

Beny, Laura Nyantung. 2005. "Do Insider Trading Laws Matter? Some Preliminary Comparative Evidence." *American Law and Economic Review* 7 (1): 144–83.

Berglöf, Erik, and Stijn Claessens. 2004. "Corporate Governance and Enforcement." Policy Research Working Paper 3409. Washington: World Bank (September).

Berglöf, Erik, and Anete Pajuste. 2003. "Emerging Owners, Eclipsing Markets? Corporate Governance in Central and Eastern Europe." In *Corporate Governance and Capital Flows in a Global Economy*, edited by P. Cornelius and B. Kogut. Oxford University Press.

Bergsten, C. Fred, Bates Gill, Nicholas R. Lardy, and Derek Mitchell. 2006. *China: The Balance Sheet*. New York: Public Affairs.

Berkowitz, Daniel, Katharina Pistor, and Jean-Francois Richard. 2003a. "Economic Development, Legality, and the Transplant Effect." *European Economic Review* 47: 165–95.

———. 2003b. "The Transplant Effect." *American Journal of Comparative Law* 51: 163–203.

Berman, Harold J. 1983. *Law and Revolution: The Formation of the Western Legal Tradition*. Harvard University Press.

———. 2003. *Law and Revolution II: The Impact of Protestant Reformations on the Western Legal Tradition*. Cambridge: Belknap Press.

Berndt, Markus. 2002. *Global Differences in Corporate Governance Systems*. Wiesbaden: Deutscher Universitäts-Verlag.

Bhattacharya, Utpal, and Hazem Daouk. 2004. "When No Law Is Better than a Good Law." Working Paper (papers.ssrn.com/abstract_id=558021).

Biancalana, Joseph. 2001. *The Fee Tail and the Common Recovery in Medieval England, 1176–1502*. Cambridge University Press.

Bierlen, Ralph, Larry N. Langemeier, Bruce L. Ahrendsen, and Bruce L. Dixon. 2000. "Land Leasing and Debt on Farms: Substitutes or Complements?" *Quarterly Journal of Business and Economics* 39 (2): 18–38.

Birdsall, Nancy, Dani Rodrik, and Arvind Subramanian. 2005. "How to Help Poor Countries." *Foreign Affairs* 84 (4): 136–53.

Black, Bernard S. 2001. "The Legal and Institutional Preconditions for Strong Securities Markets." *U.C.L.A. Law Review* 48: 781–855.

Black, Bernard, and Reinier Kraakman. 1996. "A Self-Enforcing Model of Corporate Law." *Harvard Law Review* 109: 1911–82.

Black, Bernard, Reinier Kraakman, and Anna Tarassova. 2000. "Russian Privatization and Corporate Governance: What Went Wrong?" *Stanford Law Review* 52: 1731–1808.

Black, Bernard S., and Anna S. Tarassova. 2002. "Institutional Reform in Transition: A Case Study of Russia." *Supreme Court Economic Review* 10: 211–77.

Blackstone, Sir William. 2001. *Commentaries on the Laws of England,* edited and with an introduction by Wayne Morrison. London: Cavendish Publishing Limited.

Blair, Margaret M. 2003. "Locking In Capital: What Corporate Law Achieved for Business Organization in the Nineteenth Century." *U.C.L.A. Law Review* 51: 387–455.

Blumberg, Phillip I. 1986. "Limited Liability and Corporate Groups." *Journal of Corporation Law* 11: 573–631.

Booth, Charles. 2004. "Drafting Bankruptcy Laws in Social Market Economies: Recent Developments in China and Vietnam." *Columbia Journal of Asian Law* 18: 93–147.

Bostick, C. Dent. 1987. "Land Title Registration: An English Solution to an American Problem." *Indiana Law Journal* 63: 55–111.

Botero, Juan Carlos, Rafael LaPorta, Florencio López-de-Silanes, Andrei Shleifer, and Alexander Volokh. 2003. "Judicial Reform." *World Bank Research Observer* 18 (1): 61–88.

Bottazzi, Laura, Marco Da Rin, and Thomas Hellman. 2005. "What Role of Legal Systems in Financial Intermediation? Theory and Evidence." Working Paper (strategy.sauder.ubc.ca/hellmann/pdfs/legal06.pdf) (June).

Boyreau-Debray, Genevieve, and Shang-Jin Wei. 2004. "Can China Grow Faster? A Diagnosis of the Fragmentation of Its Domestic Capital Market." Working Paper WP/04/76. Washington: International Monetary Fund (May).

Bradley, A. W., and K. D. Ewing. 2003. *Constitutional and Administrative Law,* 13th ed. Harlow: Pearson Longman.

Brainard, Lael, Carol Graham, Nigel Purvis, Steven Radelet, and Gayle E. Smith. 2003. *The Other War: Global Poverty and the Millennium Challenge Account.* Brookings.

Brandt, Loren, Jikun Huang, Guo Li, and Scott Rozelle. 2002. "Land Rights in Rural China: Facts, Fictions and Issues." *China Journal* 47: 67–97.

Brewer, John. 1989. *The Sinews of Power: War, Money and the English State, 1688–1783.* New York: Alfred A. Knopf.

Brittan, Samuel. 1978. "How British Is the British Sickness." *Journal of Law and Economics* 21 (2): 245–68.

Brown, Jennifer. 2004. "Ejidos and Comunidades in Oaxaca, Mexico: Impact of the 1992 Reforms." Report on Foreign Aid and Development 120. Seattle: Rural Development Institute (February).

Brown, L. Neville, and John S. Bell. 1998. *French Administrative Law.* Oxford: Clarendon Press.

Browne, Andrew. 2005. "China Agency Spurs Bank Rift; State Firm's Role as Investor Heats Up Financial-System Tussle." *Wall Street Journal,* August 22, 2005, p. C14.

Burghof, Hans-Peter, and Adrian Hunger. 2003. "Access to Stock Markets for Small and Medium-Sized Growth Firms: The Temporary Success and Ultimate Failure of Germany's Neuer Markt." (papers.ssrn.com/abstract_id=497404).

Burnside, Craig, and David Dollar. 2000. "Aid, Policies, and Growth." *American Economic Review* 90 (4): 847–68.

———. 2004. "Aid, Policies, and Growth: Reply." *American Economic Review* 94 (3): 781–84.

Buscaglia, Edgardo, and Pilar Domingo. 1997. "Impediments to Judicial Reform in Latin America." In *The Law and Economics of Development*, edited by Edgardo Buscaglia, William Ratliff, and Robert Cooter, pp. 291–313. Greenwich: JAI Press Inc.

Cappelletti, Mauro. 1971. *Judicial Review in the Contemporary World*. New York: Bobbs-Merrill Company, Inc.

———. 1989. *The Judicial Process in Comparative Perspective*. Oxford: Clarendon Press.

Caprio, Gerard, Luc Laeven, and Ross Levine. 2004. "Governance and Bank Valuation." Policy Research Working Paper 3202. Washington: World Bank (February).

Carroll, Alex. 2003. *Constitutional and Administrative Law*, 3d ed. Harlow: Pearson Longman.

Carruthers, Bruce G. 1996. *City of Capital: Politics and Markets in the English Financial Revolution*. Princeton University Press.

Casner, A. James, W. Barton Leach, Susan Fletcher French, Gerald Korngold, and Lea VanderVelde. 2000. *Cases and Text on Property*, 4th ed. New York: Aspen Law & Business.

Cass, Ronald A. 2001. *The Rule of Law in America*. Johns Hopkins University Press.

Castan Tobeñas, Don Jose. 1988. "Contemporary Legal Systems of the Western World." *Comparative Juridical Review* 25: 105–71.

Cerra, Valerie, and Sweta Chaman Saxena. 2005. "Did Output Recover from the Asian Crisis?" *IMF Staff Papers* 52 (1): 1–23.

Chaudhuri, K. N. 1965. *The English East India Company: The Study of an Early Joint Stock Company, 1600–1640*. London: Frank Cass & Co. Ltd.

Cheffins, Brian R. 2002. "Corporate Governance Convergence: Lessons from Australia." *Transnational Lawyer* 16: 13–43.

Chen, Hongyi. 2000. *The Institutional Transition of China's Township and Village Enterprises: Market Liberalization, Contractual Form Innovation and Privatization*. Aldershot: Ashgate.

Chen, Zhiwu. 2003. "Capital Markets and Legal Development: The China Case." *China Economic Review* 14: 451–72.

China Bank Regulatory Commission. 2005. "Latest Developments in China's Banking Reform, Opening-up and Supervision" (www.china.org.cn/e-news/news051205.htm) (December 5).

China Construction Bank Corporation. 2005. "Global Offering" (on file with author).

China Law and Governance Review. 2004. "Enforcement of Civil Judgments: Harder than Reaching the Sky." June (www.chinareview.info).

Chow, Daniel C. K. 2003. *The Legal System of the People's Republic of China in a Nutshell*. St. Paul: West Group.

Claessens, Stijn, Simeon Djankov, Joseph Fan, and Larry Lang. 1999. "Expropriation of Minority Shareholders: Evidence from East Asia." Policy Research Working Paper 2088. Washington: World Bank (June).

Claessens, Stijn, Simeon Djankov, and Larry H. P. Lang. 2000. "The Separation of Ownership and Control in East Asian Corporations." *Journal of Financial Economics* 58: 81–112.

Claessens, Stijn, Simeon Djankov, and Ashoka Mody, eds. 2001. *Resolution of Financial Distress: An International Perspective on the Design of Bankruptcy Laws.* Washington: World Bank.

Clagett, Helen Lord. 1952. *The Administration of Justice in Latin America.* New York: Oceana Publications.

Clapham, Sir John. 1945. *The Bank of England: A History, Volume I: 1694–1797.* Cambridge University Press.

Clark, David S. 2002. "The Organization of Lawyers and Judges." In *International Encyclopedia of Comparative Law*, vol. 16, *Civil Procedure*, edited by Mauro Cappelletti. Dordecht/Boston: J. C. B. Mohr.

———. 1975. "Judicial Protection of the Constitution in Latin America." *Hastings Constitutional Law Quarterly* 2: 405–42.

Clarke, Alvaro. 2003. "Annex B: Case Studies, Lessons of Recent Reform Efforts. The Politics of Implementing Corporate Governance Reform: Some Lessons from the Chilean Experience." In *White Paper on Corporate Governance in Latin America*, 40–45. Paris: Organization for Economic Cooperation and Development.

Clarke, Donald C. 1996. "Power and Politics in the Chinese Court System: The Enforcement of Civil Judgments." *Columbia Journal of Asian Law* 10: 1–92.

———. 2003. "Corporate Governance in China: An Overview." *China Economic Review* 14: 494–507.

———. 2005. "The Chinese Legal System" (donclarke.net/public/ChineseLegal System.html).

———. 2006. "The Independent Director in Chinese Corporate Governance." *Delaware Journal of Corporate Law* 36 (1): 125–228.

Clay, Karen, and Gavin Wright. 2003. "Order without Law? Property Rights during the California Gold Rush." John M. Olin Program in Law and Economics Working Paper 265. Stanford Law School (June).

Clemens, Michael, Steven Radelet, and Rikhil Bhavnani. 2004. "Counting Chickens When They Hatch: The Short Term Effect of Aid on Growth." Working Paper 44. Washington: Center for Global Development (July, revised November).

Coatsworth, John H. 1978. "Obstacles to Economic Growth in Nineteenth-Century Mexico." *American Historical Review* 83: 80–100.

Coffee, John C., Jr. 1999. "Privatization and Corporate Governance: The Lessons from Securities Market Failure." *Journal of Corporate Law* 25: 1–39.

———. 2001. "The Rise of Dispersed Ownership: The Roles of Law and the State in the Separation of Ownership and Control." *Yale Law Journal* 111: 1–82.

Cole, David C., and Yung Chul Park. 1983. *Financial Development in Korea*. Harvard University, Council on East Asian Studies.

Coleman, James S. 1990. *Foundations of Social Theory*. Cambridge: Belknap Press.

Congressional-Executive Commission on China. 2004. *Annual Report 2004*. Government Printing Office.

———. 2005. *Annual Report 2005*. Government Printing Office.

Cools, Sofie. 2005. "The Real Difference in Corporate Law between the United States and Continental Europe: Distribution of Powers." *Delaware Journal of Corporate Law* 30: 697–766.

Cooper, Richard N. 2002. "Prepared Statement of Richard N. Cooper: Chinese Economic and Budgetary Prospects." In *Compilation of Hearings Held before the U.S.-China Security Review Commission*. 107th Congress, First and Second Sessions, pp. 791–96. Government Printing Office.

———. 2004. "A Glimpse of 2020." Working Paper (post.economics.harvard.edu/faculty/cooper/papers/A%20Glimpse%20of%202020.pdf).

———. 2005. "A Half Century of Development." In *Proceedings of Annual World Bank Conference on Development Economics, 2005: Lessons of Experience,* edited by François Bourguignon and Boris Pleskovic, pp. 89–117. Washington: World Bank.

Cooter, Robert D. 1997. "The Rule of State Law and the Rule-of-Law State: Economic Analysis of the Legal Foundations of Development." In *The Law and Economics of Development*, edited by Edgardo Buscaglia, William Ratliff, and Robert Cooter, pp. 101–48. Greenwich: JAI Press.

Cox, James D., Thomas Lee Hazen, and F. Hodge O'Neal. 1997. *Corporations*. New York: Aspen Law & Business.

Cross, Frank B. 2005. "Identifying the Virtues of the Common Law." Law and Economics Working Paper 063. University of Texas (September) (ssrn.com/abstract= 812464).

Cull, Robert, and Lixin Colin Xu. 2000. "Bureaucrats, State Banks, and the Efficiency of Credit Allocation: The Experience of Chinese State-Owned Enterprises." *Journal of Comparative Economics* 28: 1–31.

Dahan, Frédérique. 2000. "Secured Transactions Law in Western Advanced Economies: Exposing Myths." *Law in Transition* (Autumn): 37–43.

Dahan, Frédérique, and John Simpson. 2004. "Secured Transactions in Central and Eastern Europe: European Bank for Reconstruction and Development (EBRD) Assessment." *Uniform Commercial Code Law Journal* 36 (3): 77–102.

Dahlman, Carl J. 1980. *The Open Field System and Beyond: A Property Rights Analysis of an Economic Institution*. Cambridge University Press.

Dakolias, Maria. 1995. "A Strategy for Judicial Reform: The Experience in Latin America." *Virginia Journal of International Law* 36: 167–231.

———. 1999. "Court Performance around the World: A Comparative Perspective." *Yale Human Rights and Development Law Journal* 2: 87–142.

Dam, Kenneth W. 1976. *Oil Resources: Who Gets What How?* University of Chicago Press.

Danziger, Danny, and John Gillingham. 2003. *1215, the Year of the Magna Carta.* London: Hodder & Stroughton.

Davis, John P. 1905. *Corporations: A Study of the Origin and Development of Great Business Combinations and of Their Relation to the Authority of the State,* vol. I. New York: P. Putnam's Sons.

Davis, Kevin E. 2004. "What Can the Rule of Law Variable Tell Us about Rule of Law Reforms?" *Michigan Journal of International Law* 26 (1): 141–61.

Davydenko, Sergei A., and Julian Franks. 2004. "Do Bankruptcy Codes Matter? A Study of Defaults in France, Germany, and the U.K." London Business School (December 21).

Dawson, John P. 1968. *The Oracles of the Law.* University of Michigan Law School.

De Alessi, Louis. 2003. "Gains from Private Property: The Empirical Evidence." In *Property Rights: Contract, Conflict, and Law,* edited by Terry L. Anderson and Fred S. McChesney, pp. 90–111. Princeton University Press.

De Figueiredo, Rui J. P., Jr., and Barry R. Weingast. 2001. "Russian Federalism: A Contradiction in Terms." *Hoover Digest* (4) (www.hooverdigest.org/014/weingast.html).

———. 2005. "Self-Enforcing Federalism." *Journal of Law, Economics, and Organizations* 21 (1): 103–35.

Deininger, Klaus. 2003. *Land Policies for Growth and Poverty Reduction.* Washington: World Bank and Oxford University Press.

Deininger, Klaus, Raffaella Castagnini, and María A. González. 2004. "Comparing Land Reform and Land Markets in Colombia: Impacts on Equity and Efficiency." Policy Research Working Paper 3258. Washington: World Bank (April).

Deininger, Klaus, and Songqing Jin. 2002. "Land Rental Markets as an Alternative to Government Reallocation? Equity and Efficiency Considerations in the Chinese Land Tenure System." Policy Research Working Paper 2930. Washington: World Bank (November).

Deininger, Klaus, Songqing Jin, Berhanu Adenew, Samuel Gebre-Selassie, and Mulat Demeke. 2003. "Market and Non-market Transfers of Land in Ethiopia: Implications for Efficiency, Equity, and Non-farm Development." Policy Research Working Paper 2992. Washington: World Bank (March).

Demirgüç-Kunt, Asli. 2006. "Finance and Economic Development: Policy Choices for Developing Countries." Policy Research Working Paper 3955. Washington: World Bank (June).

Dempsey, Mary A. 2005. "In the Crosshairs." *LatinFinance* 165 (April): 44–48.

de Soto, Hernando. 1989. *The Other Path: The Invisible Revolution in the Third World.* New York: Harper Row.

———. 1993. "The Missing Ingredient: What Poor Countries Will Need to Make Their Markets Work." *The Economist,* September 11, 1993, pp. 8–12.

———. 2000. *The Mystery of Capital: Why Capitalism Triumphs in the West and Fails Everywhere Else.* New York: Basic Books.

———. 2002. *The Other Path: The Economic Answer to Terrorism.* New York: Basic Books.

Diamant, Neil J., Stanley B. Lubman, and Kevin J. O'Brien. 2005. "Law and Society in the People's Republic of China." In *Engaging the Law in China: State, Society, and Possibilities for Justice*, edited by Neil J. Diamant, Stanley B. Lubman, and Kevin J. O'Brien, pp. 3–27. Stanford University Press.

Diamond, Jared. 2005. *Collapse*. New York: Penguin Group.

Dicey, Albert Venn. 1893. *Introduction to the Study of the Law of the Constitution*, 4th ed. London: MacMillan and Co.

Dickie, Paul, and Emma Xiaoquin Fan. 2005. "Banks and Corporate Debt Market Development." Economics and Research Department Working Paper 67. Manila: Asian Development Bank (April).

Dickson, P. G. M. 1967. *The Financial Revolution in England: A Study in the Development of Public Credit*. London: MacMillan.

Djankov, Simeon, Caralee McLiesh, and Andrei Shleifer. 2005. "Private Credit in 129 Countries." Working Paper 11078. Cambridge, Mass.: National Bureau of Economic Research (January).

Djankov, Simeon, Rafael La Porta, Florencio López-de-Silanes, and Andrei Shleifer. 2001. "Legal Structure and Judicial Efficiency: the Lex Mundi Project, Table 2." Working Paper (October) (siteresources.worldbank.org/INTWDR2002/Resources/2488_djankov.pdf.pdf).

———. 2003. "Courts." *Quarterly Journal of Economics* 118 (2): 453–517.

———. 2005. "The Law and Economics of Self-Dealing" (December) (papers.ssrn.com/abstract_id=875734).

Doidge, Craig, G. Andrew Karolyi, and René M. Stulz. 2004. "Why Do Countries Matter So Much for Corporate Governance?" Working Paper 10726. Cambridge, Mass.: National Bureau of Economic Research (August).

Dollar, David, and Jakob Svensson. 1998. "What Explains the Success or Failure of Structural Adjustment Programs?" Policy Research Working Paper 1938. Washington, World Bank (June).

Dolven, Ben, and Susan V. Lawrence. 2002. "Playing By the Rules." *Far Eastern Economic Review*, January 31, pp. 52–53.

Dolven, Ben, Howard Winn, and David Murphy. 2004. "HSBC Bests Big on China." *Far Eastern Economic Review*, August 14, pp. 42–44.

Donahue, Charles, Jr. 2004. "Medieval and Early Modern *Lex mercatoria*: An Attempt at the *probation diabolica*." *Chicago Journal of International Law* 5: 21–37.

Douglas, David C., ed. 1975. "Statute of Westminster I (3 Edw. 1), 1275, c.23." In *English Historical Documents: 1189–1327*, vol. III, 404. Oxford University Press.

Dukeminier, Jesse, and James E. Krier. 1993, *Property*, 3d ed. Boston: Little, Brown and Company.

Durlauf, Steven N., and Marcel Fafchamps. 2005. "Social Capital." In *The Handbook of Economic Growth*, edited by Philippe Aghion and Stephen Durlauf. Amsterdam: Elsevier.

Dyck, Alexander, and Luigi Zingales. 2004. "Private Benefits of Control: An International Comparison." *Journal of Finance* 59 (2): 537–600.

Dyer, Geoff. 2005a. "Beijing Doubles Stock Quota for Foreign Investors in Drive to Energise Markets." *Financial Times,* July 12.

———. 2005b. "China to Expand Scheme to Unwind Non-Tradeable Shares." *Financial Times,* June 28.

———. 2005c. "HK Is China's Preferred Stock Market." *Financial Times,* December 23.

———. 2005d. "Shanghai Stock Market Slides on News of State Holdings Sale." *Financial Times,* May 10.

Dyer, Geoff, and Francesco Guerrera. 2005a. "China Commits to Market Overhaul Shareholder Reforms." *Financial Times,* August 25.

———. 2005b. "Unfair Shares: A Mishandled Market Structure Raises the Prospect that China 'Will Get Old Before It Gets Rich.'" *Financial Times,* March 29.

Easterbrook, Frank H. 1997. "International Corporate Differences: Markets or Law?" *Journal of Applied Corporate Finance* 9 (4): 23–29.

Easterbrook, Frank H., and Daniel R. Fischel. 1991. *The Economic Structure of Corporate Law.* Harvard University Press.

Easterly, William. 2001. *The Elusive Quest for Growth: Economists' Adventures and Misadventures in the Tropics.* MIT Press.

———. 2003. "Can Foreign Aid Buy Growth?" *Journal of Economic Perspectives* 17 (3): 23–48.

———. 2005. "What Did Structural Adjustment Adjust? The Association of Policies and Growth with Repeated IMF and World Bank Adjustment Loans." *Journal of Development Economics* 76: 1–22.

Easterly, William, and Ross Levine. 2002. "Tropics, Germs, and Crops: How Endowments Influence Economic Development." Working Paper 9106. Cambridge, Mass.: National Bureau of Economic Research.

Easterly, William, Ross Levine, and David Roodman. 2004. "Aid, Policies, and Growth: Comment." *American Economic Review* 94 (3): 774–80.

EBRD (European Bank for Reconstruction and Development). 2001a. "Law in Transition: Concessions. Mobilizing Private Finance for Development" (Spring) (www.ebrd.com/pubs/legal/4857.pdf).

———. 2001b. "Law in Transition: Contract Enforcement" (Autumn) (www.ebrd.com/pubs/legal/5083.pdf).

Economist Intelligence Unit. 2005. *Country Finance: China.* London (August).

———.2006a. *Country Report: China.* London (March).

———. 2006b. *China Country Report.* London (April).

———. 2006c. *Country Report: China.* London (May).

Eder, Phanor James. 1950. "Impact of the Common Law on Latin America." *Miami Law Quarterly* 4 (4): 435–40.

Eichengreen, Barry, and Pipat Luengnaruemitchai. 2004. "Why Doesn't Asia Have Bigger Bond Markets?" Working Paper 10576. Cambridge, Mass.: National Bureau of Economic Research (June).

Ellickson, Robert C. 1993. "Property in Land." *Yale Law Journal* 102: 1315–1400.

Elster, Jon. 1989. "Social Norms and Economic Theory." *Journal of Economic Perspectives* 3 (4): 99–117.

English, Barbara, and John Saville. 1983. *Strict Settlement: A Guide for Historians.* University of Hull Press.

Epstein, Richard A. 2004. "Reflections on the Historical Origins and Economic Structure of the Law Merchant." *Chicago Journal of International Law* 5: 1–20.

Evans, Frank. 1908. "The Evolution of the English Joint Stock Limited Trading Company." *Columbia Law Review* 8 (5): 339–61 and 8 (6): 461–80.

Faccio, Mara, Larry H. P. Lang, and Leslie Young. 2003. "Debt and Expropriation." European Financial Management Association Working Paper (July 1 draft) for 2001 Lugano meetings (papers.ssrn.com/abstract_id=239724).

Fairgrieve, Duncan, and Mads Andenas. 2000. "Securing Progress in Collateral Law Reform: The EBRD's Regional Survey of Secured Transactions Laws." *Law in Transition* (Autumn): 28–36.

Fallon, Richard H., Jr., Daniel J. Meltzer, and David L. Shapiro. 2003. *The Federal Courts and the Federal System,* 5th ed. New York: Foundation Press.

Favoreu, Louis. 1990. "Constitutional Review in Europe." In *Constitutionalism and Rights: The Influence of the United States Constitution Abroad,* edited by Louis Henkin and Albert J. Rosenthal, pp. 38–62. Columbia University Press.

Feder, Gershon, and D. Feeney. 1991. "Land Tenure and Property Rights: Theory and Implications for Development Policy." *World Bank Economic Review* 5 (1): 135–53.

Feder, Gershon, Tongroj Onchan, Yongyuth Chalamwong, and Chira Hongladarom. 1998. *Land Policies and Farm Productivity in Thailand.* Johns Hopkins Press.

Feld, Lars P., and Stefan Voigt. 2003. "Economic Growth and Judicial Independence: Cross-country Evidence Using a New Set of Indicators." *European Journal of Political Economy* 19 (1): 497–527.

———. 2004. "Making Judges Independent—Some Proposals Regarding the Judiciary." Working Paper 1260. Munich: CESifo (April).

Felipe, Jesus. 1997. "Total Factor Productivity Growth in East Asia: A Critical Survey." Report Series 65. Manila: Asian Development Bank, Economics and Development Resource Center (September).

Field, Erica. 2004. "Property Rights, Community Public Goods, and Household Time Allocation in Urban Squatter Communities: Evidence from Peru." *William and Mary Law Review* 45: 837–87.

Finer, S. E. 1997. *The History of Government from the Earliest Times, Volume III: Empires, Monarchies, and the Modern State.* Oxford University Press.

Finer, S. E., Vernon Bogdanor, and Bernard Rudden. 1995. *Comparing Constitutions.* Oxford: Clarendon Press.

Fishman, Ted C. 2005. *China, Inc.: How the Rise of the Next Superpower Challenges America and the World.* New York: Scribner.

Fleisig, Heywood. 1996. "Secured Transactions: The Power of Collateral." *Finance and Development* 33 (2): 44–46.

Fogel, Robert. 2006. "Why China Is Likely to Achieve Its Growth Objectives." Working Paper 12122. Cambridge, Mass.: National Bureau of Economic Research (March).

Franks, Julian, and Oren Sussman. 1999. "Financial Innovations and Corporate Insolvency." Working Paper. London Business School (August).

Friedman, David D. 2000. *Law's Order: What Economics Has to Do with the Law and Why It Matters*. Princeton University Press.

Fukuyama, Francis. 2000. "Social Capital." In *Culture Matters: How Values Shape Human Progress*, edited by Lawrence E. Harrison and Samuel P. Huntington, pp. 98–111. New York: Basic Books.

Fuller, Lon L. 1964. *The Morality of Law*. Yale University Press.

Furnish, Dale Beck. 2000. "Judicial Review in Mexico." *Southwestern Journal of Law and Trade in the Americas* 7: 235–45.

Gambetta, Diego. 1993. *The Sicilian Mafia: The Business of Private Protection*. Harvard University Press.

Gao, Sheldon. 2002. "China Stock Market in a Global Perspective." Dow Jones Indexes (September) (djindexes.com/mdsidx/downloads.china_mkt_WP.pdf).

Garber, Peter M. 2000. *Famous First Bubbles*. MIT Press.

García Herrero, Alicia, Sergio Gavilá, and Danial Santabárbara. 2005. "China's Banking Reform: An Assessment of Its Evolution and Possible Impact." Documentos Ocasionales 0502. Madrid: Banco de España.

García Herrero, Alicia, and Daniel Santabárbara. 2004. "Where Is the Chinese Banking System Going with the Ongoing Reform?" Documentos Ocasionales 0406. Madrid: Banco de España.

Garner, Bryan A., ed. 2004. *Black's Law Dictionary*, 8th ed. St. Paul, Thomson/West.

Garretsen, Harry, Robert Lensink, and Elmer Sterken. 2004. "Growth, Financial Development, Societal Norms and Legal Institutions." *International Financial Markets, Institutions and Money* 14: 165–83.

Gates, Paul W. 1968. *History of Public Land Law Development*. Government Printing Office.

Gewirtz, Paul. 2001. "Approaches to Constitutional Interpretation: Comparative Constitutionalism and Chinese Characteristics." *Hong Kong Law Journal* 31 (2): 200–23.

Gil Diaz, Francisco. 2003. "Don't Blame Our Failures on Reforms that Have Not Taken Place." *Fraser Forum* June 2003: 7–11.

Giles, Chris, and Francesco Guerrera. 2005. "China Poised to Displace Britain as World's Fourth Largest Economy." *Financial Times*, December 21.

Giuseppi, John. 1966. *The Bank of England: A History from Its Foundation in 1694*. London: Evans Brothers Limited.

Glaeser, Edward, Simon Johnson, and Andrei Shleifer. 2001. "Coase versus the Coasians." *Quarterly Journal of Economics* 116 (3): 853–99.

Glaeser, Edward L., Rafael La Porta, Florencio López-de-Silanes, and Andrei Shleifer. 2004. "Do Institutions Cause Growth?" *Journal of Economic Growth* 9: 271–303.

Glaeser, Edward L., and Andrei Shleifer. 2002. "Legal Origins." *Quarterly Journal of Economics* 117: 1193–1229.

Goldman, Marshall I. 2003. *The Piratization of Russia: Russian Reform Goes Awry*. London: Routledge.

Green, Stephen. 2003. *China's Stock Market: A Guide to Its Progress, Players and Prospects*. London: Profile Books Ltd.

———. 2004. "Enterprise Reform & Stock Market Development in Mainland China." *Deutsche Bank Research, China Special*. March 25 (Frankfort).

———. 2005. "The Privatization Two-Step at China's Listed Firms." In *Exit the Dragon? Privatization and State Control in China*, edited by Stephen Green and Guy S. Liu. London: Chatham House.

Greif, Avner. 1989. "Reputation and Coalitions in Medieval Trade; Evidence on the Maghribi Traders." *Journal of Economic History* 49 (4): 857–82.

———. 2004a. "Impersonal Exchange without Impartial Law: The Community Responsibility System." *Chicago Journal of International Law* 5: 109–38.

———. 2004b. "Institutions and Impersonal Exchange: The European Experience." John M. Olin Working Paper 284 (May). Stanford Law School.

Greif, Avner, Paul Milgrom, and Barry R. Weingast. 1994. "Coordination, Commitment, and Enforcement: The Case of the Merchant Guild." *Journal of Political Economy* 102 (4): 745–76.

Guerrera, Francesco, and Richard McGregor. 2005. "China's Banks Smarten Up as They Switch from State Control to Commercial Lending." *Financial Times*, June 20.

Guiso, Luigi, Paola Sapienza, and Luigi Zingales. 2003. "People's Opium? Religion and Economic Attitudes." *Journal of Monetary Economics* 50: 225–82.

———.2004a. "Cultural Biases in Economic Exchange." Working Paper 11005. Cambridge, Mass.: National Bureau of Economic Research.

———. 2004b. "The Role of Social Capital in Financial Development." *American Economic Review* 94 (3): 526– 56.

———. 2006. "Does Culture Affect Economic Outcomes?" *Journal of Economic Perspectives* 20 (2): 23–48.

Haber, Stephen, Armando Razo, and Noel Maurer. 2003. *The Politics of Property Rights: Political Instability, Credible Commitments, and Economic Growth in Mexico, 1876–1929*. Cambridge University Press.

Hail, Luzi, and Christian Leuz. 2005. "International Differences in the Cost of Equity Capital: Do Legal Institutions and Securities Regulation Matter?" (ssrn.com/abstract=641981).

Halperin, Morton H., Joseph E. Siegle, and Michael M. Weinstein. 2005. *The Democracy Advantage: How Democracies Promote Prosperity and Peace*. New York: Routledge.

Hamowy, Ronald. 2003. "F. A. Hayek and the Common Law." *Cato Journal* 23 (2): 241–64.

Hanbury, Harold Greville, and Ronald Harling Maudsley. 1989. *Modern Equity*, 13th ed., edited by Jill E. Martin. London: Stevens & Sons.

Hansen, Henrik, and Finn Tarp. 2000. "Aid Effectiveness Disputed." *Journal of International Development* 12 (3) 375–98.

Hansmann, Henry, and Reinier Kraakman. 2001. "The End of History for Corporate Law." *Georgetown Law Journal* 89: 439–68.

———. 2004a. "Agency Problems and Legal Strategies." In *The Anatomy of Corporate Law: A Comparative and Functional Approach,* edited by Reinier R. Kraakman and others, pp. 21–31. Oxford University Press.

———. 2004b. "The Basic Governance Structure." In *The Anatomy of Corporate Law: A Comparative and Functional Approach,* edited by Reinier R. Kraakman and others, pp. 33–70. Oxford University Press.

———. 2004c. "What Is Corporate Law?" In *The Anatomy of Corporate Law: A Comparative and Functional Approach,* edited by Reinier R. Kraakman and others, 1–19. Oxford University Press.

Hansmann, Henry, Reinier Kraakman, and Richard Squire. 2006. "Law and the Rise of the Firm." Working Paper 57/2006. Brussels: European Corporate Governance Institute (papers.ssrn.com/ abstract_id=873507).

Hardin, Garrett. 1968. "The Tragedy of the Commons." *Science* 162: 1243–48.

Harris, Ron. 2000. *Industrializing English Law: Entrepreneurship and Business Organization, 1720–1844.* Cambridge University Press.

———. 2004. "The Formation of the East India Company as a Deal between Entrepreneurs and Outside Investors" (papers.ssrn.com/abstract_id=567941).

———. 2005. "The Formation of the East India Company as a Cooperation-Enhancing Institution." Working Paper (papers.ssrn.com/ abstract_id=874406).

Harrison, Lawrence E. 2000. "Introduction." In *Culture Matters: How Values Shape Human Progress,* edited by Lawrence E. Harrison and Samuel P. Huntington, pp. xvii–xxxiv. New York: Basic Books.

Harvard Law Review. 2004. "The Statistics." 118 (1): 497–509.

Hayek, F. A. 1960. *The Constitution of Liberty.* University of Chicago Press.

———. 1973. *Law, Legislation and Liberty,* vol. 1: *Rules and Order.* University of Chicago Press.

———. 1976. *Law, Legislation and Liberty,* vol. 2: *The Mirage of Social Justice.* University of Chicago Press.

———. 1979. *Law, Legislation and Liberty,* vol. 3: *The Political Order of a Free People.* University of Chicago Press.

Heckelman, Jan C., and Stephen Knack. 2005. "Foreign Aid and Market-Liberalizing Reform." Policy Research Working Paper 3557. Washington: World Bank (April).

Hellman, Joel S., and Daniel Kaufmann. 2002. "Inequality of Influence." Working Paper. Washington: World Bank (December) (ssrn.com/abstract=386901).

Helmholz, Richard, and Reinhard Zimmermann, eds. 1998. *Itinera Fiduciae: Trust and Treuhand in Historical Perspective.* Berlin: Duncker & Humblot.

Hendley, Kathryn. 1999. "Demand for Law, Rewriting the Rules of the Game in Russia: The Neglected Issue of the Demand for Law." *Eastern European Constitutional Review* 8 (4) (www.law.nyu.edu/eecr/Vol8num4/feature/rewriting.html).

Herman, Shael. 1984. "From Philosophers to Legislators, and Legislators to Gods: The French Civil Code as Secular Scripture." *University of Illinois Law Review* 1984: 597–620.

Hertig, Gerard, and Hideki Kanda. 2004. "Related Party Transactions." In *The Anatomy of Corporate Law: A Comparative and Functional Approach*, edited by Reinier R. Kraakman and others, pp. 101–30. Oxford University Press.

Heytens, Paul, and Harm Zebregs. 2003. "How Fast Can China Grow?" In *China: Competing in the Global Economy*, edited by Wanda Tseng and Markus Rodlauer, pp. 8–29. Washington: International Monetary Fund.

Ho, Peter. 2001. "Who Owns China's Land? Policies, Property Rights and Deliberate Institutional Ambiguity." *China Quarterly* (166): 394–421.

Hoffman, David E. 2002. *The Oligarchs: Wealth and Power in the New Russia.* New York: Public Affairs.

Hofstede, Geert H. 2001. *Culture's Consequences: Comparing Values, Behaviors, Institutions, and Organizations,* 2d ed. Thousand Oaks, Calif.: Sage Publications.

Holderness, Clifford G., and Dennis P. Sheehan. 1988. "The Role of Majority Shareholders in Publicly Held Corporations." *Journal of Financial Economics* 20: 317–46.

Holdsworth, W. S. 1956. *A History of English Law,* vol. 1, edited by A. L. Goodhart and H. G. Hanbury. 7th ed. Boston: Little, Brown.

———. 1909. *A History of English Law,* vol. 2. Boston: Little, Brown.

Holmes, Geoffrey. 1993. *The Making of a Great Power: Late Stuart and Early Georgian Britain 1660–1722.* London: Longman.

Holmes, Oliver Wendell. 1963. *The Common Law.* Boston: Belknap Press.

Holz, Carsten A. 2006. "Why China's New GDP Data Matters." *Far Eastern Economic Review* 169 (January/February): 54–57.

Huang, Yasheng. 2005. "Institutional Environment and Private Sector Development." In *Asia Program Special Report 129, China's Economy: Retrospect and Prospect,* edited by Loren Brandt, Thomas O. Rawski, and Gang Lin, pp. 26–32. Washington: Woodrow Wilson International Center for Scholars.

Hudson, John. 1996. *The Formation of the English Common Law: Law and Society in England from the Norman Conquest to Magna Carta.* New York: Longman.

Hung, Veron Mei-Ying. 2004. "China's WTO Commitment on Independent Judicial Review: Impact on Legal and Political Reform." *American Journal of Comparative Law* 52: 77–132.

———. 2005. "Judicial Reform in China: Lessons from Shanghai." Carnegie Papers 58. Washington: Carnegie Endowment for International Peace (April).

Huntington, Samuel P. 2000. "Forward." In *Culture Matters: How Values Shape Human Progress,* edited by Lawrence E. Harrison and Samuel P. Huntington, pp. xiii–xvi. New York: Basic Books.

Hutchens, Walter. 2003. "Private Securities Litigation in China: Material Disclosure about China's Legal System?" *University of Pennsylvania Journal of International Economic Law* 24: 599–689.

Hviid, Morten. 2000. "Long-Term Contracts and Relational Contracts." In *Encyclopedia of Law and Economics*, vol. 3: *The Regulation of Contracts*, edited by Boudewijn Bouckaert and Gerrit De Geest, pp. 46–72. Cheltenham: Edward Elgar Publishers Limited.

Ibbetson, David. 1999. *A Historical Introduction to the Law of Obligations*. Oxford University Press.

IIF Equity Advisory Group. 2004. "Corporate Governance in China: An Investor Perspective," Task Force Report (April 2004).

IMF (International Monetary Fund). 2003. *World Economic Outlook: A Survey by the Staff of the International Monetary Fund*. Washington.

————. 2005a. *Global Financial Stability Report: Market Developments and Issues*. Washington (September).

————. 2005b. *World Economic Outlook: Building Institutions*. Washington.

————. 2006. *World Economic Outlook: Globalizaion and Inflation*. Washington.

Inglehart, Ronald. 2000. "Culture and Democracy." In *Culture Matters: How Values Shape Human Progress*, edited by Lawrence E. Harrison and Samuel P. Huntington, pp. 80–97. New York: Basic Books.

Ireland, Paddy. 1996. "Capitalism without the Capitalists: The Joint Stock Company Share and the Emergence of the Modern Doctrine of Separate Corporate Personality." *Journal of Legal History* 17 (1): 41–73.

Islam, Roumeen. 2003. "Institutional Reform and the Judiciary: Which Way Forward." Policy Research Working Paper 3134. Washington: World Bank (September).

Jackson, Howell E. 2005. "Variation in the Intensity of Financial Regulation: Preliminary Evidence and Potential Implications." Harvard Law School (August) (ssrn.com/abstract=839250).

Jappelli, Tullio, Marco Pagano, and Magda Bianco. 2005. "Courts and Banks: Effects of Judicial Enforcement on Credit Markets." *Journal of Money, Credit, and Banking* 37 (2): 223–44.

Johnson, Simon, Peter Boone, Alasdair Breach, and Eric Feldman. 2000. "Corporate Governance in the Asian Financial Crisis." *Journal of Financial Economics* 58: 141–86.

Johnson, Simon, Jonathan Ostry, and Arvind Subramanian. 2006. "Levers for Growth." *Finance and Development* 43 (March): 1.

Johnston, David. 1988. *The Roman Law of Trusts*. Oxford: Clarendon Press.

Jolowicz, J. A. 1982. "Development of Common and Civil Law—the Contrasts." *Lloyds Maritime and Commercial Law Quarterly* 1982 (1): 87–95.

Kadens, Emily. 2004. "Order within Law, Variety within Custom: The Character of the Medieval Merchant Law." *Chicago Journal of International Law* 5: 39–65.

Kagawa, Ayako, and Jan Turksta. 2002. "The Process of Urban Land Tenure Formalization in Peru." In *Land, Rights and Innovation: Improving Tenure Security for the Urban Poor*, edited by Geoffrey Payne, pp. 57–75. London: ITDG Publishing.

Kahn, Joseph. 2006. "A Sharp Debate Erupts in China over Ideologies." *New York Times*, March 12.

Kanda, Hideki, and Curtis J. Milhaupt. 2003. "Re-examining Legal Transplants: The Director's Fiduciary Duty in Japanese Corporate Law." *American Journal of Comparative Law* 51: 887–901.

Kaplan, Steven N., Frederic Martel, and Per Strömberg. 2003. "How Do Legal Differences and Learning Affect Financial Contracts?" Working Paper 10097. Cambridge, Mass.: National Bureau of Economic Research (November).

Kaufmann, Daniel. 2003a. Comment on "Appropriate Institutions." In *Annual World Bank Conference on Development Economics: The New Reform Agenda,* edited by Boris Pleskovic and Nicholas Stern, pp. 302–13. Washington: World Bank.

———. 2003b. "Rethinking Governance: Empirical Lessons Challenge Orthodoxy." Working paper (www.worldbank.org/wbi/governance/pdf/rethink_gov_stanford.pdf).

———. 2004a. "Governance Redux: The Empirical Challenge." In *The Global Competitiveness Report,* edited by Xavier Sala-i-Martin, pp. 137–64. Oxford University Press.

———. 2004b. "Human Rights and Governance: The Empirical Challenge." New York University Center for Human Rights and Global Justice (March).

Kaufmann, Daniel, Aart Kray, and Massimo Mastruzzi. 2005. "Governance Matters IV: New Data, New Challenges." Washington: World Bank (May).

Kemp, Betty. 1957. *King and Commons: 1660–1832.* Westport: Greenwood (1957, reprinted 1984).

Kindleberger, Charles P. 1984. *A Financial History of Western Europe.* London: George Allen & Unwin.

Kindleberger, Charles P., and Robert Aliber. 2005. *Manias, Panics, and Crashes: A History of Financial Crises,* 5th ed. Hoboken: John Wiley and Sons.

Klerman, Daniel M., and Paul G. Mahoney. 2005. "The Value of Judicial Independence: Evidence from Eighteenth Century England." *American Law and Economics Review* 7: 1–27.

Knack, Stephen, and Philip Keefer. 1997. "Does Social Capital Have an Economic Payoff? A Cross-Country Investigation." *Quarterly Journal of Economics* 112 (4): 1251–88.

Koopmans, Tim. 2003. *Courts and Political Institutions: A Comparative View.* Cambridge University Press.

Kossick, Robert. 2004. "The Rule of Law and Development in Mexico." *Arizona Journal of International and Comparative Law* 21 (3): 715–834.

Kozolchyuk, Boris. 1979. "Fairness in Anglo and Latin American Adjudication." *Boston College International and Comparative Law Review* 2: 219–67.

Krueger, Anne O. 2000. "Introduction." In *Economic Policy Reform: The Second Stage,* edited by Anne O. Krueger, pp. 3–20. University of Chicago Press.

Krugman, Paul. 1994. "The Myth of Asia's Miracle." *Foreign Affairs* 73 (6): 62–78.

———. 1998. "What Happened to Asia?" (January) (web.mit.edu/krugman/www/DISINTER.html).

Kuczynski, Pedro-Pablo, and John Williamson, eds. 2003. *After the Washington Consensus: Restarting Growth and Reform in Latin America.* Washington: Institute of International Economics.

Kuijs, Louis. 2005. "Investment and Saving in China." Policy Research Working Paper 3633. Washington: World Bank.

Kuo, Patricia. 2006. "Dreaming of Robust Bond Sales in China." *International Herald Tribune*, May 25.

Kuran, Timur. 2003. "The Islamic Commercial Crisis: Institutional Roots of Economic Underdevelopment in the Middle East." *Journal of Economic History* 63: 414–46.

———. 2004a. "The Economic Ascent of the Middle East's Religious Minorities: The Role of Islamic Legal Pluralism." *Journal of Legal Studies* 33: 475–515.

———. 2004b. *Islam and Mammon: The Economic Predicaments of Islamism.* Princeton University Press.

Kwan, Chi Hung. 2004. "Why China's Investment Efficiency Is Low—Financial Reforms Are Lagging Behind." *China in Transition* (June 18) (www.rieti.go.jp/en/china/04061801.html).

Kynge, James. 2004. "China to Punish Officials behind Showy Projects." *Financial Times (Asia ed.)*, May 19.

Laeven, Luc, and Giaovanni Majoni. 2003. "Does Judicial Efficiency Lower the Cost of Credit?" Policy Research Working Paper 3159. Washington: World Bank (October).

Lague, David. 2005. "China Pressured on Death Penalty." *International Herald Tribune*, August 15.

Laixiang, Sun. 2005. "Ownership Reform in China's Township and Village Enterprises." In *Exit the Dragon? Privatization and State Control in China*, edited by Stephen Guen and Guy Shaojia Lin. London: Chatham House.

Lamoreaux, Naomi R., and Jean-Laurent Rosenthal. 2005. "Legal Regime and Contractual Flexibility: A Comparison of France and the United States during the Era of Industrialization." *American Law and Economic Review* 7 (1): 28–61.

Landes, David. 2000. "Culture Makes Almost All the Difference." In *Culture Matters: How Values Shape Human Progress*, edited by Lawrence E. Harrison and Samuel P. Huntington, pp. 2–13. New York: Basic Books.

Langbein, John H. 1985. "The German Advantage in Civil Procedure." *University of Chicago Law Review* 52: 823–66.

Lanjouw, Jean O., and Philip Levy. 2004. "A Default Question in Deed: A Cost-Benefit Framework for Titling Programs." *William and Mary Law Review* 45: 889–951.

La Porta, Raphael, Florencio López-de-Silanes, and Andrei Shleifer. 1999. "Corporate Ownership around the World." *Journal of Finance* 54 (2): 471–517.

———. 2002. "Government Ownership of Banks." *Journal of Finance* 57 (1): 265–301.

———. 2006. "What Works in Securities Laws?" *Journal of Finance* 61 (1): 1–33.

La Porta, Rafael, Florencio López-de-Silanes, and Guillermo Zamarripa. 2003. "Related Lending." *Quarterly Journal of Economics* 118 (1): 231–68.

La Porta, Raphael, Florencio López-de-Silanes, Cristian Pop-Eleches, and Andrei Shleifer. 2004. "Judicial Checks and Balances." *Journal of Political Economy* 112 (2): 445–70.

La Porta, Raphael, and others (Florencio López-de-Silanes, Andrei Shleifer, and Robert Vishny). 1997a. "Legal Determinants of External Finance." *Journal of Finance* 52 (3): 1131–50.

———. 1997b. "Trust in Large Organizations." *American Economic Review* 87 (2): 333–38.

———. 1998. "Law and Finance." *Journal of Political Economy* 106 (6): 1113–55.

———. 2000. "Investor Protection and Corporate Governance." *Journal of Financial Economics* 58: 3–27.

———. 2002. "Investor Protection and Corporate Valuation." *Journal of Finance* 57 (3): 1147–70.

Lardy, Nicholas R. 1998. *China's Unfinished Economic Revolution*. Brookings.

———. 2003. "When Will China's Financial System Meet China's Needs." In *How Far across the River? Chinese Policy Reform at the Millennium*, edited by Nicholas C. Hope, Dennis Tao Yang, and Mu Yang Li, pp. 67–96. Stanford University Press.

———. 2004. "State-Owned Banks in China." In *The Future of State-Owned Financial Institutions*, edited by Gerard Caprio and others, pp. 93–120. Brookings.

Lasser, Mitchel de S.-O.-L'E. 1994–95. "Judicial (Self-)Portraits: Judicial Discourse in the French Legal System." *Yale Law Journal* 104: 1325–1410.

———. 2004. *Judicial Deliberations: A Comparative Analysis of Judicial Transparency and Legitimacy*. Oxford University Press.

Lau, Lawrence. 2006. "Property Market Headed for Deflation." *Asia Times*, May 19.

Lau, Lawrence J., Yingyi Qian, and Gérard Roland. 2000. "Reform without Losers: An Interpretation of China's Dual-Track Approach to Transition." *Journal of Political Economy* 108 (1): 120–43.

Lawler, J. John, and Gail Gates Lawler. 1940. *A Short Historical Introduction to the Law of Real Property*. Chicago: Foundation Press, Inc.

Leach, W. Barton, and Owen Tudor. 1952. "The Common Law Rule against Perpetuities." In *American Law of Property: A Treatise on the Law of Property in the United States*, vol. 6, edited by A. James Casner. Boston: Little, Brown and Company.

Lerner, Joshua, and Antoinette Schoar. 2004. "Transaction Structures in the Developing World: Evidence from Private Equity." MIT Sloan Working Paper 4468-04 (March).

Levine, Ross. 2004. "Finance and Growth: Theory and Evidence." Working Paper 10766. Cambridge, Mass.: National Bureau of Economic Research (September).

Levine, Ross, Norman Loayza, and Thorsten Beck. 2000. "Financial Intermediation and Growth: Causality and Causes." *Journal of Monetary Economics* 46: 31–77.

Levine, Ross, and Sara Zervos. 1998. "Stock Markets, Banks, and Economic Growth." *American Economic Review* 88 (3): 537–58.

Lewis, William W. 2004. *The Power of Productivity: Wealth, Poverty, and the Threat to Global Stability*. University of Chicago Press.

Li, Ke, and Tongliang An. 2004. "Chinese Industrial Policy and the Reduction of State-Owned Shares in China's Listed Companies." *Pacific Economic Review* 9: 377–93.

Libecap, Gary D. 1981. *Locking Up the Range: Federal Land Controls and Grazing*. San Francisco: Pacific Studies in Public Policy.

Licht, Amir N. 2001. "The Mother of All Path Dependencies: Toward a Cross-Cultural Theory of Corporate Governance Systems." *Delaware Journal of Corporate Law* 26:147–205.

Licht, Amir N., Chanan Goldschmidt, and Shalom H. Schwartz. 2005. "Culture, Law, and Corporate Governance." *International Review of Law and Economics* 25: 220–55.

———. 2004. "Culture Rules: The Foundations of the Rule of Law and Other Norms of Governance" (ssrn.com/abstract=314559).

Lichtenstein, Natalie G. 2003. "Law in China's Economic Development: An Essay from Afar." In *Understanding China's Legal System: Essays in Honor of Jerome A. Cohen*, edited by C. Stephen Hsu, pp. 274–94. New York University Press.

Lieberthal, Kenneth. 2004. *Governing China: From Revolution through Reform*, 2d ed. New York: W. W. Norton & Company.

Lim, Youngjae. 2002. "The Corporate Bankruptcy System and the Economic Crisis." In *Economic Crisis and Corporate Restructuring in Korea: Reforming the Chaebol*, edited by S. Haggard, W. Lim, and E. Kim. Cambridge University Press.

Lin, Chris X. 2003. "A Quiet Revolution: An Overview of China's Judicial Reform." *Asian-Pacific Law and Policy Journal* 4: 255–319.

Liu, Lawrence S. 2001. "Corporate Governance Development in the Greater China: A Taiwan Perspective" (ssrn.com/abstract=293081).

Lohman, Bryan, Agapi Somwaru, and Keith Wiebe. 2002. "The Ongoing Reform of Land Tenure Policies in China." *Agricultural Outlook*. Economic Research Service 15-18. U.S. Department of Agriculture (September 2002).

López-de-Silanes, Florencio. 2002. "The Politics of Legal Reform." G-24 Discussion Paper Series 17 (April) (www.unctad.org/en/docs/pogdsmdpbg24d17.en.pdf).

Lora, Eduardo, Carmen Pages, Ugo Panizza, and Ernesto Stein. 2004. "A Decade of Development Thinking." Washington: Inter-American Development Bank.

Lu, Guiping. 2003. "Private Enforcement of Securities Fraud Law in China: A Critique of the Supreme People's Court 2003 Provisions Concerning Private Securities Litigation." *Pacific Rim Law and Policy Journal* 12: 780–805.

Lubman, Stanley B. 1999. *Bird in a Cage: Legal Reform in China after Mao*. Stanford University Press.

Ma, Ngok, Ka-ho Mok, and Anthony B. L. Cheung. 2001. "Advance and Retreat: The New Two-Pronged Strategy of Enterprise Reform in China." *Problems of Post-Communism* 48 (5): 51–61.

Macauley, Stewart. 1985. "An Empirical View of Contract." *Wisconsin Law Review* 465–82.

Mackay, Charles. 1841. *Memoirs of Extraordinary Popular Delusions*, vol. 1. London: Richard Bentley.

Maddison, Angus. 2001. *The World Economy: A Millennial Perspective*. Washington: OECD.

———. 2002. "The West and the Rest in the International Economic Order." In *Development Is Back*, edited by Jorge Braga de Macedo, Colm Foy, and Charles P. Oman, pp. 31–46. Paris: OECD.

———. 2003. *The World Economy: Historical Statistics*. Paris: OECD.

Mahoney, Paul G. 2001. "The Common Law and Economic Growth: Hayek Might Be Right." *Journal of Legal Studies* 30 (2): 503–25.

Maitland, F. W. 1931. *The Constitutional History of England: A Course of Lectures Delivered*. Cambridge University Press.

Masten, Scott E. 1996. "Introduction." In *Case Studies in Contracting and Organization*, edited Scott E. Masten, pp. 3–25. Oxford University Press.

———. 2000. "Contractual Choice." In *Encyclopedia of Law and Economics*, vol. 3: *The Regulation of Contracts*, edited by Boudewijn Bouckaert and Gerrit De Geest, pp. 25–45. Cheltenham: Edward Elgar Publishers Limited.

Mattei, Ugo. 1997. *Comparative Law and Economics*. University of Michigan Press.

McCloskey, Donald N. 1989. "The Open Fields of England: Rent, Risk, and the Rate of Interest, 1300–1815." In *Markets in History: Economic Studies of the Past*, edited by David W. Galenson, pp. 5–51. Cambridge University Press.

———. 1991. "The Prudent Peasant: New Findings on Open Fields." *Journal of Economic History* 51: 343–55.

McDonnell, Brett H. 2004. "Lessons from the Rise and (Possible) Fall of Chinese Township-Village Enterprises." *William and Mary Law Review* 45: 953–1009.

McGregor, Richard. 2005a. "China Bank Chiefs Attack Role of Communist Party." *Financial Times*, April 29.

———. 2005b. "Cultivating the Countryside: Hu Takes Pains to Keep China Free from a Peasants' Revolt." *Financial Times*, September 8.

———. 2006 "Views of the World: China." *Financial Times*, May 21.

Meier, Gerald M. 2001. "The Old Generation of Development Economists and the New." In *Frontiers of Development Economics: The Future in Perspective*, edited by Gerald M. Meier and Joseph E. Stiglitz, pp. 13–50. Oxford University Press.

Merrill, Thomas W., and Henry E. Smith. 2001. "What Happened to Property in Law and Economics?" *Yale Law Journal* 111: 357–98.

Merryman, John Henry. 1985. *The Civil Law Tradition*, 2d ed. Stanford University Press.

———. 1996. "The French Deviation." *American Journal of Comparative Law* 44 (1): 109–19.

Merryman, John Henry, David S. Clark, and John O. Haley. 1994. *The Civil Law Tradition: Europe, Latin America, and East Asia*. Charlottesville, Va.: Michie Co.

Miceli, Thomas J., Henry J. Munneke, C. F. Sirmans, and Geoffrey K. Turnbull. 2002. "Title Systems and Land Values." *Journal of Law and Economics* 45: 565–82.

Migot-Adholla, Shem, Peter Hazell, Benoît Blarel, and Frank Place. 1991. Indigenous Land Rights Systems in Sub-Saharan Africa: A Constraint on Productivity? *World Bank Economic Review* 5 (1): 155–75.

Milhaupt, Curtis J., and Mark D. West. 2000. "The Dark Side of Private Ordering: An Institutional and Empirical Analysis of Organized Crime." *University of Chicago Law Review* 67: 41–98.

Miller, Jonathan M. 2000. "Evaluating the Argentine Supreme Court under Presidents Alfonsin and Menem (1983–1999)." *Southwestern Journal of Law and Trade in the Americas* 7: 369–433.

Milsom, S. F. C. 1969. *Historical Foundations of the Common Law.* London: Butterworths.

Mingli, Zhang, and Hui Liu. 2001. "People's Republic of China." In *Government Bond Markets in Asia,* edited by Yun-Hwan Kim, pp. 141–90. Manila: Asian Development Bank.

Mirow, M. C. 2004. *Latin American Law: A History of Private Law and Institutions in Spanish America.* University of Texas Press.

Mishkin, Frederic S. ed. 2001. *Prudential Supervision: What Works and What Doesn't.* University of Chicago Press.

Montinola, Gabriella, Yingyi Qian, and Barry R. Weingast. 1995. "Federalism, Chinese Style: The Political Basis for Economic Success." *World Politics* 48 (1): 50–81.

Moore, Ellen Wedemeyer. 1985. *The Fairs of Medieval England: An Introductory Study.* Toronto: Pontifical Institute of Mediaeval Studies.

Morton, F. L. 1988. "Judicial Review in France: A Comparative Analysis." *American Journal of Comparative Law* 36: 89–110.

Moss, Todd, and Arvind Subramanian. 2005. "After the Big Push: Fiscal and Institutional Implications of Large Aid Increases." Working Paper 71. Washington: Center for Global Development.

Murphy, Antoin E. 2004. "Corporate Ownership in France: The Importance of History." Working Paper 10716. Cambridge, Mass.: National Bureau of Economic Research (August).

Murrell, Peter. 2005. "Institutions and Firms in Transition Economies." In *Handbook of the New Institutional Economics,* edited by Claude Menard and Mary M. Shirley, pp. 667–99. Dordrecht: Springer.

Naisbitt, John. 1997. *Megatrends Asia: Eight Asian Megatrends That Are Reshaping Our World.* New York: Touchstone.

Naughton, Barry. 1995. *Growing Out of the Plan: Chinese Economic Reform, 1978–1993.* Cambridge University Press.

Nef, John U. 1940. *Industry and Government in France and England, 1540–1640.* New York: Russell & Russell.

Nelson, Richard R., and Bhaven N. Sampat. 2001. "Making Sense of Institutions as a Factor Shaping Economic Performance." *Journal of Economic Behavior and Organization* 44: 31–54.

Nenova, Tatiana. 2003. "The Value of Corporate Voting Rights and Control: A Cross-Country Analysis." *Journal of Financial Economics* 68: 325–51.

North, Douglass C. 1981. *Structure and Change in Economic History.* New York: W.W. Norton & Company.

————. 1987. "Institutions, Transactions Costs and Economic Growth." *Economic Inquiry* 25 (3): 419–28.

————. 1990. *Institutions, Institutional Change and Economic Performance*. Cambridge University Press.

North, Douglass C., and Robert Paul Thomas. 1973. *The Rise of the Western World: A New Economic History*. Cambridge University Press.

North, Douglass C., and John Joseph Wallis. 1982. "American Government Expenditures: A Historical Perspective." *American Economic Review* 72 (2): 336–40.

North, Douglass C., and Barry R. Weingast. 1989. "Constitutions and Commitment: The Evolution of Institutions Governing Public Choice in Seventeenth-Century England." *Journal of Economic History* 49: 803–32.

OECD (Organization for Economic Cooperation and Development). 2002. *China in the World Economy: The Domestic Policy Challenges*. Paris.

————. 2005a. *Governance in China*. Paris.

————. 2005b. *OECD Economic Survey: China*. Paris.

Oliver, Dawn. 2003. *Constitutional Reform in the United Kingdom*. Oxford University Press.

Ong, Lynette. 2006. "Local Government Debt: Another Bail-out Job." *China Economic Quarterly* 10 (1): 48–55.

Osgathorpe, John D. 1995–96. "A Critical Survey of the People's Republic of China's New Company Law." *Indiana International and Comparative Law Review* 6: 493–515.

Ostrom, Elinor. 1990. *Governing the Commons: The Evolution of Institutions for Collection Action*. Cambridge University Press.

————. 2000. "Private and Common Property Rights." In *Encyclopedia of Law and Economics*, vol. 2: *Civil Law and Economics*, edited by Boudevijn Bouckaert and Gerrit De Geest, pp. 332–79. Cheltenham: Edward Elgar Publishers Limited.

Padilla, Atilano Jorge, and Alejandro Requejo. 2000. "The Costs and Benefits of the Strict Protection of Creditor Rights: Theory and Evidence." Research Network Working Paper R-384. Washington: Inter-American Development Bank (May).

Pagano, Marco, and Paolo F. Volpin. 2005. "The Political Economy of Corporate Governance." *American Economic Review* 95 (4): 1005–30.

Payne, Geoffrey. 2002. "Introduction." In *Land, Rights and Innovation: Improving Tenure Security for the Urban Poor*, edited by Geoffrey Payne, pp. 3–22. London: ITDG Publishing.

Peerenboom, Randall. 2001. "Globalization, Path Dependency and the Limits of Law: Administrative Law Reform and Rule of Law in the People's Republic of China." *Berkeley Journal of International Law* 19: 161–264.

————. 2002. *China's Long March toward the Rule of Law*. Cambridge University Press.

Perkins, Dwight H. 2000. "Law, Family Ties, and the East Asian Way of Business." In *Culture Matters: How Values Shape Human Progress*, edited by Lawrence E. Harrison and Samuel P. Huntington, pp. 232–43. New York: Basic Books.

Persson, Torsten. 2005. "Forms of Democracy, Policy and Economic Development." Working Paper 11171. Washington: National Bureau of Economic Research (March).

Picker, Randall C., Douglas G. Baird, and Thomas H. Jackson. 2002. *Security Interests in Personal Property*, 3d ed. New York: Foundation Press.

Ping Li, J. D. 2003. "Rural Land Tenure Reforms in China: Issues, Regulations, and Prospects for Additional Reform." In *Land Reform, Land Settlement and Cooperatives*, 2003/3 Special Edition. Rome: Food and Agriculture Organization (www.fao. org/docrep/006/y5026e/y5026e06.htm).

Pirenne, Henri. 1937. *Economic and Social History of Medieval Europe*. New York: Harcourt, Brace and Company.

Pistor, Katharina, Yoram Keinan, Jan Kleinheisterkamp, and Mark D. West. 2003. "Evolution of Corporate Law and the Transplant Effect: Lessons from Six Countries." *World Bank Research Observer* 18 (1): 89–112.

Pistor, Katharina, Martin Raiser, and Stanislaw Gelfer. 2000. "Law and Finance in Transition Economies." *Economics of Transition* 8 (2): 325–68.

Pistor, Katharina, and Chenggang Xu. 2005. "Governing Stock Markets in Transition Economies: Lessons from China." *American Law and Economics Review* 7: 184–210.

Plant, Roger, and Soren Hvalkof. 2001. "Land Titling and Indigenous People." Sustainable Development Department Technical Papers Series. Washington: Inter-American Development Bank.

Plato. 1952. *Laws IV,* edited by Robert Maynard Hutchins. Great Books of the Western World 7. Chicago: Encyclopedia Britannica.

Platteau, Jean-Philippe. 2000. *Institutions, Social Norms, and Economic Development*. Amsterdam: Harwood Academic Publishers.

Plucknett, Theodore F. T. 1940. *A Concise History of the Common Law,* 3d ed. London: Butterworth & Co. Ltd.

———. 1949. *Legislation of Edward I*. Oxford University Press.

Plucknett, Theodore F. T., ed. 1960. *English Constitutional History: From the Teutonic Conquest to the Present Time,* 11th ed. London: Sweet & Maxwell Limited.

Podpiera, Richard. 2006. *Progress in China's Banking Sector Reforms: Has Bank Behavior Changed?* Working Paper 06/71. Washington: International Monetary Fund.

Pomerleano, Michael. 1999. "The East Asia Crisis and Corporate Finances: The Untold Micro Story." Policy Research Paper 1990. Washington: World Bank (November).

Posner, Eric. 2000. *Law and Social Norms*. Harvard University Press.

Posner, Richard A. 1998. "Creating a Legal Framework for Economic Development." *World Bank Research Observer* 13 (1): 1–11.

Postan, M. M., E. E. Rich, and Edward Miller. 1965. *Cambridge Economic History of Europe*, vol. 3: *Economic Organization and Policies in the Middle Ages*. Cambridge University Press.

Potter, Pitman B. 2004. "Legal Reform in China: Institutions, Culture, and Selective Adaptation." *Law and Social Inquiry* 29: 465–95.

Prillaman, William C. 2000. *The Judiciary and Democratic Decay in Latin America: Declining Confidence in the Rule of Law*. Westport: Praeger.

Przeworski, Adam, and Fernando Limongi. 1993. "Political Regimes and Economic Growth." *Journal of Economic Perspectives* 7 (3): 51–69.

Qian, Yingyi. 2000a. "The Institutional Foundations of China's Market Transition." In *Annual World Bank Conference on Development Economics 1999*, edited by Boris Pleskovic and Joseph Stiglitz, pp. 289–310. Washington: World Bank.

———. 2000b. "The Process of China's Market Transition (1978–1998): The Evolutionary, Historical, and Comparative Perspectives." *Journal of Institutional and Theoretical Economics* 156 (1): 151–71.

———. 2003. "How Reform Worked in China." In *In Search of Prosperity: Analytic Narratives on Economic Growth*, edited by Dani Rodrik, pp. 297–333. Princeton University Press.

Qian, Yingyi, and Barry R. Weingast. 1997. "Federalism as a Commitment to Preserving Market Incentives." *Journal of Economic Perspectives* 11 (4): 83–92.

Quinn, Stephen. 2001. "The Glorious Revolution's Effect on English Private Finance: A Microhistory, 1680–1705." *Journal of Economic History* 61 (3): 593–615.

Rabel, Ernst. 1949–50a. "Private Laws of Western Civilization: Part II. The French Civil Code." *Louisiana Law Review* 107–19.

———. 1949–50b. "Private Laws of Western Civilization: Part III: The German and the Swiss Civil Codes." *Louisiana Law Review* 265–75.

Radelet, Steven. 2005. "Supporting Sustained Economic Development." *Michigan Journal of International Law* 26(4): 1203–22.

Radelet, Steven, and Jeffrey Sachs. 1997. "Asia's Reemergence." *Foreign Affairs* 44 (November/December): 44–59.

Rajan, Raghuram G. 2005. "Aid and Growth: The Policy Challenge." *Finance and Development* 42: 4.

Rajan, Raghuram G., and Arvind Subramanian. 2005a. "Aid and Growth: What Does the Cross-Country Evidence Really Show?" Working Paper 05/127. Washington: International Monetary Fund.

———. 2005b. "What Undermines Aid's Impact on Growth?" Working Paper 11657. Cambridge, Mass.: National Bureau of Economic Research.

Rajan, Raghuram G., and Luigi Zingales. 1998. "Financial Development and Growth." *American Economic Review* 88 (3): 559–86.

———. 2003a. "The Great Reversals: The Politics of Financial Development in the Twentieth Century." *Journal of Financial Economics* 69: 5–50.

———. 2003b. *Saving Capitalism from the Capitalists: Unleashing the Power of Financial Markets to Create Wealth and Spread Opportunity*. New York: Crown Business.

Ramseyer, J. Mark. 1994. "The Puzzling (In)Dependence of Courts: A Comparative Approach." *Journal of Legal Studies* 23: 721–47.

Ramseyer, J. Mark, and Frances McCall Rosenbluth. 1993. *Japan's Political Marketplace*. Harvard University Press.

Rawski, Thomas G. 2005. "China's Growth Prospects." In *Asia Program Special Report 129, China's Economy: Retrospect and Prospect*, edited by Loren Brandt, Thomas O. Rawski, and Gang Lin, pp. 55–61. Washington: Woodrow Wilson International Center for Scholars.

Ray, S. K. 1996. "Land System and Its Reforms in India." *Indian Journal of Agricultural Economics* 51: 220–37.

Raz, Joseph. 1983. *The Authority of Law: Essays on Law and Morality.* Oxford University Press.

Redding, S. G. 1990. *The Spirit of Chinese Capitalism.* New York: Walter de Gruyter.

Reid, Jr., Charles J. 1995. "The Seventeenth-Century Revolution in the English Land Law." *Cleveland State Law Review* 43: 221–302.

Rekosh, Edwin. 2002. "Emerging Lessons from Reform Efforts in Eastern Europe and Eurasia." In *Guidance for Promoting Judicial Independence and Impartiality*, rev. ed., pp. 53–71. Washington: U.S. Agency for International Development.

Rheinstein, Max, and Mary Ann Glendon. 2003. "Civil Law." *Encyclopedia Britannica Online.*

Rock, Edward, Hideki Kanda, and Reinier Kraakman. 2004. "Significant Corporate Actions." In *The Anatomy of Corporate Law: A Comparative and Functional Approach*, edited by Reinier R. Kraakman and others, pp. 131–55. Oxford University Press.

Rodrik, Dani. 1996. "Understanding Economic Policy Reform." *Journal of Economic Literature* 34: 9–41.

———. 2000. "Institutions for High-Quality Growth: What They Are and How to Acquire Them." *Studies in Comparative International Development* 35 (3): 59–86.

———. 2003. "Introduction: What Do We Learn from Country Narratives?" In *In Search of Prosperity: Analytic Narratives on Economic Growth*, edited by Dani Rodrik, pp. 1–19. Princeton University Press.

———. 2005. "Growth Strategies." In *Handbook of Economic Growth*, edited by Philippe Aghion and Steven Durlauf, chapter 14. Amsterdam: Elsevier.

Rodrik, Dani, Arvind Subramanian, and Francesco Trebbi. 2004. "Institutions Rule: The Primacy of Institutions over Geography and Integration in Economic Development." *Journal of Economic Growth* 9: 131–65.

Rodrik, Dani, and Roman Wacziarg. 2002. "Do Democratic Transitions Produce Bad Economic Outcomes?" *American Economic Review* 95 (2): 50–55.

Roe, Mark J. 2003. *Political Determinants of Corporate Governance: Political Context, Corporate Impact.* Oxford University Press.

———. 2006. "Legal Origins and Stock Markets in the Twentieth Century." Harvard Law School (papers.ssrn.com/abstract_id.=908972).

Rogoff, Adam, Ingrid Bag, and Charlie Wang. 2004. "China Takes Active Steps toward Reform; Changes to Insolvency Regime Are Key to Encouraging Foreign Investment." *New York Law Journal* 232, no. 99 (November 22): 9.

Roland, Gérard. 2000. *Transition and Economics: Politics, Markets, and Firms.* MIT Press.

Rosenfeld, Michel. 2000–2001. "The Rule of Law and the Legitimacy of Constitutional Democracy." *Southern California Law Review* 74: 1307–51.

Rosenn, Keith S. 1974. "Judicial Review in Latin America." *Ohio State Law Journal* 35: 785–819.

———. 1990. "The Success of Constitutionalism in the United States and Its Failure in Latin America: An Explanation." *University of Miami Inter-American Law Review* 22: 1.

———. 2000. "Judicial Review in Brazil: Developments under the 1988 Constitution." *Southwestern Journal of Law and Trade in the Americas* 7: 291–319.

Rudden, Bernard. 1991. *A Source-Book on French Law: Public Law: Constitutional and Administrative, Private Law: Structure, Contract,* 3d rev. ed. Oxford: Clarendon Press.

Sachs, Jeffrey D. 2001. "Tropical Underdevelopment." Working Paper 8119. Cambridge, Mass.: National Bureau of Economic Research.

———. 2003a." Institutions Don't Rule: Direct Effects of Geography on Per Capita Income." Working Paper 9490. Cambridge, Mass.: National Bureau of Economic Research.

———. 2003b. "Institutions Matter but Not for Everything." *Finance and Development* (June): 38–41.

Sachs, Jeffrey D., and Andrew Warner. 1995. "Economic Reform and the Process of Global Integration." *Brookings Papers on Economic Activity* 1995: 1–118.

Sajó, András, ed. 2004. *Judicial Integrity.* Boston: Martinus Nijhoff Publishers.

Santiso, Carlos. 2003. "The Elusive Quest for the Rule of Law: Promoting Judicial Reform in Latin America." *Brazilian Journal of Political Economy* 23 (3): 112–34.

Sapienza, Paola. 2004. "The Effects of Government Ownership on Bank Lending." *Journal of Financial Economics* 72: 357–84.

Schama, Simon. 2000. *A History of Britain: At the Edge of the World? 3500 B.C.–A.D.1603.* New York: Hyperion.

Schauer, Frederick. 2004. "The Failure of the Common Law." *Arizona State Law Journal* 36: 765–82.

Schipani, Cindy A., and Junhai Liu. 2002. "Corporate Governance in China: Then and Now." *Columbia Business Law Review* 1–69.

Schlesinger, Rudolf B., Hans W. Baade, Peter E. Herzog, and Edward M. Wise. 1998. *Comparative Law: Cases, Text, Materials,* 6th ed. New York: Foundation Press.

Schmidt, Reinhard H. 2004. "Corporate Governance in Germany: An Economic Perspective." In *The German Financial System,* edited by Jan Pieter Krahnen and Reinhard H. Schmidt, pp. 386–424. Oxford University Press.

Schröder, Meinhard. 2002. "Administrative Law in Germany." In *Administrative Law of the European Union, Its Member States and the United States: A Comparative Analysis,* edited by René Seerden and Frits Stroink, pp. 91–144. Groningen: Intersentia.

Scoggins, Hugh T. 1990. "Between Heaven and Man: Contract and the State in Han Dynasty China." *Southern California Law Review* 63: 1325–1404.

Scott, William Robert. 1912. *The Constitution and Finance of English, Scottish and Irish Joint-Stock Companies to 1720*, vol. I. Cambridge University Press.

Sen, Amartya. 1999. *Development as Freedom*. New York: Knopf.

Shapiro Martin. 1981. *Courts: A Comparative and Political Analysis*. University of Chicago Press.

Shen, Sibao, and Jing Jia. 2005. "Will the Independent Director Institution Work in China?" *Loyola Los Angeles International and Comparative Law Review* 27: 223–48.

Shirk, Susan L. 1993. *The Political Logic of Economic Reform in China*. University of California Press.

Siems, Mathias M. 2006. "Legal Origins: Reconciling Law & Finance and Comparative Law." University of Cambridge, Centre for Business Research (July 2006) (ssrn. com/abstract=920690).

Simpson, A. W. B. 1986. *A History of the Land Law*, 2d ed. Oxford: Clarendon Press.

Simpson, John, and Joachim Menze. 2000. "Ten Years of Secured Transaction Reform." *Law in Transition* (Autumn): 20–27.

Sitkoff, Robert H., and Max Schanzenbach. 2005. "Jurisdictional Competition for Trust Funds: An Empirical Analysis of Perpetuities and Taxes." *Yale Law Journal* 115: 356–437.

Smith, Henry E. 2000. "Semicommon Property Fields and Scattering in the Open Fields." *Journal of Legal Studies* 29: 131–69.

Smith, Munroe. 1928. *The Development of European Law*. Columbia University Press.

Sokoloff, Kenneth L., and Stanley L. Engerman. 2000. "Institutions, Factor Endowments, and Paths of Development in the New World." *Journal of Economic Perspectives* 14 (3): 217–32.

Solow, Robert M. 1995. "But Verify." *New Republic* 213 (September 11): 36–39.

Spamann, Holger. 2006. "On the Insignificance and/or Endogeneity of La Porta et al.'s 'Anti-Director Rights Index' under Consistent Coding." Harvard Law School (ssrn.com/abstract=894301).

Spiller, Pablo T., and Mariano Tommasi. 2003. "The Institutional Foundations of Public Policy: A Transactions Approach with Application to Argentina." *Journal of Law Economics and Organization* 19 (2): 281–306.

Spring, Eileen. 1993. "Law, Land, & Family: Aristocratic Inheritance in England, 1300 to 1800." University of North Carolina Press.

Srinivas, P. S., and Djauhari Sitorus. 2004. "State-Owned Banks in Indonesia." In *The Future of State-Owned Financial Institutions*, edited by Gerard Caprio and others, pp. 123–80. Brookings.

Srinivasan, T. N. 2004. "Development: Domestic Constraints and External Opportunities from Globalization." *Michigan Journal of International Law* 26 (1): 63–98.

Stasavage, David. 2002. "Credible Commitment in Early Modern Europe: North and Weingast Revisited." *Journal of Law, Economics, and Organization* 18 (1): 155–86.

———. 2003. *Public Debt and the Birth of the Democratic State: France and Great Britain, 1688-1789*. Cambridge University Press.

Stephenson, Matthew C. 2003. "'When the Devil Turns. . .': The Political Foundation of Independent Judicial Review." *Journal of Legal Studies* 32: 59–86.

Stiglitz, Joseph E. 2001. "Bankruptcy Laws: Basic Economic Principles." In *Resolution of Financial Distress: An International Perspective on the Design of Bankruptcy Laws*, edited by Stijn Claessens, Simeon Djankov, and Ashoka Mody, pp. 1–23. Washington: World Bank.

Stout, Lynn A. 2004. "On the Nature of Corporations." Law and Economics Research Paper 04-13. University of California, Los Angeles, School of Law.

Stulz, René M., and Rohan Williamson. 2003. "Culture, Openness, and Finance." *Journal of Financial Economics* 70: 313–49.

Summer, Robert S. 1999. "The Principles of the Rule of Law." *Notre Dame Law Review* 74: 1691–1712.

Sunstein, Cass R. 1995. "Problems with Rules." *California Law Review* 83: 953–1023.

———. 1996. "Social Norms and Social Roles." *Columbia Law Review* 96: 903–68.

———. 1997. *Free Markets and Social Justice*. Oxford University Press.

Sylla, Richard. 2002. "Financial Systems and Economic Modernization." *Journal of Economic History* 62: 277–92.

Tabellini, Guido. 2005. "Culture and Institutions: Economic Development in the Regions of Europe." Working Paper 1492. Munich: CESifo.

Tanner, Christopher. 2002. "Law-Making in an African Context: The 1997 Mozambican Land Law." Legal Papers Online 26. Rome: Food and Agriculture Organization (March) (www.fao.org/legal/prs-ol/lpo26.pdf).

Tanner, J. R., C. W. Previté-Orton, and Z. N. Brooke, eds. 1932. *Cambridge Legal History,* vol. 7: *The Cambridge Medieval History*. Cambridge University Press.

Tawney, R. H. 1941. "The Rise of the Gentry, 1558–1640." *Economic History Review* 11: 1–38.

Tenev, Stoyan, and Chunlin Zhang. 2002. *Corporate Governance and Enterprise Reform in China: Building the Institutions of Modern Markets*. Washington: World Bank and the International Finance Corporation.

Thompson, Mark A. 1938. *A Constitutional History of England: 1642 to 1801*. London: Methuen & Co., Ltd.

Tierney, Brian. 1963. "Bracton on Government." *Speculum* 38 (2): 295–317.

Tsai, Kellee S. 2002. *Back-Alley Banking: Private Entrepreneurs in China*. Cornell University Press.

Turner, Michael. 1986. "English Open Fields and Enclosures: Retardation or Productivity Improvements." *Journal of Economic History* 64: 669–92.

UNDP (United Nations Development Program). 2005. *2005 China Human Development Report*. New York.

Vagts, Detlev. 2002. "Comparative Company Law—The New Wave." In *Festschrift für Jean Nicolas Durey*, edited by Rainer J. Schweizer, Herbert Burkert, and Urs Gasser, pp. 595–605. Zurich: Schulthess Juristiches Medien AG.

Valencia, Juan G. Matus. 1958. "The Centenary of the Chilean Civil Code." *American Journal of Comparative Law* 7: 71–83.

Valente, Marcela. 2003. "Argentina: Third Judge on Corruption-Tainted Court Resigns." IPS-Inter Press Service, October 23.

Van Caenegem, R. C. 1988. *The Birth of the English Common Law,* 2d ed. Cambridge University Press.

Van de Walle, Nicolas. 2005. *Overcoming Stagnation in Aid-Dependent Countries.* Washington: Center for Global Development.

Van Gerven, Walter. 2005. *The European Union: A Polity of States and Peoples.* Stanford University Press.

Vines, Stephen. 2000. *The Years of Living Dangerously: Asia—From Financial Crisis to the New Millennium.* New York: Texere.

Von Mehren, Arthur Taylor, and James Russell Gordley. 1977. *The Civil Law System: An Introduction to the Comparative Study of Law,* 2d ed. Boston: Little, Brown.

Wade, E. C. S. 1961. "Introduction." In *Introduction to the Study of the Law of the Constitution,* 10th ed., edited by A. V. Dicey. London: MacMillan Press.

Walker, John L. 2000. "Building the Legal and Regulatory Framework." In *Building an Infrastructure for Financial Systems,* edited by Eric S. Rosengren and John S. Jordan. Conference Series 44: 31–66. Federal Reserve Bank of Boston.

Wallis, John Joseph. 2004. "The Concept of Systematic Corruption in American Political and Economic History." Working Paper 10952. Cambridge, Mass.: National Bureau of Economic Research (December); forthcoming in *Corruption and Reform,* edited by Claudia Goldin and Edward L. Glaeser.

Watson, Alan. 1977. *Society and Legal Change.* Edinburgh: Scottish Academic Press.

Weber, Max. 1954. *Law in Economy and Society,* translated by Max Rheinstein. New York: Simon and Schuster.

———. 1958. *The Protestant Ethic and the Spirit of Capitalism.* New York: Charles Scribner.

Wei, Yuwa. 2003. "An Overview of Corporate Governance in China." *Syracuse Journal of International Law and Commerce* 30: 23–48.

Weingast, Barry R. 1993. "Constitutions as Governance Structures: The Political Foundations of Secure Markets." *Journal of Institutional and Theoretical Economics* 149 (1): 286–311.

———. 1995. "The Economic Role of Political Institutions: Market-Preserving Federalism and Economic Development." *Journal of Law, Economics, and Organization* 11 (1): 1–31.

———.1997a. "The Political Foundations of Democracy and the Rule of Law." *American Political Science Review* 91 (2): 245–63.

———. 1997b. "The Political Foundations of Limited Government: Parliament and Sovereign Debt in 17th- and 18th-Century England." In *The Frontiers of the New Institutional Economics,* edited by John N. Drobak and John V. C. Nye, pp. 213–46. San Diego: Academic Press.

West, Mark D. 2001. "The Puzzling Divergence of Corporate Law: Evidence and Explanation from Japan and the United States." *University of Pennsylvania Law Review* 150: 527–601.

Westbrook, Jay Lawrence. 2004. "The Control of Wealth in Bankruptcy." *Texas Law Review* 82: 795–862.

Wheatley, Jonathan. 2005. "Brazil's Judicial Nightmare Brings Gridlock for Growth." *Financial Times*, May 24.

Wiarda, Howard J., and Harvey F. Kline. 2000. "The Latin American Tradition and Process of Development." In *Latin American Politics and Development*, 5th revised ed., edited by Howard J. Wiarda and Harvey F. Kline, pp. 3–91. Boulder: Westview Press.

Wilhelm, Katherina. 2004. "Rethinking Property Rights in Urban China." *UCLA Journal of International Law and Foreign Affairs* 9: 227–300.

Williams, E. Neville. 1960. *The Eighteenth-Century Constitution 1688–1825: Document and Commentary*. Cambridge University Press.

Wolf, Martin. 2003. "The Long March to Prosperity: Why China Can Maintain Its Explosive Rate of Growth for Another Two Decades." *Financial Times*, December 9.

———. 2005. "China Has Further to Grow to Catch Up with the World." *Financial Times*. April 13.

World Bank. 1997. *China 2020: Development Challenges in the New Century*. Washington.

———. 2001a. *Principles and Guidelines for Effective Insolvency and Creditor Rights Systems.* (April 1) (www.worldbank.org/ifa/ipg_eng.pdf).

———. 2001b. *World Development Report 2002: Building Institutions for Markets*. New York. World Bank and Oxford University Press.

———. 2004a. *Doing Business in 2004: Understanding Regulation*. Washington: World Bank and Oxford University Press.

———. 2004b. *World Development Report 2005: A Better Investment Climate for Everyone*. New York: World Bank and Oxford University Press.

———. 2005. *Doing Business in 2005: Removing Obstacles to Growth*. Washington: World Bank and Oxford University Press.

———. 2006a. *Doing Business in 2006: Creating Jobs*. Washington: World Bank and the International Finance Corporation.

———. 2006b. *World Development Indicators*. Washington.

———. 2006c. *World Development Report 2006: Equity and Development*. Washington.

World Bank Office Beijing. 2005. "Quarterly Update."

Wu, Jinglian. 2005. *Understanding and Interpreting Chinese Economic Reform*. Belmont, Calif.: Thomson South-Western (www.thomsonedu.com).

Yang, Dali L. 2006. "Economic Transformation and Its Political Discontents in China: Authoritarianism, Unequal Growth, and the Dilemmas of Political Development." *Annual Review of Political Science* 9: 143–64.

Yang, Xiao. 2006. "Work Report of the PRC Supreme People's Court" (lawprofessors.typepad.com/china_law_prof_blog/files/spc_work_report.html).

Young, Alwyn. 2003. "Gold into Base Metals: Productivity Growth in the People's Republic of China during the Reform Period." *Journal of Political Economy* 111 (6): 1220–61.

Yusuf, Shahid, and Joseph E. Stiglitz. 2001. "Development Issues: Settled and Open." In *Frontiers of Development Economics: The Future in Perspective*, edited by Gerald M. Meier and Joseph E. Stiglitz, pp. 227–68. Oxford University Press.

Zhang, Joe. 2005. "China's Private Sector Is in the Shadow of the State." *Financial Times*, October 5.

Zhang, Le-Yin. 2004. "The Roles of Corporatization and Stock Market Listing in Reforming China's State Industry." *World Development* 32: 2031–47.

Zweigert, Konrad, and Hein Kötz. 1987. *Introduction to Comparative Law: The Framework I*, 2d ed., translated by Tony Weir, pp. 82–85. Oxford: Clarendon Press.

———. 1992. *Introduction to Comparative Law*, 2d rev. ed. Oxford: Clarendon Press.

———. 1998. *Introduction to Comparative Law*, 3d rev. ed. Oxford: Clarendon Press.

Index

Acemoglu, Daron, 18, 57

Act of Settlement (England; *1701*), 81–82, 83, 112

Adams, John, 13

Adoption and transplantation. *See* Legal issues

Africa: bankruptcy in, 214; crime and corruption in, 123; crony bias in, 55; economic growth of, 17–18, 34; effects of geography in, 58; judiciary in, 51, 102–03; legal systems in, 33–34, 49, 52; property and property rights in, 134–35, 138, 149, 150; rule-of-law issues in, 52; study of, 226

Agency, 129, 177–78

Agricultural issues: credit, 199; in developing countries, 9, 35; economic development, 58; property and property rights, 92, 134, 135–38, 145, 146–47, 152–53, 225; sharecropping, 147; strip farming, 153

Albania, 94

Alford, William P., 253

Allen, Franklin, 234–35, 237

Alston, Lee J., 114–15

Angola, 59

Aoki, Masahiko, 3

Argentina: banks and banking in, 195, 201; business and corporate issues in, 181, 184; civil code in, 43, 44; judiciary in, 103. 114–15

Asia and East Asia: Asian Tigers, 18, 243, 244, 277; banks, banking, and bankruptcy in, 194, 205, 212, 214, 215; business and corporate issues in, 237; contracts in, 125, 236; credit and creditor issues, 236; economic issues, 17, 18, 239; financial crisis of *1990*s

in, 192, 205, 212, 215, 240, 241, 277; judiciary in, 50, 51, 102; legal systems in, 52; property and property rights in, 135, 138; social norms and values in, 66, 67–68; trade in, 72

Asian Development Bank, 104, 117–18

Australia, 19, 34, 101, 206–07, 234

Austria, 34

Aziz, Jahangir, 257, 258

Aztecs, 19

Bai, Chong-En, 266

Baird, Douglas G., 212–13

Balz, Manfred, 215–16

Bangladesh, 52, 146

Bank of England, 81

Bank of Spain, 260

Banks and banking issues: bankruptcy, 25, 95, 162, 190, 194–98, 199, 204–06, 210–18; competition and, 193; collateral, 198–203, 204; contracts and, 92, 129, 160; corporate governance of, 193, 229–30; credit and creditors, 194–203, 210–12, 218–19; crony capitalism and, 192–93, 230; default and default rates, 194–95, 197, 200–201; equity markets and, 190; judiciary and, 95, 143, 202–03; lending by, 191–92, 193–94, 229–30; ownership of, 191; property issues, 143–44; regulation of, 188, 192, 193; related lending by, 193; relevance of legal origins, 204–07; role of, 190–91; substantive law rules, 206. *See also* Business and corporate issues; Financial sector

313